DEVELOPING SERIOUS GAMES

DEVELOPING SERIOUS GAMES

BRYAN BERGERON

CHARLES RIVER MEDIA, INC.

Hingham, Massachusetts

Cover Design: Tyler Creative

CHARLES RIVER MEDIA, INC.
10 Downer Avenue
Hingham, Massachusetts 02043
781-740-0400
781-740-8816 (FAX)
info@charlesriver.com
www.charlesriver.com

This book is printed on acid-free paper.

Bergeron, Bryan P. *Developing Serious Games*
ISBN: 1-58450-443-9

Library of Congress Cataloging-in-Publication Data

Bergeron, Bryan P.
  Developing serious games / Bryan P. Bergeron.
      p. cm.
  Includes index.
  ISBN 1-58450-444-7 (pbk. : alk. paper)
  1. Computer games—Programming. 2. Computer games—Design. I. Title.

  QA76.76.C672B43 2005
  794.8'1526—dc22
                    2005032329

Printed in the United States of America
05 7 6 5 4 3 2 First Edition

CHARLES RIVER MEDIA titles are available for site license or bulk purchase by institutions, user groups, corporations, etc. For additional information, please contact the Special Sales Department at 781-740-0400.

CONTENTS

CHAPTER 3   TECHNOLOGY TRENDS   79

CHAPTER 4   STANDARDS   125

CHAPTER 5   BEST PRACTICES   173

CHAPTER 9   OUTLOOK   365

INTRODUCTION

Play is at least partly responsible for the survival of the human species. Through play, our ancestors honed their hunting skills, established a dominance hierarchy, learned the importance of following rules, and discovered the values of their societies. Today, it's common knowledge that hanging out with the wrong crowd—that is, playing with the wrong rules and people that espouse them—can adversely affect the trajectory of character development and an individual's ability or desire to integrate into society.

Games—formalized play—are a uniquely human behavior associated with enhanced individual and group survival. Not only is the penalty for failure within a game much less than in the real world, but lurking within every good game is a general message about how to think and act when confronted with real problems.

Games assume different forms, each with different types and degrees of learning. For example, the value of board games in developing specific problem-solving skills is highlighted by Ivan Moscovich's *1000 Play Thinks*, in which games are classified in areas ranging from geometry and logic to probability, topology, and perception [Moscovich01]. War games and their derivatives—sports—combine physical elements with real-time problem solving. The added value of sports and other games with an active, physical component over primarily mental games is the vicarious enjoyment and learning that can be experienced by spectators. This emotional involvement made possible through virtual role playing can be as intense in a crowd watching a game of tennis as it is in another group watching baseball or soccer. The particular sport is irrelevant, as long as the onlookers are fans of the sport and the players.

For many sports fans, watching their team compete with an opposing team is a serious matter, down to the physiological level. Male fans have been shown to have higher levels of testosterone in their bloodstream shortly after their team wins, while the fans of the losing team have depressed testosterone levels [Bernhardt98]. For the team owners, advertisers, TV networks, and others in the entertainment industry who can benefit monetarily from the focused attention and physiology of vicarious play, games are *very* serious business.

Games have several key features in common, whether they are played on a field, around a table, or in front of an LCD monitor. Games have clear rules, goals, and objectives that push the player to compete and overcome an adversary. And, as in real life, games present problems that must be solved and overcome by taking action. However, games depart from reality in the consequences of success or failure and in the clarity of outcomes. That is, a player losing a campaign in *Halo 2* to a Major Elite won't suffer any physical harm after succumbing to a plasma grenade. Furthermore, the outcome is immediate and indisputable. This clarity and immediacy of outcome is one of the attractions of games. In the real world, not only are outcomes murky, but they might not be evident for months or even years.

Computer games, a nascent industry compared with sports franchises and board game empires, have established a following that extends beyond hard-core computer types. In the vernacular of business, computer games have crossed the chasm between the few technology enthusiasts and visionaries and the much larger population of pragmatists [Moore99]. According to the report *Generation M: Media in the Lives of 8–18-Year-Olds* by the Kaiser Family Foundation, 83 percent of 8 to 18-year-olds have a computer game console at home [Rideout05]. In addition, a majority (56 percent) have two or more consoles, and more than half (55 percent) have a handheld computer game player. The report also reveals that members of Generation M, which includes many of today's consumers and tomorrow's workforce, spend an average of almost an hour a day playing computer games.

Like other forms of entertainment, computer games are valued because their use results in an emotional state change in the player. However, unlike the typical novel or movie that places ordinary people in extraordinary circumstances, the state change associated with computer gameplay is often the result of the player wielding extraordinary power in extraordinary situations. With a Playstation 2 and CD-ROM, a novice golfer is transformed into a pro who can compete with Tiger Woods at Augusta. Similarly, a group of teenagers in a quiet backwoods town can log in to Xbox Live after school and together defeat an army of aliens in some distant galaxy. In the world of computer games, with enough practice and perseverance, a scrawny 10-year-old can defeat the most power-ful creatures in the universe.

As a natural outgrowth of the rapid expansion of the games industry, game developers, educators, marketing firms, and domain experts are excit-edly envisioning serious applications for computer game technologies. These applications—serious games—represent opportunities for game developers to apply their talents to areas outside of the entertainment industry.

SERIOUS GAMES

At first glance, *serious games* seems like an oxymoron. After all, computer games are often associated with the frivolity of adolescence. But games, computer and otherwise, have long been used as training for serious en-deavors from childhood to adulthood. *Developing Serious Games* details what is involved in developing serious computer games, from crafting a design document to identifying sources of capital and affordable develop-ment tools.

A serious game is an interactive computer application, with or with-out a significant hardware component, that

- has a challenging goal;
- is fun to play and/or engaging;
- incorporates some concept of scoring;
- imparts to the user a skill, knowledge, or attitude that can be applied in the real world.

This empirically derived definition is based on the author's work over two decades designing, developing, evaluating, and managing the devel-opment of simulations and serious games for the Harvard Medical School/MIT curriculum, the pharmaceutical industry, medical boards, and the military.

Acknowledging that developers working in other disciplines might have somewhat different opinions of what constitutes serious games, the definition offered here provides the needed basis for the discussions that follow. Furthermore, to avoid unnecessary repetition, unless otherwise noted, the terms "computer game" and "video game" are synonymous.

Note that even though there might be significant differences between serious and entertainment game development in terms of toolset, user in-terface design, and development approach, this needn't be the case. Several generalizations about serious games can be made, however. For example, a major characteristic of serious games is that the designation cuts across the traditional game taxonomy. For example, a serious game developed to train U.S. Army medics in surface anatomy could be a first person shooter, with the usual Easter eggs, power-ups, and boss characters. Serious games are also platform agnostic, in that they have been developed for hardware platforms ranging from computer-controlled mannequins, motorized helicopter cockpits, and game consoles, to laptop computers and cell phones. Although several examples of serious games based on specialized hardware are discussed in the text, it is assumed that most readers are interested in developing serious games on an accessible personal computer platform.

The term serious games is relatively new. A search for the term through HighBeam Research reveals that it was first used in the context of a computer game in 1992 [Gold92]. More recently, the term has been popularized by Ben Sawyer of Digitalmill (*www.dmill.com*). Together with the Woodrow Wilson International Center for Scholars, Digitalmill founded the Serious Games Initiative. As the chief serious games evangelist, Ben has been instrumental in raising developer awareness of—and interest in—serious games.

Even though serious games may be new to the vernacular of game development, the paradigm isn't. Serious games have been used by the U.S. military, medical schools, and the general academic community long before the term was coined. For example, the programming language LOGO is arguably an early serious game. It was designed in the 1960s as a programming language that would encourage small children to grasp mathematical principles and learn constructive principles [Papert80]. With LOGO, children can create complex geometric shapes by instructing a mechanical or on-screen turtle to move iteratively in specified directions for specific distances. See the LOGO foundation Web site, *el.media.mit.edu/logo-foundation*, for examples of games written in LOGO. Chapter 1, "Historical Perspective" provides many more examples of early serious games.

What of the current interest in using computer gaming as a means of imparting knowledge, skills, and attitudes? A search on the Web reveals that there is renewed interest in basic research into the role of computer games in learning and literacy [Gee04], the relative efficacy of computer-based training [Fordis05], the educational potential of specific game genres [BonkDennen05], as well as the potential for harm [Mitchell-Savil-Smith04]. This new activity, which is reminiscent of the fervor surrounding computer-based instruction in the late 1980s and early 1990s, reflects the evolution of game development along economic, technical, and socio-organizational lines.

"It's not about the money" might be a popular phrase among dedicated professionals in every industry, but the economic performance of the game industry is difficult to ignore, even for those who live and breathe games. Admittedly, there are a few developers who rise to the ranks of celebrities, but most work with the quiet satisfaction that they're contributing to a fun and worthwhile project. Even in Korea and other Asian markets, where top gamers enjoy the cult status and financial perks normally reserved for movie and rock stars, game developers aren't granted special status. The U.S. market is barely aware of top game players, despite significant advertising dollars behind gaming competitions [Svensson05].

The fact is, computer games are a multibillion dollar industry. Although the contribution of serious games development to the overall game market is difficult to quantify, the U.S. military alone is spending millions annually on the development and analysis of serious games. It's important to underscore the investment in analysis, because it represents one of the defining qualities of serious games. The sometimes sizeable investment in serious games development has to be backed up by evidence of efficacy relative to comparable expenditures in alternative approaches to imparting knowledge, skills, and attitudes. In addition to this push from military investment, there is the pull of potential cost and/or time savings associated with using serious games in applications ranging from training basketball players to marketing for Madison Avenue.

From a technological perspective, the upsurge in interest in serious games from the user and developer communities is fueled by the availability of affordable, powerful development tools and hardware platforms. The pervasiveness of digital technology in the classroom and workplace, as well as the popularity of gaming as a pastime for a large segment of the population, serve to strengthen the position that the use of serious games as educational vehicles is part of the natural evolution of educational technology.

A favorable economic environment and the availability of affordable enabling technologies are necessary but insufficient to explain the recent emergence of the SimWorkshops at Stanford Medical School (*simworkshops. stanford.edu*), the biannual Serious Games Summit (*www.seriousgamessummit.com*), the annual Games for Health Conference (*www.gamesforhealth.*

org), the *Journal of Game Development* (*www.jogd.com*), and the numerous additional electronic and print resources available for users and developers of serious games. These offerings reflect a critical mass of professional educators, game developers, researchers, and traditional multimedia developers who are drawn to serious games.

A socio-organizational trend in the evolving serious games community is the rapid intra- and interdisciplinary formation of communities of practice. As soon as discipline-specific communities of serious games developers are established, there is inevitably mutually beneficial cross-fertilization with communities from other disciplines. To illustrate this phenomenon, consider the events at the second annual Games for Health Conference in the fall of 2005. As part of the conference, the U.S. Army's Telemedicine and Advanced Technology Research Center (TATRC) underwrote a series of roundtable discussions between experts in the traditional medical modeling and simulation world, representatives from TATRC, professional game developers, and researchers.

During the discussions, we explored a variety of possible topics for mutual benefit, from adding physiology modeling features to game engines and sharing design methodologies to securing funding for the efforts from the Department of Defense. The overarching theme of the discussions was sharing and collaboration toward common goals. Such a meeting would have been untenable only a few years earlier.

WHY THIS BOOK?

As of the fourth quarter of 2005, academic institutions have yet to offer degrees in serious games development, and there is little information in the way of serious games developer demographics. Like most of the figures used to define the serious games development community, demographics are at best intelligent guesstimates. Assuming serious games developers are not significantly different from developers in the entertainment industry, the artists, designers, and programmers involved in serious games development tend to be young relative to their counterparts in the general software industry.

In support of this claim is a survey conducted in 2004 by the International Game Developers Association's Quality of Life Committee, which reveals that more than 81 percent of the 1,000 developers surveyed were under 35 years old [Bonds04]. Stated differently, the majority of game developers questioned was born well after the invention of computer games. Although a young, enthusiastic work force might be advantageous in an industry that often demands long hours, the survey suggests that many serious games developers might not have experienced the previous technological and economic cycles that rocked the early computer game industry.

Attempting to fit serious games developers into a simple demographic slot might be futile. For example, the IGDA survey didn't consider the seasoned veterans experienced in military or medical modeling and simulation who supplement traditional approaches to development with game development technologies. Regardless of the demographics of those in the serious games development community, it is the common challenges and constraints faced by developers that bind attendees to the serious games conferences and that attract readers to the related online and print publications.

Consider a scenario in which the developers of an online military game for training medics are required to adhere to SCORM, a suite of standards for online education [ADL05]. The developer, unfamiliar with the standard, especially as it relates to medical content, could invest resources in learning the nuances of the standard on its own. Alternatively, the developer could look to other developers and organizations experienced in developing SCORM-compliant games. For example, the developer could reach beyond the military community to the MedBiquitous Consortium (*www.medbiq.org*), a developer of information technology standards for healthcare education and competence assessment. To avoid reinventing many of the methodologies previously developed by members of the consortium, the developer would have to become aware of work relevant to serious games development occurring beyond of the developer's discipline.

Although summits and conferences provide invaluable opportunities for this sort of cross-fertilization and sharing, there has been no book that compiles the topics relevant to serious game development. *Developing Serious Games* is designed to fill that void.

KEY FEATURES

Through numerous examples, readers will come to understand that serious games aren't the result of genre-bending to create an artificial niche or adding a veneer of gameplay to an otherwise dull simulation or computer-based instruction experience.

This book contains the following key features:

- Defines the serious games industry from multiple perspectives
- Presents tools and techniques that can be applied to real-world development challenges
- Explains relevant technical and business concepts with a minimum of jargon
- Provides an extensive resource section for established and burgeoning game developers

INTENDED AUDIENCE

Developing Serious Games is written for students, established game developers, and professionals in related fields, such as modeling and simulation or instructional design, who are skilled in training with traditional approaches and tools. As a branch point to further exploration, the content should be equally applicable to programmers, graphic artists, and management—anyone contemplating or involved in the development of serious games. Although this book considers a range of technical and business topics, it does not assume a technical background or experience managing a game development shop.

THE CONTENT

Serious games development is an evolving, diverse field, and the content of *Developing Serious Games* reflects this diversity. Although there are exceptions, at this stage in the development of the serious games industry, small developers—independents as well as shops working within large institutions or businesses—are more likely to be involved in serious games development than are the Electronic Arts of the world. Many development shops, especially those in academia and medicine, are resource-constrained and lack the funding that typically accompanies an extensive serious military game. As such, accessible tools, techniques, and approaches to serious games development are emphasized, while recognizing the practices employed by the large development shops that create AAA games for the entertainment industry.

Although this book is written in self-standing chapters, the concepts discussed in the first seven chapters culminate in a serious games design document discussed in Chapter 8, "Serious Games Design." Furthermore, experienced game developers might want to skip to Chapter 3, "Technology Trends." Readers familiar with instructional design and traditional modeling and simulation or courseware development but new to game development, as well as students new to the field, will likely benefit from the survey provided by the first two chapters.

Chapter 1, "Historical Perspective":   Offers a review of the factors that have contributed to the emergence of serious games as a viable niche in the multibillion dollar gaming industry. In particular, it catalogs the role of the industrial-military complex and the medical information communities within the context of sweeping developments in the commercial game and computer hardware industries. Developments in the medical community are used to illustrate issues common to contemporary serious games development, from the need for domain expertise and emphasis on content accuracy to designs that reflect the primary learning styles of the player population.

Chapter 2, "Working Context":   Offers examples of contemporary serious games, including games with an agenda, news games, political games, realistic games, and core competency games. In addition, serious games derived from repurposed COTS games and modifications (mods) are considered because of the popularity of these approaches to acquiring or developing serious games. This chapter also examines the value proposition offered by serious games, primarily in the area of economics, educational effectiveness, efficacy, and social impact.

Chapter 3, "Technology Trends":   Introduces the enabling technologies that address the complexity and resource demands of serious games development. The latest innovations in computer hardware and architectures are discussed in the context of increased development pipeline throughput. The central role of custom and repurposed COTS peripherals in serious games development and design is introduced, and the various forms of middleware, from game engines to AI engines, are discussed. Network developments that increase gameplay options and extend gameplay longevity are introduced, followed by a review of technologies aimed at reducing complexity by supporting management strategies and technological challenges at every stage of the development pipeline.

Chapter 4, "Standards":   Discusses the standards relevant to serious games development, including those related to hardware platforms, development tools, and asset formats and those that provide for communications and interoperability. Genre and rating standards for serious games destined for widespread commercialization and distribution are discussed. Data Flow diagrams and Use Case models, two game design notation standards, are defined and illustrated, and asset standards that support the economical repurposing and sharing of models, images, and other media are discussed. Wired and wireless communications standards are discussed in the context of increasingly popular networked gaming. Finally, SCORM and similar interoperability standards initiatives are discussed in terms of their potential impact on serious games developers.

Chapter 5, "Best Practices":   Reviews best practices that apply to serious games development in the areas of user interfaces design, programming, working with assets, actor and level design, as well as archiving and reporting. User interface best practices are discussed in terms of the six-tier model, with the physical interface at the bottom and the emotionally intelligent interface at the top. Programming best practices considers languages, data structures and algorithms, program flow, and code review practices. Methods of handling assets, such as the creation of a master asset list, are discussed, followed by best practice methods of defining game actors. Level design practices using both level logic and level maps are introduced, followed by a discussion of archiving. Finally, assessment best practices, namely expressing goals in terms of measurable behavior changes with a standard nomenclature, following proven protocols, and reporting user activity with standards such as XML are introduced.

Chapter 6, "Tools":   Provides an overview of the potentially confusing array of tools that can be used to develop serious games. There is an emphasis on the less complex and more affordable tools that might be used by developers working in simulation or instructional design. Design software options are reviewed, followed by data acquisition and development hardware. A section on embedded hardware is provided for readers who require functionality or mobility unavailable with standard hardware. Options for prototyping software are reviewed, with an emphasis on tools for working with serious content. There is also a discussion of game engines and approachable development environments and tools for code and asset creation and management, followed by tools for management and deployment. A final section provides examples of software development suites used for serious game development projects.

Chapter 7, "Serious Business":   Examines the economic realities of the serious games industry. Using the entertainment game market as a reference point, business models, markets, stakeholders, and customer base of the serious games business are discussed. Legal issues relevant to serious games, including intellectual property rights associated with government contract work are introduced, followed by a review of relevant risk management strategies. Finally, the public relations challenges inherited from the entertainment games industry are discussed.

Chapter 8, "Serious Games Design":   Introduces the serious games design document, which marks the transition of a game from an idea to an actionable plan. The major sections of the document are discussed within the context of serious games development, including: the requirements specification; a description of technical architecture; the overall game design; programming plan; details of asset acquisition and development; the plan for testing and debugging; deployment details; assessment as a vehicle for measurable behavior change; provision for maintenance and troubleshooting; project management; and legal issues.

Chapter 9, "Outlook":   Offers a view on the likely trajectory of serious gaming, from the perspectives of both developers and emerging markets. It examines the potential future of serious games based on technological trends and explores the prospects for developers who have domain expertise in addition to knowledge of game development.

Appendix A, "Glossary":   Provides a collection of terms serious game developers are likely to encounter in the course of financing, developing, and marketing a serious game. In addition to terms used in the text, there are definitions related to funding opportunities with the military and other organizations.

Appendix B, "Acronyms":   Lists acronyms used in the text, supplemented with additional acronyms associated with the military and government funding agencies relevant to serious games development.

Appendix C, "File Formats":   Provides a ready reference to file extensions linked to format standards for graphics, fonts, animation and video, audio, databases, and game engines. A separate section on medical formats is provided to illustrate the range of domain specific formats that might be involved in serious games development.

Appendix D, "Serious Games Design Document Outline":   Offered to readers as the basis for a serious games design document.

Appendix E, "A Brief Business Plan Primer":   Provided for readers new to business plan development. As with the other appendices, relevant references are provided for readers who want to explore the topic more fully.

Appendix F, "Resources":   An extensive list of online and print resources, organizations, conferences, tools, and vendors relevant to serious games development.

As with most printed publications that deal with the game industry, the half-life of the content presented in this book is inversely proportional to the rate of change in the rapidly evolving field. Readers who follow the field know that magazines and Web sites are continually reporting on development shops that wither away or grow to absorb their competitors, new development tools, and the latest short-lived poster child for the top serious game. Given this reality, readers are encouraged to examine the online and print references at the end of each chapter so that they can better follow the inevitable twists and turns of the serious games development industry as it evolves. Readers new to game development should pay particular attention to Appendix F, "Resources," which provides links to organizations and newsgroups that monitor the pulse of the serious games industry.

REFERENCES

[ADL05] ADL, *Content Object Reference Model*. 2005. *http://www.adlnet.org*, accessed September 11, 2005.

[Bernhardt98] Bernhardt, P. C., J. M. Dabbs, Jr, et al., "Testosterone Changes during Vicarious Experiences of Winning and Losing among Fans at Sporting Events." *Physiol Behav* 1(1998): pp. 59–62.

[Bonds04] Bonds, Scott, Jamie Briant, et al., *Quality of Life in the Game Industry: Challenges and Best Practices*. International Game Developers Association, 2004.

[BonkDennen05] Bonk, Curtis, and Vanessa Dennen, *Massive Multiplayer Online Gaming: A Research Framework for Military Training and Education*. Advanced Distributed Learning, 2005.

[Fordis05] Fordis, Michael, Jason King, et al., "Comparison of the Instructional Efficacy of Internet-Based CME with Live Interactive CME Workshops: A Randomized Controlled Trial " *JAMA* (2005): pp. 1043–51.

[Gee04] Gee, James, *What Video Games Have To Teach Us about Learning and Literacy*. Palgrave Macmillan, 2004.

[Gold92] Gold, Steve, "Atari Falcon 030 Now Shipping." *Newsbyte News Network*, 1992.

[MitchellSavil-Smith04] Mitchell, Alice, and Carol Savil-Smith, *The Use of Computer and Video Games for Learning: A Review of the Literature*. Learning and Skill Development Agency. 2004. *www.lsda.org.uk/files/PDF/1529.pdf.*, Accessed September 11, 2005.

[Moore99] Moore, Geoffrey, *Crossing the Chasm: Marketing and Selling High-Tech Products to Mainstream Customers*. HarperBusiness, 1999.

[Moscovich01] Moscovich, Ivan, *1000 Play Thinks: Puzzles, Paradoxes, Illustrations & Games*. Workman Books, 2001.

[Papert80] Papert, Seymour, *Mindstorms: Children, Computers and Powerful Ideas*. Basic Books, 1980.

[Rideout05] Rideout, Victoria, Donald Roberts, et al., *Generation M: Media in the Lives of 8–18-year-olds*. Kaiser Family Foundation, 2005.

[Svensson05] Svensson, Peter, *Videogame Tourneys Draw Big-Time Sponsors*. Yahoo News. 2005. *news.yahoo.com/news?tmpl=story&u=/ap/20050914/ap_on_hi_te/emerging_e_sports*, accessed September 14, 2005.

HISTORICAL PERSPECTIVE

In This Chapter

- Contribution of the industrial-military complex to serious games
- Evolution of serious games in medicine
- Growth of commercial games and computing platforms

INTRODUCTION

Every serious games developer should be aware of how tools, hardware, business models, and the art of game development have coevolved. The most important developments in the serious games space have been related to the evolution of the industrial-military complex, the use of computers in medical education, the popularity of commercial games and growth of the computer industry.

THE INDUSTRIAL-MILITARY COMPLEX

The genesis of the commercial video game industry was the development of simulators for the military. Initial accounts of serious gaming and the modern military date back to the late 1920s, when Edwin Link built the first flight simulator [Kelly70]. The impetus to build a simulator was economic. It was the time of the Great Depression, and Link couldn't afford to develop his aviation skills through flying time alone. Using organ parts and air compressors from his father's shop, Link built a crude flight simulator to supplement his training.

Initially, Link only managed a few sales of what came to be known as the Link Trainer to amusement parks, because the flying community regarded his contraption as an expensive toy. Link's fortunes changed with an accident in which several air force pilots were killed because of poor visibility due to fog. After personally demonstrating how his system could train pilots to take off and land at night, the military came to accept his technology. Within a few years, Link had sold trainers to the Army Air Corps and, ironically, the Japanese Imperial Navy.

World War II was an economic boon for Link, and his company sold thousands of the electro-mechanical simulators to the U.S. military. The ANT-18 trainer, shown in Figure 1.1, was known as the *Blue Box*. Each flight simulator was equipped with a full instrument panel.

During WW II, approximately 10,000 Link Blue Boxes were produced and used to train a half-million Allied aviators. Following the war, Link's company continued to develop simulators for the military, NASA, and the commercial airline industry. One of Link Simulation and Training's latest products, the Aviation Combined Arms Tactical Trainer-Aviation (AVCATT-A), shown in Figure 1.2, enables up to six crews to train together on a virtual-reality battlefield [Roxana04].

Moving from the Blue Box to the AVCATT-A required 50 years of progress in computers, electronics, and game development. The first computer games appeared shortly after WW II. Arthur Samuel designed a checker-playing computer in 1947; this was followed by a design for a chess-playing computer in 1950 by the mathematician and father of information theory, Claude Shannon [Asimov94].

FIGURE 1.1   The ANT-18 trainer, or Link Blue Box. Operators seated around the desk instruct the pilot through various maneuvers and record the results. © Link Simulation and Training. Reprinted with permission.

FIGURE 1.2   Aviation Combined Arms Tactical Trainer-Aviation. © Link Simulation and Training. Reprinted with permission.

The first computer-based military simulation games were developed at the Rand Air Defense Lab in Santa Monica in 1952. The audience for these games was limited to research scientists because of security issues, the cost of computer time, and the limited number of computers. The conceptual framework for the computer game was formalized the following year in the first primer on game theory, *The Compleat Strategyst* [Williams86]. Many firsts were soon to follow—the first non-military game, a pool game, in 1954, the first theater-level war game in 1955, and the first multiplayer game in 1958.

Jumping ahead to the mid-80s, the U.S. Army's Simulation Network, SIMNET, enabled tank crews to maneuver simulated tanks and fighting vehicles against enemy helicopters [Sharp97]. Like the network games available through game consoles, crews could communicate with each other to coordinate their moves. The virtual reality training system led to the creation of the more advanced Close Combat Technical Trainer (CCTT) in the late 1990s [Craven05].

The military was involved in the development of hundreds of relatively small, independent game systems during the 1990s, such as *Electro Adventure*, part of the Navy's Basic Electricity and Electronics training program (BEESIM). The simulation-based adventure game was used to teach basic electrical theory [Halff94]. Other Navy projects at that time included Submarine Skills-Training Network (*SubSkillsNet*), a simulation-based game for the PC, and *Bottom Gun*, a radar training game that allowed players to fire missiles at targets [Walters01]. One of the limitations of these systems was the inability to share content between programs in the navy and other branches of the military—a limitation that the U.S. military has attempted to rectify.

It took decades for military computer games to diffuse into the consumer market. Interestingly, the flow of innovation was not one-way. Consider that Mattel introduced the PowerGlove in 1989 as a game controller for the Nintendo Entertainment System. The glove, which enabled players to use finger motion and wrist roll to control a game, was a commercial failure. However, the military parlayed the technology into useful systems, including the Navy's Virtual At-Sea Training (VAST) project [Chatham03]. The war game uses real ships and weaponry and computer-generated targets to enable seamen to practice at sea, saving the time and expense of traveling to and from remote training ranges. The heart of the game is a system of acoustic sensing buoys equipped with GPS sensors that enable the accurate triangulation of the ordinance—akin to the TV-mounted sensors used to determine the position of the PowerGlove.

More recent serious games projects are underway at the MOVES Institute Naval Postgraduate School in Monterey (*www.movesinstitute.org*). The institute has been involved in a wide range of game-relevant work, from developing more realistic AI for first-person shooters to supporting the development of *America's Army* [Darken04]. MOVES uses off-the-shelf computer hardware and the *Delta3D* open source software (*www.delta3d.org*) to avoid licensing fees and vendor lock-in.

The most significant military serious games project is the Defense Advanced Research Project Agency (DARPA) on-demand training superiority program DARWARS (*www.darwars.com*). As with MOVES, the concept is to use low-cost, Web-centric, simulation-based systems that take advantage of the ubiquity of the PC and of the Internet.

EVOLUTION OF SERIOUS GAMES IN MEDICINE

Medicine is second only to the military in directing the evolution of serious games. The reasons for this influence include a tradition of biomedical modeling and simulation, significant government funding for research into computer-based instruction for physicians, and the attractiveness of the lucrative medical market to hardware vendors and software developers.

Computer-Aided Instruction

Serious games in medicine emerged from a milieu of computer-aided instruction (CAI) and simulation that began at Oregon State University (OSU), Massachusetts General Hospital Laboratory of Computer Science (MGH-LCS), and the University of Illinois. OSU introduced the first computer-based instruction systems in medicine, the *Tutorial Evaluation System* (TES), in 1967 [Shortliffe01]. MGH-LCS and the University of Illinois introduced their own character-based systems shortly thereafter.

These three systems set the standard for computer-based instruction in medicine. Because the underlying technology was expensive to create and maintain, it was beyond the technical and economic reach of most other medical institutions. The National Library of Medicine (NLM) addressed this problem in 1972 when it sponsored the creation of a nationwide network for CAI in medicine.

Enabling Hardware

Interest in using computers for serious tasks surged with the introduction of the IBM PC in 1981. Despite the PC's appeal to corporate America, the Apple II was favored over the IBM PC by many clinicians. *Gas Man*, a simulation-based learning environment for anesthesiologists, was developed at Brigham & Women's Hospital, Boston, on the Apple II in 1982 [Philip84]. The program enabled users to visualize the dynamics of respiratory, vascular, and tissue anesthetic concentrations in a patient under inhalation anesthesia (*www.gasmanweb.com*). *Gas Man* was significant in that it was one of the first products from the medical modeling and simulation community designed with an interface for clinicians instead of researchers, who were used to a command line interface [Randall87].

The problem of incompatibility due to multiple hardware platforms, operating systems, and languages resurfaced in the mid-1980s. There were thousands of medical simulations and teaching programs that couldn't interoperate. Even sharing the media stored in standard formats was problematic.

Development Examples

In the mid-1980s, one focus of Harvard's Decision Systems Group (DSG) was supporting the HST curriculum with computer-based simulations and courseware. The first courseware developed in the DSG was *HeartLab* (see Figure 1.3), a simulation-based serious game designed to teach cardiac auscultation [Bergeron86].

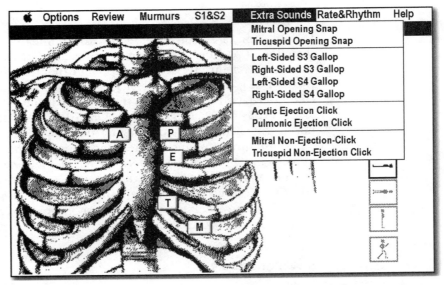

FIGURE 1.3   *HeartLab*, the first commercial multimedia patient simulator on a microcomputer and one of the first serious games in clinical medicine. © 1986 Bryan Bergeron.

From the perspective of the evolution of serious games in medicine, *HeartLab* was significant in that it attempted to accurately replicate the visual and audio components of a real patient encounter. Although the graphics shown in Figure 1.3 are rudimentary by modern standards, in 1985, the concept of onscreen graphics for nongame applications was revolutionary.

Around the same time, researchers at Stanford were experimenting with AI concepts that would eventually drive serious games development. The most significant program was *GUIDON*, which used teaching strategy rules that interacted with diagnostic rules from an expert system [Clancey87].

In 1989 the author worked with John Fallon and students of the HST program to develop *PathGame,* a serious medical game that requires players to differentiate between normal and abnormal pathology images (see Figure 1.4). *PathGame* is significant in that it is one of the first serious games expressly developed as a *fun* game for a medical school curriculum. A study of *PathGame* showed that students voluntarily played the game in their off hours to prepare for exams [Bergeron 90]. The program is also significant in that it used a neural network to control the progression of difficulty [Bergeron90b].

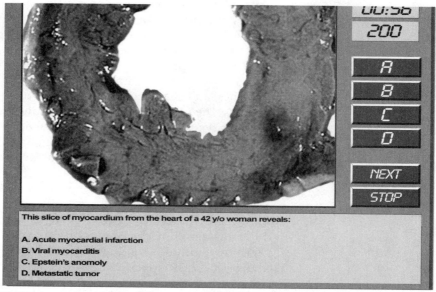

FIGURE 1.4   *PathGame* is a serious medical game in which players are required to respond to questions keyed to images of medical pathology. © 1989 Bryan Bergeron.

Significance

The evolution of serious games in medicine illustrates several domain-independent issues related to serious games development. The key issues include the following:

   Content accuracy: The serious content must be verified for accuracy. Close approximations of images, sounds, and other content that might be good enough for an entertainment game may be unusable in a serious game. Because of this need for accuracy, the time and resources expended on content creation and acquisition might overshadow game development coding.

Domain expertise: Related to content accuracy is the need for domain expertise in the development group. The subtle details of a domain that might not be noticeable to someone without domain expertise are often critical to game success. Knowledge of the correct tint of tissues in a pathology image, the sound characteristics of a barely perceptible rumble in a heart murmur, and the exact orientation of a blood vessel often can't be learned from a book in five minutes or from a quick Web search. Developers of serious military games without military experience have been known to sleep in military barracks, eat military rations, and observe live weapons fire to better represent the sounds and images of military activity in their games [Bennett04].

Design principles: Developing a serious game is more than simply building a graphical interface and adding gameplay to an existing mathematical model. A serious games design should reflect a requirements specification that defines gameplay and user interaction. Serious games needn't include 3D graphics, physics engines, and character AI to be effective.

Staffing: The need for domain expertise and content accuracy places specific demands on staffing requirements. For example, an artist just out of game development school might do a great job designing superheroes for a video game, but fail at drawing anatomically correct figures for a surgical procedure. Serious games developers typically come from other disciplines, such as the modeling and simulation community.

Domain-specific techniques: There is often a need to integrate domain-specific techniques with traditional game development techniques in the serious games development process.

Domain- and task-specific user interfaces: Serious games might require domain-specific software and hardware interfaces that are integral to gameplay. Physicians typically listen to heart sounds with stethophones, for example, even though headphones and other superior technologies are readily available.

Player profile: Developers working with specific populations should know whether there is a preferred learning style and, if so, design their serious games accordingly.

Visibility: There are many more serious games in use throughout academia, corporate America, and the military than the press releases suggest.

Product mix: None of the medical serious games described in this chapter were developed in a game shop, and none of the developers would have described themselves as game developers. And yet, the groups produced serious games. This raises the issue of what product mix constitutes a serious game shop.

Standards: The experience of the medical education community illustrates the need for standards so that content and code can be readily shared. Unfortunately, many content standards are still discipline dependent, as illustrated in Appendix C, "File Formats."

Investment: Significant investment from government and private sector sources is necessary to maintain research and development efforts in serious games.

Platform and tool evolution: Most of the medical education applications developed only a decade ago are no longer available because of changes in computer hardware and software platforms.

Assessment component: Assessment is often an integral part of the serious games lifecycle. Educational institutions, like private industry and the government, want to know whether their investment in serious games is resulting in the desired behavior change.

The contribution of the evolution of commercial game technology and computing platforms to the development of serious games is considered in the following section.

COMMERCIAL GAMES AND COMPUTING PLATFORMS

The first widespread gameplay experiences in the civilian world were on academic mainframes and minicomputers. The first game invented specifically for the computer, *Spacewar*, was developed in 1962 by Steven Russell at MIT [Lok05]. The game was never commercialized, largely because there wasn't a large user base for the computing platform—the PDP-1 from Digital Equipment Corporation.

The field of CAI was kick started by two events in 1964. The first was the development of a general-purpose, multimedia CAI system at Stanford and the introduction of the BASIC language at Dartmouth College. A variety of graphic displays soon appeared on the market, enabling Evans and Sutherland to create an electronic flight simulator in 1969—40 years after Link built his electromechanical simulator. Evans and Sutherland (*www.es.com*) went on to become a major supplier of commercial and military simulators.

Widespread use of computers by the civilian population was encouraged by the government. Federal funding from the National Science Foundation (NSF) in the 1960s encouraged the use of computers in high school and college. One notable NSF-funded game, *Malaria*, was developed in 1969 at the Brooklyn Polytechnic Institute. Players had to control an outbreak of malaria using a combination of pesticides, inoculations, and other treatments without bankrupting the country. Within three years, the first role playing games (RPGs), *Adventure* and *Dungeons and Dragons*, were usurping the off-hours computer time of academic mainframes and minicomputers.

Apple introduced the first home computer with color graphics, the Apple II, in 1977. It was the product of two game developers from Atari—Steve Jobs and Steve Wozniak. That same year, Lucasfilm, Ltd., released *Star Wars*, which features special effects made with plastic models and laborious manual manipulation of film. The Apple II laid the groundwork for the computer hobby industry, which was catapulted even higher by David Ahl's book *101 Basic Computer Games*, the first computer book to sell more than a million copies [King03]. Ahl's book and his magazine, *Popular Computing*, popularized game development as a hobby [Freiberger00].

Paradoxically, even though the personal computing industry was initially based on gaming, the long-term survival of the personal computer as a computing platform was dependent on leaving behind the gaming and hobby machine image. The first chink in the personal-computer-as-game-machine image came in 1979 with the first *killer app* for the personal computer, *VisiCalc*. The spreadsheet program was reason enough for some small business to invest in a computer to keep their books.

The tipping point came in 1981, when IBM entered the personal computer market and changed the public perception of personal computers as game and hobby machines to business tools. The availability of the *Lotus 123* spreadsheet in 1982 pushed the IBM PC into small businesses and corporate America, where its Windows-compatible descendents remain entrenched.

The personal computer reemerged as a significant gaming platform in 1993 with the release of two landmark games—Cyan's *Myst* and Id Software's *DOOM*. *Myst*, with its picturesque, pre-rendered 3D landscapes—and opened PC (and Macintosh) gaming to a mass audience. PC gamers could finally experience 3D graphics and sound reminiscent of those available through console players a decade earlier. *DOOM* was significant in that it supported network play and could be easily modified, or modded, by players.

In addition to redefining the first person shooter (FPS) genre and driving the popularity of PC-based multiplayer games, Id Software revolutionized video game development. Id offered the core code of *DOOM*—the *DOOM engine*—to other developers to decrease time to market for their games [Daley01]. Microsoft's Windows Games SDK, the progenitor of DirectPlay, and OpenGL from Silicon Graphics added to the momentum of the game engine approach to game development by offering predefined libraries of graphics functions. Although the competing APIs divided the development community, they made it possible for hobbyists to develop fully functional game engines in a matter of months.

Id again shook the game industry with the release of *QUAKE* in 1996. Like *DOOM*, the first person shooter supported network play and the underlying engine was easily modded. What distinguished *QUAKE* from its predecessors was true 3D graphics that were rendered in real-time. In addition to innovations such as dynamic lighting and the use of 3D models for characters, *QUAKE* was influential as a driver in the video card and display industries. Players who wanted to experience the space marine's adventure in higher fidelity were happy to pay for video cards with more than a few kilobytes of RAM and for higher quality color displays. Screen shots of Id's games, from *Commander Keen: Invasion of the Vorticons* trilogy to the latest incarnations of *QUAKE* and *DOOM*, are available on the Id Software Web site (*www.idsoftware.com*).

Prior to the use of game engines, code and data were usually intermingled in one file. Following the lead of the artificial intelligence community, which advocated separate data and code, the new game architecture established a standard approach for the development of more complex and powerful back ends, especially the artificial intelligence component of modern console and PC games. Game engines lowered a major barrier to entry and shortened time to market for small, independent game development shops. See Appendix F, "Resources," for examples of the many game engines and game development environments available to serious games developers.

Arcade Games

The golden age of arcade games began in 1972 with the debut of the first commercially successful coin-operated computer game, Atari's *Pong*. By 1982—only a decade after the debut of *Pong*—the arcade computer game business was worth $7 billion [Reid-Green00], thanks to a run of games that included *PacMan*, *Space Invaders*, and *Asteroids*.

The game industry's bubble burst in 1983, ostensibly because of an overabundance of mediocre games and a saturated market with companies competing for game market share. The industry rebounded after 1985 with the release of the Nintendo Entertainment System (NES), but with the increasing popularity of home computers and portable game devices, the arcade business never repeated the performance of its first decade.

The arcade game industry is significant to the development of the serious games industry in how it positioned games negatively in the mind of the general public, and in its contribution to the use of serious games in the military. The controversy surrounding gratuitous violence and sex in *Grand Theft Auto* (Rockstar Games) seems trite compared with the arcade game *Death Race* (Exidy), released in 1976. Gamers scored points in the cross-country automobile race game by hitting pedestrians along the way. The publicity might have temporarily resulted in a run on quarters, but it also tarnished the image of gamers and of the gaming industry.

The public perception of video games as contributors to juvenile delinquency came to a head in 1993, when U.S. Senators Lieberman and Kohl initiated an investigation on video game violence. Facing stiff regulations, the video game industry *volunteered* to establish and maintain rating systems. The result was the Entertainment Software Rating Board (ESRB) and Internet Content Rating Association (ICRA), which rate packaged games and online game sites, respectively [ESRB 05; ICRA 05]. Of the two rating systems, the ICRA is more relevant, in that independent serious games developers frequently rely on the Internet as an inexpensive distribution channel.

Arcade games were the vehicle for the U.S. military's first foray into the use and repurposing of commercially developed entertainment video games for serious training purposes. In 1980 the Army's Training and Doctrine Command (TRADOC) commissioned the development of a prototype based on Atari's tank game, *Battlezone* [Battlezone05]. Instead of the space tanks and flying saucers found in the arcade game, *Army Battlezone* featured realistic silhouettes of enemy and friendly tanks, helicopters, and armored personnel carriers [Trachtman81]. The tradition of repurposing COTS games continues today. For example, the Navy's digital game-based learning initiative MISSILE is focused on identifying consumer games that can be used by the Navy for training [NAVY03].

Consoles

Games on general-purpose computer hardware and operating systems have consistently lagged behind what is possible on dedicated console platforms. The first game console available to consumers, the Magnavox Odyssey, was an evolutionary anomaly in 1971. The video game console used rudimentary graphics and colored plastic overlays designed to stick to a TV screen (see Figure 1.5). The mix of games available for the unit was comparable to contemporary console offerings and included sports, educational, warfare, adventure, puzzler, gambling, and driving games. Players selected games by inserting "dumb" cards into the console, which physically rewired the unit's internal circuitry. Some games required several card changes during gameplay, and it was up to one of the players to know when to insert a different card in the console.

The graphics and logic available on the Odyssey were limited. The games relied on plastic overlays for color and context (akin to a level in modern games), a pair of die for randomization, and playing cards for additional content. Several of the games were supplemented with a cardboard game board and plastic playing pieces to add context and an element of chance.

FIGURE 1.5   Magnavox Odyssey *Simon Says,* the first anatomy game on a console. © Archetype Technologies, Inc.

The *Simon Says* game, shown in Figure 1.5, is an anatomy game for two players. During gameplay, a third person is supposed to turn over one of the cards from the deck of anatomy landmarks and read it aloud. The first player to move his block cursor from the starting position (one of the two rectangles in Figure 1.5) to the proper body part wins the round. In this example, the goal is the elbow, which is correctly identified on the figure of the girl. Although simplistic by modern standards, *Simon Says* was the first commercial console-based anatomy trainer.

The Odyssey was doomed from day one because it was an *analog* computer, without a general purpose digital CPU, programmable ROM, or memory found in modern consoles. Gameplay was based on circuit dynamics defined by a few dozen resistors, capacitors, and diodes, and only 31 transistors, distributed among 10 plug-in circuit cards (see Figure 1.6) and the motherboard. As a result, the gameplay varied little from one game to the next, and new games couldn't be accommodated by the unit. Because the unit lacked memory, rudimentary capabilities such as maintaining a list of high scores, was impossible.

If not for the development of the digital integrated circuit and the digital CPU, game development today would require a soldering iron, discrete transistors from the local electronics store, and a steady hand. But Intel did develop the first single chip digital microprocessor, the Intel 4004, in 1971 [Wittie00].

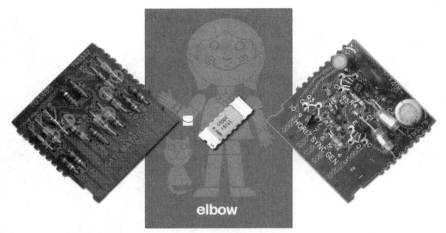

FIGURE 1.6   Two of the 10 analog computing modules from the Magnavox Odyssey and the digital Intel 4004 (center) responsible for the Odyssey's demise. The playing card is from the *Simon Says* anatomy game. © Archetype Technologies, Inc.

The technological leap from the analog circuitry of the Odyssey to the digital microprocessor is almost evident from the packaging, shown in Figure 1.6. Compared with three or four transistors per 4.5×4.5 cm card, the much smaller 4004 held 2,124 transistors. Furthermore, whereas the functions of the analog circuitry were defined by the physical connection of discrete components, the functions of the 4004 could be modified quickly and inexpensively by programming a ROM. In comparison, modifying a game on the Odyssey required a physical circuit change, and a modification for one game affected all other games. The flexibility and power of the microprocessor enabled Atari to enter the game market with an affordable, extensible digital game system that outperformed the Odyssey [Slater01].

Consoles are relevant to the serious games development community as standards against which players judge PC games. Consoles are closed systems and, except for non-extensible systems, console revenue is tied directly to game sales. Game titles define the profit and loss for the game console manufacturers because Microsoft, Sony, and Nintendo receive a significant royalty with every game sold [Wingfield05]. In this regard, the big three console manufacturers follow the business model perfected by Gillette and sell the hardware at or below manufacturing cost.

Just as razorblade manufacturers take a loss on the shaving handle and make money on the high-margin consumables, the major console manufacturers count on game sales for revenue. To sell more consumables (game CD-ROMs, DVDs, and cartridges), console developers pour research and development (R&D) dollars into improving the quality and speed of their console's graphics and the power and realism of their sound systems. In addition, game console makers entice developers to develop exclusively for their platform by offering them lucrative contracts that include special development software and hardware at extreme discounts—a practice borrowed from desktop computer manufacturers. The initial success of the Apple Macintosh, for example, was due largely to the efforts of Apple at enjoining a group of certified developers who were given access to proprietary information on Apple's hardware and software in exchange for their loyalty.

The exception to the consumables model noted earlier refers to the emergence of handheld TV games in the late 1990s. These miniature, battery-powered consoles, also referred to as Play TV™, TV Arcade™, Plug It In And Play TV Game™, and Video Maxx™, plug directly into a TV monitor [Jakks05]. As shown in Figure 1.8, TV games are sealed controllers the size and shape of either a small joystick or a controller pad. In other words, the game hardware and firmware are embedded in the controller, just as microcomputers are increasingly embedded in appliances, cell phones, and toys. See the Jakks Pacific Web site (*www.jakkstvgames.com*) for more information on TV games.

FIGURE 1.7   Examples of Plug It In And Play TV Games™ *Spider Man, Atari 10-in-1,* and *Ms. Pacman.*

Many of the classic arcade titles, from *Ms. Packman* to *Frogger*, have been ported to the TV games format. The latest TV games feature multiple games and built-in memory, and sell for about the price of a standard controller. The *Atari 10-in-1* game, shown in Figure 1.7, provides 10 classic Atari video games, including *Pong, Centipede, Missile Command*, and *Asteroids*, in one Atari 2600 joystick replica.

NETWORKED DESKTOP AND CONSOLE GAMES

LAN parties and modern subscription-based massively multiplayer online games (MMOGs), such as *Lineage, EverQuest, Ultima Online*, and *Star Wars Galaxies*, are rooted in technology first popularized in 1981 by the Play-Cable Company [Herman97]. The PlayCable adapter allowed subscribers to download Intellivision games over cable TV to their consoles. Failures by Nintendo, Sega, and dozens of lesser-known companies in the networked gaming space paved the way for the game networks supporting Sony, Microsoft, and Nintendo. In particular, Sega's short-lived SegaNet service for Dreamcast players was introduced in 2000 with the first console-based MMOG role playing game, *Phantasy Star Online*.

Unlike gamers in Korea, Japan, and Hong Kong, who flock to PC gaming cafes to interact with other players through multiplayer gameplay, most gamers in the United States play at home [Rideout05]. Not surprisingly, networked gaming has been targeted by the big three console manufacturers as a cornerstone to the success of their latest generation machines. The Xbox 360, Playstation 3, and Nintendo Revolution are all designed to facilitate networked gameplay [Wingfield05b]. The Playstation 3 enables players to videoconference during gameplay, and Xbox Live Gold supports intelligent gameplay matchmaking, video chat, and video messaging.

The popularity of networked gaming that started with *DOOM* hasn't been limited to MMOGs and console games. However, while most of the top entertainment titles on the PC support multiplayer use, the serious games community has yet to exploit the potential of the social phenomenon of networked gaming on the PC. Exceptions are multiplayer military games and the previously mentioned *DARWARS* project. The military is also actively researching the effectiveness of MMOGs as vehicles for military training [BonkDennen05].

Handheld Games

The first cartridge-based handheld video game, the Milton Bradley MicroVision, was introduced in 1979 [Herman97]. Since then, dozens of handheld video game systems have come and gone, from the Nintendo Game &

Watch, Atari Lynx, Nintendo Game Boy, and NEC TurboExpress, to Sega's Game Gear. In addition to these extensible systems, there have been hundreds of inexpensive, dedicated handheld games, such as Bandai's *Tamagotchi*, Hasbro's *Battleship*, and Mattel's *Classic Baseball*. Most of these dedicated entertainment games were manufactured in Asia and distributed through toy stores in the United States. Dedicated game systems remain a viable niche in the toy industry and range from inexpensive, reincarnated versions of retro arcade games to wireless educational toys that enable children to solve puzzles together.

Educational electronic toys are among the fastest growing segments of the otherwise lackluster toy market [Kang05]. Figure 1.8 shows an example of an educational handheld, the Leapster™ Multimedia Learning System, which was introduced in 2003 [Leapfrog05]. The game, which can be extended with childproof cartridges, enables a child to play a variety of serious games, read electronic books, draw, and watch interactive videos.

FIGURE 1.8   Leapster Multimedia Learning System running *Spider Man The Case of the Sinister Speller.*

For most serious game developers, the latest handheld offerings from Nintendo and Sony, the WiFi-enabled Nintendo DS and Sony PSP, have been the most desirable adult handheld deployment platforms. Other contenders for the handheld game market, such as the Gizmondo from Tiger Telematics and the N-Gage QD from Nokia, have failed to attract significant attention from gamers or game developers [Mott05]. However, accessibility to the DS and PSP has been limited to serious games developers working on games with significant commercial potential, such as *DS Training for Adults: Work Your Brain* (Nintendo) for the DS and *Smart Bomb* (Eidos) for the PSP.

Although the development tools and distribution licenses for the DS and PSP are closely controlled by Nintendo and Sony, software development kits (SDKs) are readily available for PDAs compatible with the Palm OS and Microsoft Windows Mobile platforms. For example, we used a third-party compiler, *NS Basic*, to develop the *Mixed Reality Auscultation Trainer* for the PocketPC (see Figure 1.9).

This serious game is designed to provide Harvard medical students with exposure to a variety of abnormal heart and lung sounds in the context of a live patient presentation. Not shown in the figure is the wireless sensor harness, composed of a dozen quarter-sized, sensors designed to clip on to the underside of a garment over specific points over the instructor's chest and back. In operation, the instructor, who controls the iPAQ and wears the sensor harness, complains of shortness of breath, pain radiating to her left arm, or other cardiac symptoms.

FIGURE 1.9   Instructor interface of the *Mixed Reality Auscultation Trainer* on an iPAQ 2755. The student user interface is a wireless sensor harness worn by the instructor. © Archetype Technologies, Inc.

Even the Apple iPod can be used as a serious games platform. *iHeart-Lab*, shown in Figure 1.10, presents students with prerecorded heart and lung sounds. Students respond by manipulating the iPod's wheel controller. Students are awarded points for correctly answering multiple-choice questions keyed to specific auscultation sounds. Documentation on programming within the Note Reader environment is available through Apple's developer site, *developer.apple.com/hardware/ipod/ipodnotereader.pdf.*

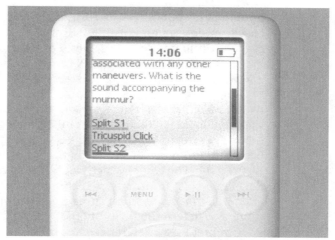

FIGURE 1.10   *iHeartLab,* a cardiac auscultation quiz game for the Apple iPod © Archetype Technologies, Inc.

The obvious advantage of the iPod as a delivery platform for audio-centered games is its popularity among medical students. Another is that because the audio characteristics of the iPod audio system and the standard ear buds are known, the physiologic sounds can be adjusted to closely resemble the sounds heard through a stethoscope.

Cell Phone Games

Cell phone technology originated in the United States in the early to mid-1970s, but businessmen in Tokyo were using cell phones in 1978, years before the first cellular licenses were available in the United States [Bergeron01]. At the start of the new millennium, cellular subscribers throughout Europe and Japan were enjoying games, multimedia, and a host of other services over high-bandwidth digital networks. Meanwhile, subscribers in the United States were still struggling with a mix of incompatible handsets, slow analog connections, and incompatible digital systems.

As of the end of 2005 the U.S. cellular network was still far behind much of Europe, Asia, and even many third-world countries [Drucker05]. Even so, leading domestic cellular carriers were downloading on average one million games per month in mid-2005 [Cooke05]. Another sign that the domestic market for cell phone games has finally taken off is that Trip Hawkins, the founder of Electronic Arts, created Digital Chocolate (*www.digitalchocolate.com*) to offer mobile games. Thus far, the major cell phone game publishers, such as JAMDAT (*www.Jamdat.com*), have focused on entertainment titles. However, several of these programs can also be considered serious games. For example, JAMDAT offers *Lemonade Tycoon*, a business simulation, *Kasparov Chessmate*, a chess game, and several word games, including *Wireless Scrabble*, *Boggle*, and *Text Twist*.

Although gaining access to and developing for multiple cell phone platforms remains a hurdle for serious games developers, the primary design challenge is creating a useful serious game within the confines of tiny color screen and miniature keypad. Responses to this challenge have been numerous, as illustrated by the *SymBall* table tennis game shown in Figure 1.11. The game, which can be freely downloaded from the Finnish developer VTT Information Technology Multimedia Group (*www.vtt.fi/multimedia/index_dm.html*), uses images from the cell phone's onboard camera to determine the motion of the unit, using a colored object in the environment as a reference. According to VTT's Multimedia Research Professor Charles Woodward, this relative motion is, in turn, used to position the virtual racket in the cell phone's display.

FIGURE 1.11 *SymBall* table tennis game for camera cell phones in two-player mode illustrates the type of user interface that can be applied to serious games. Developed by the VTT Information Technology Multimedia Group.

SUMMARY

The genesis of modern serious games can be traced back to the aircraft simulators of the late 1920s and the funding of simulator development by the military. The medical modeling and simulation, medical computer-based instruction, and medical informatics communities have each contributed to the trajectory of serious games. In many instances, developments in these and other disciplines were either limited by or enabled by the evolution of the commercial game and computing industries.

Early serious medical games development illustrates several of the distinguishing characteristics of modern serious games, namely: an emphasis on content accuracy; a need for developers with domain expertise; the need to follow design principles that consider the serious content and game components as a unified whole; staffing requirements that reflect the need for content accuracy and domain expertise; the need to incorporate techniques that might be specific to the serious content domain with what many game developers consider traditional techniques; the need to reflect the player's preferred learning style in the serious game design; variability in product mix and, therefore, what it means to be a serious games development shop; the importance of adhering to established standards for content and coding to facilitate sharing; the sizeable investment required to maintain momentum in the research and development of serious games; and the need to make provision for the inevitable evolution of hardware platforms and development tools.

REFERENCES

[Asimov94] Asimov, I., *Asimov's Chronology of Science and Discovery*. Harper Collins Publishers, 1994.

[Battlezone05] Battlezone, *Battlezone*. GameArchive. 2005. *www.gamearchive.com/Video_Games/Manufacturers/Atari/battlezone.html*, accessed April 15, 2005.

[Bennett04] Bennett, Lisa, "Camp Guernsey Event Shows What Its like To Be a Soldier." The Torrington Telegram Online. 2004.*www.torringtontelegram.com/main.php?story_id=2820&page=23*, accessed Sept 14, 2005.

[Bergeron86] Bergeron, Bryan, *HeartLab*. Williams &Wilkins Publishers, 1986.

[Bergeron90] Bergeron, Bryan, John Fallon, et al., Using a gaming approach to maximize student participation in computer-based education. *Collegiate Microcomputer* (4 1990): pp. 293–300.

[Bergeron90b] Bergeron, Bryan, Abraham Morse, et al., A generic neural network-based tutorial supervisor for computer aided instruction. *Fourteenth Annual Symposium on Computer Applications in Medical Care* (1990): pp. 435–9.

[Bergeron01] Bergeron, Bryan, *The wireless web: how to develop a winning wireless strategy*. McGraw-Hill, 2001.

[BonkDennen05] Bonk, Curtis, Vanessa Dennen, *Massive Multiplayer Online Gaming: A Research Framework for Military Training and Education*. Advanced Distributed Learning, 2005.

[Clancey87] Clancey, W., *Knowledge-Based Tutoring: The GUIDON Program*. MIT Press, 1987.

[Cooke05] Cooke, P., "Wireless Networks: Carriers and Barriers." *Game Developer* 2(2005): pp. 53.

[Craven05] Craven, Randal, *Close Combat Tactical Trainer*. 2005. *www.benning.army.mil/ SimCntr/CCTT.htm*, accessed April 16, 2005.

[Daley01] Daley, S., "In Europe, Some Fear National Languages Are Endangered." *The New York Times* (April 16, 2001): pp. 1–10.

[Darken04] Darken, Christian, David Morgan, et al., Efficient and Dynamic Response to Fire. *AAAI 04 Challenges in Game AI workshop* 2004).

[Drucker05] Drucker, Jesse, "Why You Still Can't Hear Me Now." *The Wall Street Journal* (May 25, 2005): pp. D1–D6.

[ESRB05] ESRB, *ESRB Rating System*. 2005. *www.esrb.org*, accessed April 9, 2005.

[FreibergerSwaine00] Freiberger, Paul, Michael Swaine, Fire in the Valley: The making of the personal computer. McGraw-Hill, 2000.

[Herman97] Herman, L., *Phoenix: The Rise and Fall of Videogames*. Rolenta Press, 1997.

[ICRA05] ICRA, *ICRA Rating System*. 2005. *www.icra.org*, accessed April 8, 2005.

[Jakks05] Jakks, *Jakks TV Games*. 2005. *www.jakkstvgames.com*, accessed May 20, 2005.

[Kang05] Kang, Stephanie, "Bright Spot in Toyland." *The Wall Street Journal* (May 23, 2005): pp. R13.

[Kelly70] Kelly, Lloyd, *The Pilot Maker*. Grosset & Dunlap, 1970.

[KingBorland03] King, Brad, John Borland, Dungeons and Dreamers: The Rise of Computer Game Culture from Geek to Chic. McGraw-Hill Obsborne Media, 2003.

[Leapfrog05] Leapfrog, *Leapster Multimedia Learning System*. 2005. *www.leapfrog.com*, accessed May 23, 2005.

[Lok05] Lok, Corie, "The Start of Computer Games." Technology Review (June 2005): pp. 88.

[Mott05] Mott, Tony, Hardware Overload. *Edge* (May 2005): pp. 50–7.

[NAVY03] NAVY, *Naval Reservists Enhance PC-Based Flight Trainer*. Navy Newsstand. 2003. *www.news.navy.mil/search/display.asp?story_id=9402*, accessed May 23, 2005.

[Philip84] Philip, James, *GAS MAN - Understanding Anesthesia Uptake and Distribution*. Addison-Wesley, 1984.

[Randall87] Randall, James, *Microcomputers and Physiological Simulation*. Raven Press, 1987.

[Reid-Green00] Reid-Green, Keith, "Computer Games: Arcade Games," in *Encyclopedia of Computer Science*. Groves Dictionaries, Inc., 2000.

[Rideout05] Rideout, Victoria, Donald Roberts, et al., *Generation M: Media in the lives of 8–18-year-olds*. Kaiser Family Foundation, 2005.

[Roxana04] Roxana, Tiron, Collective Simulation Essential for Pilot Leadership Training. *National Defense* (December 1, 2004).

[Sharp97] Sharp, RF, Logged On: Training on Virtual Battlefield; Tank Crews Enter Computer Combat. *Daily News* (Oct 26, 1997).

[Shortliffe01] Shortliffe, E. H., L. E. Perreault, et al., eds. *Medical Informatics: Computer Applications in Health Care and Biomedicine*, edited by Shortliffe, EH, LE, Perreault, et al. Springer, 2001.

[SlaterSullivan01] Slater, D, J. Sullivan, "Good Idea, Bad Timing." CIO (Aug. 2001): pp. 129–30.

[Trachtman81] Trachtman, Paul, "πA generation meets computers on the playing fields of Atari." Smithsonian (Sept 1981): pp. 61–72.

[Walters01] Walters, B, Training Half Dry. *Armada International* (Aug 2001).

[Williams86] Williams, J. D., *The Compleat Strategyst: Being a Primer on the Theory of Games of Strategy*. Dover Publications, 1986.

[Wingfield05] Wingfield, N, New Games, New Machines, New Winners and Losers. *The Wall Street Journal* (Monday, Jan 31, 2005): pp. R4.

[Wingfield05b] Wingfield, Nick, Rob Guth, et al., A buyer's guide to the new gameboxes. *The Wall Street Journal* (May 18, 2005): pp. D1–6.

[Wittie00] Wittie, Larry, "Microprocessors and Microcomputers," in *Encyclopedia of Computer Science*. Groves Dictionaries, 2000.

2

WORKING CONTEXT

In This Chapter

- Modern serious games
- The value proposition

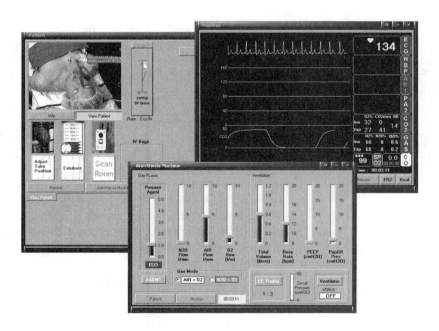

INTRODUCTION

The voluminous consumption of music, video, and video games by Generation M—those born immersed in video, music, games, and computer technology—has refocused the interest of advertisers and the entertainment industry on the goings-on of the multi-billion-dollar video game industry. This renewed interest has in turn fueled the development of game technologies, from affordable, high-performance video cards for PCs and svelte handheld units to next-generation game development software. With the tools available today, anyone with a modicum of programming skill who has played *Halo 2* or *Grand Theft Auto* can develop a *simple* first-person shooter (FPS) in an afternoon. Even the military, a long-time independent and secretive developer and user of proprietary computer-based game technology, is actively acquiring and developing spin-offs from the commercial game development arena. In these anomalous times, custom military hardware and software can no longer compete on a cost/performance basis with the technology available at the corner microcomputer center.

The possibilities created by new game-oriented hardware and software technologies have riveted the attention of educators, advocacy groups, and entertainment game developers. Enthusiasts in these groups want to develop *serious games*—games that not only entertain, but that intentionally deliver an underlying message. As a reality check, professional game developers will point out that developing a game that engages *and* imparts knowledge is a feat that requires an understanding of both gameplay and educational theory. Three excellent treatments of games and learning are Marc Prensky's *Digital Game-Based Learning*, James Gee's *What Video Games Have to Teach Us about Learning and Literacy*, and *Rules of Play: Game Design Fundamentals* by Katie Salen and Eric Zimmerman. Additional resources are listed in Appendix F, "Resources."

Unlike the billion-dollar entertainment video game industry, which has responded to increased product demand by developing increasingly complex and costly games, the serious games segment of the industry has followed an approach of cost containment and technology simplification. Although significant money can be made by serious games development shops, a half-million dollar contract to develop a serious game pales in comparison to a $20 million or $30 million entertainment game contract. Increasingly, what's low budget to an entertainment games developer is considered high-budget in the serious games world.

The genesis of the serious video games genre is full of twists, turns, and unexpected heroes. Furthermore, predicting the trajectory of serious games, including the ultimate market potential, requires an appreciation of the historical contribution of video games (including computer games) to the computing revolution. The first step in this journey is to understand the technological trends, the role of standards and tools, and the serious games market.

CONTEMPORARY SERIOUS GAMES

Based on the lackluster "edutainment" software that flooded the grade schools in the '80s and '90s, it would be easy to misconceive that serious games are primarily content- or test-oriented, with a bit of entertainment sprinkled in as an afterthought. Although edutainment fits the definition of serious games, all *good* serious games are explicitly designed to entertain. It's the serious content woven into the fabric of an entertaining game that makes a serious game a success.

In discussing the entertainment value of serious games, it's important not to get caught up in the semantics, but to understand the concept from the player's perspective. According to Koster in *Theory of Fun for Game Design* [Koster04], a game is fun if it has a challenging goal, is enjoyable to play, and incorporates some concept of scoring or winning and losing—even if only indirectly. However, players might refer to a successful serious game as simply "engaging" instead of "fun," depending on their goals and motivation for playing. For example, a paratrooper using a military game to prepare for a mission would probably refer to a positive experience with the game as "engaging." Regardless of whether a game is fun, entertaining, or engaging, the emotional connection to the game enables the player to receive maximum benefit from the experience.

Fun is a subjective feeling that can't be measured directly. Furthermore, what one person considers fun or engaging might be considered boring by another. Aside from functional MRI (fMRI) studies that show patterns of blood flow associated with various brain activities and states, one of the best methods of indirectly measuring fun is to assess the player's perceived passage of time. The saying, "Time flies when you're having fun" is relevant here, in that when someone is mentally engaged in a task, time seems to pass more rapidly than normal [Block82; Edmonds81]. Most gamers can relate to looking at the clock and committing to just one more level and then looking up, in what seems to them like moments later, surprised to find that hours have passed. Athletes and professionals who are completely engaged in a match or performance refer to this time distortion as being "in the zone" or achieving "flow" [Csikszentmihalyi91]. Conversely, everyone has experienced the opposite effect of time expansion when the task at hand is boring. Filling out an income tax form, sitting through a boring lecture, or enduring a headache can all seem to slow the passage of time.

Even in the military, where studying and other learning activities can be mandated, there is a need to create training materials that soldiers will opt to use on their own time. According to SGM David J. Litteral, chief instructor in the Department of Combat Medic Training at Fort Sam Houston, Texas, the U.S. Army needs a way to entice medics in training to learn anatomy, physiology, and medical vocabulary on their own prior to the official start of their medic training. Some enlistees arrive two weeks prior to the start of classes, and SGM Litteral is convinced that educational games would be the perfect preparation for the 6,500 combat medics—often referred to as the "91 Whiskeys"—who graduate from Fort Sam Houston annually [Litteral05].

The odds of people voluntarily using a serious game that isn't entertaining are no greater than the odds of their picking up a textbook on the subject and studying on their own. Without sufficient motivation, little or no learning will occur. As in the tagline for the Internet portal Social Impact Games (*www.socialimpactgames.com*) suggests, a good way to think about serious games is that they entertain but have nonentertaining goals. Note that this definition doesn't exclude commercial off-the-shelf (COTS) games, just as many historical novels teach history even as they tell a good story. Successful COTS games emphasize entertainment over education because entertainment value correlates positively with play time and market value. There is typically considerable tension in the serious games development community over where to move the imaginary slider positioned between entertainment value and explicit information. This is important because false training is worse than no training. Each notch toward the information end of the spectrum limits the number of players who will eventually see and potentially enjoy a game title.

Even as serious games vie for shelf space and a place in the mind of consumers, and to some degree, funding, most game developers realize that the genre has virtually unlimited market potential. In many ways, the history of serious games parallels that of science fiction, which was regarded as an insignificant aberration by the publishing community for decades. Only after science fiction developed a significant following did publishers and academia come to appreciate the talents of Arthur C. Clarke, Robert A. Heinlein, and Ray Bradbury.

As the game industry evolves, the universe of serious games is condensing into five primary categories and two secondary categories. The primary categories are games with an agenda; news games; political games; realistic games; and core competency games. The two secondary categories, repurposed COTS games and modifications (mods) are actually game technologies that could be used to create any of the primary categories of serious games. However, they are considered separate categories here because of the popularity of using repurposed COTS and mods as a means of acquiring or developing serious games.

Because games in the five primary categories can be considered a variation of educational games, that term isn't used as a separate category. Another reason to avoid the label *educational game* or *edutainment* is that the genre has a bad reputation among educators [SalenZimmerman04]. Searching through the literature on what is today considered serious gaming, one is hard-pressed to discover terms other than "simulation," "multimedia," or "graphical" to describe games. The military uses phrases such as "tactical decision making simulation system" to describe games used by tactical decision makers. Regardless of the nomenclature, each of the categories in the serious games space is ripe for exploration, in areas ranging from homeland security and home health care to management training.

GAMES WITH AN AGENDA

Games with an agenda are developed to influence opinion, share knowledge, or simply to make a point. As in a well-crafted novel or movie, the agenda of the developer behind this type of serious game might not be obvious to the untrained observer. Games with an agenda can be subdivided according to the target audience and area of influence. Although there are no hard and fast rules on the subdivisions, those considered here include activism, advergames, business games, exergaming, health and medicine games, news games, and political games. See "Social Impact Games" later in this chapter and online at *www.socialimpactgames.com* and Water Cooler Games online at *www.WaterCoolerGames.org* for additional systems of stratifying games with an agenda.

Activism Games

Activism games, sometimes referred to as advocacy games, social games, persuasive games, or public policy games, actively promote an opinion and attempt to increase public awareness in areas from vegetarianism to global warming. An example of this genre is *Steer Madness* (*www.steermadness.com*), winner of the Innovation in Audio Award at the 2005 Independent Games Festival (see Figure 2.1). This 3D action-adventure game for Macs and PCs, developed by Vancouver-based Veggie Games, features Bryce the Steer, who narrowly escapes the slaughterhouse and goes on a mission to save his animal friends. The game supports vegetarianism and environmentalism while vilifying slaughterhouses and those involved in the meat trade.

Another activism game is *World Heroes*, in which the player can volunteer on a variety of United Nations Children's Fund (UNICEF) relief missions that involve immunization, water purification, and nutrition in remote countries. In one mission, gameplay involves directing a UNICEF truck to capture air drops of tents, first aid kits, and food before they hit the ground. The Web-based game (*www.unicefgames.org*) promotes awareness of UNICEF's mission while allowing the player to take part, at least virtually, in aiding underprivileged countries.

FIGURE 2.1   *Steer Madness,* showing Bryce the Steer on a city street corner with friends. © Veggie Games. Reprinted with permission.

A *Force More Powerful* (Breakaway Games) is an activism game commissioned by the International Center for Non-Violent Conflict (*www. nonviolent-conflict.org*). In this strategic simulation game, the player assumes the role of chief of staff of a nonviolent movement who learns how to organize to initiate political change. Gameplay involves issuing orders to various characters within the movement, who attempt to carry out actions, such as making speeches and organizing demonstrations. A scenario editor can be used to localize the game to suit a particular political environment.

Emphasizing entertainment value over message, Eidos Interactive's *Whiplash* (*www.whiplashgame.com*) was awarded Best Animal-Friendly Videogame at the 2005 People for the Ethical Treatment of Animals (PETA) Award. The setting for the PS2 and Xbox game is a high-tech lab in which innocent animals are used to test products for human consumption. Gameplay involves helping a weasel and a rabbit in their attempt to break out of the facility. Through the mayhem, the pitting of human versus animal is emphasized, drilling home the point that research labs are dangerous, cruel places for animals. *Whiplash* illustrates the importance of a game's entertainment value in getting a message out to a large number of players. See the links on Ludology.org (*www.ludology.org*) and other sites listed in Appendix F, "Resources," for additional examples of activism games and other games with an agenda.

Advergames

Advergames promote a product, service, or organization. Some of the first advergames promoted Buick cars using 3D simulations of engines and games designed to illustrate superior braking power. These Macintosh-based games allowed the player to rev the engine and watch a cutaway of the engine block to view the reciprocating pistons, firing sparkplugs, and a rotating crankshaft. Players could test their reaction time with a braking game. A more recent example of an advergame for the automobile industry is Ford's *No Boundaries* game that pits the player against a series of obstacles in a race against the clock. The game was bundled with owner's manuals for 2003 Ford trucks [Cole05].

Online games are particularly attractive as advergames because of the low cost of mass distribution. One of the early adopters of online advergames, Chrysler, offers a branded, downloadable golf game, *Chrysler World Tours Golf* (*www.chrysler.com/games*). Registered users can play either on a realistic course or in a fantasy world. Other advergames include *Chrysler West Coast Rally*, in which players race somewhat recklessly through an urban jungle, and its antithesis, *Road Steady Streetwise*, which, paradoxically, promotes public safety. In 2003 Chrysler gave visitors to their site the option of obtaining vehicle information in the form of a game or brochure. More chose the game format [Geist04], suggesting either acceptance of advergaming or simply that potential customers surfing the Internet were a self-selected group comfortable with video games. Regardless of the underlying reason, Chrysler placed *Laura Croft, Tomb Raider: The Cradle of Life* online the same year. A quarter million people registered to play the game, which has a tie-in with Jeep, during the first six months [Geist04]. Chrysler also secured product placements in the entertainment video game *MidNightClub 3* for the Playstation 2, Xbox, and PSP (*www.rockstargames.com/midnightclub3*) and worked with Microsoft to design a version of *Project Gotham Racing 2* to include the 2005 Chrysler 300 and Dodge Magnum. One of the attractive features of games is that use is more measurable than with traditional media.

Coca-Cola's presence in the advergaming space is obvious in *NCAA Championship Run 2005* (*www.champrun.com*). The arcade-style basketball game places the Coca-Cola brand in the center-stage logo, on the scoreboard, and in the signage. During gameplay, power-ups, in the form of Coke cans, float above the floor. Players who run over a can are able to run and slam-dunk faster.

Nike Europe built a loyal online following by offering a soccer game every year since 2003. The 2005 release, *Goooooooal!*, is a real-time multiplayer game that pits thousands of participants from around the world against each other (*www.nikefootball.com*). Dial Corporation, which markets Coast soap, released *Coast BMX Full Grind*, a biking game targeting 18–34-year-old active males with an interest in games and active sports (*www.coastsoap.com*). The publisher, WildTangent, reports that the game resulted in a 300 percent increase in traffic on the Dial Web site [Wild-Tangent05].

BMW and Cadbury Schweppes are among the other companies using advergames to reach potential customers. The *BMW X3 Adventure game* (*www.bmwusa.com/newX3*) features three different driving experiences combined with mountain biking, snowboarding, and a kayaking adventure. A follow-up game for mobile phones, *Formula BMW*, pits the player against five opponents on a series of Formula One tracks.

Cadbury's approach to advergaming is unique in that it brands existing titles, such as a simple board game of checkers, instead of inventing new games [Mack04]. The downside of this approach is the number of equally compelling and freely available games competing for mindshare.

The poster child for advergame is the phenomenally successful *America's Army* (*www.americasarmy.com*), launched on July 4, 2002. The PC-based multiplayer game, based on the *Unreal Tournament 2003* engine, consists of more than 40 linked missions. After successful completion of basic combat training, players can join multiplayer online units such as the 10th Mountain Division and 172nd Infantry Brigade. In these missions, players serve as members of squads of U.S. soldiers, while opposing players appear as terrorists. In this way, players begin to identify themselves as U.S. soldiers, a potentially valuable step in the recruiting process. According to Jerry Heneghan, formerly a Black Hawk instructor and now president and CEO of the 20-person Virtual Heroes development shop and Executive Producer–Government Applications, America's Army Game Project, *America's Army* was developed as a marketing and educational tool for civilians who had no other means of learning about the opportunities and aspects of the U.S. Army [Heneghan05].

Merriam-Webster Online (*www.miriamwebster.com*) offers word games as an added incentive for users to subscribe to the site. Games are rotated on a regular basis to encourage daily visits. One game of the day is *Syn City*, in which players create skyscrapers of synonyms by adding words that have a common meaning to the appropriate building. Merriam-Webster also offers Palm and Pocket-PC versions of its online game suite.

LEGO's contribution to the advergaming genre is a range of LEGO-like puzzles that are part advertisement and part extension of their famous plastic building blocks. One of the most engaging of the puzzle games on the LEGO site (*www.lego.com*) is *Inventor Saves the Day!*, a game based on gears, motors, pulleys, and breakable eggs (see Figure 2.2). Although the puzzle can be solved without LEGOs, it might help some players to work with real LEGO pieces. Regardless of how it's achieved, a player who works through 60 levels is promoted to the rank of *Inventor Master*. Like the other games on the site, *Inventor Saves the Day!* appeals to players who prefer thinking games for themselves and their children. Of note is that the developer of this and many of the other games on *lego.com*, Eric Zimmerman's GameLab (*www.gamelab.com*), is a 12-person studio that specializes in inventing new forms of gameplay.

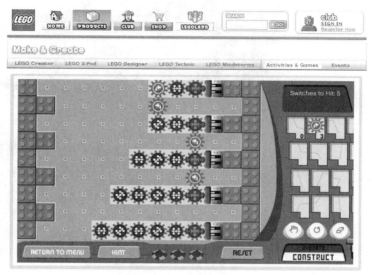

FIGURE 2.2   *Inventor Saves the Day!* © 2005 The LEGO Group. Used here with permission. All rights reserved. LEGO, the LEGO logo, and the brick configuration are trademarks of the LEGO Group, which does not sponsor this book.

One of the most unusual advergames is the virtual hunting game, *Live-Shot* (*www.live-shot.com*). Players control a .22 caliber rifle over the Internet to shoot live ammunition into paper targets set up at a Texas ranch (see Figure 2.3). Although the targets aren't as engaging as weapon-toting aliens, they're standard issue for a shooting range. In play, the scope view jumps slightly with each round and sound accompanies the puff of dust caused by the bullet as it rips through the target backing. The visual and audio cues are such that the game achieves a degree of realism that isn't achieved in high-end entertainment games such as *Halo 2*.

Although a player's monthly membership is active, he can access the viewing cameras to see how others perform, control the pan/tilt/zoom camera to take a look around the range, or schedule a reservation for online shooting. The Texas ranch, which is stocked with sheep, antelope, and hogs, also offers live hunting experiences for players who want to upgrade from virtual reality to the real thing.

FIGURE 2.3   *Live-Shot*, showing the computer, image capture, and remote-control .22 rifle. © Live-Shot.com. Reprinted with permission.

The concept of providing virtual control over real devices (*telecontrol*) as a component of advertisement is largely untapped. There would likely be a market for players eager to telecontrol a real wrecker ball or earth mover, push the button to detonate the real explosives placed to take down an old building, or turn on the sprinkler system at the local professional ball park. The challenge is tying in an appropriate advertisement with the game. For example, a remote control flying club could promote membership by allowing members to fly real model aircraft from the comfort of their office. The related technology of *telepresence*, which has been applied to areas ranging from XXX-rated teledildonics [ÓhAnluain03] to petting animals over the Internet [Cheok05], is another area ripe for serious games development.

Business Games

Business games focus on economics, ownership, management, operations, or some other aspect of business or investing. *Homes of Our Own* (Media Options) is a business game designed to teach school children the responsibilities of home ownership (see Figure 2.4). As in *The Sims*, players select a site and then build a home. In the course of gameplay, players must consider building codes, local environmental and health issues, and eventually, how to sell the house. The game is available free to educators (*www.homesofourown.org*), thanks to support from the National Association of Home Builders (NAHB), the National Housing Endowment, Freddie Mac, and the Fannie Mae foundation.

FIGURE 2.4   *Homes of Our Own*, showing a town meeting in which the player is seeking advice on site location and unseen hazards. © Courtesy Media Options, Inc. Reprinted with permission.

Better Business Game (British Telecom) is an online RPG in which the player assumes the role of CEO charged with managing the social and environmental issues in a business (*www.btplc.com/Societyandenvironment/ Businessgame*). The player can elect to take on 12-month assignment in a bull, neutral, or bear market. In contrast with this content-heavy game are business games that emphasize entertainment value, including *Wall Street Raider* (Ronin Software), *Lemonade Tycoon* (Hexacto Publishing), and *TV Manager 2* (NBSD Publishing). In *Wall Street Raider*, an RPG involving the stock market and corporate takeovers, the player builds a corporate empire while fending off the SEC, IRS, Justice Department, EPA, Congress, unions, and the competition.

Players in *Lemonade Tycoon* begin with a small lemonade stand and a few dollars. Astute business decisions are rewarded with increased cash reserves, the ability to move to a higher traffic location, upgraded equipment, and victory over the competition. As is commonplace in the turbulent video game industry, the original publisher of *Lemonade Tycoon*, Hexacto Publishing, was acquired by JAMDAT mobile (*www.jamdatmobile.com*) as part of its growing mobile entertainment portfolio. *TV Manager 2* is an RPG in which the player takes over a small and nearly bankrupt TV station and attempts to grow it to a world-class TV network.

Some business games are serious business. Students in England place their grades on the line when they play *Entrepreneur—The Game*, developed by Aqua Pacific (*www.aqua-pacific.com*) and Henley College [Pudelek05]. Within the PC-based RPG, shown in Figure 2.5, players choose between running a hairdresser studio, a pizza parlor, a pub, and a video store. Players who master financing, market research, advertising, and the other aspects of running their virtual business are awarded certificates in "Setting Up Your Own Small Business" and "Business Management."

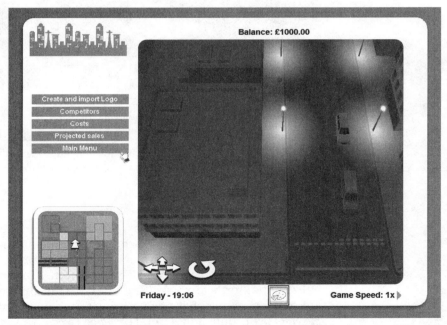

FIGURE 2.5 *Entrepreneur—The Game*, showing traffic outside the business at night (right) and a map of the city (lower left). © Courtesy Aqua Pacific. Reprinted with permission.

Game development for *Entrepreneur—The Game* was funded by the Learning and Skills Council in association with the European Social Fund. A second business title from Aqua-Pacific, *Business Tycoon*, also developed with support from the Learning and Skills Council, teaches business skills related to catering and the media sector.

Exergaming

Water and electricity might not mix, but exergaming has successfully managed to marry sweat and gaming. Exergaming is exemplified by Kanomai's *Dance Dance Revolution* series (*www.konami.com*) for the Xbox and PS2. *Dance Dance Revolution* uses pop singles and dance pad peripherals to teach players to dance or guide them through aerobic workouts. Several companies market the pressure-sensitive, meter square dance pads for the PC, GameCube, PS2, and Xbox, including RedOctane (*www.RedOctane.com*) and MadCatz (*www.MadCatz.com*). Dance pads and software are particularly popular among the youth of Korea and Japan, where they are used in clubs and at home. In addition to dance routines, there are a few sports-related programs that work with pads, such as *Athens 2004* (Eurocom) for the PS2, which directs the player through movements found in some of the 2004 Olympic events.

Sony's EyeToy® camera system (*www.eyetoy.com*) is a little more sophisticated than *Dance Dance Revolution* in that it relies on a camera peripheral that is used to overlay graphics on the player's image. In gameplay, the PS2 generates music and virtual objects that interact with the user or that the user can manipulate through movement, as captured by the motion-sensitive camera.

Titles for the EyeToy include *AntiGrav* (SCEA), in which the player rides a virtual snowboard, and *Play* (SCEA), in which up to four players are encouraged to move their bodies through a variety of moves, from Kung Fu and dancing to washing windows. Sony also launched a direct competitor to *Dance Dance Revolution* in the form of *Groove* (SCEA), in which up to four players dance in time to one of 28 songs.

Exergaming for space- and time-challenged golf aficionados is available through *Golf LaunchPad* by Electric Spin (*www.electricspin.com*). The PC/Mac game enables golfers to practice with their own clubs on a small putting green outfitted with optical sensors and a tethered golf ball. The game, which is similar in concept to the Navy's Virtual At-Sea Training system described in Chapter 1, " Historical Perspective," calculates distance, spin, and eventual location of the ball on the simulated golf course using data from the sensors on the miniature putting green.

Kilowatt Sport, one of several models of exergaming peripherals from PowerGrid Fitness, replaces a handheld controller with the equivalent of a supersized joystick (see Figure 2.6). Strain gauges in the console column translate isometric pushing, pulling, and side-to-side pressure into the equivalent thumb movements on a controller, and an LCD dashboard shows total workout time and total weight lifted. The sensitivity of the *Kilowatt Sport* is adjustable so that gameplay requires a few ounces to 300 pounds of force for full range of control. A smaller model, the *Kilowatt Spark*, is designed for children ages 7 to 14, and a more substantial *Kilowatt Pro* is available for fitness centers. All of the units work with any PC/Mac or console game that supports an analog joystick.

FIGURE 2.6   Kilowatt Sport. The game controller on steroids provides isometric resistance for gameplay. © PowerGrid Fitness. Reprinted with permission.

A line of exergames aimed at the toy market is sold by Xavix Games (*www.xavix.com*). The company offers a line of sports-related games, including *Golf*, *Bowling*, *Baseball*, and *Tennis*, which are played through a proprietary TV console. The wireless system captures the motion information from a specially instrumented bat, golf club, bowling ball, or tennis racket, calculates the results of the player's actions, and displays the outcome in the 3D environment portrayed on a TV screen. Because the Xavix system relies on plastic instruments, the transference of skills developed in the games to real-world sports is questionable. However, as with the other exergames described here, it's difficult to use the games properly without getting physical.

An example of a software-only exergame is responDesign's *Yourself-Fitness* (*www.responDesign.com*), shown in Figure 2.7. In effect, the game is an attractive, interactive 3D interface to the diet and fitness simulations that have been on the market since the early 1980s [Bergeron84; 84b]. Although not as interactive as most other exergames, *YourselfFitness* features a virtual personal trainer, appropriately named Maya, who guides the player through aerobics, Pilates, strength training, yoga, and meditation.

FIGURE 2.7   *YourselfFitness*, showing virtual personal trainer, Maya, illustrating a movement sequence. © responDesign. Reprinted with permission.

Like a real personal trainer, Maya guides the new player through a questionnaire to capture the player's health and fitness goals. She then selects the most appropriate exercises from a library of 400 movements. Gameplay consists of signaling progress and commitment level so that

Maya can personalize subsequent training sessions. *YourselfFitness* is unique in that it is one of the few games that targets women, with emphasis on cardio, flexibility, and core body strength. The game, available on the PC, Xbox, and PS2, includes a personal nutrition advisor, along with an electronic cookbook that even generates a shopping list.

Given the realism and accuracy of the moves, it isn't surprising that the founder of the 15-person responDesign development house is a triathlete. However, the greatest hurdle the company faces is getting people to understand that the game isn't about moving Maya with a game controller, but getting up off the couch.

Health and Medicine Games

Games addressing health and medicine are the most significant of games with an agenda in terms of impact on society and individual well-being. In addition, many of the games in this category border on advergames, especially those games tied either directly or indirectly to the pharmaceutical industry. To understand the dynamics of the health and medicine serious games space, it's helpful to consider three separate subcategories or application areas of health and medicine: consumer, guided consumer, and professional.

Consumer

Consumer health and medicine games are intended for use with or without the intervention of a healthcare provider. Many of these games are available on the Internet and were developed with support from non-profit organizations, the government, or corporations, all with a particular agenda or idea to promote. An example is *Burger Man* (*www.supersizeme. com/burgerman.htm*), a 2D maze game that strongly resembles *Pac Man*, with carrots for power-ups. *Burger Man* is tied to the promotion of *Super-Size Me*, the Morgan Spurlock documentary that illustrates the relationship between obesity and the American fast food diet. Another example is *MyPyramid* (*teamnutrition.usda.gov*), a game that encourages kids to explore the USDA food pyramid and the importance of physical activity.

Three examples of consumer-oriented health and medicine games from the academic community are three games developed in Dr. Mark Baldwin's lab at McGill University in Montreal, Canada (*www.selfesteemgames.mcgill.ca*). The online games *EyeSpy: The Matrix, Wham!*, and *Grow Your Chi* (see Figure 2.8) are intended to help raise the self-esteem of children by enhancing self-acceptance. In *EyeSpy: The Matrix*, the player is charged with identifying a smiling face in a matrix of frowning faces. The exercise trains players to focus on positive rather than negative feedback.

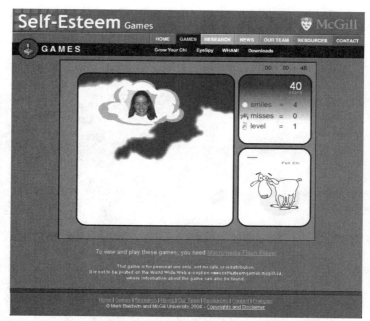

FIGURE 2.8   *Grow Your Chi.* Facial expressions embedded in clouds fly past the player (left) while the score and Chi pet reflect correct and incorrect responses. © Mark Baldwin. Reprinted with permission.

Wham!, like *EyeSpy*, asks the player to register his or her name. After the game gets going, the player's name is paired with smiling, accepting faces. The third program in the suite, *Grow Your Chi*, is a combination of *Wham!* and *EyeSpy* in that the goal is to identify smiling faces and collect enough points to cover a virtual Chi pet (akin to a pottery Chia Pet®) with green shoots. The game was co-created by Dr. Baldwin and three student collaborators: Stephane Dandeneau, Jodene Baccus, and Maya Sakellaropoulo.

The power of games to capture the attention of patients and enable them to take an active role in their medical treatment is exemplified by *Ben's Game*, which allows young cancer patients to engage in a virtual fight against their cancer. *Ben's Game*, developed by Ben, a 9-year-old leukemia patient, and Eric Johnston at LucasArts, is available free through the Greater Bay Area Make-A-Wish Foundation (*www.makewish.org*).

As shown in Figure 2.9, *Ben's Game* takes place in the body, on a playfield of blood cells. The two-player PC/Macintosh game is complete with fever monsters, mutating cells, and shields for protecting the body against nausea, hair loss, bleeding, and barfing from chemotherapy. The heads-up display (HUD) shows ammunition level (in terms of available drugs), attitude (in terms of medical setbacks), and health (based on the number of mutated cells Ben collides with during the course of gameplay). The game, which includes realistic physics, can be modified to replace Ben's image with that of another patient.

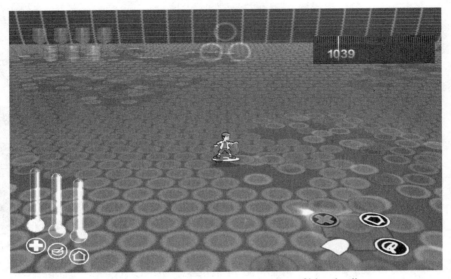

FIGURE 2.9   *Ben's Game*, showing Ben skating across a sea of blood cells. © Greater Bay Area Make-A-Wish Foundation. Reprinted with permission.

On the theme of mental well-being, *Wild Divine* (www.wilddevine.com) is a high-tech equivalent of the mood rings and biofeedback paddles that were popular in the 1970s. Instead of a game controller, the player slips on a heart rate and skin resistance sensor that plugs into a PC or Macintosh. By following the on-screen guru through various breathing and meditation exercises, the scenery can be made to change—as long as the player's biofeedback cooperates. The game, which is endorsed by wellness personality Deepak Chopra, is marketed as a tool to reduce stress and improve physical and mental health.

Guided Consumer

In contrast with consumer titles, guided consumer health and medicine games are normally used under the supervision of a clinician. Serious games in this category have been developed to ease the pain of burn victims, to treat phobias, and to treat Post Traumatic Stress Disorder (PTSD). Some of the most innovative work in this area has been performed in the

Virtual Reality Analgesia Research Center at the University of Washington Human Interface Technology Laboratory (HITLab) in Seattle (*www. hitl.washington.edu*).

The director of HITLab, Dr. Hunter Hoffman, has worked with physicians and psychologists at the University of Washington to develop active, immersive, game-based distraction known as Virtual Reality Therapy [Hoffman04]. Games played using head-mounted displays are used to immerse burn patients, particularly children and teenagers, in a virtual reality environment, easing the pain associated with wound care and physical therapy [Versweyveld99].

One of the games used with burn victims, *SnowWorld* (Paradigm Simulations), enables the patient to fly through an icy canyon with a river and a frigid waterfall, shooting snowballs at snowmen, igloos, robots, and penguins (see Figure 2.10). *SnowWorld*, which was developed with funding from Microsoft co-founder Paul Allen and the National Institutes of Health (NIH), requires the use of a head-mounted display and headphones for maximum effect. Dr. Hoffman found that simply giving patients a Game-Boy isn't as effective. A follow-on program to *SnowWorld*, *SuperSnowWorld*, allows a second player, such as the patient's mother, to accompany the patient in the exploration of the frozen virtual reality world.

FIGURE 2.10   *SnowWorld*. A patient undergoing painful therapy for a hand burn (right) uses a joystick to maneuver within the interactive virtual reality (VR) environment filled with snowmen and ice (left). © Dr. Hunter Hoffman, Virtual Reality Analgesia Research Center at the University of Washington's HITLab. Reprinted with permission.

ChocolateWorld, a zero calorie pain distracter for chocolate lovers, is a mixed-reality therapeutic game in which players see a virtual chocolate bar that is linked through position sensors to an actual candy bar. As the patient eats the real chocolate bar, bite marks appear on the virtual bar [Hoffman04]. The idea of mixing virtual and actual reality, along the lines of consumer products such as Sony's *Eye Toy*® and *Golf Launch Pad*, is to provide a deeper immersive experience for the patient. The smell, taste, and tactile feedback from a real chocolate bar amplify the illusion of reality created by the visual display of a world in which everything is made of chocolate.

Another mixed reality therapeutic system developed at the HITLab is *SpiderWorld* (Division Ltd), which is designed to reduce a patient's fear of spiders (see Figure 2.11). The patient, outfitted with a full-immersion helmet display, walks into a virtual kitchen in which she can open the drawers and cabinets, pick up teapots, and gradually approach a virtual spider.

FIGURE 2.11   *SpiderWorld*. A patient with a fear of spiders views the VR image in *SpiderWorld* as Dr. Hoffman positions a toy spider to provide the patient with tactile feedback. © Dr. Hunter Hoffman, Virtual Reality Analgesia Research Center at the University of Washington HITLab. Reprinted with permission.

Eventually, the patient, wearing a tracking glove, can reach out to touch the virtual spider while actually feeling a furry toy spider. As with the chocolate bar in *ChocolateWorld*, the combined tactile and image sensations add a sense of realism to the experience. With continued exposure, the patient's tolerance to spiders increases to the point she no longer fears them. Virtual reality therapy is growing in acceptance in the medical community and is available worldwide through clinics such as the Virtually Better chain (*www.virtuallybetter.com*). See Dr. Hoffman's Web site, *www.vrpain.com*, for additional information on virtual reality and pain control.

Professional

Professional health and medicine games are used by clinicians to acquire and maintain their clinical skills. Professional medical training has long been an application area of serious gaming. One reason for this heritage is the need for physician, nurses, and other clinicians to amass a certain number of continuing medical education (CME) credits every year to maintain their licensure. Physicians can receive CME credits by attending live lectures, by taking paper-and-pen quizzes after reading journal articles, and by using colorful, entertaining programs that also teach. In the realm of medical software for clinicians, CME is a mark of quality. Most physicians wouldn't consider buying or using a learning tool that isn't approved for CME credits.

The other factor is the deep-pocketed pharmaceutical industry, which is under constant pressure to provide physicians with eye-catching ad copy, computer programs, and anything else that will encourage them to write prescriptions for their drugs. There have been literally hundreds of serious games created for clinicians with direct pharmaceutical support for promotional purposes. Our first non-CME game directed at physicians was an FPS developed as part of a kiosk for the rollout of a new antibiotic by an international pharmaceutical firm. The player, piloting a space ship through asteroids and other space hazards, had to use weapons (antibiotics) to fend off oncoming space bugs (bacteria). Pairing the best antibiotic with the particular incoming bugs was necessary for survival. Not surprisingly, the client's product was the most powerful and versatile drug in the space craft's arsenal. The game wasn't accredited, but the lure of the game format was enough to pull physicians out of a busy convention floor into the kiosk area. Most people who make it through medical school have at least something of a competitive streak.

Because of the competition for the attention of physicians, the pharmaceutical corridor that stretches from New York to Philadelphia is a haven for multimedia marketing and communications firms. Each is engaged in a race to develop the most innovative and engaging programs—including games—for pharmaceutical sales training, clinician education, and, as noted in the advergaming section, promotion.

Not all professional games in health and medicine are developed with accreditation in mind. Some are intended to be used in educational settings that are themselves accredited activities, such as residency training programs. For example, *Body Simulation*, shown in Figure 2.12, is a simulation-based game that emphasizes the accuracy and fidelity of the simulation of patient cases. The player, who assumes the role of an anesthesiologist, must treat the patient just as a real anesthesiologist would—or the simulated patient suffers the consequences.

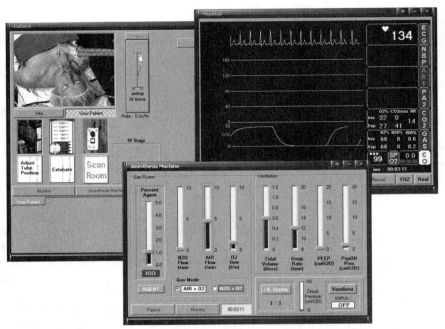

FIGURE 2.12   *Body Simulation*, showing the anesthesia machine controls (center), patient physiology tracings (right), and the patient on the operating table (left).
© Advanced Simulation Corp. Reprinted with permission.

Body Simulation, from Advanced Simulation Corp. (*www.advsim.com*) is notable in that it illustrates how the context of use defines the degree to which a simulation qualifies as a game. *Body Simulation* can be used as a review for anesthesiologists or a learning tool for anesthesiology residents. It can also be used by teaching faculty to create interactive scenarios in which the teacher can ask what-if questions and the player can view the results. In addition, the core simulation can be used in other applications. For example, the underlying Body model has been used to give 3D models in traditional game environments the ability to react realistically to trauma sustained from military activity [Zimmer03].

Another independently funded medical game for clinicians is Mad Scientist Software's *Cardiac Arrest!* (*www.madscientistsoftware.com*), shown in Figure 2.13. The PC-based game presents 45 patients in realistic cardiac arrest situations in which the player assumes the role of an emergency room physician. As in a real ER, she has the option of administering oxygen, drugs, and fluids, ordering radiology procedures, and doing a variety of other standard tests. *Cardiac Arrest!*, which is accredited by the American College of Emergency Physicians for CME credit, is an example of a

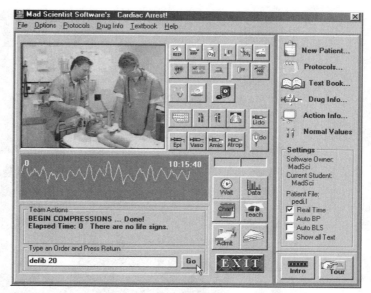

FIGURE 2.13   *Cardiac Arrest!*, a patient simulation game for emergency room physicians. © Mad Scientist Software. Reprinted with permission.

game designed for professionals that nonmedical, casual gamers would probably find too difficult or boring.

An example of a health and medicine game that could be used by professionals, medical students, or interested consumers is *Achilles*, an anatomy game that we developed with a storyline based on the tale of the central character in Homer's *Iliad*, shown in Figure 2.14. In gameplay, players are required to first score a critical hit on the opponent, which temporarily freezes the opponent. While the opponent is immobilized, the player must use his weapon's x-ray scope to identify the opponent's Achilles heel—the particular bone, muscle, organ, or blood vessel randomly identified by the game.

Many of the virtual reality principles used in therapeutic medical games, such as the superposition of real spider images over a toy spider in Dr. Hoffman's *SpiderWorld*, have also been applied to student and professional medical education. For example, the *Augmented Reality Medical Simulator™—Auscultation* combines a laptop-based 3D game engine and a wearable sensor vest to enable an instructor or a stand-in to provide the physical basis for the auscultatory component of a heart, lung, and abdomen physical examination. An instructor equipped with the system can present with an infinite variety of abnormal heart sounds, murmurs, and arrhythmias, as well as lung findings associated with pneumonia, asthma, and other pulmonary conditions.

FIGURE 2.14   *Achilles*, a first-person sneaker designed to teach functional anatomy to military medics in training. © Archetype Technologies. Reprinted with permission.

In operation, the instructor or patient wearing the vest mimics the symptoms suggested by the computer system, such as left shoulder pain. As the player examines the patient, proximity sensors embedded in the vest respond to the player's stethoscope location as well as the patient's position and communicate the data wirelessly to the laptop. The game engine generates the appropriate heart, lung, or bowel sounds, which are reproduced through the computer speakers and/or headphones. The player provides his or her diagnostic findings, such as atrial fibrillation, rales, or hyperactive bowel sounds, and enters a provisional diagnosis into the computer system. Based on the player's input, an intelligent tutoring system (ITS) in the game generates more or less challenging cases. The sensor vest can also be placed on a mannequin for single-user study and skill maintenance under direction of an ITS. Implementation details of the PC-based Augmented Reality Medical Simulator system are discussed in Chapter 6, "Tools." A PocketPC version of the serious game was introduced in Chapter 1, "Historical Perspective."

Other medical games allow players to assume the role of a medical professional but are designed primarily for entertainment and are not appropriate for the training of medical professionals. Examples include Legacy Interactive's *Combat Medic: Special Forces, ER: Code Red,* and *911*

Paramedic; Atari's *ER: Life or Death* and *ER: Disaster Strikes*; Sierra's *Emergency Room Code Red*; and Activision's *Emergency Room 3*. These PC games (with confusingly similar titles) use a combination of static graphics, video, and 3D graphics to present patients with various maladies to the player for workup and treatment. Although these games teach some medicine, they wouldn't captivate or entertain a medical professional and are not accurate enough to be accredited for physicians.

Readers interested in developing serious games for health and medicine are not encouraged to visit the Games for Health portal (*www.gamesforhealth.org*) and other health-related resources listed in Appendix F, "Resources."

News Games

News games highlight and usually question some aspect of current events. The archetype for this genre is *Kuma\War* (*www.kumawar.com*), which bills itself as an interactive chronicle of the war on terror. The games, which are on par with any entertainment titles on the market, are unremarkable in theme and gameplay in that there are dozens of military shooter games in which the player assumes the role of a soldier fighting in Iraq or another hotbed. What differentiates *Kuma\War* from other military games is that the games don't take place in some unknown desert with generic characters, but they're keyed to specific, real-world events that have been in the news. Players become intimately involved in an interactive docudrama in which they can witness the capture of Saddam Hussein or other events promoted by the news networks.

Many of the missions, which are played from a third-person perspective, have covered various aspects of the war in Iraq as they unfolded (see Figure 2.15). The developer, Kuma\Reality Games, has also addressed historical war issues in the news. For example, when presidential candidate John Kerry's military service was in the news prior to the 2004 election, the company created a game around the Swift Boat incident that resulted in Kerry's disputed Silver Star. This particular episode caused a stir because of the political ramifications of the details of the incident [Marlowe2004]

Kuma\Reality Games is developing event recreations that can be deployed over the Internet for use in training exercises. In addition, the developer has been contacted by soldiers who want their story told via the newsgame format, in part because they see the power of the medium as a communications vehicle and in part because of the *cool factor* of being in a game.

If *Kuma\War* is maintained, the site could easily become a resource for high school or college history lessons. This is possible because the single and multiplayer online games are accompanied by intelligence packs that include real-world news videos and satellite photos of the mission area.

FIGURE 2.15 *Kuma\War* showing a mission in Iraq linked to a then-current news story. © Kuma Reality Games. Reprinted with permission.

Another example of a newsgame is *September 12th* (*www.newsgaming. com*), a game based on the United States–led invasion of Afghanistan following the September 11 attacks. The developer released the game, which is a hybrid simulation and cartoon, to trigger interest in international politics [Boyd04]. Like *Kuma\War*, as time passes, *September 12th* may become useful as a historical resource.

One of the more controversial news games is *JFK Reloaded* (*www. jfkreloaded.com*), an interactive 3D reconstruction of President Kennedy's assassination in Dallas, Texas (see Figure 2.16). The FPS/RPG questions whether Lee Harvey Oswald could have assassinated Kennedy. Players assume the role of Oswald and take shots at the motorcade from his hotel room overlooking the route of the motorcade.

After taking aim and firing, the player can examine the scene, including close-up, slow-motion frames of bullet trajectories from virtually any angle. A ballistic report on the player's attempts is compared with the official report from the Warren Commission. To add to the controversy of the game, developed by Traffic Games/Traffic Management Limited of Scotland, UK, the site initially held a competition with a $100,000 prize for the player who most closely replicated the official ballistics report.

Political Games

Political games harness unresolved political tensions and tend to be steeped in controversy. Games in this category could be viewed as propaganda, de-

FIGURE 2.16 *JFK Reloaded,* showing a close-up of a virtual President Kennedy just prior to his assassination in Dallas.
© *www.jfkreloaded.com.* Reprinted with permission.

pending on the perspective of the player. For example, military games such as *Full Spectrum Warrior* (Pandemic) have been cited for trivializing killing in the name of military values and patriotism [Hyman03]. In addition, *JFK Reloaded, Kuma\War,* and *September 12th* could be considered political games because they each take a particular perspective on historical or current events. However, as defined here, political games are different from news games or ordinary military games in that the developer's intent to generate controversy seems to override other considerations.

Two exemplars of political games are *Escape From Woomera* (*www. escapefromwoomera.org*) and *UnderAsh2* (*www.underash.net*). *Escape from Woomera* deals with the treatment of illegal asylum seekers in the detention centers in Australia. The game, which is a special modification (mod) of the popular entertainment game *Half-Life,* places the player in the role of refugee who must deal with the Woomera Immigration Reception and Processing Centre. Much of the controversy of the anti-government game stems from its source of funding—the Australian Federal Government through the Australian Council of Arts.

UnderAsh2, which is also promoted as *Under Siege,* is a pro-Palestinian, FPS in which the player assumes the role of a Palestinian, Ahmed, who deals with the Israeli occupation. Figure 2.17 shows a scene from Level 3 "David and Goliath," developed by Syria-based Afkar Media (*www.afkar-media.com*). Through the course of the PC game, the player progresses from throwing rocks at Israeli soldiers to destroying Israeli military positions. The game is designed to provide an alternative to the foreign games that the producers feel distort the history and facts of the Israeli-Palestinian conflict. See Persuasive Game (*www.persuasivegames.com*) for additional examples of political games.

FIGURE 2.17   *UnderAsh2* shows the Palestinian-Israeli conflict from the Palestinian perspective. © Afkar Media. Reprinted with permission.

REALISTIC GAMES

The second major category of serious games, realistic games, attempts to mimic some subset of reality with high fidelity, typically emphasizing realistic physics. Simulation-based RPGs, such as commercial flight, submarine, and tank simulator games, are examples of this genre. The difference between a simulation and a realistic game that relies on simulation is the all-important element of engagement or fun. As defined in *Rules of Play*, to the extent that a simulation is a procedural representation of some aspect of reality, every game can be understood as a simulation [SalenZimmerman04]. However, a dry, numerical simulation might be engaging to a scientist or mathematician, but wouldn't qualify as a game.

The U.S. Navy has developed libraries of simulation-based games for sailors to use in self-study, known as the Submarine On-Board Training (SOBT) program. As part of the Submarine Skills-Training Network (SubSkillsNet), the Naval Air Warfare Center Training Division took an accurate but dry periscope simulation and converted it into a game, *Bottom Gun*, by enabling the player to fire missiles based on their periscope readings [Garris99]. By adding a chance of being blown out of the water, the high-fidelity simulation was transformed into a more engaging experience. Another PC-based game made available to sailors as part of Sub-

SkillsNet is *BPS-15H Radar Procedures Game,* which allows a player to race against the clock while working the complex user interface of the BPS-15H submarine navigation radar.

Realistic game development isn't limited to deep-pocketed military applications. An independent developer who managed to create a realistic game on a shoestring budget is Stephan Guenther, the force behind *Easy Lander,* a moon lander game (see Figure 2.18). Stephan, who has been programming as a hobby since the appearance of the Commodore 64 in 1982, transformed his passion for space and computing as a hobby into running a one-man programming and Web-development company, Space Domains (*www.SpaceDomains.com*). He programs during every waking hour, working in *DarkBasic Pro* and learning C++ at a remote learning academy.

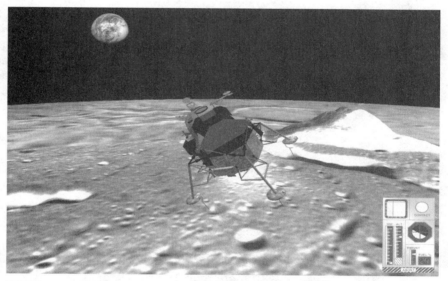

FIGURE 2.18   *Easy Lander,* a modern, 3D multimedia treatment of a classic. © Stephan Guenther of SpaceDomains. Reprinted with permission.

Easy Lander, one of Stephan's first games, took him two weeks to code in DarkBasic Pro, but he spent almost two months developing the 3D model of the lunar lander. The 3D version of the classic game adds the elements of an interactive moon surface map, multiple views of the lander and landing area, and voice communications from NASA ground control. Another one of his projects, *Saturn V Explorer,* provides a virtual tour of the Saturn V rocket. It required three weeks of coding and almost six months to build the models. Both programs can be purchased in the Spaceshop at the Kennedy Space Center.

Although they are usually affordable, software-only realistic games lack the tactile feedback that physical problems typically have in real life. For example, in a medical simulation-based game, the process of intubating a patient—inserting a plastic tube in the airway—might be a matter of timing a mouse-click. In reality, inserting a breathing tube involves the use of a laryngoscope that can lacerate the tongue and chip teeth if used improperly. Similarly, monitoring a patient during surgery entails much more than simply watching the real-time display on an anesthesia machine. Anesthesiologists periodically listen to patient's breathing, feel for pulses, and test the skin turgor for signs of perfusion and dehydration. More importantly, real-world crisis management is a contact sport that involves working closely with other clinical staff.

In response to that concern, modern mannequin simulators with life-like features were developed in the late 1980s for different applications. One system was developed by Dr. David Gaba and colleagues at Stanford University and used for training and research in human performance during critical event management. A curriculum named Anesthesia Crisis Resource Management (ACRM) was developed based on an aviation training model (Crew Resource Management). The central component of the room-sized RPG is a computer-controlled mannequin that generates heart and breath sounds, pulse, and blood pressure and responds to drugs via either manual control or based on mathematical models or preprogrammed responses (see Figure 2.19). With such computer-controlled mannequins in a full-scale operating room or other medical settings, physicians, nurses, and other healthcare providers can learn both technical and behavioral (such as, leadership, teamwork, communications, and resource management) skills. Thousands of such mannequin simulators and part-task trainers for specific medical procedures are now used around the world for these and other applications in medical education and training. As of 2004 there were 454 simulation centers worldwide, some with more than 100 simulators [Jones04]. Moreover, the number of medical simulation centers has grown exponentially since 1994, and the trend continues today.

Another example of integrating software and hardware to create the illusion of medical realism can be found in the 91W medic program at Fort Sam Houston, Texas, which uses the Human Patient Simulator (HPS) from Medical Education Technologies, Inc. (*www.meti.com*). The HPS is a computer-model driven full-sized mannequin that blinks, breathes, has a pulse, and responds to drugs injected into its plastic arteries and veins. At the heart of the HPS is a Macintosh that models human physiology.

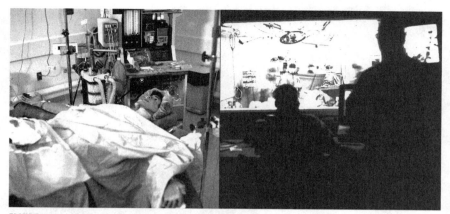

FIGURE 2.19   Mannequin and laparoscopic simulators integrated in an operating room setting during a session for team training of a full surgical team (left) and view from the control room (right). Courtesy Dr. Jeffrey Cooper. © Center for Medical Simulation (*www.harvardmedsim.org*).

In the course of their 16-week program, medics in training interact with dozens of mannequins in computer-controlled rooms in which lights, helicopter and munitions sounds, smoke generators, and other special effects are used to create the illusion of reality (see Figure 2.20). Some mannequins are placed in standard army tents, while others are in parts of helicopters or transport vehicles. Some are dressed in civilian clothes, and several are permanently modified with wounds that pulse with a blood-red liquid. Elsewhere at Fort Sam Houston, there are rooms filled with HPS mannequins lined up in cots for the trainees to use as physiology simulators—akin to dog labs in medical school. This dual use of the HPS illustrates an important concept in the simulation versus game dichotomy. The rows of mannequins are used as simulations to explore physiology; whereas the same technology is used in an emotional context to create a top gun game shown in Figure 2.20.

The use of instrumented mannequins at Fort Sam Houston illustrates one of the limitations of a hybrid mechanical-computer game or simulation system over a computer-only game. In the lab settings, physiological findings associated with a gaping chest wound, such as decreased blood pressure, rapid heart rate, and increased respiration rate, can be quickly programmed into the system. However, the mannequin's outward appearance doesn't automatically reflect the trauma. The mannequins must be moulanged—covered with latex wounds and blood painted on the plastic skin—manually. This time-consuming process limits the degree of realism that can be achieved by the system.

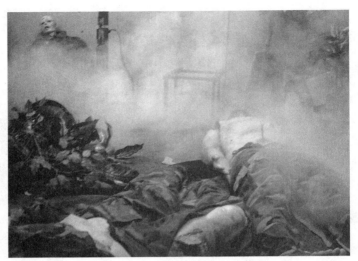

FIGURE 2.20   Computer-controlled mannequins in a "top gun" class for 91W medics training at Fort Sam Houston, Texas. Three mannequins are visible among the debris in the smoke-filled room.

An example of a mass-marketed realistic game that is integrated with hardware is *Bass Fishin'® Pro*, marketed by Sharper Image (see Figure 2.21). The unit, which can be used as a fishing simulator (Recreation mode) or as a competitive game (Tournament or Turbo Fishin' modes), consists of a dedicated handheld game attached to a 14-inch rod and life-size reel. The integrated hardware-software game features a motion sensor that assesses the direction and force of the player's cast, and haptic feedback, in the form of resistance on the reel, simulates the tug of a biting fish. The LCD display shows fishing scenes, including a sonar view of fish, along with the number of fish caught and the elapsed time. The game also produces a variety of sounds, such as fish jumping, the line playing out on a cast, and the click of the reel during trolling. The game illustrates how hardware can be integrated with a handheld computer to provide a fun learning experience that has educational value. The same type of synergy could be created with a Windows Mobile or Palm OS handheld computer and a variety of hardware, from mannequins to engine parts.

Another serious game that attempts to replicate a hobby or pastime is *Pre-Flight 2.1F*, a user-configurable flight simulator and model aircraft designer from Transcendental Technologies. The game targets radio-controlled (RC) aircraft enthusiasts who either want to practice flying but don't have time to make it to a flying field with their model aircraft or who want to experience flying a wide variety of model aircraft. Learning to fly a model helicopter, for example, is an expensive and time-consuming endeavor, especially when a single gust of wind can destroy a several-hundred-dollar

FIGURE 2.21 *Bass Fishin'® Pro* motion-activated electronic game. Game face
(left) and hardware profile (right).

model. The game enables players to select a model from a library of model
aircraft, which includes single- and double-wing airplanes, helicopters, and
even a blimp, or, using the integrated Aero Designer utility, create a model
from scratch. Because the flight characteristics of the computer models are
determined mathematically, model aircraft designers can try out a new design in the game and then create a real balsa and Mylar RC aircraft based on
the perfected computer model.

Pre-Flight 2.1F illustrates how a 3D game engine can be configured to
allow nonprogrammers to personalize a game experience (see Figure
2.22). Not only does the program support the creation of custom aircraft,
but a scenery editor enables players to replicate the layout of their local
field—including the location of trees and other hazards to RC aircraft.
The same principles could be applied to realistic games in any field, from
firefighting to driver's education. A demo of the game is available at
www.preflightsim.com.

Realistic games aren't limited to simulations of spacecraft, aircraft, and
other devices, but can be based on simulations of situations that help provide a practical framework for traditional academic studies. For example,
Aqua Pacific (*www.aqua-pacific.com*) developed *English Taxi* to help Chinese
university students in England understand colloquial spoken English. The
challenge for the British educational system was that Chinese students
were very good at reading and writing the formal English spoken in the
university, but often had difficulty listening to and understanding colloquial English. *English Taxi* addresses the problem by immersing players in

FIGURE 2.22   *Pre-Flight 2.1F* remote-controlled model aircraft simulator from Transcendental Technologies, showing the flying field (background), scenery editor (lower left), and Aero Designer (lower right).

a realistic situation in which they find themselves in a British taxi and have to communicate with the English-speaking driver. Students hear colloquial English and respond with the computer keyboard (see Figure 2.23). The game was commissioned by the British Council.

FIGURE 2.23   Chinese university students in England using *English Taxi* to learn colloquial spoken English. © Aqua Pacific. Reprinted with permission.

CORE COMPETENCY GAMES

Core competency games, the third major category of serious games, are designed to develop a core competency or area of specialized expertise. These games often contrast with realistic games that strive to replicate the learning environment accurately and in high fidelity, in that the game environment might bear little resemblance to the actual activity or skill to be learned. A useful way to think about core competency games is that they are a form of cross-training—akin to weight training to improve performance on the golf course.

Consider *Lexia Cross-Trainer*, from Lexia Learning Systems, Inc. (*www.lexialearning.com*), which is composed of a battery of PC/Mac games designed to strengthen the thinking skills that form the foundation for academic learning. *Cross-Trainer* focuses on improving the 22 distinct visual-spatial skills in a way that helps learning-disabled, special needs, and mainstream students strengthen their thinking, memory, and problem-solving abilities. The six core competencies developed by *Cross-Trainer* are visualization, visual memory, mental rotation, visual tracking, spatial orientation, and multi-perspective coordination.

Jon Bower is quick to point out that his company doesn't refer to *Cross-Trainer* as an educational game or as edutainment because both terms are stigmatized in the kindergarten through twelfth grade (K–12) market. Edutainment software was over-hyped by the computer industry in the 1980s as a means of moving computer hardware into schools and homes. Apple Computer was especially aggressive in the K–12 market and frequently bundled edutainment software with its Apple II line of computer. Work by educational researchers in the early 1990s, such as Seymour Papert, developer of the LOGO language, caused educators to step back and consider exactly what computers were teaching students, and whether the concepts and methodologies were developmentally appropriate. *Young Children and Technology*, by Susan Haugland and June Wright, provides an excellent overview of the history of edutainment and modern methods of evaluating educational software for children [HauglandWright97].

One of the games or modules within the *Cross Trainer* is *Cubes*, is shown in Figure 2.24. Using a Logitech Wingman Rumblepad, players manipulate the environment and try to envision what a scene or set of objects would look like if seen from a different angle. Jon, who employs 10 developers and an equal number of educational psychologists, says that the nonthreatening game environment is applicable to all children. However, Lexia's clinical studies of efficacy have centered on children with learning disorders because nothing else has worked for these children.

Cognitive core competency training isn't limited to children or to strictly cognitive tasks such as reading. Applied Cognitive Engineering (*www. Ace4sports.com*) offers *Intelligym*™ a 2D game marketed to professional,

FIGURE 2.24 *Lexia Cross-Trainer* showing the *Cubes* application, with 2D and 3D representations of the blocks balanced on the turtle's back. © Lexia Learning Systems, Inc. Reprinted with permission.

collegiate, and high school basketball coaches (see Figure 2.25). The PC game, which is based on technology developed for Israel's fighter pilots, is designed to improve core abilities such as coordination, attention control, peripheral vision, and perception.

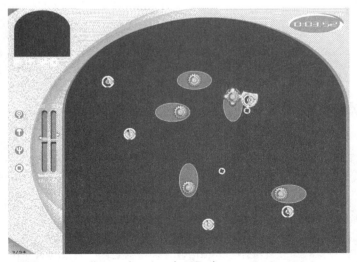

FIGURE 2.25 *Intelligym*, showing the 2D play space. © Applied Cognitive Engineering (ACE). Reprinted with permission.

Intelligym is based on research in the field of cognitive engineering. Each game is generated from a detailed training plan, and for each 15–60-second game round, the program tracks about 80 parameters. Furthermore, there is a library of hundreds of rounds and dozens of optional movement pattern dynamics. The result is a training arsenal that can be customized to a player's individual needs. Among the first installations in the United States were for the basketball teams of the University of Kentucky and the University of Memphis in 2004. The company is exploring other vertical markets, including martial arts training.

REPURPOSED COMMERCIAL OFF-THE-SHELF (COTS) GAMES

Repurposed COTS games, the fourth category of serious games, are designed for one purpose and used for other, often unrelated, purposes with little or no alteration. An example of a game in this category is *America's Army*, which proved so successful as a realistic marketing tool that it was incorporated into the training of cadets and soldiers. *America's Army* is used at West Point's Simulation Center to teach cadets teamwork, leadership skills, and basic tactics that would otherwise need to be illustrated on blackboards and sand tables or through expensive live training sessions. Cadets also use *America's Army* to learn the basics of land navigation, force protection, procedural first aid and survival, critical thinking and leadership, and maintenance and intelligence skills. Since the introduction of *America's Army* in the West Point curriculum, cadets not only progress more rapidly through training, but incoming cadets learn land navigation training a year earlier than in the past [AmericasArmy05].

Another realistic, simulation-based COTS game that has been repurposed by the military is *Falcon 4.0* (Microprose), a multiplayer air combat simulation set in the Korean peninsula. Players are thrust into a real-time war in which they assume the role of an F-16 fighter pilot. Perhaps one reason the game is popular as a training aid is the complexity and completeness of the underlying simulation. It's so complete that many casual players are turned off by the steep learning curve [Rowland99].

Following the once common model of spinning out military technology for civilian use, military games have been repurposed for civilian applications. In September 2003 Auburn University became the first civilian organization to use the Joint Conflict and Tactical Simulation (JCATS) software from the U.S. Military [Bell05]. JCATS, which is used by the military to plan battles and evaluate military situations, was adopted by the university for emergency preparedness and homeland security training exercises. The virtual reality software, developed at the Lawrence Livermore National Laboratories, models details of the environment and the humans involved—down to the calories expended during a domestic crisis [Shimamoto00].

JCATS games can take anywhere from 20 minutes to several weeks to play, depending on the complexity of the mission and the number of agencies involved. Setting up an exercise in JCATS can be just as lengthy, depending on the number and kind of combat forces and the kinds of topography that has to be modeled. As in a typical FPS, players have at their disposal a variety of weapons and military vehicles. An atypical feature of JCATS is the supply of crowd control weaponry, from rubber bullets and clubs to tear gas and stinger grenades. It's also important to note that JCATS proper is more of a simulation than a game. However, when used in the appropriate context, it can provide the basis for gameplay.

An important application of COTS is to provide readily available prototypes for more extensive serious games development. Consider the work of Believe in Tomorrow National Children's Foundation (*www.believeintomorrow.org*), a nonprofit national children's foundation affiliated with Johns Hopkins. One of the problems facing families with children requiring chronic therapy for cancer, burns, and kidney disease is the inevitable resistance from the children to submitting to the painful therapy. The Believe in Tomorrow staff hypothesized that one way to entice children to come in for treatment was to create a unique game that could be played at the doctor's office. Furthermore, it was thought that the game would also provide a distraction for the children undergoing painful procedures.

To test the pain control hypothesis, Dr. Lynnda Dahlquist, a psychologist with the University of Maryland, Baltimore County, conducted an initial study in which children played through a commercial entertainment game using a joystick and head-mounted display. Using buckets of ice water as painful but harmless stimuli, Dr. Dahlquist demonstrated that the average tolerance time for subjects to keep an arm immersed in ice water was only about 15 seconds. With gameplay, the average tolerance time was a minute [Dahlquist05].

Given the initial success of the distraction therapy demonstration, Believe in Tomorrow and Dr. Dahlquist's research team are preparing for a second phase study to determine whether children scheduled for treatment will be less reluctant to see their doctors and will experience less discomfort during their medical treatment if they have a unique game to play waiting for them in the treatment room. Breakaway Games (*www.breakawaygames.com*), a leader in the serious games industry, is developing the game, which is based on an underwater diving simulation it built for the U.S. Navy [Sheffield05]. The environment includes schools of fish, sea turtles, and plant life that behave like the real things, thanks to artificial intelligence (AI) behind each element (see Figure 2.26). For example, the fish swim away if the children get too close, and plant life grows and develops just like a real reef. The developer is extending the basic reef simulation to enable the player receiving therapy to explore the reef, hunt for hidden treasure, and take pictures of fish, all in the relaxed underwater environment.

FIGURE 2.26   *Believe in Tomorrow Project*, showing an undersea environment used to distract children receiving painful, therapy.
© Breakaway Games and Believe In Tomorrow. Reprinted with permission.

Perhaps the most unexpected emergent use of COTS video games is to aid surgeons in training. Dr. James Rosser, head of the Advanced Medical Technology Institute at Beth Israel Medical Center in New York City (*www.rosseramti.com*), has been repurposing COTS video games to train doctors in laparoscopic surgery since 2001 [Xie05]. Rosser reports that because every game is different, the degree of skill carryover to surgery is game-dependent. He tested more than 100 games and found three games that made a significant difference in developing surgical skills—*Super Monkey Ball* (Sega), *Silent Scope* (Konami), and *Star Wars: Episode I Racer* (LucasArts) [Rosser04]. Rosser found that students who played video games for more than three hours per week had 37 percent fewer errors during the procedure and finished the operation in 27 percent less time [Rosser04].

MODIFIED GAMES (MODS)

Game enthusiasts have modified commercial games for years. Modifications (mods) of game engines, the fifth major category of serious games, have been used to create new games from the engines behind *QUAKE*, *DOOM*, *Half-Life*, and other popular games [Chan04]. Most mods are intended to create new, improved, entertainment games. However, the mod process can be used to create serious games. For example, *Marine DOOM*, a mod of *DOOM II* (Id Software) that supports multiple users, is designed to teach teamwork, coordination, and decision making [Newman96].

The impetus for developing *Marine DOOM* was economic. In the mid-1990s, the Marines didn't have the money to pay for the ammo and field time they needed to keep themselves in practice, and the *DOOM* mod seemed like a cheap and efficient way to train [Riddell97]. Even though the unfunded experiment resulted in cost savings, the use of Mods also has an economic downside. Players must have the base game engine installed on their PCs to run the mod.

The Mod *Tactical Iraqi*, based on the *Unreal Tournament* engine, was developed at the Center for Advanced Research in Technology for Education (CARTE) at the USC Information Sciences Institute (*www.isi.edu/isd/carte*). The game, shown in Figure 2.27, incorporates a voice recognition engine and considerable additional AI to teach U.S. soldiers and Marines how to speak Iraqi Arabic. The game format holds the students' attention better than conventional training [Johnson04].

FIGURE 2.27   *Tactical Iraqi*, developed to train U.S. military personnel in Iraqi Arabic. Courtesy Dr. Lewis Johnson. © University of Southern California. Reprinted with permission.

Another mod, based on *Deus Ex: Invisible War* (Eidos), is being developed by the University of Abertay and Learndirect Scotland to teach Scots to read [Qureshi04]. Unlike a typical mod, which includes new items, weapons, characters, enemies, models, modes, textures, levels, and a new story line, *Deus Ex* proper is largely untouched. With the exception of toning down some of the original violent content, the modifications take the form of puzzle-solving memory and verbal reasoning tests interspersed within the game levels. Players are required to use their problem-solving skills in order to progress from one level to the next.

Mods are normally implemented by third parties. However, developers can also add multimedia and modify the gameplay of an existing title to save time and development cost. In addition to the serendipitous applicability of the unaltered *America's Army* game to real army training, the Future Application Team of the Virtual Heroes shop is developing versions of *America's Army*—actually mods of the underlying Unreal engine—for a variety of government agencies, homeland security, and military teams. Figure 2.28 shows the *America's Army* Adaptive Thinking & Leadership (ATL) training application, which was created for the JFK Special Warfare Center and School at Fort Bragg, NC.

FIGURE 2.28 *America's Army* Adaptive Thinking & Leadership (ATL) training game, a modified version of America's Army. Courtesy Jerry Heneghan. © Virtual Heroes. Reprinted with permission.

Virtual Heroes is also developing versions of *America's Army* using new modeling technology to simulate advanced weapons systems so that engineers can test the weapons virtually before committing to production. Other mods for government agencies incorporate advanced AI, physics, and physiology capabilities as well as new assets. Figure 2.29

shows an example of the assets developed for a version of *America's Army* used by the Secret Service. Additional models for the Secret Service include new weapons, additional vehicles, and NPCs.

FIGURE 2.29   *Presidential Limousine Cadillac* (left) and *Uniformed Officer* models (right) developed by Virtual Heroes for a project with the U.S. Secret Service. Courtesy Jerry Heneghan. © Virtual Heroes. Reprinted with permission.

The U.S. military is clearly the most influential of the groups working to modify game software for serious applications. In addition to the examples detailed here, the U.S. Navy uses a modified version of *Microsoft Flight Simulator* to train rookie pilots [Smith05]. There is also considerable independent work in the mod space. Readers are referred to Internet portals such as Game-Mods.com (*www.game-mods.com*) for news and information on mod packs available and under development.

THE VALUE PROPOSITION

The current interest in using, developing, and investing in serious games reflects the perceived value of the medium in terms of economics, educational effectiveness, efficacy, and social impact.

Economics

Admittedly, the economics of the serious games space is the most critical element in the value proposition. Without an economic incentive, few developers would devote their energies to furthering the field, and without multi-million-dollar simulation-based game projects, military contractors would focus elsewhere. Getting a handle on current expenditures on serious games development is difficult because of the visibility issue illustrated in Chapter 1, "Historical Perspective," and the lack of a universally accepted definition of what constitutes a serious game.

Using the definition of serious games offered in the Introduction—*an interactive computer application, with or without a significant hardware component, which has a challenging goal; is fun to play and/or engaging; incorporates some concept of scoring; and imparts to the user a skill, knowledge, or attitude that can be applied in the real world*—most serious games used for internal development and education are never marketed. Many other serious games are developed for closed markets.

As noted earlier, the pharmaceutical industry develops or commissions the development of serious games for direct and indirect product promotion. A half-million dollar game might be used for one weekend at a major trade show and then either archived or given to physicians as a take-away. According to PhRMA, the Pharmaceutical Research and Manufacturers of America (*www.phrma.org*), the U.S. pharmaceutical industry spent $6 billion on journal promotion, hospital, and office promotion in 2003 [Phrma05]. Some percentage of that figure was devoted to serious games development. The exact figure is difficult to determine because states have different reporting laws [BergeronChan04]. In addition, the developers in the shops catering to the pharmaceutical industry—as well as thousands of other industries worldwide—might not even consider themselves game developers.

Lacking figures on the internal development in industry and education, a conservative estimate of the economic potential of serious games can be estimated as some portion of the overall game industry. Consider that sales in the worldwide video game industry were $24.5 billion in 2004, with sales projected to exceed $55 billion by 2008 [Grover05]. U.S. sales of portable and console hardware, software, and accessories were $9.9 billion in 2004—a drop from $10 billion in 2003—according to the NPD Group [Riley05]. Even though dollar sales were down, unit sales were up by 4 percent over the same period the previous year. Software sales for 2004 were a record $6.2 billion, an increase of 8 percent over 2003. Moreover, sales of mobile software titles broke the $1 billion mark for the first time.

To put this performance in relative economic terms, video games pulled in more than movie box-office receipts in 2004. Video game sales is less impressive when compared with the combined gross sales and rental revenue from U.S. home videos—about $25 billion in 2004 [Sporich04]. Even so, the interactive unit of Nielsen Entertainment (*www.nielsen.com/nielsen_entertainment.html*) reports that sales of video games to U.S. males in the first half of 2005 were second only to DVD sales, for all forms of media, including music [Reuters05].

The positive performance trend of video games has attracted the attention of advertisers and media conglomerates, as well as companies immersed in the game industry. The reason for the interest by advertisers and those in traditional media is the valuable mindshare of males of all ages. Nielson Entertainment reported that nearly a quarter of all gamers are over age 40. Furthermore, skyrocketing sales of video games aren't just a U.S. phenomenon. When it comes to online games, Nielsen NetRatings found that 56 percent of boys and 42 percent of girls in the UK aged 12 to 17 visited online game sites in December of 2004 [Presswire05].

The funding for serious games development for training and recruitment from the Department of Defense is easily the largest in the serious games space. As an example of the value of serious gaming to the military, consider one rationale behind the U.S. DOD spending millions of dollars annually on simulators. Findings at the Navy's Top Gun Strike University, showed that without practice, the effect of Top Gun training is lost after only 45 days [ChathamBraddock01]. In other words, after only six weeks, an F/A-18 pilot's bombing accuracy returns to pre-training levels. However, actual flight time or simulator time can inhibit the decay of learning. Given the expense of operating and maintaining a $28 million F/A-18, even a multi-million-dollar simulator system can be a bargain.

Then there is the success of *America's Army*, which is managed by the office of the Assistant Secretary of the Army—Manpower and Reserve Affairs (ASAM&RA) through the Office of Economic & Manpower Analysis (OEMA) at West Point. *America's Army* is the most successful use of a game for marketing. OEMA reports that, as of February 2005, there were more than 4.6 million registered users, 67 million hours of game play, and 20 million downloads of the game and its upgrades, which placed *America's Army* among the top five online action games in the world [Wardynski05]. In addition, a survey found that 29 percent of young adults and 19 percent of their parents had a positive awareness of the Army based on *America's Army*—levels that exceed the total impact of all other Army sponsorships combined. Furthermore, the game accomplished this level of awareness at a fraction of the cost of traditional communications channels [Wardynski05].

Analysis by *The Wall Street Journal* suggests that the nearly $10 billion U.S. game industry is projected to grow by 20 percent annually through 2009 [Wingfield05]. There is undeniably a great deal of economic activity in the gaming industry, but not every developer is going to get rich by developing yet another FPS. In addition, the game industry, like every other modern industry, is cyclical.

In evaluating the economic potential of serious games, focusing on economic figures alone can be deceiving. For example, even as sales topped $8 billion in 2004, the industry giant, Electronic Arts, suffered financial cutbacks, and employees sued over uncompensated overtime [WongTakahashi05]. In terms of market share, Sony is clearly in first place with 54 percent of the market. Microsoft is a distant second at 24.9 percent, and Nintendo is last with only 18.7 percent of the market [Grover05]. However, from a corporate performance perspective, Sony realized only $4.5 billion in operating income for the years 1998 through 2004. During the same period, Nintendo achieved $7 billion in operating income. Microsoft, number two in revenue, reported heavy losses as it tried to break into the market by giving away hardware [Grover05].

For an appreciation of the economic disparity between serious games and those developed strictly for entertainment purposes, consider the recipients of the 2005 Game Developers Choice Awards. *The Sims* (Maxis), *Grand Theft Auto* (DMA Designs/Rockstar Games), *Metroid Prime* (Retro Studios), and S*tar Wars: Knights of the Old Republic* were all entertainment blockbusters [IGDA05]. Similarly, the entertainment mega-hit in 2004 was *Halo 2*, with single-day sales in excess of 2.4 million units and revenue of more than $120 million [McCaffrey04]. To put this in perspective, the top entertainment movie of 2004, Shrek 2 (DreamWorks), generated $108 million on opening day [BoxOfficeMojo05].

There are very few serious games funded at the level of AAA entertainment games. Breakaway Games reports that it was responsible for three of the five AAA budgeted games in development at the start of 2005 [Sheffield05]. These serious games, as well as the multi-million-dollar, multi-year entertainment video game development projects can be contrasted with low-budget projects on display at the annual Independent Game Festival, also held at the GDC. In 2005 there were about 80 entrants in categories of Innovation in Game Design, Audio, Visual Art, Technical Excellence, Audience Award, and Independent Game of the Year in each of Web/Downloadable and Open categories. Average development costs and time were approximately $50,000 over nearly 17 months, with an average team size of about five people [IGF05]. The overall winner, *Gish*, a PC/Mac game by Chronic Logic, LLC (see Figure 2.30), was developed by three developers working half-time over eight months with a budget of $5,000. The developer's main out-of-pocket cost was for sound and music, which were outsourced [Pisciotta05].

Gish, like the other winners of the IGF, was not categorized as a serious game, but it gives some indication of the economic potential of independently developed games in the serious games space. The $20 game, available as a download from the developer (*www.chroniclogic.com*), could be repurposed as an educational game in high-school physics. As players direct an amiable tar ball through tunnels and traps, they have to understand and apply physics properties such as momentum, adhesion, and surface friction. Used in the appropriate educational setting, the game could easily help a player grasp these and other physical principles.

Readers interested in formulating guesstimates of the economic potential of the serious games industry are encouraged to explore the business development and online information sources sections of Appendix F, "Resources." For example, Ben Sawyer's article on Gamasutra is worth reading [Sawyer04].

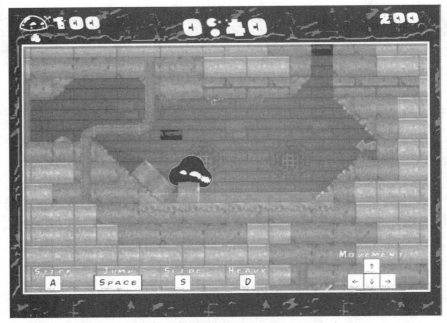

FIGURE 2.30 *Gish*, winner of the 2005 Independent Games Festival. © Chronic Logic, LLC. Reprinted with permission.

Educational Effectiveness

Few serious educators would claim that games are the most efficient way to learn facts, especially when pressed for time. However, serious games may be the most effective means of safely learning skills and attitudes—processes that are difficult to acquire through rote memorization [Gee04]. Furthermore, there is considerable evidence suggesting that even when there are more efficient methods of acquiring knowledge, learning through gameplay may be longer lasting. Witness the increasing popularity of case-based curricula in business and medical schools since the 1980s [Williams92].

Case-Based Curricula

McMaster University, Harvard Medical School, Harvard Business School, Wake Forest University, and the University of New Mexico are among the many universities that have used case-based approaches to teaching complex processes. At Harvard Medical School, for example, students are presented with patient case scenarios—live RPGs—in which they must diagnose a volunteer patient. While going through the role playing game in which students take turns as the attending physician, students may refer to textbooks on physiology, anatomy, neurology, and other areas as needed. The role playing enables medical students to experience the nuances of the diagnostic process that can't be mastered by rote memorization. Proponents of simulated patient cases or games report that the superiority of the case-based approach to medical training also applies to the use of interactive virtual patients in medical training [Bergeron89].

A large, well-controlled study on the effectiveness of computers as educational tools was conducted at Dartmouth Medical School in the late 1980s [Lyon90]. The program tested was not classified as a game at the time, but it nonetheless incorporated elements of a modern RPG in which students played the role of doctor in diagnosing patients with a blood disorder. The two-year study, which involved hundreds of medical school students, illustrated several advantages of the computer-based method. For example, students using the program were able to complete patient cases on average 43 percent faster than students using traditional methods.

Contemporary studies on the educational value of games, while rare, tend to focus on K-12 students [HauglandWright97; Morrison04]. Recently, several positive milestone studies of the educational value of games have been conducted in the UK, with government support [Sanger97; Turner04; Ulicsak04]. Even before these studies, which support the use of games in education, it was rare to find a school with a computer learning lab void of games.

Despite positive studies, proponents of the use of games in K–12 education are hard pressed to show games are the best investment of time and money. The literature is filled with studies of computer-based education systems that were developed at considerable expense, only to be used once by a few dozen students. Furthermore, educators point out that any number of factors could be responsible for positive findings in schools that use games in the curriculum. The sheer novelty of the medium could account for temporary heightened interest and effectiveness. It's also likely that more thought has gone into a game design than into a typical lecture or series of lectures. A thoroughly planned educational design—not the game per se—might be responsible for the positive results of the limited studies in the literature.

Faced with money-strapped school systems, it's difficult to defend massive expenditures of resources so that a few students can experience a game for an afternoon. One solution is to share games with other schools through an educational game consortium. In this way, every school or university contributing to the consortium can have access to a library of educational games.

Emergent Behavior

Understanding the user experience is central to quantifying the effectiveness of serious video games as educational tools. Anecdotally, every game teaches, but sometimes what is being taught may not be obvious. For example, consider the mannequin-based patient simulators used in the Top Gun medic training at Fort Sam Houston, Texas. As discussed elsewhere, mannequins made up as casualties are placed on rubble or patches of dirt surrounded by artificial trees, under camouflage canopies, and in other realistic settings. However, even with all of the attention to detail, instructors initially found that the room-sized games also taught emergent, undesirable behavior.

Several of the first medic trainees who experienced the Top Gun program were unable to move volunteer victims out of the line of fire [Litteral05]. When asked why, the trainees were hard pressed to explain. It turned out that the trainees were instructed not to move the mannequins because the expensive training devices were connected via a thick umbilical cord to power, air and fluid pumps, and the computer system. The medic trainees learned not to move mannequins, and this behavior carried over to the human volunteers in the live games. One solution under development is to use cordless mannequins that can be dragged to safety.

Recognizing that much of the research into the educational value of video games lags behind technological advances, the Advanced Distance Learning (ADL) Initiative, Office of the Under Secretary of Defense for Personnel and Readiness, has chosen to examine massively multiplayer online gaming (MMOG) as a future focus [BonkDennon05]. In particular, the ADL recognizes that even though the U.S. military has been exploring the use of MMOGs to improve the analytical and thinking skills of personnel, most of the evidence is anecdotal.

The same predicament exists in the world of mannequin-based training in medicine. Despite millions of dollars invested in the technology since the early 1990s, there are no large-scale studies that prove the use of simulators in training clinicians results in "better" clinicians. The cost and difficulty of following groups of clinicians trained with simulators and comparing them with clinicians trained without simulators is daunting. Even if hundreds of clinicians could be followed for 5 or 10 years and significant differences in, say, number of malpractice suits filed against clinicians could be shown, other factors could account for the differences. Because teachers who actively embrace new learning technologies are likely more committed to teaching than their peers, differences in clinician behavior could simply reflect better teachers, not the simulator props.

Efficacy

Most serious games are never subject to the rigorous scrutiny of scientific peer review. One of the few games studied for therapeutic efficacy is *The Matrix*, shown in Figure 2.31. The program, developed by Stephane Dandeneau in Dr. Mark Baldwin's lab, has been shown to increase implicit self-esteem—the automatic, nonconscious aspect of self-esteem—through classical conditioning. Two studies based on *The Matrix* demonstrated that implicit self-esteem can be enhanced through repeated pairing of self-relevant information with smiling faces as in *The Matrix* [Baccus04; DandeneauBaldwin04].

As described earlier, *The Matrix* is part of a suite of three games developed to enhance self-esteem. Additional studies on the game suite are underway, including an assessment of the psychological effects of *Grow Your Chi*, the most interactive of the three games [Baldwin05; Dandeneau05].

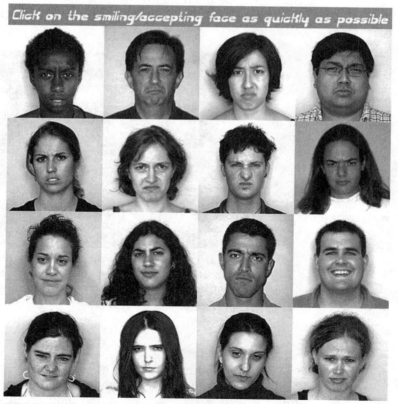

FIGURE 2.31   *The Matrix*, a serious game in medicine and healthcare that has been subject to rigorous scientific evaluation. Courtesy Stéphane Dandeneau. © Mark Baldwin. Reprinted with permission.

The efficacy of virtual reality games in treating phobias and distracting patients during burn treatment and chemotherapy are other areas that have been subject to scientific validation. Technologies such as functional MRI (fMRI) have been used to monitor changes in brain activity in patients undergoing painful therapy while they are immersed in a virtual reality game [Hoffman04]. Figure 2.32 illustrates brain activity differences in a patient who is experiencing pain with and without virtual reality, as measured by Dr. Hunter Hoffman of the Virtual Reality Analgesia Research Center.

These well-planned and executed studies are anomalies, in that most games are never evaluated for efficacy of any type. For example, the efficacy of virtual reality therapy in some disorders, such as Post-Traumatic Stress Disorder (PTSD), has yet to be validated by large-scale clinical trials. Even the use of game technology for burn patients and phobics hasn't been subject to large-scale scientific analysis. Of note, however, is that the lack of data hasn't stopped the use of VR games to control pain. In medicine, it can be unethical to withhold apparently beneficial but unproven therapies, especially if the side effects are negligible.

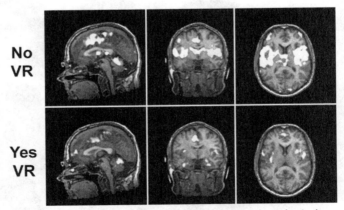

FIGURE 2.32   Functional MRI brain scans showing physiological differences in the brain when the patient is experiencing pain with and without virtual reality. © Dr. Hunter Hoffman, Virtual Reality Analgesia Research Center at the University of Washington HITLab. Reprinted with permission.

Efficacy is often evaluated in terms of cost. In 1986 the American College of Orthopaedic Surgeons convened a conference in which thought leaders from academia and industry in the field of simulation and education were asked to formulate a plan to develop a surgical simulator for training surgeons in arthroscopic knee surgery [Bergeron86]. Up to that time, the primary method available to most knee surgeons was to visit their local butcher shop and purchase cow knees. Then, using a homemade jig, surgeons mounted the knees and practiced repairing tears and avulsions while looking through the scope.

During the conference, a representative from Evans and Sutherland, known for developing flight simulators for the military, suggested that a surgical simulator was possible with then current haptic and computer display technology. However, he estimated the cost at two to three million dollars—per simulator. By the end of the conference, the leadership of the college decided that it was not in a position to fund surgical simulator research and development. The college recommend to its membership that surgeons continue with cow knees—a bargain at less than a dollar per knee.

Two decades later, despite millions invested in prototype surgical simulators, including several funded by the U.S. Army's Telemedicine and Advanced Technology Research Center (TATRC), most knee surgeons in the U.S. turn to cow knees and cadavers for practice. Cost, especially of the haptic hardware, is still a primary limitation. However, given the long-term focus of TATRC and commercial enterprises, serious surgical games will eventually be a reality. Readers interested in the latest developments in surgical simulations and serious medical games for the army are encouraged to visit the TATRC site (*www.tatrc.org*).

Social Impact Games

Developers of serious games would like to think that their work has a positive social impact. Of the serious games discussed here, *America's Army* is the one most intensely studied for social impact. However, it's an anomaly because of the money available to assess the effectiveness of the army's various marketing campaigns in attracting and retaining troops for the war effort.

The primary challenge in assessing the efficacy of serious games in terms of social impact is cost. Large-scale, statistically valid market surveys are expensive and the expense may not be warranted, given the operating budgets of many nonprofit organizations. With the exception of product-linked advergaming, in which users who play a game can be identified at the time of product purchase, it is practically impossible to quantify social impact. At best, social impact can be inferred from gameplay activity on the Internet and/or the flow of CDs through other distribution channels.

Summary

Contemporary serious games aren't limited to the military or medicine. Like the definition of serious games, the categories of serious games are not universal standards. The categories of serious games offered here are games with an agenda, news games, political games, realistic games, and core competency games. Serious games derived from repurposed COTS games and modifications (mods) are often considered categories worth separate treatment because they are popular methods of acquiring or developing serious games.

In examining the value proposition of serious games—what games have to offer—it's difficult to put a solid figure on the economic potential of the industry. Much of the activity in serious games development is invisible, and many multimedia designers and programmers involved in serious games development may not even consider themselves in the game industry. As such, a conservative guesstimate of the current and future economics of serious games development is to assume it is some slice of the total game development economy.

Linked to the economic performance of serious games are figures on the educational effectiveness, efficacy, and social impact of serious games. There is evidence that serious games may be the most effective means of learning skills and attitudes and that serious gameplay may support longer-lasting learning than traditional methods. However, there are very few unequivocal studies that show the introduction of serious games into a curriculum is the best use of limited resources.

References

[AmericasArmy05] AmericasArmy, 2005. *www.americasarmy.com*, accessed April 15, 2005.

[Baccus04] Baccus, Jodene, Mark Baldwin, et al., "Increasing Implicit Self-esteem Through Classical Conditioning." *Psychological Science* 7(2004): pp. 498–502.

[Baldwin05] Baldwin, Mark, Personal Communications, *Grow Your Chi.* McGill, April 7, 2005.

[Bell05] Bell, Beca, "Auburn U. Applies Defense Software to Civilian Situations." *The Auburn Plainsman* (March 17, 2005).

[Bergeron84] Bergeron, B. P., *Know Your Body.* Home Health Software, 1984.

[Bergeron84b] Bergeron, B. P., *The Lean Machine.* Home Health Software, 1984.

[Bergeron86] Bergeron, Bryan, "Clinical Skill-Building through Computer Simulation." *Proceedings of the Medical Simulation Foundation Conference* (1986): pp. 57–60.

[Bergeron89] Bergeron, B. P., "Providing Clinical Experience through Computer Simulation." *Medical Practice Management* (4 1989): pp. 288–93.

[Bergeron90] Bergeron, Bryan, John Fallon, et al., Using a Gaming Approach to Maximize Student Participation in Computer-Based Education. *Collegiate Microcomputer* 4(1990): pp. 293–300.

[BergeronChan04] Bergeron, Bryan, Paul Chan, *Biotech Industry: A Global, Economic, and Financial Overview.* J. Wiley & Sons, 2004.

[Block82] Block, R. A., Temporal Judgments and Contextual Change. *Journal of Experimental Psychology: Learning, Memory, and Cognition* 6(1982): pp. 530–44.

[BonkDennen05] Bonk, Curtis, Vanessa Dennen, *Massive Multiplayer Online Gaming: A Research Framework for Military Training and Education.* Advanced Distributed Learning, 2005.

[BoxOfficeMojo05] BoxOfficeMojo, *2004 Domestic Grosses.* Box Office Mojo. 2005. *www.boxofficemojo.com*, accessed March 25, 2005.

[Boyd04] Boyd, Clark, Games Blur News and Entertainment. BBC News. 2004. *news.bbc.co.uk/go/pr/fr/-/1/hi/technology/3653294.stm*, accessed April 1, 2005.

[Chan04] Chan, Norman, MODS. *PC Gamer: The Ultimate Shooter Guide* 1(2004): pp. 74–84.

[ChathamBraddock01] Chatham, R., J. Braddock, *Training Superiority and Training Surprise, Report of the Defense Science Board.* 2001.

[Cheok05] Cheok, Adrian, *The Mixed Reality Lab of the National University of Singapore Introduces Poultry-Internet—A Revolutionary New Invention for Human-to-Chicken Touch through the Internet.* 2005. *http://mixedreality.nus.edu.sg/research-TI-infor.htm*, accessed May 20, 2005.

[Cole05] Cole, David, *Ford No Boundaries 3D Game.* 2005. *www.dave-cole.com/portfolio*, accessed April 1, 2005.

[Csikszentmihalyi91] Csikszentmihalyi, Mihaly, *Flow: The Psychology of Optimal Experience.* Perennial, 1991.

[Dahlquist05] Dahlquist, Lynnda, Personal Communications, *Believe in Tomorrow Project.* April 14, 2005.

[Dandeneau05] Dandeneau, S., J. R. Baccus, et al., "Attention Training Modifies Perception of Social Threat and Reduces Stress. In preparation.

[DandeneauBaldwin04] Dandeneau, S., Mark Baldwin, The Inhibition of Socially Rejecting Information among People with High versus Low Self-Esteem: The Role of Attentional Bias and the Effects of Bias Reduction Training. *Journal of Social and Clinical Psychology* 2004): pp. 584–602.

[Edmonds81] Edmonds, E. M., D. Cahoon, et al., The Estimation of Time as a Function of Positive, Neutral, or Negative Expectancies. *Bulletin of the Psychonomic Society* (1981): pp. 259–60.

[Garris99] Garris, Rosemary, Submarine Skills-Training Network (SubSkillsNet). *Undersea Warfare: The Official Magazine of the U.S. Submarine Force* (Winter 1999).

[Gee04] Gee, James, *What Video Games Have to Teach Us about Learning and Literacy.* Palgrave Macmillan, 2004.

[Geist04] Geist, Laura, "Marketing to the Joystick Nation: Chrysler Group Uses Gaming to Lure Youth to Its Brands. *Automotive News* (April 12 2004).

[Grover05] Grover, Ronald, Cliff Edwards, et al., Game Wars. *Business Week* (March 28 2005).

[HauglandWright97] Haugland, Susan, June Wright, *Young Children and Technology.* Alyn & Bacon, 1997.

[Heneghan05] Heneghan, Jerry, Personal Communications, April 4, 2005.

[Hoffman04] Hoffman, Hunter, Virtual-Reality Therapy. *Scientific American* 12(2004): pp. 58–65.

[Hyman03] Hyman, Paul, War! "What Is It Good For? Propaganda in the form of game-playing, for One Thing." *Computer User* (Sept 2003).

[IGDA05] IGDA, *The Game Developers Choice Awards.* 2005. *www.igda.org/awards*, accessed March 24, 2005.

[IGF05] IGF, *2005 IGF Results.* 2005. *www.igda.org/awards*, accessed March 24, 2005,

[Johnson04] Johnson, W., Carole Beal, et al., *Tactical Language Training System: An Interim Report.* Information Sciences Institute, 2004.

[Jones04] Jones, Alan, *Geographic Breakdown of Simulation Centres.* University of Bristol. 2004. *www.bris.ac.uk/depts/bmsc/geog.htm*, accessed June 22, 2005.

[Koster04] Koster, Ralph, *Theory of Fun for Game Design*. Paraglyph, 2004.

[Litteral05] Litteral, David, Personal Communications, *Training Medics at Fort Sam Houston*. March 30, 2005.

[Lyon90] Lyon, H. C., J. C. Healy, et al., "Computer-Based Exercises in Anemia and Chest Pain Diagnosis: An Interim Evaluation of the PlanAlyzer project." *Fourteenth Annual Symposium on Computer Applications in Medical Care* (1990): pp. 483–7.

[Mack04] Mack, Ann, "The Branded Connection: From Cola Makers to Car Companies, Marketers Are Using Online Gaming to Get Their Messages Through." *Brandweek* (2004).

[Marlowe04] Marlowe, Chris, "Gamers May Re-enact Kerry's Swift Boat Mission" Chicago Sun-Times. 2004. *www.suntimes.com/output/elect/cst-ftr-swift18.html*, accessed Sept 14, 2005.

[McCaffrey04] McCaffrey, Ryan, "The History of Halo." *Ultimate Guide to Halo 2* (March 2004): pp. 5–6.

[Morrison04] Morrison, Joe, *Showcase-Savannah*. 2004. *www.nestafuturelab.org/showcase/savannah/savannah.htm*, accessed April 17, 2005.

[Newman96] Newman, R. J., Warfare 2020: "Ones and Zeroes, Not Bombs and Bullets, May Win Tomorrow's Battles." *U.S. News & World Report* (1996).

[ÓhAnluain03] ÓhAnluain, Daithí, "Reaching through the Net to Touch." Wired News. 2003. *wired-vig.wired.com/news/print/0,1294,59462,00.html*, accessed September 14, 2005.

[Phrma05] Phrma, *Annual Report 2005-2006: New medicines, new hopes*. PhRMA. 2005. *www.phrma.org/publications/publications//2005-07-21.1191.pdf*, accessed September 14, 2005.

[Pisciotta05] Pisciotta, Josiah, Personal Communications, *Chronic Logic, LLC*. March 25, 2005.

[Presswire05] Presswire, M2, "Teens Rock on the Internet." *M2 Communications, LTD* (February 17, 2005).

[Pudelek05] Pudelek, Jenna, "Education Matters: One Game That Is a Certified Success." *The Birmingham Post* (March 14, 2005).

[Qureshi04] Qureshi, Yakub, "Violent Video Game Helps Scots to Read." *Scotland on Sunday* (May 30, 2004).

[Reuters05] Reuters, *Men Spend More on Video Games than Music*. Reuters. 2005, accessed April 7, 2005.

[Riddell97] Riddell, Rob, "Doom Goes to War." *WIRED* 4 (1997).

[Riley05] Riley, David, *The NPD Group Reports Annual 2004 U.S. Video Game Industry Retail Sales*. NPD Funworld. 2005. *www.npdfunworld.com*, accessed April 13, 2005.

[Rosser04] Rosser, James, "Video Game and Laparoscopic Surgery." *Medicine Meets Virtual Reality* (2004).

[Rowland99] Rowland, Emory, *Falcon 4.0*. 1999. *www.gamezilla.com*, accessed April 3, 2005.

[SalenZimmerman04] Salen, Katie, Eric Zimmerman, *Rules of Play: Game Design Fundamentals*. MIT Press, 2004.

[Sanger97] Sanger, J., J. Wilson, et al., *Young Children, Videos and Computer Games: Issues for Teachers and Parents*. Falmer Press, 1997.

[Sawyer04] Sawyer, Ben, *Getting Serious about New Opportunities: On Game Developers and the 'Serious Gaming' Market*. Gamasutra. 2004. *www.gamasutra.com/features/20041015/sawyer_02.shtml*, accessed September 15, 2005.

[Sheffield05] Sheffield, B., "Breaking the waves." *Game Developer* 2(2005): pp. 25–6.

[Shimamoto00] Shimamoto, Faith, *Simulation Warfare is No Video Game: Livermore's JCATS Combat Simulation Program Proves Invaluable for Training Officers and Rehearsing Missions*. Lawrence Livermore Laboratories. 2000, accessed April 4, 2005.

[Smith05] Smith, Wes, "Hurt Soldiers Still Help Country—Virtually." *The Orlando Sentinel* (April 13, 2005).

[Sporich04] Sporich, Brett, DVD "Sales Growth in 2004 Gets Biggest Push from TV: Figures Climb 60%, Studios Report. *Hollywood Reporter* (Dec 23 2004).

[Turner04] Turner, Jim, Carl Gavin, et al., "Racing Academy." *Physics Education* 5(2004): pp. 429–33.

[Ulicsak04] Ulicsak, Mary, *Astroversity*. Nesta FutureLab. 2004. *www.nestafuturelab.org/research/projects/astro_report_02.htm*, accessed April 17, 2005.

[Versweyveld99] Versweyveld, Leslie, *Hospital Therapists to Experiment with Virtual Reality Techniques for Burn Pain Control*. 1999. *www.hoise.com/vmw/99/articles/vmw/LV-VM-07-99-7.html*, accessed April 10, 2005.

[Wardynski05] Wardynski, Casey, *Information Paper—America's Army Game*. Office of Economic & Manpower Analysis, 2005.

[WildTangent05] WildTangent, 2005. *www.wildtangent.com*, accessed April 18, 2005.

[Williams92] Williams, S. R., "Putting Case-Based Instruction into Context: Examples from Legal, Business, and Medical Education." *Journal of the Learning Sciences* 2(1992): pp. 367–427.

[Wingfield05] Wingfield, N., "New Games, New Machines, New Winners and Losers." *The Wall Street Journal* (Monday, January 31, 2005): pp. R4.

[WongTakahashi05] Wong, Nicole, Dean Takahashi, Electronic Arts to Convert Some of Its Salaried Employees to Hourly Pay. *San Jose Mercury News* (March 10, 2005).

[Xie05] Xie, Fei, University Wire. 2005. *Video games aid doctors in training*, accessed April 4, 2005.

[Zimmer03] Zimmer, James, Paul Kizakevich, et al., *The Technology Behind Full-Body 3D Patients*. RTI International, 2003.

TECHNOLOGY TRENDS

In This Chapter

- Hardware platforms
- Middleware technologies
- Technologies for managing complexity

ITS and Traditional CAI

ITS and Serious Games

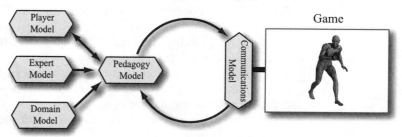

INTRODUCTION

Developing a serious game in a small, understaffed shop is nirvana for those of us afflicted with Attention Deficit Disorder (ADD). After a morning of programming, it's on to game design and perhaps a bit of animation work before heading home with the general ledger tucked in bicycle pannier. For many others, an environment reminiscent of a 24/7 dot-com in perpetual startup mode is a recipe for mental thrashing and has a great potential burnout.

Even in a shop with sufficient staff for programming, art and animation, game design, audio, and production, there is constant pressure to do more with less. Although astute management is essential to mend the inherent cultural divide that separates the engineering types from the artistic staff, maximizing the effectiveness of the development staff also depends on leveraging time with technology. Multiplying a shop's time and talents with technology requires knowledge of the tasks at hand and of the tools available.

Developing a quality game on time and on budget that delights players is impossible without the appropriate technologies. The most effective technologies automate the tedium of low-level tasks and transform them to processes at a higher level of abstraction. These time-saving technologies, applied judiciously to the business of development as well as the development process proper, can minimize time to market, staffing headaches, and production costs.

When a workstation had less processing power than a modern Palm Pilot, game developers had no choice but to work in native assembly language to squeeze every bit of performance out of the hardware. With modern, high performance CPUs and video cards, even low-level graphics routines can be coded in a high-level shader language (HLSL) without noticeable degradation in game quality compared to hand-coded assembler [Gray03]. Technological advances, such as high level languages, result in more effective use of limited programming resources and more readable and portable code.

A major challenge faced by resource-limited serious games developers is how to determine which hardware and software technologies will provide the best return on investment (ROI) while minimizing the risk of failure or breaking the bank. To appreciate this challenge, consider the game development pipeline, shown in Figure 3.1, which begins with definitions of the conceptual, technical, business, and knowledge, skills, and attitude (KSA) requirements. These four factors, which are normally defined in the game design document (see Chapter 8, "Serious Games Design"), provide the rationale and driving force behind the remainder of the development pipeline.

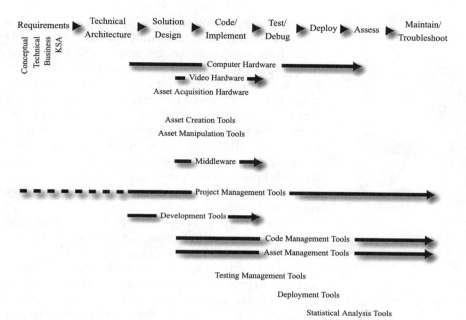

FIGURE 3.1   Game development pipeline and the enabling technologies at the various stages.

A solid technical architecture definition drives the solution design and the resource-intensive coding and asset development stages of the pipeline. It might seem paradoxical that the technical architecture drives the solution design and not vice versa. However, from a practical perspective, a development shop has expertise with specific tools and game engines, and this expertise has been gained over months and sometimes years of working with specific tools. If the requirements of a particular project can't be addressed adequately with an existing technology base, then development time will be extended while the development staff learns the new technology. A shop that specializes in developing games written in *Macromedia Flash* will likely take considerable time and resources to become equally fluent with a complex 3D graphics engine.

After successful testing and debugging, perhaps involving several minor rewrites, the game is distributed over the Web and/or burned to CD-ROM. Before the effects of the game launch party have worn off, the staff assigned to maintain and troubleshoot the game begins their work. Depending on the game, the data collected by support staff might drive the development of a patch or major product update, or simply update a reference file for the next title.

With the development pipeline in mind, consider the enabling technologies at each stage. The computer hardware used by the development shop, from workstations and peripherals to servers, affects the pipeline throughput from solution design through maintenance and troubleshooting. As detailed in the "Hardware Platforms" section of this chapter, the evolution of CPU chips from pipelined devices to parallel processors with multi-core architectures similar to those found in mainframe computers opens new vistas for developers who can cope with the increased complexity. Advances in video hardware, which primarily affects the coding/implementation to testing/debugging stages of the pipeline, are also redefining what is possible. Graphic accelerator cards have broken the 512 MB RAM barrier and the power of onboard processing rivals that of common desktop PCs.

Once a luxury limited to high-end entertainment shops, body and object scanners are becoming commonplace in serious games shops that develop character-based titles. Digital scanners that capture 3D models and motion can rapidly create media with the realism that players have come to expect from entertainment video games. New technologies for asset creation and manipulation that integrate with workflow can be leveraged to streamline the flow of assets through the pipeline.

The most controversial technologies, collectively known as middleware, are viewed as a necessary evil by some small developers and as a godsend by others. No one disputes the power and versatility of the latest generation of physics and AI engines, networking tools, or video codecs, but they come at a price. Exorbitant license fees can decimate the bottom line, and programmers may be loath to find themselves immersed in an uninspiring task of creating the glue to connect middleware *black boxes* together. Like game designers, many game programmers are driven by the creative aspects of game development.

From a management perspective, advanced product management technologies can be used to improve pipeline throughput from the solution design stage to maintenance and troubleshooting. The latest in development technologies, from affordable performance profilers to cross-platform development environments, can multiply the effectiveness of limited programming staff and open markets otherwise beyond the reach of a small development shop.

Given the increasing complexity of games of all genres, testing is more important than ever before. Shops without a dedicated quality assurance (QA) team can invest in the latest generation of testing management tools to maximize the effectiveness of the resources that are available. Finally, given the sophistication of the serious games player community, development tools that provide engine, asset, and copy protection are essential to guard against theft and cheating.

Reviewed here are the technology trends in hardware platforms and middleware and the numerous tools available to manage complexity and maximize throughput in the game development pipeline. This discussion is largely vendor agnostic; a description of specific tools appears in Chapter 6, "Tools."

HARDWARE PLATFORMS

Game developers have a reputation for pushing the hardware envelope further and faster than any other group of computer users. After all, consumers don't see much improvement in the functionality of *Microsoft Word* by moving from 50 MHz Pentium II to a 3.6 GHz Pentium IV. However, the 2005/2006 generation consoles and PCs are positioned to provide the game development community with the means by which they can redefine the gameplay experience and games market for the remainder of the decade.

The PS3 Cell Processor, a 64-bit, multi-core (multiple CPU) chip jointly developed by Sony, Toshiba, and IBM, contains eight parallel coprocessors [Griffin05]. The PS3 promises unparalleled animation capabilities. Similarly, the Xbox 360, based on a 64-bit triple-core PowerPC processor and an ATI graphics processor unit (GPU), has the potential to improve on the original Xbox graphics to the degree that nearly photo-realistic games are possible. Nintendo's response to the PS3 and Xbox 360, the Revolution purportedly offered motion-sensitive game controllers and new gameplay possibilities. Nintendo demonstrated the wireless controller, a device that looks like a TV remote that can be used as a conductor's wand, virtual bat, sword, or racket, at the Tokyo Game Show [Kageyama05]. In addition to defining and defending their niche markets, Sony, Microsoft, and Nintendo all stress connectivity with the Internet, WiFi devices, and entertainment peripherals as central to their designs and marketing plans [Griffin05].

The next-generation PC games, like the games written expressly for the latest consoles, will run on multi-core CPUs with better graphics, physics, AI, and sound and promise more compelling user interaction than is possible with single-core CPU designs [Bennett05]. Small shops catering to niche market that demand this level of realism and performance may have to contend with the complexity of a mixed delivery environment until the legacy systems are replaced. Described here are technology trends in PC-based computer, video, and asset acquisition hardware relevant to serious games development.

Computer Hardware

Barring a major overhaul of the console industry, the personal computer, perhaps supplemented with hand-held game platforms, will remain the primary development and delivery platform for serious games developers.

Given the heightened player expectations created by dedicated game consoles, serious games developers catering to the AAA market might be compelled to leverage the latest computer hardware technology or risk developing titles that are outdated as before they're released. However, as illustrated in the first two chapters, serious games needn't push 3D graphics engines to the limit to achieve the design goals. In simulations, games, and other teaching applications, the appropriate level of detail and realism is a function of the knowledge, attitude, and skills to be learned by the player [BergeronRouse92]. Unnecessary eye candy might not be distracting, but it might negatively impact the performance of the entire system.

Multi-Core CPUs

Since the invention of the first single-chip microprocessor in 1971, Intel, AMD, Motorola, and others have increased performance through innovations such as wider data paths and registers, shorter intrachip connections through miniaturization, more bits per instruction, reduced instruction sets, and faster clock rates. Because of miniaturization limits imposed by heat dissipation challenges, exponentially increasing production costs, and the laws of physics, the processor speed of personal computer microprocessor chips from Intel and AMD have topped out at about 4 GHz [Dickey05; Dickey05b]. Following the lead of the game console manufacturers and the supercomputer industry, Intel and AMD have identified parallel processing as the evolutionary path for the CPUs that drive desktop PCs and servers. Parallel or concurrent processing achieves greater throughput than sequential pipelining methods by assigning different tasks to separate execution threads. For example, one thread might handle game AI, one might handle physics, and a third might be assigned to terrain graphics.

In exchange for more dynamic gameplay, game developers will have to deal with the chief headache associated with parallel processing—managing the synchronization and load of the concurrent threads [Leopold01]. That is, if the game physics, graphics, and audio aren't properly synchronized, the player might hear a collision before seeing it on the screen, and the physical interaction of the colliding objects might appear unnatural.

Of the several methods of achieving parallel processing, Intel and AMD chose a model in which multiple, fully configured CPUs or cores are placed on a single wafer of silicon. The first-generation multi-core chips from Intel and AMD, the Intel EM64T and AMD Opteron, are dual-core designs, with two CPUs per chip. Intel's contribution to the space is the dual-processor Pentium® Extreme Edition processor, shown in Figure 3.2. Each core of the 3.20 GHz, 64-bit processor can run two independent threads [Intel05]. Furthermore, the close physical proximity of the cores results in much lower latency than parallel processing using separate chips. The result is greater throughput and higher performance.

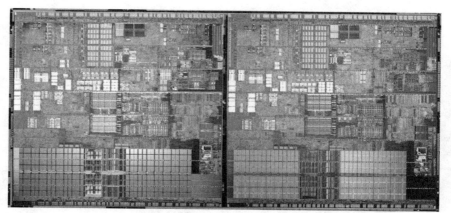

FIGURE 3.2   Intel® Pentium® Processor Extreme Edition processor with dual-processor architecture. © Intel®. Reproduced with permission.

This use of multiple threads, or multithreading, to increase chip performance is not limited to multi-core chips, but can be simulated on a single CPU. Intel's Hyper-Threading technology for the Pentium IV simulates multithreading by creating two logical processors out of a single processor [Marr02]. However, true multithreading on a multi-core processor provides greatly enhanced throughput compared with simulated multithreading. For example, although the overhead of Hyper-Threading can actually harm chip performance, AMD's multi-core chip has been shown to provide between 85 and 64 percent improvement over its single-core chip [Yager05]. The performance increase isn't double that of a single core because of the overhead of coordinating processing within the two cores.

Intel predicts that by 2010, its personal computer microprocessor line will contain 10 cores per chip [RamanathanThomas05].This projection (illustrated in Figure 3.3) seems conservative given the multi-core chips in the PS3 and Xbox 360 and the multi-core chip announced by Sun Microsystems only a week before the debut of the Xbox 360. While the triple-core, 3.2 GHz IBM PowerPC processor in the Xbox 360 can handle two hardware threads per core, the Sun Microsystems' UltraSparc T1 is an eight core chip that supports four threads per core.

To compete successfully with games designed for the latest game consoles, PC-based game engines will have to take full advantage of multi-core chip technology. Similarly, as applied to the development pipeline, the multi-core CPUs will be a boon to the small development shop as soon as development software capitalizes on the new multithreading capabilities. Multi-processor servers using AMD's 64-bit single-core chips can take advantage of the multi-core design by simply plugging in the

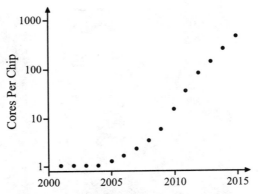

FIGURE 3.3   Intel's projections for multi-core processors
through 2015 [Ramanathan Thomas05].

Opteron [Yager05]. However, most of the applications used for development will have to be rewritten to take advantage of the new hardware and 64-bit Windows environment.

This tool conversion might require years, given the record of third-party ports to Hyper-Threading technology. Three years after introducing Hyper-Threading Pentium IV's, Intel listed only a few dozen applications that were capable of exploiting the technology [Intel05]. Among the development tools were *Adobe Photoshop* and *Premiere Deep Paint 3D*, *Acid Music*, and *Audio Cleaning Lab*. Furthermore, Intel identified only seven games capable of using Hyper-Threading: *Lineage II* (NCSoft), *Trainz* (Auran), *Dungeon Siege* (Microsoft), *EverQuest* (Sony), *Shining Lore Online* (Phantagram), *StarTrek Armada II* (Activision), and *Warrior Kings* (EmpireInteractive).

Intel's own projections show a mix of parallel and pipelined PC applications through 2012 [RamanathanThomas05], suggesting that industry-wide conversion of pipelined to parallel applications will require at least seven years. Of historical note is that both Intel and AMD released their first dual-core processors in April 2005, 40 years to the month after Gordon Moore made his oft-quoted prediction that the number of components on a processor would double every year. AMD followed up its initial offering of a dual-core microprocessor for servers with one for desktops only few weeks later [Fordahl05].

Distributed Processing

While tool vendors port their products to multi-core CPUs, small development shops can make the most of their existing single-core hardware investment by capitalizing on distributed processing technologies for their computationally-intensive development tasks. In this form of parallel processing, a server and local area network (LAN) are configured so that rendering or compiling can run simultaneously on multiple workstations, as in Figure 3.4. The software that makes this possible distributes data on the network, dynamically configures whatever machines are available for processing and handles error recovery from machine crashes and power failures.

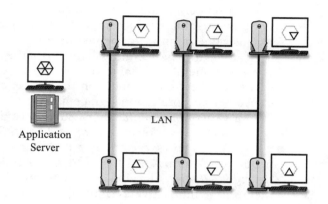

Rendering Workstations

FIGURE 3.4   Distributed processing architecture illustrating shared image rendering.

Distributed processing add-ons to processor-intensive programs like *Maya*, *Softimage*, *Lightwave*, and *3ds max* allow a small shop with limited hardware resources to use surplus processing power from dormant machines to create assets it would otherwise be unable to generate. Distributed processing is especially relevant when the programming staff is working on a game in which build times exceed a few hours. Properly configured, a distributed processing system can reduce iteration time and expensive programmer idle time, and increase pipeline throughput.

As with the other productivity-enhancing technologies discussed here, the ROI must be considered in terms of lost opportunity costs and competing technologies. For example, in order to avoid violating license agreements, additional copies of an application may be required for each workstation that will share the workload. The cost of extra licenses, or a site license, has to be compared with the cost of leasing or purchasing dedicated, high-end hardware for the production staff or of leasing time from commercial Internet-accessible rendering farms.

Peripherals

Despite repeated attempts from numerous technology vendors, nothing has been able to retire the mouse or trackball and graphics tablet on the artist's workstation. Several manufactures have devised 3D mice for working with 3D editing environments. However, a major limitation of these editing peripherals for the serious games developer is the lack of drivers for less expensive, second-tier software tools. Furthermore, the cost of specialized 3D controllers can be double or triple the price of second-tier rendering and animation packages.

Domain- and task-specific peripherals—a laser-tag M-16 for a military serious game or an instrumented mannequin for residents learning how to treat sucking chest wounds—are one of the hallmarks of serious games. These peripherals can take the form of custom devices or repurposed COTS peripherals, depending on the budget and number of peripherals. Consumer and professional-grade aircraft yoke peripherals are available from a variety of manufacturers, such as Guillemot (*www.guillemot.com*), CH Products (*www.chproducts.com*), and Logitech (*www.logitech.com*).

An example of a computer peripheral is the instrumented mannequin used in the VIRGIL Chest Trauma Training System (*www.medical-sim.org/virgil.htm*), developed at Harvard's Center for Integration of Medicine & Innovative Technology (CIMIT). The PC-based system presents the user with a 3D view of chest anatomy and tube positions, while the mannequin accepts chest tubes. As part of the training, students use a scalpel and scissors to cut a hole in the chest wall in the space between the ribs and then properly place a chest tube in the chest cavity. The incision is through an area of the life size mannequin fitted with a replaceable latex panel that replicates the tactile properties of a real chest wall. Moreover, the panel is fitted with small sacks of a red fluid that provides visual feedback from an improper incision that is too close to one of the mannequin's ribs. The disposable, palm-sized panel is replaced after each training session.

Custom peripherals may add substantial cost to a serious game destined for widespread distribution, but they can also serve as effective copy protection devices. This approach was used with the *HeartLab* program described in Chapter 1, "Historical Perspective." The program wasn't copy protected, and fully functional copies of the software were distributed freely. Potential purchasers could examine the features of the program with low-quality audio and then order an official copy—with stethophones and in-line filter.

Servers

Game developers attempting to duplicate the functionality of Sony's *EverQuest* massively multiplayer online game (MMOG) will have to contend with server and communications overhead. Until recently, server farms consisted of hundreds of generic desktop PCs stacked on racks in a warehouse. A better solution is to use racks of server *blades* that can pack the equivalent of 40 to 50 desktop PCs in a single 19-inch rack. However, even these easy-to-maintain devices require someone on staff to monitor and maintain the system. As such, many small shops continue to outsource server and communications hardware services so that they can focus on game development.

Video Hardware

Because computer graphics are central to the video game experience, they have received the most attention from game developers and video hardware manufacturers. For example, GPUs are generally optimized for either OpenGL or DirectX graphics engines.

While CPU speeds may have reached a temporary limit, video hardware has been evolving at a rapid pace since the 4MB Voodoo cards revolutionized gaming in 1996. Less than a decade later, 512 MB video cards from nVIDIA and ATI vied for first place in the high-performance games market. Thanks to the vastly increased buffer size, wider video bus bandwidths, and powerful onboard GPUs, scenes from games like *Half-Life 2* (Valve) can be rendered at full resolution without affecting frame rates. For serious games developers, workstations with high bandwidth video bus architectures are a welcome time saver. Professional video cards with high-performance GPUs and several GB of virtual memory have redefined performance and productivity price points for the technology.

Display technology hasn't improved picture quality appreciably since the flat screen CRT was introduced in the mid-1990s. Aesthetics of LCD and plasma panels aside, phosphor screens still define the price/performance benchmarks for brightness, refresh rate, color balance, and latency. However, the physical constraints imposed by limited desk space and concerns over electromagnetic radiation from high-voltage CRT monitors favor the flat panel displays over CRTs in the increasingly popular 20–24-inch range.

Asset Acquisition Hardware

The sense of realism achieved in the latest character-based entertainment games is due in part to the use of digital motion capture. The traditional method of animating characters in a game environment relies on keyframing, a technique in which an artist directs the computer to fill in missing data. Although digital motion capture (mocap) systems were originally expensive and difficult to work with, the trend is toward affordable, easy-to-use optical, magnetic, and mechanical systems.

For character-oriented games, digital mocap is the path to increased realism, and the technology is continually improving. Prototype optical systems can capture scenes in 3D and, within seconds, create models of rooms or objects, complete with textures. Until these systems, which use a pair of digital cameras mounted in parallel, become commonplace, digital mocap is the best technology available for capturing movement.

Of course, the overall quality of the motion capture data depends on the quality of movements made by the actor wearing the motion capture hardware. An affordable alternative to live motion capture is to use a service that sells libraries of animation sequences. Like any other commercially developed asset, the challenge is fitting what is available into the game design.

As with mocap, there are competing technologies for static object and scene capture. With magnetic data capture, a magnetic wand is used to outline the 3D shape of an object, and the 3D data points are used to create a 3D mesh that describes the object. The common element in these systems is greater speed, which translates to better quality and enhanced throughput in the development pipeline.

MIDDLEWARE

Middleware, the software tools designed to facilitate the graphics, sound, physics, fighting, AI, and other gameplay attributes, was popularized by Id's game engine. In theory, by incorporating third-party middleware in a game, the role of everyone contributing to the development pipeline can be optimized more easily . With the appropriate middleware, sound-related issues can be resolved by the sound designer and lighting by the lighting or art director—not the programming staff. Armed with a full suite of middleware, the programming staff can shift the focus of their work from developing tools to the integration and tuning of middleware components.

Middleware isn't universally accepted in the game development world. Some developers complain that the level of abstraction afforded by middleware limits their creativity. However, it can also free developers to focus on the big picture—delivering a quality game that's fun to play and delivers a message. For serious games developers without a team of programmers on staff, middleware is especially useful in prototyping and in learning game development while avoiding low-level programming issues.

Consider CMU's Entertainment Technology Center (ETC), where students are given only 14 weeks to develop game-based projects. There simply isn't time for students to build a game from scratch [Schell03]. One notable project from the ETC, *Project Biohazard,* is a game-based interactive training system dealing with terrorism attacks. Working in conjunction with MIT and using the *Unreal 2003* engine (Epic), students had enough time-saving technology at their disposal to create in only one semester a training scenario that simulated a chemical attack on a shopping mall.

The game, renamed HazMat HotZone (see Figure 3.5), was enhanced by the ETC and adopted by the Fire Department of New York, where it has been used to train firemen on how to respond to hazardous material emergencies (*www.hazmatproject.org*). According to Dr. Jesse Schell, advisor on the HazMat team, the prototype has been very successful. The ETC is working to create a complete biohazard response training system that can be distributed to fire training centers nationwide.

FIGURE 3.5   HazMat HotZone, showing a firefighter scene during a chemical attack at a mall. © CMU's Entertainment Technology Center. Reprinted with permission.

An Electronic Arts or THQ may have the luxury of developing a custom shader and a physics engine for a new game title. However, a small studio developing a serious game for a nonprofit client typically doesn't have the capital or time to work at that level. To stay competitive, small developers may have no choice but to use the latest generation of middleware to enable their limited staff. Increasingly, successful serious games developers are tool users, as opposed to tool builders.

Using the latest middleware—especially the open-source variety—is often an obvious, viable solution to limited development resources. However, commercial middleware may cost from $50 to more than $50,000, depending on the package and the licensing arrangement. Investing in a $50,000 middleware solution with $25,000 maintenance contract is usually limited to special cases in which the customer requires a game with capabilities that are beyond the development capabilities of the shop's staff. For example, a military game that requires realistic, real-time simulation of missile trajectories may demand the use of a particular physics engine. Fortunately, open-source projects such as Delta3D, offer powerful, affordable alternatives to commercial middleware solutions.

Game Engines

The most often used middleware in serious games development is the game engine. The challenge in discussing this type of middleware is precisely defining what constitutes a game engine. Examples of game engines used in serious games development include the *Unreal Engine 3*, *QUAKE*, *Torque*, and others listed in Appendix F, "Resources." A functional definition is that it's the core software component of a video game that handles activities such as rendering, AI, and physics, separate from the sounds, images, textures, and other media in the game.

Structurally, a game engine is simply what's left over after the code and assets specific to a particular game have been removed. Take any game written from scratch and remove the assets and what remains could be sold as a game engine. Of course, the ease of dropping in new assets and modifying the gameplay code to suit another game depends on how the original game was constructed. A clean, modular construction in which code and assets are maintained separately is more useful than a design in which code and data are intermingled.

Microsoft's DirectX 9 can be considered a minimalist game engine—or at least a library of game engine components. As illustrated in Figure 3.6, DirectX 9 is made up of three major components: DirectX Graphics, DirectInput, and DirectSound [MSDN05]. DirectX Graphics is a single application programming interface (API) to DirectDraw and Direct3D that is designed to simplify graphics programming tasks. DirectInput supports input devices, from mice and keyboards to force-feedback joysticks. DirectSound supports various functions that capture and play sound and music.

Using DirectX components in a game design can streamline the development pipeline, support the repurposing of code, and enable programmers to work with drawing and sound routines in BASIC, C++, or another high-level language. One reason for the acceptance of DirectX by the game development community is that it is free, well-documented, and rigorously maintained.

Most game developers expect a game engine to provide considerably more functionality than what is offered by the raw DirectX APIs. Whether a game engine is a full-featured program like the *Unreal* engine or an entry-level prototyping and game development environment such as *DarkBasic Pro* (GameCreators), the goal is to transform a primarily pro-

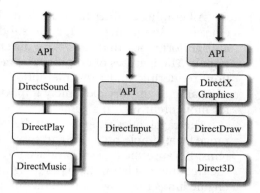

FIGURE 3.6   DirectX 9 architecture, illustrating APIs to DirectInput, DirectSound, and DirectX Graphics.

gramming task into one of software engineering in which the game design is fit into the features supported by the engine.

A game engine may also simplify the port to multiple platforms. Armed with a cross-platform game engine, porting a game to a new platform often entails little more than tuning the game to system nuances, such as the remapping of game pad buttons. More work is involved when the port involves moving a game that is intimately associated with platform-dependent components, such as DirectX.

Most of the technological advances in game engines have been made in engine components that focus on graphics, physics, AI, and sound. These game engine components are discussed here, along with middleware technologies that support connectivity and the utilities that help bridge the gap between low- and high-end PC platforms.

Graphics Engines

Graphics engines, which are central to every game engine, simplify the handling and display of 2D and 3D data and graphics. Microsoft's Direct3D, part of DirectX, and OpenGL are both APIs that represent the extreme low end of what can be considered graphics engines. Although these interfaces and associated tools can free programmers from mundane, low-level tasks, most developers work with software that provides a much higher level of abstraction.

Gamebryo (NDL) is an example of a heavyweight, full-featured, true graphics engine. *Gamebryo* is a stand-alone product, providing developers with the freedom to integrate third-party middleware from a variety of vendors. NDL helps relieve the angst of working with third-party middleware from a variety of vendors by suggesting compatible middleware for audio, video, AI, networking, and physics.

All graphic engines have a role in displaying the eye candy that play-ers see during gameplay. It's the subtle differences in engine capability and performance that make the difference between fantastic and so-so visuals. The features of graphics engines fall into three categories: anima-tion, rendering, and run-time optimization. The animation components of a game engine are extremely important because they provide the basis for movement within a game.

The capabilities supported by the latest generation of graphics engines range from simple rotations and sprites to light animation and particle sys-tems. Because the realism produced by a graphics engine is largely due to the treatment of light, the types of light animation supported by a graphics engine limits the range of presentation possibilities. Particle systems, which are used to generate rain, bullets, fire, beams, and smoke, vary significantly in quality and capability from one graphics engine to the next.

Virtually all graphics engines provide animation through simple linear interpolation or more advanced Bezier, TCB, or spline interpolation. More advanced engines additionally support skeletal or bone animation, in which a mesh is deformed over a framework of interconnected bones, as in Figure 3.7. Developing the animation entails describing the movement and path of the bones; the mesh follows automatically. Bones animation can provide more natural movement than interpolation animation, espe-cially when combined with forward and inverse kinematics animation utilities that use joint articulation to define possible bone positions.

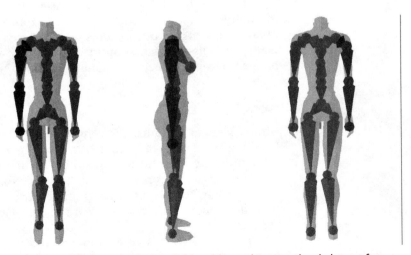

FIGURE 3.7   Bones animation. A deformable mesh covers the skeleton of interconnected bones. The right shoulder joint bone is darker than the other bones in the model.

The rendering tools within a graphics engine define the fluidity of gameplay and the limits of resolution. Fully describing the range of rendering features found in the latest graphics engines would require several volumes, but all graphics engines have some form of shader program that determines the surface properties of object in the game. Vertex and pixel shaders execute in the GPU and operate at the vertex or pixel level of a 3D mesh. Some graphic engines support extensible shaders that can be modified or replaced with code written in HLSL and/or Assembler. Despite the variability in implementation from one engine to the next, most full-featured graphic engines handle basics such lighting, shadows, motion effects, textures, and sky systems.

As in still and motion photography, the quality of lighting limits the quality and emotional context of the graphics displayed on the computer monitor. The range of possible lighting variables supported by a full-featured graphics engine includes a variety of static and dynamic lighting, specular highlights, spot, and directional light sources. Special effects typically include bullet holes, mirrors, water, lens flares, distortions, and mapping of images onto irregular surfaces. Outdoor games can benefit from a sky system with animated layers and backdrop bitmaps, and multi-texture terrains with bump and environment mapping.

Run-time optimization minimizes the load on the CPU, leaving processing power for physics, AI, sound, and other activity within the game, while maximizing GPU throughput during gameplay. Run-time optimization features supported the major 3D game engines include background loading, batching of primitives, culling, varying level of detail, memory management, and selective updates.

Background loading improves performance by pre-fetching textures and other memory-intensive graphic components before they're needed. Batching of primitives with identical rendering attributes saves set-up time.

Culling, the rejection of scene elements that don't need to be rendered from a particular vantage point, is one of the most talked about topics in game engine design and selection. Culling is based on the premise that if an object isn't visible to the player character or third person vantage point, it needn't be drawn (see Figure 3.8). There are dozens of culling methods, but most can be categorized as either precompiled or runtime [Pietari00].

An algorithm commonly used for precompiled culling is Binary Space Partitioning (BSP), in which the space within a game is partitioned in half and then in half again, recursively. The object is to define which surface is in front of the other, from all potential perspectives in the game, prior to runtime. An advantage of precompiled culling is the runtime load on the computer hardware. The major disadvantage is often extended compile times.

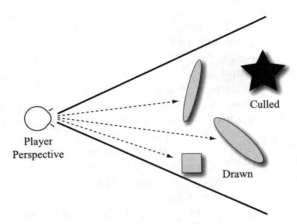

FIGURE 3.8   Culling an object obscured from the player's perspective.

An example of real-time culling, portal culling, can be thought of as a method of using doors and windows (portals) to determine what is visible and what isn't. When a player character walks through a door or turns a corner, there is no need to draw anything behind the player character. Because portal culling is dynamic and occurs at runtime there is more CPU overhead compared with pre-compiled culling. However, with the high-performance GPUs available on consumer hardware, the game performance penalty for using real-time culling is often insignificant. In addition, culling isn't limited to either runtime or pre-compiled methods, but can be a hybrid approach that uses elements of each form of culling.

In addition to culling, varying the level of detail at runtime can save processor cycles and enables a game to run on a range of PC hardware platforms. By allowing the graphics engine to vary the level of detail automatically to suit the capabilities of the hardware platform, a game is capable of infinite extensibility. Players with high-end computer systems can enjoy enhanced, high-definition graphics, and those with low-end systems can play the same game, but with fewer graphic details.

The memory management routines in a graphics engine remove infrequently used textures and other data from video memory. Selective updating of objects in the view frame saves processor time and increases frame rate without sacrificing image quality. For example, stationary objects usually require fewer updates than rapidly moving objects.

Physics Engines

Physics engines simplify the simulation of real-world physical properties, such as mass, gravity, torque, elasticity, and object interactions, freeing the game developer to focus on gameplay instead of vector and matrix algebra. An example of a physics engine is *Havok* (*www.havok.com*), which is used in the entertainment titles *Half-Life 2* and *Halo 2*.

Most physics engines are based on rigid-body dynamics, which assume there is no change in the geometry of interacting bodies [Conger04]. This approximation ignores real-world physics, in which colliding bodies, such as two aircraft, deform significantly upon impact. Solving soft-body dynamics, the physics of interactions among deformable bodies, is computationally demanding and rarely used in real-time gaming. With enough processing power, soft-body dynamics can be approximated by modeling hundreds or thousands of rigid bodies. Fluid dynamics, the most computationally intensive of the physics problems that apply to games, can be approximated with thousands of rigid body calculations as well. However, solving several thousand rigid-body dynamics problems in real-time while handling the graphics, sound, and other elements of a game are beyond the capabilities of a PC with a standard, single-core Intel or AMD processor [van den Bergen03].

A technical innovation that could redefine gameplay physics on the PC is the development of hardware-assisted physics, in the form of Physics Processor Units (PPUs). Just as GPUs have revolutionized game graphics, a PPU offloads the computational overhead from the CPU and handles the matrix and vector math and other calculations related to physics [Ageia05].

The first announced PPU, the PhysX chip from Ageia (*www.ageia. com*), is supported by *Unreal Engine 3* [Cross05] as well as the multi-core architecture of the latest processor architectures. For PC game developers, widespread adoption of PPU or equivalent technology will open up creative possibilities, just as the GPU revolutionized game graphics. For example, instead of spending hours deciding which objects in a scene to model with physics and which ones to ignore, every object can be modeled.

According to Ageia, the PhysX chip supports the physics of material properties, rigid body dynamics and collision detection, joints and springs, fluids, smart particle systems like fire and smoke, and cloth. Unlike a general-purpose microprocessor, the PhysX chip achieves increased performance by hard coding the major algorithms used in physics simulations [Mott05]. Developing games that take full advantage of the PPU will initially increase production costs as developers invest time and resources to learn how to exploit the technology. It remains to be seen which PPU will be accepted by the market, but Ageia has attempted to ease the process of learning its chip by buying and then giving away the Novodex physics API, the software equivalent of its PhysX chip. A major question regarding the future of hardware-assisted processes is whether the multi-core CPUs will obviate the need for ancillary hardware. With multi-core microprocessors, a separate core could be used to process graphics, AI, physics, sound, and other specialized game engines or functions.

As with most engines, modifications and extensions may be necessary to provide the realism required by serious games that don't fit the typical genres. For example, a game based on a surgical procedure may need to provide realistic haptic feedback that approximates skin elasticity and soft tissue deformation. Two excellent references on game physics are David Conger's *Physics Modeling for Game Programmers* [Conger04] and David Bourg's *Physics for Game Developers* [Bourg02]. Both books provide grounding in the mathematics of game physics along with practical examples in C.

AI Engines

When combined with the intelligence from an AI engine, the graphics and physics of a game come to life. Much of the success of titles in the entertainment game industry has been attributed to increased nonplayer character AI that has paralleled increases in graphic fidelity [Johnson02]. Players expect advances in graphics to be accompanied by concomitant increases in AI, just as they expect adults to act more mature than children.

As with graphics and physics engines, AI engines are available in a wide variety of flavors and capabilities and rely on just as wide a variety of underlying technologies, from neural networks, Bayesian inferencing, and rule-based AI to fuzzy logic, finite state machines, and genetic algorithms. The most sophisticated engines learn from experience, while entry-level engines are limited to fixed AI or scripted extensions [Champandard04]. Many of the capabilities provided by AI engines, such as chasing, evading, guarding, and weapon selection, are geared to character-oriented shooters.

A with physics engines, an AI engine may not fulfill a serious game's behavior requirements out of the box, even for military serious games of the FPS genre. For example, instead of simply walking past a wounded player character, a combat medic nonplayer character (NPC) might drag the player character to safety and then administer first aid.

All professional AI engines provide tools with which they can be extended to incorporate user-defined behaviors. These customization features can be used to implement domain-specific behaviors that support the underlying serious games message. For example, consider a game designed to teach medical students how to recognize and interact with patients suffering from a bipolar behavior disorder. In this scenario, an extensible AI engine could be used to define a character with moods and behaviors associated with mania and depression. However, because AI engines differ in their degree and method of extensibility, it's difficult to determine the applicability of a particular engine for a particular task without hands-on experience.

Sound Engines

Sound engines handle the basics of playing WAV and MP3 files, as well as the subtle, sophisticated manipulations involving 3D sound localization that can underscore the graphical elements in a game. Simple 2D or stereo sound, first introduced in the arcade games of the 1970s, might be sufficient for simple 2D serious games. However, 3D sound localization, various filters and effects, and support for Dolby Surround Sound are the norm for entertainment titles. Voiceover IP, the basis for voice communications in multiuser online games, is also handled by the full-featured sound engines.

Given the rising user expectations due to developments in the entertainment game genre, serious games developers should consider using a full-featured sound engine. At a minimum, developers can use the sound middleware from Microsoft, DirectMusic and DirectSound, or the open source OpenAL. Whereas Microsoft's sound-handling APIs are limited to the Windows platform, OpenAL is a cross-platform API for the rendering of 3D positional audio and effects such as Doppler shifts.

Serious Games Engines

It may be impossible to find engine components that fill a particular serious game design. For example, a medically accurate serious game might require a physiology engine that handles the calculation of blood pressure, pulse, respiration, and other physiological parameters. One option would be to simply write the physiology routines as quickly as possible and get on with coding the remainder of the game. Another option is to invest time in creating an engine that could be shared or sold to other serious games developers.

Given the number of medically related serious games likely to be developed over the next decade, it's likely that a physiology engine would save a number of developers the time and headaches of developing their own library of physiology routines. Although the market for this might be small compared with the market for entertainment-related engines, marketing and distribution on a serious gaming network would be one way for the original developer to recoup some of the cost of creating an engine.

A major contender for a custom engine that would appeal to educators in the serious games community is an Intelligent Tutoring System (ITS). Functionally, an ITS improves the efficiency and/or effectiveness of the educational process by presenting content according to the learner's ability or preference. The underlying hypothesis is that systems that adapt to the learner's skills, aptitudes, and abilities provide the most effective educational experiences [ForbusFeltovich01]. This capability requires embedded intelligence or knowledge in three areas: the domain, the learner, and pedagogy or teacher strategy [HartleySleeman73]. The embedded intelligence is often conceptualized as separate models [Wolf92], as illustrated in Figure 3.9 and outlined here:

Student model: A model of the learner, based on his or her understanding of the material being taught, as measured by exams, response delays, or self-directed preferences, the more detailed and specific the student model, the more specific the intervention and instruction possible

Pedagogy model: Defines the teaching process, including decisions about the topic, the problem, and the appropriate feedback, based on input from the student model

Communications model: Defines interaction with the learner, especially how the ITS user interface is configured

Domain model: A model of the information the ITS is teaching

Expert model: A representation of a domain expert's domain knowledge and problem-solving ability

Because adaptation requires learner interaction, games are the ideal delivery mechanism for ITS. Whereas a traditional computer aided instruction (CAI) system might present the learner with a question or two after a concept has been presented, games typically require player interaction every few seconds. The continuous feedback in a game can provide more and more frequent data for an ITS without interrupting the learning experience.

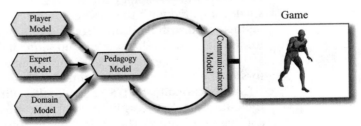

FIGURE 3.9   Intelligent Tutoring Systems using a traditional CAI architecture (top) versus ITS in a continuous feedback serious games environment (bottom). Details of the ITS Assessment and Content Adjustment Module are omitted for clarity.

Many of the same AI tools and techniques used in AI engines are also used to create intelligent tutoring systems. [OngRamachandran00]. For example, we are involved in the design and implementation of a nuclear, chemical, and biological multimedia collaboratory for TATRC that uses an ITS based on neural network and genetic algorithm technology [Bergeron05]. A goal of the project is to demonstrate the effectiveness of ITS-directed text, images, simulations, and games in training first responders, relative to live instructor training.

The ITS is central to the project because it allows a single environment to be used for training first responders at levels of difficulty and fidelity appropriate to their level of expertise in medicine and disaster life support. This ITS-based approach obviates the need to create multiple versions of the training environment, with separate version for first responders from firemen to physicians. A fireman needs to know how to handle a victim suffering from burns associated with a nuclear detonation, and perhaps the concept of the effect of radiation on white blood cells. A physician, in contrast, relies on the white blood cell count to determine the radiation exposure and prognosis for survival. A single environment under an ITS can adjust the content accordingly. In addition, at the individual level, the ITS can set the difficulty level and content, providing an appropriately challenging learning experience in the shortest time possible. Regardless of the domain, the technological hurdle remaining for serious games developers is the creation of standard interfaces that work with the commonly used game engines.

Connectivity

Multiplayer, networked games are increasingly popular because of emergent gameplay and extended game longevity. Whereas a single-user, stand-alone game might provide 20 or 30 hours of developer-limited gameplay, gameplay and total play time in a multiplayer game are a function of the other players. However, adding network connectivity to a game, whether it's a simple multiplayer game or the massively multiplayer variety, is typically outside of the core competency of small development shops. Dealing with the gameplay in a multiuser game is challenging enough without the need to worry about packet size across a network.

In lieu of a dedicated network support staff, most shops outsource multiuser connectivity or purchase the appropriate middleware. While the basic connectivity challenges of managing packets, sockets, and client-server messaging can be mastered by a competent programmer in a day or two, the more intricate networking issues, such as synchronization, require a higher level of skill.

Network middleware handles low-level machine issues, such as synchronization, dropped packets, and message-passing from one player to the next, using various forms of latency management, such as dead reckoning. Latency management enables players to interact in real time over network connections of varying quality, making realistic, fair gameplay over the Internet possible. Without latency (delay) management, players with the best Internet connection have an unfair advantage over players who have to contend with delays due to poor Internet connections.

Dead reckoning addresses latency—the time it takes to get information through a network—by minimizing the bandwidth required for players to communicate with one another or with the server hosting a game. Instead of sending a constant stream of data with every keystroke or game pad movement, a dead-reckoning system predicts the future state of the game. It only sends information across the network if the player's interactions result in a state significantly from what was predicted.

The hard problems today in supporting networked gaming are credit card fraud, identity theft, and cheating plug-ins [Scammell04]. Middleware that implements player authentication and encryption methods, such as industry-standard public key cryptography (PKCS) and symmetric key cryptography (SKCS), can minimize fraud and theft. Network middleware with strong cryptography can pay for itself in avoiding legal fees that might be spent defending the development shop against irate players who have had their credit care information stolen.

Utilities

The top utilities in the serious games developer's bag of tricks address the challenge of developing for a coarsely defined hardware platform. An entertainment developer for the PlayStation consoles may have to deal with at most three models, and the clock speed, RAM, and graphics capability of each model are fixed. Not so for personal computer development. Although it's difficult to find a serious game that runs on DOS, there is a lineage of Windows operating systems to contend with, video cards with only a few megabytes of RAM, and processors limping along at a few hundred megahertz. One option is to require the latest operating system, a multi-GHz clock speed, and the latest video technology. However, doing so severely limits the potential audience.

One way to ensure that game graphics can run on ancient hardware is to use software renderers. These run-time utilities, which are the equivalent of a DirectX- or OpenGL-compatible video card in software, enable a game to bypass the drivers and video card hardware installed on the system. Similarly, video codecs (coder-decoders) allow developers to add DVD-quality video cut scenes to a game without regard to the hardware capabilities of the delivery platform.

MANAGING COMPLEXITY

Manufacturing a fun and/or engaging experience is a complex, difficult process, especially when the underlying goal is to convey a serious message to the player. Serious games developers need all the help they can get in managing this complexity, including accounts of best practices, post-mortems from those who have learned the hard way, and models that provide a roadmap to success. Models, by their very nature, assume a particular perspective that oversimplifies other perspectives for the sake of clarity. For example, the development pipeline model we saw in Figure 3.1 doesn't indicate where the developers should add "pixie dust." Although not indicated in the model, most developers recognize the Solution Design stage of the pipeline as the point where the fun of gameplay is defined.

Creating games that are fun and/or engaging is also a resource-intensive process. The development pipeline doesn't address the capital, staff, and other resources needed to keep the development process moving toward completion during the months of development. One point that should be clear from the pipeline is that business requirements, in terms of timing, investment of resources, and expected ROI, drive all subsequent activities.

Readers familiar with the postmortem articles in every issue of *Game Developer* or the compilation edited by Austin Grossman [Grossman03] will appreciate the finding that even the top developers in the industry make profound blunders at every level. Most of these mistakes don't deal with code errors or problems with the game engine, but with managing the resources of the development shop. People problems, faulty business plans, failing to monitor the bottom line, and, in general, failure to adhere to proven business strategies are the greatest challenges most development shops face. Clearly, technological and strategic innovations in the business of game development are at least as important as the type of culling used by a particular game engine.

Given that many entertainment games never make it through development, and those that do may never reach profitability, developing large, complex serious games is a risky business. Not only are serious games developers required to create an entertaining or engaging game, but they must do so while attending to the serious content. Following is a discussion of the business- and industry-specific technologies and strategies that can be used to manage the complexity of serious games development.

Business Strategies

Achieving business goals in an evolving area like serious games doesn't happen by chance—it requires a high-performance organization. In *The Four Pillars of High Performance*, Paul Light identifies the four characteristics of robust, high-performance organizations as alertness, agility, adaptability, and alignment [Light05]. Alert organizations don't assume they know what the future will bring. They think in future tense and develop strategies that address a spectrum of possibilities. Agile organizations recruit staff with a goal of attaining the greatest flexibility with the smallest team possible. Adaptable organizations challenge the prevailing wisdom of how things should be done to maximize the benefits from limited resources. Finally, aligned organizations grow leadership from within, facilitate and reward communications, and learn to ignore the irrelevant.

Managing the complex business of serious games development can be a stressful, high-risk proposition. It can also be a rewarding experience if management is knowledgeable of fundamental business strategies and can leverage time-compression technologies that keep the development pipeline running smoothly.

Knowledge and wisdom come with time and experience—but not just any experience. As Michael Gerber notes in his book *The E-Myth Revisited: Why Most Small Companies Don't Work and What to Do about It*, a common fallacy in small organizations is that technical expertise translates to management proficiency [Gerber95]. The best artist in a team rarely makes the best art director, just as the fastest coder rarely makes the best technical director. Although robust, high-performance organizations grow leaders from within, in a small development shop with a loose structure and tight deadlines, technical experts with an interest in management should look to outside resources to gain management expertise.

The process of game development often seems like magic to an outsider. After all, unlike building a house, there isn't much to see with each passing day of activity. Anyone watching a house under construction can see how the materials are coming together and get a good idea of the final structure long before the finishing touches are applied. Even first-time home owners can asses the progress and quality of construction at any point in the process—assuming they grew up in a house.

As documented in *The Mythical Man-Month* in 1975—the same year Bill Gates and Paul Allen founded Microsoft—software development is fundamentally different from building a house or other physical structure because of the relative invisibility of the progress [Brooks75]. The situation is different today, given the degree of computer literacy in the general population. Furthermore, there is an abundance of technologies available for the creation of games. The challenge is identifying and applying the technologies appropriately, and that requires an understanding of the underlying business strategies.

The National Institute of Standards and Technology (NIST) has identified values and concepts common to high-performance organizations [NIST05]. These metrics, which apply directly to serious games development, form the basis of the Malcolm Baldrige National Quality Program. As listed in Table 3.1, high-performance organizations focus on business results, but not to the detriment of customers or employees. These organizations also have strong leadership that engages in strategic planning. Leaders of winning organizations don't let it happen; they make it happen. In addition, high-performance organizations quantify progress every step of the way through repeated measurement and analysis using a systematic, process management approach.

TABLE 3.1   Malcolm Baldrige Award Core Values and Concepts

MALCOLM BALDRIGE AWARD CORE VALUES AND CONCEPTS
Business Results
Customer and Market Focus
Human Resource Focus
Leadership
Measurement, Analysis, and Knowledge Management
Process Management
Strategic Planning

NIST is only one of several organizations promoting excellence. The International Organization for Standardization (ISO), a federation of national standards bodies, is recognized worldwide as a promoter of quality initiatives. The ISO 9000 family of international quality management standards address quality management and promote continual performance improvement in terms of quality, customer satisfaction, and adherence to regulatory requirements [ISO04].

Adhering to national and international quality and performance standards may seem like an academic exercise to a development shop with a half-dozen employees struggling to meet a deadline. Admittedly, many small developers may not be able to implement the systems described here. However, the strategies used by high-performance organizations may suggest a more effective means of creating a successful serious game while maintaining the bottom line.

As the postmortems in *Game Developers* illustrate, there is no one best business strategy when it comes to running a development shop. However, following the recommendations of NIST and ISO, managers should be familiar with the business concepts embodied in Performance Management, Knowledge Management and Customer Relationship Management.

Performance Management

The basis of Performance Management (PM) is the effective use of resources, as measured by quantifying processes and outcomes. Performance

Management is a composite of techniques that have roots in the manufacturing industry of the 1920s. Around the time Link was building his first flight simulators, Statistical Process Control (SPC) emerged as the best means to determine whether a business process was functioning within statistical norms. Statistical analysis was used to determine whether observed changes in a variable, such as the number of widgets manufactured per hour, were due to random variation or to some other factor that could be controlled by adjusting the process or the environment.

The challenge of relying on Statistical Process Control alone is that changing a process in response to data due to random variation can create an unstable process. Conversely, if nonrandom data are mistakenly interpreted as random variation, the process will become increasingly unstable as the factor contributing to the variability becomes more prominent. For example, if compile errors are becoming more frequent because of poor compiler scalability, but they're written off as random error or related to programmer sleep deprivation, then the errors will continue to escalate.

Knowing when to call statistical variation significant depends on the standards established by management. Anyone who has spent a few years in the development industry probably has an intuitive idea of what constitutes normal rates, but Statistical Process Control is about establishing solid metrics. As an extreme example of statistical standards, consider the standards established for Six Sigma. This extension of Statistical Process Control pioneered at Motorola attempts to eliminate nonrandom variation to the point that the likelihood of an error is six standard deviations (six sigmas) from the mean—or about three errors per million.

Performance Management is a strategy—meaning a behavior change—that is normally implemented with the help of so-called business intelligence software that automates data management, operations, financial planning and strategizing. If all goes according to plan, the strategy should enable the shop to deliver a quality game on time and within budget.

Every game development shop has problem areas that can benefit from gathering metrics—referred to as Key Performance Indicators (KPIs) in the business intelligence community. Examples of KPIs range from the number of hours worked by each employee per week to the number of assets created by the art staff every day. Because it's easy to go overboard measuring every nuance of a business, even large corporations limit the indicator list to a couple dozen metrics.

The purpose of collecting the performance indicators is to help management direct the use of the organization's resources more effectively, promote best practices, and improve the bottom line. It's up to management to decide which indicators to monitor, establish acceptable ranges of indicator values, analyze the data, and then act on the analysis. Although there are obvious metrics that should be tracked, such as profit and loss, most indicators are shop specific.

Graphical dashboards are a popular method of viewing the status of KPIs over time. Properly designed dashboards can present a large number of key indicators in one consolidated, easily understood view. The dashboard illustrated in Figure 3.10 provides a consolidated view of end-of-month metrics for asset development, code rewrites, and project slippage (bottom right), budget variance by day of the month and pipeline stage (top), and royalty income status (bottom left). Performance Management is a strategy independent of dashboards and other bells and whistles. A manager comfortable with Microsoft® Excel™ needn't invest in a graphical reporting package. However, if a dashboard is used, the graphics must reflect the problem at hand. For example, a pie chart would be of little value to a manager trying to identify potential sources of nonrandom error in the productivity of the art production staff. In fact, the pie cart would likely hide the problem. A better solution is to use a control chart—a type of line chart that shows relative fluctuations in the value of a metric over time.

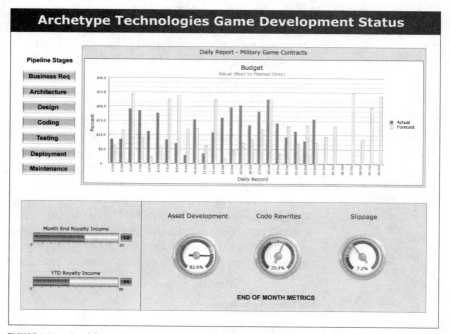

FIGURE 3.10   Dashboard view of development activity for a game development company. Created with Xcelsius (*www.infommersion.com*).

Key Performance Indicators are seldom used alone, but are combined in a scorecard or table listing various indicator values. A sudden drop in the number of assets generated by the art department is more informative when paired with the number of hours worked by the staff, for example.

Some people refer to any listing of indicators as a balanced scorecard. However, as defined Kaplan and Norton in their seminal article, "The Balanced Scorecard—Measures that Drive Performance," a balanced scorecard is a Performance Management strategy that looks at indicators from four balanced perspectives: financial; customer; internal business process; and employee learning and growth [KaplanNorton92]. The central idea is that if management simply measures financial indicators, individuals will change their behavior to look good financially, often at the expense of fellow staff, self development, and other aspects of normal work life.

Taking a balanced scorecard look at a development shop, the financial perspective examines how the organization looks to investors and other stakeholders, using indicators such as return on investment and net income. The innovation/learning perspective measures employee satisfaction. The internal perspective measures operational processes, such as cycle time and number of program bugs. The customer perspective quantifies how well the shop satisfies the customer's needs. The obvious challenge is devising a scheme that accurately measures each of these parameters.

Typically, the most difficult parameters to measure are true costs of people, activity, and technology. To this end, Activity Based Costing (ABC) is an accounting practice that can help support Performance Management by determining costs and savings associated with the changes brought about through Performance Management. ABC generates more accurate cost and performance indicators than traditional accounting by focusing on the costs of performing specific processes, such as rendering in-house instead of using an outside service. Traditional accounting records only the aggregate cost at the department level.

Performance Management derives some of its methodology from the Total Quality Management (TQM) movement, to the extent that TQM promotes perpetual improvement. However, unlike Performance Management, organizations often use Total Quality Management methods to cut employee count while maintaining the level of output.

Knowledge Management

Knowledge Management (KM), a business optimization strategy that focuses on the creation, use, and communication of information, is practiced to some degree in every successful organization [Bergeron03]. The value of following a KM strategy in a development shop is that it treats intellectual capital as an asset that can be tracked, measured, and analyzed with performance indicators, just like a material asset.

KM contributes to the business of game development in the way that it treats intellectual capital. KM defines intellectual capital as a major organizational asset of four types: human, customer, structural, and intellectual property (IP). Human capital includes the knowledge, skills, and competencies of the programmers, artists, and other employees. Without a KM strategy in place, when designers or programmers leave the organization, they take their skills, competencies, and knowledge with them. Customer capital is the value of the organization's relationships with its customers, which might include third parties as well as players. Structural capital includes the processes, structures, information systems, financial relations, and intellectual properties that are independent of the staff who create them. The fourth type of intellectual capital, intellectual property, consists of patents, licenses, trademarks, and copyrights held by the development shop.

Customer Relationship Management

Customer Relationship Management (CRM) is a strategy that promotes a mutually beneficial relationship between buyers and sellers [Bergeron02]. The business strategy may be relevant to shops that deal directly with large numbers of customers, as opposed to shops that hand off finished programs and to a client and then go on to the next project. A shop that distributes serious games over the Internet, or that supports an online game, often can benefit from knowing about customer habits, demographics, and interactions with the support staff. Jessica Mulligan and Bridgette Patrovsky provide an excellent overview of how to apply CRM methods to ensure the success of online games in their book *Developing Online Games, An Insider's Guide* [MulliganPatrovsky03]. An excerpt of the book that describes the application CRM in managing an online game is also available on Gamasutra [MulliganPatrovsky03b].

Business Technologies

Dealing with business technologies is usually simpler than learning the nuances of business strategies because technology can be purchased. However, like development hardware and software, business technologies have to suit the game development environment—particularly the demeanor of the staff. Forcing a shop to adopt business technologies that don't follow a coherent strategy or that overly constrain the staff can destroy the creative atmosphere a game development shop needs to thrive. The six major categories of business technologies reviewed here are operations applications, communications, infrastructure, data capture, decision support, and training.

Operations Applications

Every business has to deal with payroll, customers, and the government, and yet, the same development shops that invest in the latest graphics tools often ignore the back office software and hardware that can significantly improve day-to-day operations. Fortunately, many technologies can be applied to the business processes of every game development project, including those at small, independent shops. Examples of general-purpose management technologies applicable to serious games development include administrative support, contact management, Enterprise Resource Planning (ERP), finance, human resources, payroll, and project management.

Administrative support software that addresses the specific needs of inventory, mailroom, printing, records management, and supply applications can be purchased separately or as an integrated administrative support package. Contact management software is usually provided as a suite of integrated tools designed to track and manage customer contact. A typical full-featured contact management system includes a customer database, a method of recording the topic discussed in each call or email, an automatic time and date stamp, and a calendar with reminders. Full-featured contact management applications provide a variety of tools to create reports, including lists of customers who have unresolved problems.

ERP software is designed to improve the internal processes of a company. These packages typically contain loosely integrated database management, statistics, and operations management tools. More powerful software suites, commonly marketed as business intelligence (BI) application tools for Performance Management, offer integrated general accounting, payroll processing, purchasing, taxes, and transaction processing and can help streamline the financial process. As with other suites, the degree of integration enhances the efficiency of the technology. In general, the tighter the integration, the less work there is for the employee working with the system.

Human Resource (HR) application suites automate the process of recruiting, relocation, staffing, training, and dealing with the paperwork associated with workers' compensation. Ideally, the head of Human Resources can use the technology to leverage her time to the degree that support staff isn't required.

A major activity in Human Resources is recruiting and screening potential employees. Assessment technologies available for screening range from the personality-heavy Myers-Briggs type assessment [Quenk99] to the competency-oriented McClelland/McBer job competence assessment (JCA) [SpencerSpencer93]. Most, if not all of the major assessment tests can be administered or processed online by an HR director with the relevant qualifications.

A new manager working with an established shop may have little success in getting everyone to submit to extensive personality tests. Fortunately, there are quick, low-tech approaches to classifying employees that may give a manager a better idea of how to deal with the inevitable flare-ups that occur during crunch time. In their book *People Styles at Work*, Robert Bolton and Dorothy Grover Bolton classify employees as either analytical, amiable, driver, or expressive, based on their relative assertiveness and responsiveness (see Figure 3.11). Following the Bolton & Bolton classification scheme, analytical types score low on the assertiveness and responsiveness scales, whereas expressives score high on both. Drivers are more assertive and less responsive, and amiables are less assertive but more responsive. Knowledge of where employees fit in the grid can help management understand what everyone in the shop needs to be happy and productive.

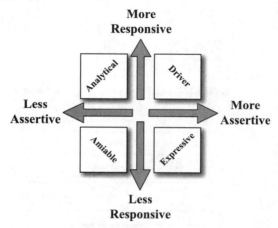

FIGURE 3.11   Bolton & Bolton style classification scheme.

Project management software can help management determine how to use human resources as effectively as possible, monitor progress along the development pipeline, and communicate timelines and milestones to the development staff. Most people equate project management software with the charting tools, especially the Program Evaluation and Review Technique (PERT) chart and the resource and task matrix. A PERT chart (see Figure 3.12) displays the tasks in a project along with the dependencies among the tasks. A resource and task matrix, shown in Figure 3.13, provides a tabular view of resources mapped to tasks. Project management software automates the generation of these and additional views of resources, time, and tasks so that the documents serve as dynamic models of activity along the development pipeline.

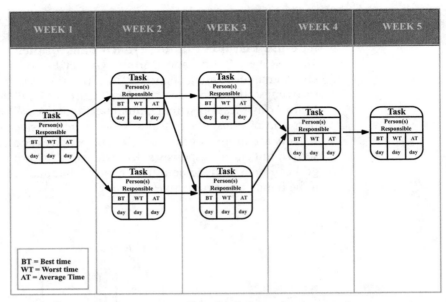

FIGURE 3.12 PERT chart showing tasks and task dependencies over time.

Resource and Task Matrix

Resources	Tasks								
	Task	Task	Task	Task	Task	Task	Task	Task	Task
Lead Programmer									
Art Director									
AI Programmer									
Lead Artist									
Animator									
Video Editor									
Hardware Engineer									
Technical Director									
Level Designer									
QA/Tester									
Sound Designer									

◉ Primary responsibility ○ Team members △ Provide Resources

FIGURE 3.13 Resource and task matrix.

Communications

The line between voice, data, and media communications continues to blur, but the value of email, wireless data transfer, and network technologies to a development shop are indisputable. The Internet and email are the main support modalities for development shops of any size. Instant messaging, wireless handheld computers, and problem-tracking databases can be integrated with voice and data systems or Interactive Voice Response (IVR) and are only a few of the technologies that can help a small business save time.

Infrastructure

In addition to high-speed Internet connections and a robust LAN, game development shops can benefit from an infrastructure of databases, database encryption, and means of mining the database. As information-intensive organizations, game development shops rely on timely and accurate business, customer, and process data for operations.

Business data must be collected and stored in a form that supports rapid search and analysis as well as longevity. Data archiving hardware and software technologies include automatic tape backup units, large disc farms that can be hung off the LAN, and offsite, outsourced storage that can be accessed via the Internet. A Database Management System (DBMS), separate from the asset management system used for production, can simplify and regulate the process of working with employee and customer records, including housekeeping tasks related to security.

Data encryption software and hardware is valuable in any shop with employees who work remotely or who routinely send sensitive data across the Internet. A variety of encryption software and hardware technologies is available to support the secure transfer of data. Data mining software, which supports the process of extracting meaningful patterns from data stored in databases, can be used to derive player preferences and predict future demands for game titles or specific services.

Data Capture

Accurate, complete, timely data capture is easily the highest priority in automating the management of a development shop. It's one thing to design a Performance Management system with a dozen key performance indicators and quite another to have the indicator values in a spreadsheet or database. Compiling statistics on programming errors, asset development rate, and other metrics that management can use to measure progress can be a costly, time-consuming process. Data capture technologies worth considering include the following:

- Voice recognition systems for free-text dictation and transcription
- Flatbed scanners equipped with optical character recognition (OCR) and optical mark recognition (OMR) software for capturing text and employee or customer responses on printed forms

- Bar code systems to track computers, software, books, and other physical assets
- Digital camera for HR records
- Activity monitoring software for logging staff activity on workstations

Decision Support

The same decision support tools used for programming AI engines—decision trees, flow diagramming, linear programming, and statistical analysis—have a role in business operations. Automated decision tree software enables a manager with the necessary data to build a decision table in minutes instead of hours. Automated flow diagramming, an operations management technique, can help management answer production capacity questions by mapping out the workflow in the development pipeline in a way that highlights potential inefficiencies. For example, flow diagram software can pinpoint areas where production methods could be improved by changing from sequential to parallel operations.

Automated forecasting programs use historical data to forecast the status of business processes at some point in the future. Linear Programming, a mathematical optimization technique, can be used to explore production capacity and determine the optimum use of human resources and capital. Finally, statistical analysis software has wide applicability as a management tool, from identifying quantifiable characteristics of staff production to highlighting player preferences.

Training

In the fast moving world of game development, management and staff can't afford to be left behind technologically or without the benefit of the latest best practices. Continual growth for individuals and the entire development shop is a requirement, not an option, in an industry that is consolidating and rewarding cost containment and innovation. CD-ROM, online training videos, and interactive CBT courses can obviate or minimize the need for employees to travel across the country to attend seminars.

Development Technologies

In addition to addressing the business needs of a serious games development shop, there is the obvious need to do the actual work of filling the development pipeline with code, assets, fun, and a final product. With the possible exception of the fun component, there have been a flood of technological innovations since the invention of the video game that make it tenable for a few devoted developers with a clear vision to create a quality game without spending two years chained to a workstation. The major time-multiplying technologies applicable to the stages of the development pipeline are reviewed here.

Coding and Implementation

Coding and implementation is typically the most time- and resource-intensive stage in the development pipeline. The programming team is busy either coding low-level routines or tweaking the game engine components. In parallel, graphics artists are creating or assembling the characters, textures, and other graphical assets for the game, and the sound artist is assembling or creating sound effects and music.

Before all of the activity begins in earnest, there is usually a period of a few weeks to months devoted to developing a prototype to test the concepts in the design document—the detailed plan for the full game. Thanks to literally hundreds of introductory-level game shells and engines marketed primarily to hobbyists and students, it's possible to click together a reasonable prototype game in a few hours. Figure 3.14 shows one of the click-together game creation tools within *The 3D Gamemaker*, by The GameCreators (*www.thegamecreators.com*), a game development environment that can be used for code-free rapid prototyping. This example shows the selection of the nonplayer character hivebrain—one of the many prefabricated objects provided with the inexpensive tool (about $40, including shipping from the UK). Regardless of the toolset used, a prototype that enables the team to experiment with level layout, the location of login, help, and options panels, and other elements that will appear in the game, is invaluable.

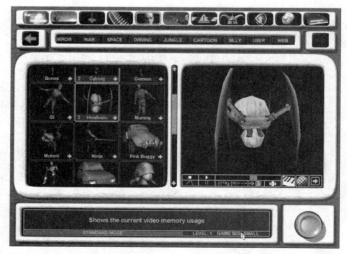

FIGURE 3.14   *The 3D Gamemaker*, by The GameCreators, a click-together game development tool that can be used for rapid prototyping.

Pointing and clicking might be adequate for creating a rough proto-type, but developing a game that's going to be released to the public requires programming. Although games can be developed in any language, from BASIC, *Flash*, and *PHP* to *JAVA* and Assembler, the most popular development language is some variant of C/C++. Thanks to the popularity of C/C++ in the general computing community, there are catalogs of utilities designed to help the C programmer at every level of development. For example, the Standard Template Library provides generic C++ data structures and algorithms that can be used across many compilers and platforms [Meyers01]. Applications such as distributed C/C++ compilers allow programmers to decrease compile time by recruiting other workstations in the development shop to help with the compile operation.

Version control utilities can speed the task of game programming by automating the organization and tracking of source code. File comparison and merging tools empower multiple programmers to work on the same files and then combine their work. Cross-platform development environments enable programmers to port their code to multiple platforms with little programming. Cross-platform development utilities are especially relevant for games developed for cell phones, because there are hundreds of combinations of operating systems, programming languages, screen resolutions, keypad layouts, and sound capabilities.

Asset development and management is at least as challenging and time-consuming as coding. As shown in Figure 3.15, creating a asset for a game involves much more than simply working in a graphics application for a few hours, dropping the image or character in a folder, and then moving on to the next asset. After the graphic, sound, or other asset has been created (or acquired), it has to be archived for safe keeping.

Archiving requires some form of version control so that, for example, an asset three versions back can be reworked and repurposed for another part of the game or some other project. Version control, in turn, can be facilitated by an automated standardized naming convention so that a particular asset can be located quickly and easily. Some assets may be repurposed for use in other internal projects, or, as is common practice, sold to other game developers. However, there might be digital rights issues with some of the assets licensed from external artists that limit asset exports.

Assets that have been either created or acquired are rarely used in native format, but exported in a format suitable for the game under development. For example, a multi-layered, high-resolution image in TIFF format may undergo several stages of processing before it is exported as a single-layer, low-resolution BMP image (see Figure 3.16). Similarly, a sound might be generated or captured at 44 KHz and 16 bits, only to be exported as an 8 KHz, 8-bit sound file. The asset management issue in both cases is choosing which intermediate versions of the data should be archived.

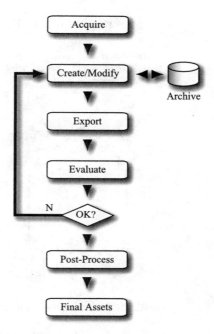

FIGURE 3.15   Asset management process. The iterative create-export-evaluate or modify-export-evaluate loop is the most time-consuming part of the process.

After the asset is placed in the game environment, it is evaluated in the context of the other assets in the game. Frequently, the asset requires modification, and the artist retrieves the original from the archive and modifies it according to the new information. This iterative process, which can be the most time consuming aspect of asset development, continues until the asset is acceptable. At this point, the asset undergoes postprocessing to the final game data format. Eventually, the asset becomes part of the game release.

Not only is the process of asset management complex, but an artist may be saddled with tracking thousands of assets, each at various stages in the asset management process. Unassisted, an artist's productivity might dip precipitously as the number of assets in the project increases. Fortunately, technologies are available to assist artists in the creation and to manage the textures, characters, environments, props, and sounds developed or acquired, including digital rights management. As a result, artists use their time to do what they do best—make art.

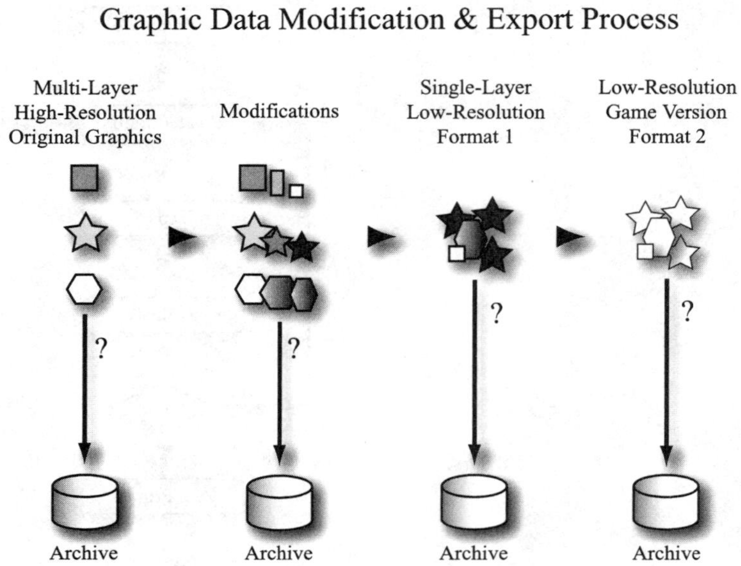

Graphic Data Modification & Export Process

FIGURE 3.16   Data modification and export process.

Testing and Debugging

The activities in the testing and debugging phase of the game development pipeline depend on the nature of the game and the topic domain. Multiplayer online games need to be load tested to determine the number of users that can be supported with a given hardware and software configuration. Single-user and multiplayer games should be tested with a profiling utility that determines where the game is slow.

While some game development environments have modest integrated profiling tools that provide a real-time report of frame rates at various video settings (see Figure 3.17), the latest generation of specialized tools provides finer granularity reports, allowing programmers to identify which functions and routines need to be optimized.

Large testing and debugging projects, such as the beta testing of a massive multiplayer online game with hundreds of beta testers, can benefit from one of the many test scheduling and error tracking products on the market. These applications, which are used throughout the software development industry, simplify the capture and tracking of errors, allowing the programming staff to focus on fixing bugs instead of managing the beta testers.

The topic domain of a serious game can profoundly complicate the testing and debugging phase of development. For example, a simulation-based medical game may need to be validated as a teaching or training

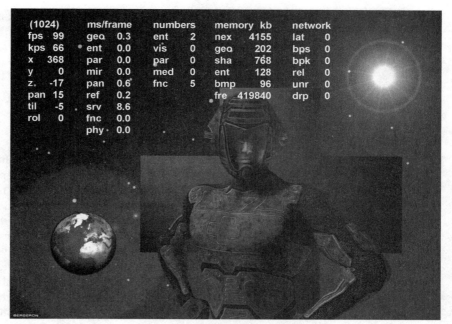

(1024)		ms/frame		numbers		memory kb		network	
fps	99	geo	0.3	ent	2	nex	4155	lat	0
kps	66	ent	0.0	vis	0	geo	202	bps	0
x	368	par	0.0	par	0	sha	768	bpk	0
y	0	mir	0.0	med	0	ent	128	rel	0
z.	-17	pan	0.6	fnc	5	bmp	96	unr	0
pan	15	ref	0.2			fre	419840	drp	0
til	-5	srv	8.6						
rol	0	fnc	0.0						
		phy	0.0						

FIGURE 3.17   Integrated, real-time profiling tool within 3D GameStudio showing frame rate and other performance indicators (top, left). Game © 2005, Archetype Technologies, Inc.

tool, even if the underlying simulation has been verified. Aside from the added overhead of verification and validation, beta testing of serious games might require tools that can be used by domain experts who might not have development experience. Testing games for the military might also involve catering to the needs of testers with security clearance.

Deployment

A game isn't usually ready for release or deployment fresh off the testing line, but it must be processed for distribution. Whether the game is distributed over the Internet or as a shrink-wrapped CD-ROM, game engine and assets must be encrypted to prevent someone from creating an illegal mod or using the sounds, graphics, DLLs, and other assets in their games or projects. Cryptographic toolkits also can lock online games to prevent cheating by hackers. The parallel operation on games distributed on CD-ROM, copy protection, can at least impede unauthorized duplication of the code and assets.

Developers that double as publishers typically prefer the Internet as a distribution medium because of the wide reach, low cost, and ease of tracking distribution. Even developers of games intended for free distribution rarely simply place game on a public Web server, but use distribution software to track number, geographic distribution, and time of downloads. Developers who charge for their games can use distribution software to handle the login process, charge card verification, and email notification (with links to a download area), and can otherwise monitor and control the distribution channel.

Reality Check

While discussing the leading-edge technologies that enable game developers to create realistic interactive environments, it's important to remember that many serious games developers use far simpler tools. Although they might not make the headlines, many serious games developers have been quietly churning out quality games based on traditional multimedia technologies for years. Prior to the widespread availability of high-speed Internet connections, hundreds of serious games were developed for the K–12 and higher education markets with Apple's *HyperCard* and Silicon Beach Software's *SuperCard*. Unfortunately, lowering development barriers resulted in a flood of programs from domain experts who lacked training in educational design or knowledge of basic educational principles. As with content on the Web, the challenge was identifying the high-quality serious games in the sea of edutainment offerings.

More recently, Macromedia's *Flash* and *Shockwave* have been used to create readily accessible serious games for the Web and on CD-ROM. While serious games created with these and similar tools might lack the immersive qualities available through the latest 3D game engines, game developers can make a living working with traditional tools.

Fantastic Food Challenge, shown in Figure 3.18, is representative of the many serious games developed with a traditional multimedia tool. The development team, which consisted of a game designer, a programmer, an artist, a content expert, and a narrator, created the program with Macro-Media *Director* and *Flash*, Apple *Soundtrack* wave editor, and *Adobe Photoshop* image editor. The program is actually a suite of four games, available from Michigan State University Extension, Family & Consumer Sciences (*commtechlab.msu.edu/products/foodchallenge.html*). The suite of games, which includes *The Great Meal Deal*, *Store It Safely*, *What Can You Make*, and *The Price Makes Sense*, is designed to motivate young adults to learn about nutrition, how to store food safely, food preparation, and how to compare food prices. With colorful 2D graphics, voice coaching, sound effects, bonus game element, and a high scorers list, the developers have created an informative game that is fun to play.

For example, in *What Can You Make*, players compete with a robot name Johnny Not So Swift to use foods available through food programs such as the Special Supplemental Food Program for Women, Infants, and

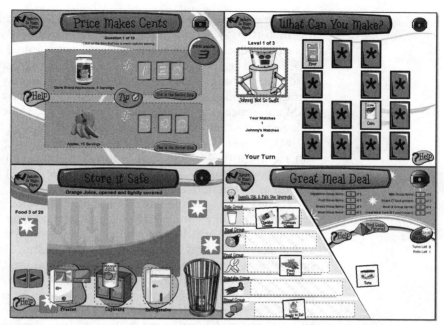

FIGURE 3.18   *Fantastic Food Challenge*, from MSU Extension, Family & Consumer Sciences.

Children. Using a memory game format, players learn that food combinations such as lasagna and canned tomatoes are valid, whereas combinations such as bananas and canned tomatoes are not.

Fantastic Food Challenge, which runs on Windows and the Mac OS, was developed through a partnership between the MSU Extension's Family Nutrition Program and Communication Technology Laboratory and partially funded through the USDA Food Stamp Program. The CD-ROM is available for $4, which includes shipping and handling.

SUMMARY

Numerous technologies are at the serious games developer's disposal that can be used to save time, reduce the complexity of game development, and, in general, do much more with less. The latest innovations in computer hardware, multi-core processors, promise-enhanced graphics, physics, artificial intelligence, and overall gameplay. Distributed processing architectures enable shops with limited resources to use surplus computing power to reduce iteration times, programmer idle time, and increase pipeline throughput.

Domains-and task-specific peripherals, in the form of commercial, off-the-shelf (COTS) peripherals and custom devices, are often used with serious games. Custom peripherals are frequently limited to internal, nonpublished serious games because of the expense of duplication. Other enabling hardware includes servers, which support massively multiplayer online games, and video duplication hardware with hefty amounts of onboard RAM and processing power. Motion capture and static object capture technologies can streamline asset acquisition.

Middleware, a major enabling technology in games development, can facilitate the handling of graphics, sounds, physics, AI, and other gameplay attributes. The cost of this increased level of abstraction, integration and tuning of middleware components.

Game engines are the most common middleware used in serious games development. They handle activities such as rendering, AI, and physics with separate engines or subcomponents. Graphics engines simply the handling and display of 2D and 3D graphics. Physics engines simplify the process of simulating real-world physical properties, such as gravity, friction, and elasticity. AI engines provide nonplayer characters with the semblance of intelligence by controlling behaviors such as weapon selection, following, and avoidance. Sound engines handle the playing of sound files as well as 2D and 3D sound manipulations. Although these core engines are applicable across a variety of entertainment and serious games applications, developers of serious games are often lacking in middleware for niche engines in areas such as intelligent tutoring and physiology.

Designing serious game with network connectivity can increase gameplay options and extend gameplay longevity. As with AI, physics, and graphics engines, most developers opt to use third-party solutions that allow them to focus on game design. Numerous utilities are also available to simply the development process, including software renderers, video codecs. The best game engine designs maintain code and game assets separately, and simply the process of porting from one platform to another.

Techniques that can help developers manage the complexity of serious games development include a variety of business strategies, including Performance Management, Knowledge Management, and Customer Relationship Management. Business technologies that serious games developers can use to manage complexity range from operations applications, communications technologies, and high-speed network infrastructure, to applications designed to facilitate data capture, decision support, and training. Development technologies relevant to serious games development include coding and implementation utilities, testing and debugging, and deployment.

It's important to note that every one of the technologies discussed in this chapter could be applied equally to entertainment and serious games development projects. Even the proposed specialized engines in physiology and intelligent tutoring could be used to increase the level of believability in entertainment games.

REFERENCES

[Ageia05] Ageia, *A White Paper: Physics, Gameplay and the Physics Processing Unit.* AGEIA, 2005.

[Bennett05] Bennett, Kyle, "Multithreaded Gaming: Terminal or Reality." *Computer Power User* 2(2005): pp. 32.

[Bergeron02] Bergeron, B., *Essentials of CRM: Customer Relationship Management for CEOs.* John Wiley & Sons, 2002.

[Bergeron03] Bergeron, B., *Essentials of Knowledge Management.* John Wiley & Sons, 2003.

[Bergeron05] Bergeron, B., "Nuclear, Biological, and Chemical Multimedia Collaboratory." *DOD Baseline Review of Medical Training Research, Advanced Technology Applications for Combat Casualty Care Conference* (2005).

[BergeronRouse92] Bergeron, Bryan, Ron Rouse, *Cognitive Aspects of Modeling and Simulating Complex Biological Systems*, in *Structuring biological systems: A Computer Modeling Approach.* CRC Press, 1992.

[Bourg02] Bourg, David, *Physics for Game Developers.* O'Reilly & Associates, 2002.

[Brooks75] Brooks, Frederick, *The Mythical Man-Month.* Addison-Wesley, 1975.

[Champandard04] Champandard, A. J., *AI Game Development: Synthetic Creatures with Learning and Reactive Behaviors.* New Riders Publishing, 2004.

[Conger04] Conger, D., *Physics Modeling for Game Programmers.* Thomson Course Technology, 2004.

[Cross05] Cross, Jason, "Is the world ready for Physics Acceleration?" *ExtremeTech* 3(2005): pp. 43.

[Dickey05] Dickey, K., Top of the line from AMD. *PC Modder: Reference Series* 2(2005): p. 15.

[Dickey05b] Dickey, K., Top of the line from Intel. *PC Modder: Reference Series* 2(2005): p. 16.

[ForbusFeltovich01] Forbus, Kenneth D., Paul J. Feltovich, *Smart Machines in Education: The Coming Revolution in Educational Technology.* AAAI Press; MIT Press, 2001.

[Fordahl05] Fordahl, Matthew, *AMD Unveils Dual-Core Chips for Desktops.* Associated Press. 2005. *news.yahoo.com/s/ap/20050531/ap_on_hi_te/amd_dual_core*, accessed May 30, 2005.

[Gerber95] Gerber, Michael, *The E-Myth Revisited: Why Most Small Companies Don't Work and What to Do About It.* HarperBusiness, 1995.

[Gray03] Gray, Kris, *DirectX 9 Programmable Graphics Pipeline.* Microsoft Press, 2003.

[Griffin05] Griffin, Mike, "The Next Generation." *Play* (4 2005): pp. 28–29.

[Grossman03] Grossman, Austin, *Postmortems from Game Developer: Insights from the Developers of Unreal Tournament, Black and White, Age of Empires, and Other Top-Selling Games.* CMP Books, 2003.

[HartleySleeman73] Hartley, J., D. Sleeman, "Towards More Intelligent Teaching Systems. *International Journal of Man-Machine Studies* 2(1973): pp. 215–36.

[Intel05] Intel, *Featured software.* Intel. 2005. *www.intel.com/cd/personal/computing/apac/eng/experience/software/84479.htm*, accessed April 19, 2005.

[Intel05] Intel, *Intel Pentium Processor Extreme Edition Product Brief.* Intel, 2005.

[ISO04] ISO, *ISO 9000 and ISO 14000—in brief.* International Organization for Standardization. 2004. *www.iso.org/iso/en/iso9000-14000/index.html*, accessed April 24, 2005.

[Johnson02] Johnson, S., "Wild Things." *WIRED* 3 (2002): pp. 78–83.

[Kageyama05] Kageyama, Yuri, *Nintendo Produces New Remote Control* Yahoo News. 2005. *news.yahoo.com/news?tmpl=story&u=/ap/20050916/ap_on_hi_te/japan_game_show*, accessed September 16, 2005.

[KaplanNorton92] Kaplan, R. S., D. P. Norton, The Balanced Scorecard—Measures That Drive Performance. *Harvard Business Review* (Jan–Feb 1992): pp. 71–79.

[Leopold01] Leopold, C., *Parallel and Distributed Computing: A Survey of Models, Paradigms, and Approaches*. John Wiley & Sons, 2001.

[Light05] Light, Paul, *The Four Pillars of High Performance: How Robust Organizations Achieve Extraordinary Results*. McGraw-Hill, 2005.

[Marr02] Marr, Deborah, Frank Binns, et al., *Hyper-Threading Technology Architecture and Microarchitecture: A Hypertext History*. Intel Technology Journal. 2002. *developer.intel.com/technology/itj/2002/volume06issue01*, accessed April 19, 2005.

[Meyers01] Meyers, Scott, *Effective STL*. Addison-Wesley, 2001.

[Mott05] Mott, Tony, "Beyond the Valley of the Rag Dolls." *Edge* (May 2005): pp. 66–71.

[MSDN05] MSDN, *DirectX 9.0 Components*. Microsoft Developers Network. 2005. *http://msdn.microsoft.com/library/default.asp?url=/library/en-us/directx9_c/directx/directxsdk/dx9components.asp*, accessed April 20, 2005.

[MulliganPatrovsky03] Mulligan, Jessica, and Bridgette Patrovsky, *Developing Online Games: An Insider's Guide*. New Riders, 2003.

[MulliganPatrovsky03b] Mulligan, Jessica, and Bridgette Patrovsky, *Managing an Online Game Post-Launch*. Gamasutra. 2003. *www.gamasutra.com/features/20030521/mulligan_pfv.htm*, accessed September 16, 2005.

[NIST05] NIST, *2005 Baldrige National Quality Program: Criteria for Performance Excellence*. National Institute of Standards and Technology, 2005.

[OngRamachandran00] Ong, J., S. Ramachandran, "Intelligent Tutoring Systems: The What and the How." *Learning Circuits (ASTD)* (February 2000).

[Pietari00] Pietari, Laurila, *Geometry Culling in 3D Engines*. GameDev.net. 2000. *www.gamedev.net/reference/articles/article1212.asp*, accessed April 22, 2005.

[Quenk99] Quenk, Naomi, *Essentials of Myers-Briggs Type Indicator® Assessment*. John Wiley & Sons, 1999.

[RamanathanThomas05] Ramanathan, R. M., and Vince Thomas, *Platform 2015: Intel Processor and Platform Evolution for the Next Decade*. Intel Corporation, 2005.

[Scammell04] Scammell, Rupert, "Cryptography for Game Developers. *Game Developer* 11(2004): pp. 20–33.

[Schell03] Schell, Jesse, "Shaping an Entertaining Future at Carnegie Mellon." *Computer Magazine* 8(2003): pp. 96–8.

[SpencerSpencer93] Spencer, L. M., S. M. Spencer, *Competence at Work: Models for Superior Performance*. John Wiley & Sons, 1993.

[van den Bergen03] van den Bergen, Gino, *Collision Detection in Interactive 3D Environments*. Morgan Kaufmann, 2003.

[Wolf92] Wolf, B., "AI in Education," in *Encyclopedia of Artificial Intelligence*. John Wiley & Sons, 1992.

[Yager05] Yager, Tom, "AMD's Opteron Finds a New Gear." *InfoWorld* 17(2005): pp. 28–30.

STANDARDS

In This Chapter

- Platform standards, from consoles to cell phones
- Game genre and rating standards
- Game design notation standards
- Asset standards
- Wired and wireless communications standards
- Interoperability standards and initiatives

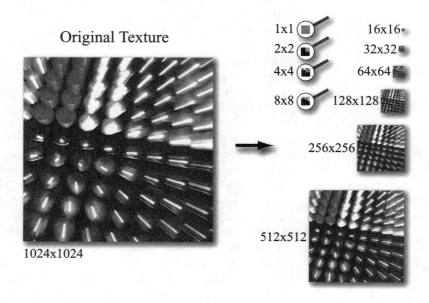

Original Texture

1024x1024

1x1
2x2
4x4
8x8

16x16
32x32
64x64
128x128

256x256

512x512

INTRODUCTION

During the Industrial Revolution, assembly lines of interchangeable parts replaced thousands of custom shops, creating a new economy dominated by industrial giants. In the Post-Industrial Era, the computer is the engine that drives a global knowledge economy in which thoughts are things and the rate of innovation is increasing exponentially. Whereas mass production was introduced over decades, software products such as videogames can run through their entire product lifecycles, from inception to obsolescence, within a matter of months [Bergeron02]. If not for standards, games might never make it to market because of a constantly moving deployment platform.

The relationship between standards, the constant churn of technology, and the accelerated rate of innovation isn't limited to software products, but is evident in all computer-enabled markets, including the cell phone industry. Although the Darwinian environment should eventually result in better cell phones and service, even with current political and legal constraints on the rate of technological change, standards are necessary for the growth of the industry. Without standards that enable customers with different handsets and cellular carriers to talk with each other or engage in a multiplayer game, the technology churn would be replaced by a free-for-all.

Whereas universal standards for voice communications have been established by national and international organizations, the cell phone gaming industry is plagued by an overabundance of standards. The myriad combinations of screen color depths, latencies, resolutions and layouts, operating system nuances, and network connectivity present a serious barrier to entry for deep-pocketed game developers, much less serious games developers. Cross compilers and other tools for the PC have matured to the degree that creating games for the most popular cell phone standards is feasible [Bergeron01a].

An example of a PC-based cell phone game development environment is *Omega Basic*, shown with the supporting J2ME (Java 2 Micro Edition) toolkit in Figure 4.1. This cross-platform development tool enables games developers to leverage the standard compilers and tools available on Windows, Linux, and the Mac OS to develop games on the several cell phone platforms. *Omega Basic* enables developers to code in BASIC or JAVA and use standard PC-based graphic tools to create games that run in native code on cell phones that support J2ME. PC-based cross compilers are possible only because of standardized enabling technologies. J2ME, which was introduced in 1988 [Baer98], is one of the major mobile and cell phone standards for game development and deployment.

When it comes to establishing standards, the serious games community is too small to influence standards adopted by the general computing or entertainment gaming communities. Even the top entertainment game developers are at the mercy of the console developers, who create their own *de facto* standards whenever they release a new console.

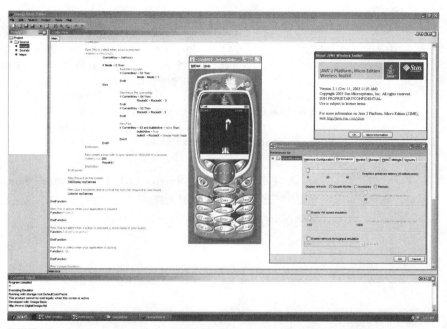

FIGURE 4.1   *Omega Basic* and the J2ME development environment provide serious games developers with a PC-based game development platform for cell phones and handheld devices. The cell phone emulator is running a version of *Space Invaders*, and the BASIC source code for the game is visible in the editor.

The realities of the games marketplace illustrate how abiding by sometimes fleeting standards is necessary but insufficient for serious games developers to survive in certain segments of the games market. For example, by controlling development tools and licensing access to their consoles, Microsoft, Sony, and Nintendo determine who can develop for their game consoles. Serious games developers who aspire to enter the potentially lucrative console market must not only abide by the standards established by the manufacturers, but they must satisfy a variety of additional criteria, such as the potential market share and likely revenue stream for the manufacturer.

This chapter provides an overview of the technological standards important to serious games developers, with an emphasis on the accessible PC platform.

PLATFORM STANDARDS

The major deployment platforms available to game developers are listed in Table 4.1. At first glance, it would seem that game developers who want to have a presence in every market would have to contend with more than 20 gaming platform standards. On closer examination of the list of deployment platforms, it should be obvious that developers who want to cover the spectrum of platforms have to deal with hundreds of so-called standard platforms. Whereas there are only three PlayStation and two Xbox console standards to contend with, the Windows, Linux, and MacOS desktop systems represent a virtually unlimited combination of operating system version, processor speed, system and video RAM, sound capabilities, and network connectivity.

TABLE 4.1   Game Deployment Platforms. Platforms marked (*) are particularly available/suitable for serious games development.

GAME DEPLOYMENT PLATFORMS
Arcade/Coin-Op
Cellphones*
Game Boy Advance
Game Boy Color
Linux*
Mac OS X*
Microsoft Xbox
Microsoft Xbox 360
Nintendo DS
Nintendo GameCube
Nintendo Revolution
Nokia N-Gage
Palm OS*
Playstation 2
Windows Mobile 2003/5*
Sony Playstation
Sony Playstation 3
Sony PSP
Tapwave Zodiac 2
Tiger Telematics Gizmondo
Windows 2000/XP*

Regardless of the exact number of possible PC platforms, few development shops have the resources to develop for 2 platforms, much less 20. The retooling necessary for a shop versed in the Xbox or PlayStation

2 to the move to the Xbox 360 or PlayStation 3 is enough to tax the resources of even the largest development shops.

The Palm OS and Windows Mobile platforms are not as diverse, with each representing perhaps dozens of hardware configurations. However, cell phones are even more diverse than PC platforms, with hundreds of models on the market, and hundreds of legacy models still in use. About a third of the platform categories listed in Table 4.1 are open to serious games developers who aren't backed by deep pockets and political connections, and most of these are defined by multiple, sometimes conflicting, standards.

As indicated in Table 4.1, the top serious games deployment platforms are various flavors of cell phones, Linux, MacOs X, Palm OS, Windows, and Windows Mobile. Of the desktop platforms, the MacOS is the least stable in the short term. After years of running on PowerPC chips from IBM and Freescale Semiconductors, Apple switched to Intel as its source of microprocessors [WingfieldClark05]. In the long-term, a common hardware architecture might bode well for the game development community, which has favored Windows-Intel/AMD over MacOS-PowerPC for years.

Standards are respites in the otherwise constant forward march of technology. They allow investors to recoup their investments and encourage other companies to develop ancillary technologies. If console manufacturers introduced new platforms every year instead of every five, few game developers could create a game and make a profit before the console and their game became obsolete. The same tension between progress and profit is also evident in the U.S. cell phone industry, where the functionality provided by one carrier lags behind that of another. Carriers have not jettisoned their first- and second-generation cellular network standards because of their desire to extract the last bit of profit from their previous investments in the antiquated infrastructure [Bergeron01a]. An additional barrier to change is the tactic employed by cellular operators of locking in customers with one or two year contracts so that they won't jump to a carrier with a superior network—and better technology standards. At odds with this strategy are carriers who need to attract new customers by offering premium services, such as games.

Console Standards

Console standards are worth reviewing because a handful of serious titles have made it to the consoles. Furthermore, by raising player expectations, consoles establish minimum standards of what is acceptable for PC-based games. In establishing new standards of performance, console manufacturers play the technological leapfrog game with one another at a slower pace than PC manufacturers because of lengthy game development time, significant research and development costs, and market demand.

When the PlayStation 2, Xbox, and GameCube consoles were introduced, they were comparable in power and storage to the average PC. As a point of reference, *PC Magazine* selected the Dell Dimension 4100 as the Best Computer of 2000. The $1,200 system featured a Pentium III/866 CPU, 128MB of RAM, a 10GB hard drive, and a 16MB graphics card [Machrone01]. The Xbox, released in 2001, was more powerful than either the PlayStation 2 or GameCube, but less powerful than the Dell 4100. However, the advantage of the Xbox over the Dell as a game deployment platform has been a standard configuration for five years, versus a target that was upgraded and replaced every six months.

As illustrated in Table 4.2, the latest offerings from the three console manufacturers provide significant performance enhancements over their predecessors. Raw processing power aside, the most important standards for the console-based serious games developers are the provision for networking, including WiFi; the higher capacity media on the PlayStation 3; and the HDTV video resolution available on the latest generation consoles. The more exacting HDTV video standard is clear evidence that PC-based serous game asset developers and programmers will have to become more facile with their trade.

TABLE 4.2   Console Specifications for the Top Three Console Manufacturers

MANUFACTURER	MICROSOFT		SONY		NINTENDO	
Console	Xbox	Xbox 360	PS2	PS3	GameCube	Revolution
Year Introduced	2001	2005	2000	2006	2001	2006
Processor	Pentium 3	IBM tri-core PowerPC	Toshiba & Sony Emotion Engine	IBM Cell	IBM PowerPC Gekko	Intel Broadway
Processor Speed	0.733 GHz	3.2 GHz	0.3 GHz	3.2 GHz	0.485 GHz	—
Video	Unified RAM, 720p	Unified RAM, 10MB cache, 1080p HDTV	4 MB, 720p	256MB, 1080p HDTV	2MB Frame Buffer, 480p	128 MB, HDTV
Audio	3D Stereo	Surround Sound	Stereo	Surround Sound	Stereo	—
Base RAM	64MB	512MB	32MB	256MB	24MB	512MB
Media	DVD-ROM	DVD-ROM	CD-ROM, DVD-ROM	CD-ROM, DVD-ROM, Blu-ray Disc	Mini-DVD	12cm disc, mini-DVD
Wireless Controllers	NA	4 user	NA	7 user, plus PSP	NA	Yes
Network	Wired	Wired, WiFi, Bluetooth	Wired	Wired, WiFi, Bluetooth	NA	WiFi
Storage	8GB HD, Flash	20GB re-movable HD, Flash	NA	Optional HD, Memory Stick, SD, CompactFlash	Flash	SD

Configurations for the PlayStation 3 and Nintendo Revolution are based on prerelease announcements. The table is based on reviews available in Q4 of 2005 [CNET05; Microsoft05; Ung05].

PC Standards

The standards relevant to the most pervasive serious game deployment plat-form, the Windows-based PC, can be described in terms of the main loop, system architecture, configuration, video, and performance benchmarks.

Main Loop

Windows, like Linux and the Mac OS, is an event-driven operating sys-tem, meaning that games compete with other programs for attention from the processor. In games, this competition for PC resources is de-scribed in terms of the *main loop*, which is a high-level abstraction of the inner workings of the game engine.

After initialization, Windows-based game engines employ an event driven message handling and dispatching system in which the system waits for messages such as keyboard, mouse, or joystick interactions. As shown in Figure 4.2, the engine then dispatches the appropriate messages to the specific handlers for graphics, AI, physics, sound, and other com-ponents of the game. Various permutations of the standard pipelined or sequential game loop are possible, such as running the sound and music on a second thread, parallel to the graphics, AI, and other handlers. With true multithreading hardware and software, the graphics, AI, physics, sound, and networking operations can be executed in parallel.

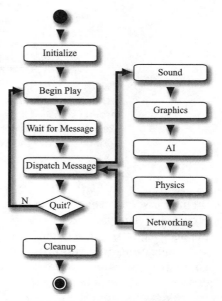

FIGURE 4.2   The game main loop associated with a typical pipelined game engine.

PC Architecture

The main loop is a high-level abstraction of the PC that is in turn based on the standard Windows-based architecture. As shown in Figure 4.3, this architecture includes several layers of abstraction, in that the engine and various components, such as the gamepads and other peripherals, interface with software drivers that in turn communicate with low-level basic input/output services (BIOS) that are linked directly to memory, processors, controller chips, and other hardware.

The game engine interfaces with standard software extensions to the operating system, which in turn interfaces with low-level device drivers. The operating system and extensions handle the mouse, keyboard, and controller events in the user interface, as depicted in the main loop.

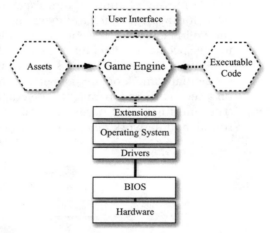

FIGURE 4.3 The relationship between standard PC architecture (solid lines), game engine, and game resources (dashed lines). Assets and executable code, like the applications used to create them, are positioned above the extensions level.

Although not part of the PC architecture proper, the relative placement of assets and executable code in the overall architecture is shown in Figure 4.3. The game engine incorporates assets and executable code as needed. Like the game engine, the programming and asset creation tools are applications that run at the application level of the architecture, just above the operating system extensions. Figure 4.3 illustrates how game engine execution is dependent on the chain of standards that enable the unbroken link from the game engine, through operating system, drivers, down to the central processing unit and other hardware.

PC Configuration

Whereas the architecture illustrated in Figure 4.3 is a logical abstraction of PC hardware and software, the physical architecture involves real components, and standards are the glue that enables the disparate hardware and software to work as a coordinated whole. Examples of the combinations of standard technologies that go into a PC, referred to as the configuration, are listed in Table 4.3.

At the most basic level is the bus architecture, which involves a cascade of other standards involving devices, ranging from the hard drive to video and system memory. From the serious games developer's perspective, the bus architecture is relevant to the extent it limits or enhances overall system performance. PCs with older bus architectures can be found in hospitals, schools, and other potential serious games deployment sites.

TABLE 4.3   The Matrix of Standards Associated with the Configuration of Desktop PCs That Might Pose Challenges to Serious Games Developers

TECHNOLOGY	EXAMPLES	SERIOUS GAMES DEVELOPMENT ISSUES
Audio	Integrated audio	Compatibility, bit-depth, support for 3D sound
BIOS	Manufacturer specific	Compatibility with operating system
Bus Architecture	ISA, EISA, MCA, VLB, PCI	Overall performance
Coprocessor	Graphics Coprocessor	Software driver compatibility, stability
Drivers	Hard drive, CD-ROM	Compatibility with operating system
Storage	CD/DVD-ROM, hard drive, Tape, floppy, flash memory	Longevity of media and device, compatibility
Microprocessor	Intel P4 EE, AMD Opturon	Brand, performance, clock speed, cores, compiler availability
RAM	SDRAM	Quantity, performance
Chipset	Intel 925XE	Bus speed, system performance
Monitor	CRT, LCD, Plasma	Color temperature, refresh rate, resolution
Network Connection	ISDN, DSL, T1, WiFi, Bluetooth	Bandwidth, security, range
Operating System	Windows XP, Linux	Game engine compatibility, extension, and driver software compatibility
Peripherals	Game controller, mouse,	Layout, functions, driver availability keyboard
Ports	USB-2, Firewire, LAN	Speed, compatibility, number
Video Hardware	GeForce 6800, Radeon 9000	RAM bit depth, resolution, color calibration, video RAM, OpenGL/DirectX support

Microprocessor technology for the PC has standardized on technology from Intel and Advanced Micro Devices (AMD). This contrasts with the microprocessor used in the Xbox 360, a tri-core PowerPC chip developed by IBM. Similarly, Sony, Toshiba, and IBM developed the multi-core Cell processor. Like bus architecture, the relevance of microprocessor design to serious game designers is performance. In addition, developers who want to take advantage of the dual core microprocessors from Intel and AMD must use tools and utilities that support parallel processing.

Audio and video standards are increasingly important in serious games design. Graphic resolution and rendering quality are approaching HDTV quality, and audio components for *multimedia* PCs often support 3D sound technology once reserved for high-end home theatre systems.

Even though PC configurations directly affect serious games development, PC configuration data that game developers provide end users is rarely as detailed as the information given in Table 4.3. More often, developers describe a subset of the configuration data listed in the table in terms of minimum and suggested system requirements. Minimum system requirements reflect oldest legacy system that is capable of running the game at an acceptable performance level. Because the potential market for a game increases as the minimum system requirements are eased, there is motivation for developers to support old systems. However, support and development costs also increase when provision is made for low-performance, outdated equipment. An example of a suggested minimum system requirements statement for a serious medical game is shown in Listing 4.1.

LISTING 4.1   Suggested Minimum System Requirements for a Medical Serious Game

```
CPU Type & Speed: Pentium® III 667 MHz
Video Card: Direct 3D video card with 32 MB RAM, 1024 x 768
Operating System: Windows® 98
System Memory: 256 MB
Hard Drive Space: 750 MB available
CD-ROM Speed: 4X
DirectX: 4.0c
Sound Card: Windows® compatible
Controller: Windows® compatible mouse
```

Recommended system requirements represent a standard of performance that is optimal for gameplay. They should include optional interface components such as enhanced sound, game controllers, and other elements that are integral to optimal gameplay. Recommended requirements don't address the best possible gameplay. However, recommending a bleeding edge system configuration may limit the market size of the game. The recommended system requirements statement for the same serious medical game is shown in Listing 4.2.

LISTING 4.2   Recommended System Requirements for a Serious Medical Game

```
CPU Type & Speed: Pentium ® IV 3.6 GHz
Video Card: Direct 3D card with 128 MB RAM, 1024 x 768
Operating System: Windows ® XP SP2
System Memory: 1 GB
Hard Drive Space: 1 GB
CD-ROM Speed: 16X
DirectX: 4.0c
Sound Card: Dolby® Digital audio compatible
Controller: Logitech® Rumblepad II
```

If the system configuration is known prior to development, it can serve as the basis for game design. For example, if a first responder learning lab for firefighters and EMTs is filled with 1.2 GHz Pentium machines with 32 MB of video RAM and GPUs optimized for OpenGL, then the limited video RAM and lack of Direct 3D acceleration should be reflected in the game design document (see Chapter 8, "Serious Games Design"). In selecting a game engine, developers can either choose to use the OpenGL engine or test a DirectX-compatible engine on the hardware configuration to determine if non-accelerated Direct 3D will support acceptable gameplay.

PC Video

The constant evolution of wide bandwidth bus architectures, powerful graphical coprocessors, and high-speed, dedicated video RAM have transformed the face of game computing from blocky sprites in primary colors to rich, realistic 3D environments. Most PCs are sold with integrated graphics chipsets on the motherboard, and the leading supplier of these chipsets is Intel [Harris05]. However, there is a significant market for discrete video cards on the high and low end of the performance spectrum. At the high end are cards with onboard GPUs and ample video RAM that compete for media attention by claiming to have the fastest video card on the planet. At the low end are cards that share system memory. The performance of these unified memory cards depends on the other components in the system, making a programmatic assessment of video capabilities problematic for game developers.

The quantity of RAM directly affects game performance because too little RAM requires machine cycles from the CPU to repeatedly load textures and other image files from the hard drive or CD-ROM into video memory instead of loading the data once at the start of a level. The resulting disruption in gameplay can break the illusion of reality that many good games foster. Inadequate video RAM may also limit the number of frames per second a given game engine can display. Game engines render a scene to an off-screen buffer and then blast the contents of the buffer to the monitor when it is refreshed. The better engines employ several layers of buffering to achieve smooth gameplay at high frame rates. However, this technique requires adequate video memory. As of 2005, the better video cards provide between 128 MB and 512 MB of video RAM—a big improvement over the few kilobytes of video RAM that were standard on the first IBM PC. However, corporate America and the educational system are filled with legacy systems with at most 16 MB to 32 MB of video ram.

While the raw quantity of video RAM affects performance by determining how often the CPU has to fetch assets from the CD-ROM or hard drive, bit depth determines the number of colors that can be displayed at any one time on the computer monitor. The more bits and more colors, the more realism possible for the displayed images.

The standard pixel depth for modern video cards, such as the NVIDIA GeForce 6800 series, is 32-bits. In the 32-bit mode, there are 8 bits available for the red, green, and blue (RGB) components of a pixel, plus 8 bits for the alpha channel [Cogley05]. The alpha channel defines the transparency of each RGB component, allowing blending of colors.

It's difficult to find a PC that ships with less than 32-bit color today, even in a system with only 16MB of video RAM. However, many legacy video systems use 24 or 16-bit standards. In the 24-bit standard, there are 8 bits each for red, green, and blue, and no alpha or transparency channel. With 16 bits, there are 5 bits for each RGB component, plus one extra bit for green—so called 565 video cards. The relationship between video RAM bit depth and the number of simultaneous colors available is illustrated in Table 4.4. A pixel driven by 24-bit or 32-bit video hardware can be assigned any one of 2^{24} or 16.7 million colors, but a 16-bit hardware can support only 2^{16} or 65,536 colors. This limitation would be visible when displaying discrete bands in a linear spectrum, such as the colors associated with a rainbow. The same rainbow would be rendered as a smooth gradation from one color to the next in a 24-bit system.

TABLE 4.4   Video RAM Bit-Depth versus Number of Possible Simultaneous Colors and Bits Available for a Transparency or Alpha Channel

BIT-DEPTH	COLORS	ALPHA BITS
8	$2^8 = 256$	0
16	$2^{16} = 65,535$	0
24	$2^{24} = 16.78M$	0
32 (24 + 8)	$2^{24} = 16.78M$	8

A twist on handling game graphics is to use 8-bit color palettes to define images with 256 or fewer 24-bit colors. The pixel colors of these palletized images are defined indirectly by a lookup table, as illustrated by Figure 4.4. This method of handling colors is popular with graphics in browser-based games and textures in platform-based games because palletized images can be very compact. Furthermore, unlike other space-saving methods, the use of palletized images is lossless, in that the color data encoded with a color lookup table can be extracted without error. Instead of loading dozens or hundreds of 24-bit images into video RAM, each with 8-bit R, G, and B values per pixel, smaller 8-bit palletized images can be loaded, along with an 8-bit palette or color lookup table (CLUT).

To appreciate the magnitude of space saved by palletized images, consider the first four entries from a color lookup table shown in Figure 4.4. The first entry specifies a color with RGB values of 12, 3, and 88, which is a dark blue. The second entry specifies a Red value of 200, a Green value of 54, and a Blue value of 250, which is purple. The CLUT continues in this way until the 8-bit palette index table is filled. Using the CLUT, the color data associated with each pixel in a palletized image is reduced from 24 to 8 bits—a savings of two-thirds per image. Assuming a 128 × 128 pixel texture, RGB to palletized image size is approximately 390 KB to 130 KB—a savings of 260K per image.

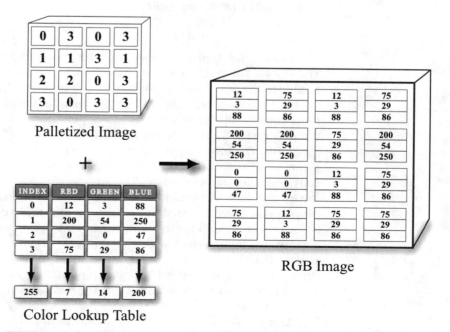

FIGURE 4.4   Palletized image (top, left), color lookup table (bottom, left), and reconstructed RGB image (right).

This space savings has a modest computational cost. There is the CPU overhead of fetching the RGB values from the CLUT before rendering a texture, which is minimal. More significant from the developer's perspective is that the continuous range of 16.7 million colors may not be available, especially for games optimized for viewing in a Web browser. This limitation can be seen in the color picker utility within Adobe Photoshop. As shown in Figure 4.5, there is pronounced banding in the palletized image, indicating lack of continuity from one color to the next.

 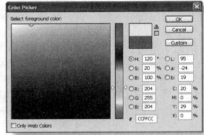

FIGURE 4.5 Color picker within Adobe Photoshop, showing lack of continuity in the range colors available for palletized images destined for the Web (left) versus a continuous 24-bit RGB image (right).

Video resolution is another constraint associated with game design. The 1024×768 resolution is standard today, but some legacy systems are limited to the 800×600 or even 640×480 standard. On new systems, the 1600×1200 standard is increasingly popular as 20-inch monitors become more affordable. Serious games developers need to make provision for the 640×480, 800×600, 1024×768, and 1600×1200 pixel resolution standards. The most elegant approach is to scale graphics, fonts, and characters to fit the distribution platform's resolution—either programmatically or under player control. The alternative, designing a game for the lowest common denominator resolution, dates the game and penalizes players who have invested in hardware that is more capable.

The relationship between maximum resolution, bit depth, and color quality can be explored with the Window's Display Properties control panel. As illustrated in Figure 4.6, a video card with 16 MB RAM set to drive a monitor at 1600×1200 pixel resolution is limited to 16-bit color, whereas a card with 256 MB of video RAM can support 32-bit color at the same resolution.

As with video resolution, the practical implication of limited color quality is that serious games developers must make provision for video

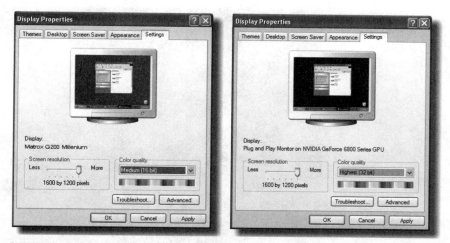

FIGURE 4.6   Display properties are limited to 16-bit color on the video card with 16 MB of RAM (Left) versus 32-bit color on the card with 256 MB of video RAM (Right) at 1600 × 1200 resolution.

cards with less than the optimal amount of RAM. Developing games for the lowest color quality standard may result in banding artifacts from limited bits per pixel. Another approach is to use the full bit depth supported by the game environment and use a variety of tricks to degrade the rendered scene gracefully as defined by the available RAM. For example, a fog effect can be used to limit the detail required of textures distant from the viewer, and the game engine can be configured not to draw the textures on distant objects until there are resources available to load the bitmaps. This technique of progressive texture mapping is illustrated in Figure 4.7.

The scene from *Microsoft Flight Simulator* (Figure 4.7) shows a view over Hong Kong, with the darker textures for vegetation loaded on about a third of the land in view. One of the heuristics for minimizing the visual disruption of progressive texture mapping is to load textures closer to the player first. As in Figure 4.7, textures near the city, in the background, are not loaded, whereas textures for the dark greenery nearest the player are partially loaded.

Even with several hundred kilobytes of video RAM, a dedicated GPU can dramatically improve video performance by implementing OpenGL and/or Direct3D in hardware. Many video cards and integrated video systems are capable of supporting both standards. For example, the nVIDIA GeForce 6800 series of video cards are optimized for Direct X 4.0, with extensions for OpenGL [NVIDIA05].

FIGURE 4.7   *Microsoft Flight Simulator 2004* illustrating progressive texture mapping to compensate for insufficient video RAM.

As illustrated in Figure 4.8, many 3D game engines can leverage a GPU to accelerate Direct3D or OpenGL routines. Each standard has strengths and weaknesses, and numerous commercial entertainment games have been developed with each standard. Graphics acceleration may not be an absolute necessity, especially with high-performance CPUs. As long as the OpenGL or Direct3D routines are loaded in the PC, it may not be a question of a particular game engine running or not, but one of acceptable graphic performance. Of course, there are exceptions.

Another video standard that applies to many serious games is that of color, which can play an important role in the content of the game. Every monitor displays colors differently due to variances in monitor design and manufacture, video hardware, the computer configuration, and ambient room lighting. The standard that applies to the color of computer displays is the ICC specification for device profiles, which is maintained by the International Color Consortium (*www.color.org*).

Most graphic artists are familiar with spectrophotometers that take a reading directly off of the monitor face. These hardware devices offer the most precise means of adjusting a display to render standard colors. Visual methods using interactive calibration screens are also available, but they are less accurate than instrumented methods.

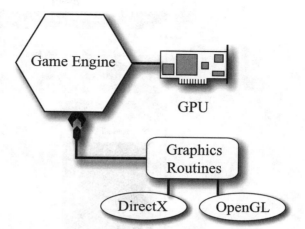

FIGURE 4.8   A 3D game engines leveraging a graphical processing unit (GPU) to accelerate DirectX or OpenGL routines.

Because variance in color accuracy between monitors of the same make and model is small compared with monitors from different manufacturers, an economical way to ensure that every monitor in a classroom or training facility renders colors accurately is to calibrate one monitor with a spectrophotometer and then apply the same correction factors or monitor profile to the other computer systems. Monitor profiles provide color management systems with the information they need to convert monitor color data to device-independent color.

The most critical calibration setting is the gamma, which affects color rendering by modifying the brightness and contrast of the middle tones. A higher gamma value yields an overall darker image. Many video drivers have a color correction utility that can be used to specify the gamma setting, as in Figure 4.9.

PC Performance Benchmarks

Regardless of what's under the hood of a PC, as a gaming platform, it all comes down to performance. Doubling the video RAM doesn't necessarily improve video performance, just as swapping a single-core processor for a dual-core model doesn't guarantee better game physics. To the contrary, the overhead of extra video RAM in an underpowered video card or of a dual-core CPU in a computer without an operating system or game designed to take advantage of the parallel processing can result in decreased game performance.

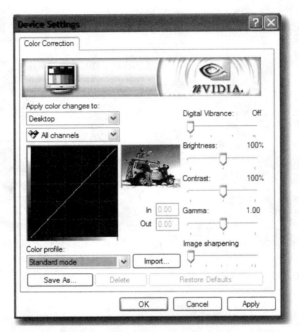

FIGURE 4.9 A monitor control panel showing controls for modifying the monitor profile, including gamma correction.

Given the complex interplay of computer hardware components and the operating system, it's difficult to assess the performance of a PC based solely on variables such as the microprocessor type and clock speed, quantity of video and system RAM, and bus architecture. Prior to the advent of Windows, PCs were assessed or benchmarked with raw processor tasks, such as the number of floating point operations per second. However, these benchmarks often failed to translate into real-world performance with applications.

A more pragmatic approach to assessing PC performance as a gaming platform is to use benchmarks based on real games, such as *DOOM*, *Halo*, *QUAKE*, and *Unreal Tournament*. For example, in the reviews of video cards featured in *Maximum PC*, the performance results are reported in terms of frames per second (fps) at a given resolution and game segment of *QUAKE 3* and *Unreal Tournament 2003* [MaximumPC03]. Another popular standard for assessing PC system performance is the suite of applications from Futuremark Corporation, including the *3DMark* series for gaming platforms and *SYSmark 2004* for developers. *3DMark 2005* is designed to test the performance of systems with video hardware that support DirectX. It combines 3D game tests, feature tests, and image quality tests to derive a total score that game developers and players can use to compare their computer system with other systems over the Internet.

The three game tests within *3DMark 2005* target different game environments (see Figure 4.10). Game test 1, a segment from *Return to Proxycom*, is an indoor shooter that relies heavily on lighting effects and multiple animated characters. Game test 2, *Firefly Forest*, is a segment of the small space outdoor game, and a segment from *Canyon Flight*, an expansive outdoor game, is used in Game test 3. The relevance of each test to a serious games developer depends on how closely it approximates the serious game.

During each test, the frame rate is displayed on the screen. In addition to the real-time displays, the *3DMark 2005* generates an extensive report of the video hardware and CPU performance. A freeware version of the full product can be downloaded through the Futuremark Web site (*www.futuremark.com*).

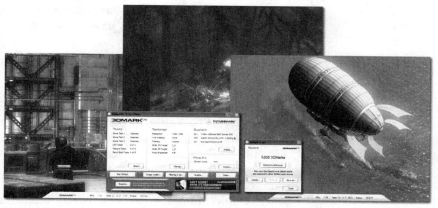

FIGURE 4.10   *3DMark 2005* game performance benchmark suite, showing screens from *Return to Proxycom* (left), *Firefly Forest* (center), and *Canyon Flight* (right).

Gameplay performance isn't relevant when it comes to evaluating the performance of a development workstation. More important is how a workstation can support the creation and editing of art, compiling of game code, and other development tasks. *SYSmark 2004*, developed by Business Application Performance Corporation (BAPCo), is an application-based benchmark standard used by game developers.

The benchmark is relevant to serious game developers because it reflects performance in the areas of content creation and office productivity, based on a suite of programs that includes popular game content development tools such as *Adobe Photoshop* and *Discreet 3ds max* [Bapco04]. BAPCo is a nonprofit consortium of computer industry publications, independent testing labs, PC hardware manufacturers, and software publishers, including AMD, CNET Labs, Dell, Hewlett-Packard, IBM, Intel, and Microsoft.

Handheld Standards

Handheld game deployment platforms have come a long way in only a few years. When Sony released the PSP handheld console in 2005, it had the same basic configuration of the PlayStation 2—a 333 MHz processor and 32MB of RAM—with the additional capabilities of handling video, MP3 music, JPEG snapshots, and WiFi for multiplayer gaming. However, for developers with plans for only limited internal distribution of a game, the PSP may be effectively off limits because of the hassles of working with Sony.

Of the major handheld platforms on the market, Palm OS and Windows Mobile machines are the most approachable handheld standards for serious game development because the development tools are inexpensive and readily available, and developers can self-publish through any number of Web portals. Even so, developers have to content with multiple standards for each environment.

Palm OS

Palm offers a free software development kit (SDK) for game developers (*www.palm.com*). The Palm OS platforms suitable for serious games provide from 2 to 32 MB of base RAM, a display resolution from 160×160 to 320×480 pixels, and from 4- to 16-bit grayscale or color. To add to the variability in platforms, there are also options for WiFi and Bluetooth communications using plug-in cards.

An example of a game on a handheld platform is shown in Figure 4.11. The game, *Lemonade Tycoon*, is a strategy game that relies on business simulation to enable players to manage a lemonade business, including pricing, inventory and marketing. Players pick locations for their stands, check the weather forecast, adjust recipes, set prices and manage inventory. By making good business decisions and increasing cash reserves, players can move to better locations, buy a refrigerator, and automate their business processes. Although limited in comparison to a PC-based game, even the low-end M500, with its 160×160 pixel, 4-bit gray-scale display is an adequate game platform.

In addition to supporting native Palm hardware, the Palm OS has been licensed to companies such as Aceeca, AlphaSmart, Handspring, Samsung, Kyocera, Symbol, Tapwave and Sony, for products ranging from smart phones to educational toys and competing PDAs [Palm-Source05]. Some of the products from these companies are attractive game deployment platforms, while other platforms are marginal. For ex-

FIGURE 4.11   *Lemonade Tycoon* on the
Palm M500 PDA.

ample, although the Palm OS-based Zodiac 2 from Tapwave beat the
Sony PSP to market, it failed to attract a significant following. After only
two years in the market, it was discontinued in the third quarter of 2005
[Tapwave05].

Windows Mobile

After several false starts, sales of Microsoft's Windows Mobile (formerly
Windows CE) platform standard surpassed those of the Palm OS in the
third quarter of 2004 [Bell04], and it has continued to accumulate market
share. In addition to its greater popularity, the Windows Mobile platform
is even more varied than the Palm OS platform. Microsoft licenses the operating system to vendors ranging from Acer, Asus, Garmin, Fujitsu, and
Mio, to Sony, HP, and Dell, and there is significant product differentiation
from one brand to the next. Even within HP's line of Pocket PCs, screen
resolution varies from 240 × 320 to 480 × 640, with between 32 MB and
256 MB of base RAM. Some HP handhelds have WiFi, Bluetooth, and cellular wireless connectivity built in, and others can be extended with plug-
in cards. Microsoft offers an SDK for free download (*www.Microsoft.com*).
As with the Palm OS, several companies offer kits that can simplify game
creation.

Cell Phone Standards

Cell phone standards are the most fragmented of all game platforms. In the United States, standards revolve around three areas: form, function, and cost. Form varies from one manufacturer to the next, with differences in screen size and resolution, device weight, audio capabilities, and interface design, including the function and placement of controls. For example, some multifunction cell phones rely on a stylus to select names to dial, whereas others use buttons and thumbwheels. Cell phone function varies in terms of mobility, battery life, security, privacy, availability, modes of operation, and location awareness. From a customer cost perspective, there are significant differences between both handsets and carriers in term of operating charges and game download charges. From the perspective of the cellular network owner, there is variability in content costs and hardware and software licensing. Despite the lack of standards, cell phones have the greatest growth potential of all serious games development platforms.

GAME STANDARDS

The successful marketing of entertainment and serious games is dependent on simple, unambiguous categories or genres of gameplay to inform potential customers about the type of content in games. The standard game genre categories have been defined by the top selling titles. Similarly, content ratings reflect the reaction of certain groups to those titles.

Game Genres

The standard genre definitions listed here are used to define entertainment and serious games include:

Action: Involves the player in combat, sports, and/or shooting.
Adventure: Emphasizes exploration.
Arcade (Retro):   Mimics the early arcade games.
Combat (Fighting):   Features hand-to-hand combat in an action game.
Driving: Involves driving or racing a vehicle.
First-Person Shooter (FPS):   A fast-paced action game in which the object is to shoot other characters, from a first-person perspective.
Military Shooter: A first- or third-person shooter in a military environment.
Multiplayer: Supports more than one player simultaneously.
Puzzle: Involves the solution of logic puzzles or mazes.
Real-Time Simulation (RTS):   Multiple players can attack, defend, or build simultaneously.

Role Playing Game (RPG):   The player carefully controls and manages the development of either a single or multiple characters. Storyline is stressed over action.

Shooter: An action game in which the object is to shoot other characters from a first (FPS) or third person (TPS) perspective.

Simulation: Mimics reality, typically with an emphasis on game physics and/or AI.

Sneaker: A shooter that emphasizes subterfuge and precision strikes over non-stop action.

Sports: Mimics traditional sports, such as basketball, baseball, or football.

Strategy: Emphasizes planning and resource management over action

Third-Person Shooter (TPS):   A shooter in which the perspective is above and behind the player.

Trivia: Tests the player's knowledge of trivia.

Turn-Based: Supports more than one player, one player at a time.

Because many serious games are not intended for commercial distribution, developers often have freedom to create serious games that cross over or blend several genres. For example, a shooter in which the player character is a combat medic that can attend to the wounded could be classified as a Shooter/RPG

Game Rating Standards

The two rating systems for videogames are the Entertainment Software Rating Board (ESRB) for packaged games and the Internet Content Rating Association (ICRA) for online game sites [ESRB05; ICRA05]. Whereas ESRB Ratings are printed on game packaging, ICRA ratings are designed to be read by a search engine. Web-based game developers who want their site rated simply complete an online ICRA label generator (*www.icra.org/label/generator*) and paste the label into the <HEAD> section of every Web page on their site for which it is valid. The ESRB rating system and ICRA rating vocabulary are listed here.

ESRB Rating

EC (Early Childhood):   Content suitable for ages 3 and older. Contains no material that parents would find inappropriate.

E (Everyone):   Content suitable for ages 6 and older. Titles in this category may contain minimal cartoon, fantasy or mild violence and/or infrequent use of mild language.

E10+ (Everyone 10 and older):   Content suitable for ages 10 and older. Titles in this category may contain some cartoon, fantasy or mild violence, mild language, and/or minimal suggestive themes.

T (Teen):   Content suitable for ages 13 and older. Games may contain violence, suggestive themes, crude humor, minimal blood and/or infrequent use of strong language.

M (Mature):   Content suitable for persons ages 17 and older. Titles in this category may contain intense violence, blood and gore, sexual content, and/or strong language.

AO (Adults Only):   Content suitable for persons ages 18 and older. May contain prolonged scenes of intense violence and/or explicit sexual content and nudity.

RP (Rating Pending):   Content has been submitted to the ESRB and is awaiting final rating. The "RP" symbol appears only in advertising prior to a game's release.

ICRA Rating Vocabulary

Nudity and Sexual Material: Content may contain genitals, breasts, and explicit sexual acts. The context can be specified as artistic, educational, or medical.

Violence: Content may include sexual violence, blood and gore, killing, and deliberate killing of humans, animals, or fantasy characters. The context can be specified as artistic, educational, medical, or sports.

Language: Content may include explicit sexual language, crude words or profanity, or mild expletives.

Other Topics: Content may promote tobacco, alcohol, or drug use, gambling, use of weapons, discrimination, or otherwise set a bad example for young children.

Chat: The site may support unmoderated chat or moderated chat suitable for children and teens.

GAME DESIGN NOTATION STANDARDS

Because of the complexity of modern game design, it's virtually impossible for one person to design, build, and market a game without help from others. Even the few who are able to go it alone need tools to help them think through the problems inherent in game design. In both cases, software notation conventions used by the general programming community also apply in game design.

For group development, a standard notation provides everyone in the group with an unambiguous means of communications, typically in conjunction with a design document—the topics of Chapter 8, "Serious Games Design." Similarly, the use of a standard notation allows the lone developer to leverage the experience of others, including by using software tools designed to help automate the notation process. The two major notation standards discussed here are Data Flow diagrams and the Unified Modeling Language or UML.

Data Flow Diagrams

Data Flow diagrams are used to illustrate a game in terms of processes that act on input data and produce output data. The player, referred to as an entity, is typically the source of the data input and output. The top-level Data Flow diagram that describes a game, called a context diagram, provides a view of the game as a single process (see Figure 4.12). This diagram illustrates data flow in and out of a game that supports local as well as networked players and that saves player scores in a database.

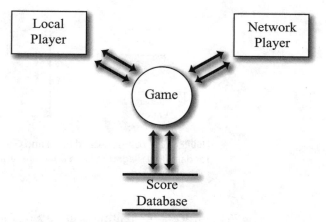

FIGURE 4.12   Top-level Data Flow diagram (context diagram) of a networked game.

Two popular notation standards used to create data flow diagrams are Yourdon and Coad [Coad90] and Game and Sarson [GaneSarson77]. The differences between the two standards are minor, and there are only four basic symbols, as illustrated in Figure 4.13:

External Entity: Objects outside the game with which the game communicates. These are represented by rectangles labeled with the entity name.

Dataflow: Pipelines that carry packets of data. Dataflow is represented by unlabeled lines with unidirectional arrowheads indicating direction of data flowing through the system.

Datastore: Repositories of data in the game system. These are represented by open rectangles labeled with the datastore name.

Process: The transformation of an incoming data flow into an outgoing data flow. Processes are represented by labeled circles or rounded rectangles. A number can be used to represent the process number or level.

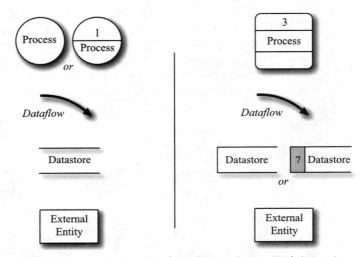

FIGURE 4.13   Yourdon-Coad (Left) and Game-Sarson (Right) notations for data flow diagrams. Data flows are represented by unlabeled lines with arrowheads.

The process of creating a library of Data Flow diagrams that shows the general flow of information through a game is one of decomposition. After defining the top-level process, as in Figure 4.12, the game is recursively decomposed into subprocesses until further decomposition yields no additional information. In this way, the system of four symbols can be used to represent any game at any level of detail. Terminal processes elements are often replaced by or supplemented with pseudocode.

There is no standard, universal pseudocode used in game design notation. However, every pseudocode must address three basic structures: sequence, selection, and iteration [Aktas87]. Examples of each structure are provided in Listing 4.3.

LISTING 4.3   Pseudocode for sequence, selection, and iteration.

```
/Sequence/
Read data from disk
Write data to disk
```

```
/Selection/
If <condition>
    then perform action-1
    else perform action-2
Endif

/Iteration/
While <condition> do
    Perform action
Endwhile
```

An advantage of Data Flow diagrams and the analysis they represent over ad hoc methods is simplicity. The Data Flow diagram presents only a network of potential paths—not quantity, frequency, timing, or other parameters. It achieves this in a hierarchical, logical representation that models what the game does, as opposed to how the game accomplishes the task.

The steps for developing Data Flow diagrams for a game are as follows:

1. Determine the external entities and data stores that define the top-level data flow diagram, as in Figure 4.12.
2. Decompose the single-game process into constituent processes, such as player input handling, rendering, sound output, and scoring.
3. Determine the data stores and data flow to/from the identified processes.
4. Evaluate the data flow diagram for consistency and accuracy.
5. Continue decomposing the processes until each processes can be represented by a single function in pseudocode.

Figure 4.14 is an example of a data flow diagram that illustrates the flow of data involved with collecting and processing game scoring data. As with the previously discussed program flow diagrams, each node in the data flow diagram should be decomposed into layers of additional processes to the point that pseudocode is more informative.

The data flow diagram in Figure 4.14 describes data flow in a game that scores player interactions with the game. According to the diagram, the player engages in gameplay, which results in a score that is saved to a local database. The score is compared with others in the database. If it is a new high score, then the server is updated to reflect that. Staff can monitor student progress by requesting reports from the server. A half-dozen data flow diagrams like the one in Figure 4.14 might be sufficient to describe a simple game. In contrast, 20 or more diagrams might be required to define data flow in a multiplayer, online game with 20 levels.

Unified Modeling Language (UML)

The Unified Modeling Language (UML) is a graphical language accepted by the Object Management Group (*www.OMG.org*) as the standard for

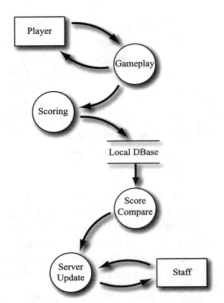

FIGURE 4.14   Data Flow diagram of score data handling.

modeling object-oriented programs. The UML consists of nine types of diagrams that apply in varying degrees to different aspects of designing and documenting game functionality, regardless of whether the programming follows an object-oriented paradigm [Pender03]. The nine types of diagrams and their primary application area are summarized in Table 4.5.

TABLE 4.5   UML Diagram Types and Their Application to Game Programming

UML DIAGRAM TYPE	USED TO DESCRIBE
Activity	Dynamic flow of control from activity to activity
Class	Static structure
Collaboration	Static structure and dynamic behavior
Component	Organization of software components
Deployment	Physical resources
Object	Static structure at a point in time
Package	Static structure organized into related groups (packages)
Sequence	Interactions among classes
State Chart	Dynamic behavior in response to stimuli
Use Case	Functionality provided by the game to users

All of the UML diagram types can be applied to game design. However, the most broadly applicable diagram type for inclusion in the game design document is the use case, because it is not limited to games developed using an object-orientated methodology [Jacobson92]. A Use Case is a model of the interaction between a player and a game that captures some player-visible function and achieves a discrete goal for the player.

It's important to distinguish between the use case model and the UML diagram, which is only one of several approaches to define the model. For example, Use Case models can be defined in text [Cockburn00]. The advantage of graphical Use Cases is simplicity and, with the appropriate tools, speed of documentation. The UML graphing of Use Cases emphasizes the high-level relationships between elements in the model, whereas text Use Cases can address precise specifications suitable for detailed analysis and functional specifications [Gelperin04]. Properly written Use Cases can be less ambiguous than graphical models, but take more time to produce.

In the graphical Use Case model shown in Figure 4.15, the game boundary is indicated by a large rectangle that encompasses labeled ovals that represent functions or services. Players and others who interact with the game, the so-called actors, are drawn as stick figures. Relationships between functions are depicted as lines with arrowheads, labeled as either "uses" or "extends." A "uses" relationship line points to a function that is used by another function. An "extends" relationship line points to a function extended by another function.

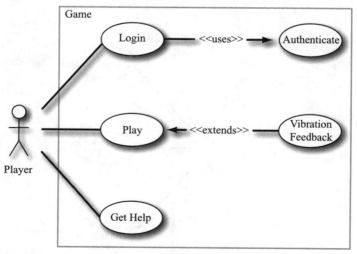

FIGURE 4.15   Use Case diagram. Functions are drawn as ovals, and lines define the relationship between functions.

Use Case modeling has application in user interface design, to define requirements specifications, and to support software design. In this simplistic example of a Use Case model, the player has three options of interacting with the game: login, play, and get help. The login function uses an authentication function within the game. In this player-centric model, the details of the authentication process are undefined. Similarly, the play function is extended or supported by vibration feedback provided by the game. The play function could be extended by other functions and services, such as sound feedback, 3D graphics rendering, and other functions supportive of gameplay. From the player's perspective, the get help function is freestanding in this model. However, a second model could focus on the help function supported by the game, which might be extended by local content as well as hyperlinks to the game vendor's Web site.

It's possible to define fully the range of possible player interactions with a game with UML Use Cases, supplemented with detailed text descriptions when necessary. In defining the Use Cases, consider the duality of serious games as part entertainment, part pedagogy. In the world of entertainment games, use case models that depict player-game interactions may be sufficient for the design document. However, with serious games industry, Use Cases should additionally describe the pedagogical nature of the game.

The Use Case model shown in Figure 4.16 illustrates game interaction in the context of knowledge, skill, and attitude acquisition, from the player's perspective. Instead of focusing on how the player interfaces with the functions supported by the game, the model highlights the educational functions associated with the interactions.

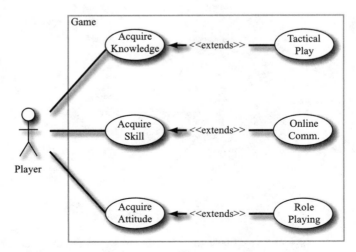

FIGURE 4.16   Use Case model of gameplay in the context of knowledge, skills, and attitudes transferred to the player.

ASSET STANDARDS

Serious games developers rarely have the time, money, or human resources to create every asset from scratch or to create assets that can't be easily repurposed for follow-up projects. Even deep-pocketed entertainment game developers use prefabricated techniques whenever possible. Just as using commercial game engines, middleware, and DLLs is more efficient than developing custom game environments, off-the-shelf texture libraries, sounds, music, and 3D models can minimize artistic staff requirements and time to market.

Developers must attend to both internal and external asset standards. For example, the optimal scale of 3D models and other objects in a game is often defined by the size and complexity of levels supported by the game engine. Without internal standards of scale, the characters created by one artist might not fit through doorways created by another artist in the development shop.

Abiding by external standards is necessary for incorporating content from any of the vast libraries of graphics textures, 3D models, sounds, and other assets available on the Web. Furthermore, armed with knowledge of the standard formats, developers can identify the tools they need to translate assets into a form that they can use in their game. Described below are general issues associated with graphic and sound standards. See Appendix C, "File Formats," for a compendium of standard formats for graphics, animation, video, audio, databases, fonts, and game engines commonly used in game development.

Graphic Formats

The standard formats for graphics, models, and images are established by the most popular authoring tools and, to a lesser extent, the most successful game engines. Because the top 3D authoring tools are *3ds max*, followed by *Maya* and *Softimage XSI* [Thacker05], virtually every lesser-known tool can read files created by one of these tools.

Many of the standard formats have outlived their original applications. For example, the GIF standard was introduced by CompuServe as a lightweight graphic format, suitable for the then popular telephone modem connections to the online service provider. Similarly, if there are any Amigas still running, it isn't likely that they're being used for game development. Nevertheless, the Amiga Interchange File Format (IFF) lives on. In addition, with new graphics applications entering the marketplace every year, the number of graphic file formats continues to increase.

Game engines rarely use the formats created by authoring tools because of size and efficiency constraints. An important step in asset development is packaging assets into a format that is optimized for quick loading during gameplay. Moreover, many of the formats used by the popular game engines, such as the *Unreal* engine, can be read by authoring and editing tools.

In addition to the standard graphics formats used in game design, serious games developers may have to work with file formats native to the serious content domain. For example, a developer using MRI and CT medical images in a medical game might have to work with ACR/NEMA and DICOM formats, two of the more common file formats produced by medical imaging devices.

Medical imaging and biomedical signal formats, examples of which are listed in Appendix C, "File Formats," are typically vendor and modality specific. For example, GE and Siemens, two major competitors in the MRI market, each have proprietary formats. Files from these imaging devices have to be converted to a standard format before they can be incorporated into a game. An alternative, which we have used on several occasions, is to digitize films of ultrasound, CT, or other imaging modality into a TIFF or other standard format with a high-resolution laser scanner. With the appropriate scanner system, the added noise and loss of detail associated with the scanning process is imperceptible [Greenes94].

The medical research community has also developed file standards around popular applications and databases. For example, one of the most often used physiological signal databases is the PhysioBank (*www.physionet.org/physiobank*), an archive of over 1000 recordings of EKGs and other signals [Goldberger00]. Similarly, the bioinformatics community, which is involved in the 3D imaging of proteins and other organic molecules, uses well-documented but nonstandard file formats [Bergeron02]. Information on these file formats, as well as freely available data and rendering programs, is available through the Entrez life sciences search engine (*www.ncbi.nlm.nih.gov/gquery/gquery.fcgi*).

Form

Assets vary in form as well as format. For example, a game engine may require textures in JPG format. However, if the engine uses a binary space partitioning (BSP) algorithm, then the optimal dimensions of the JPG textures will commonly be powers of 2 (for example, 64, 128, or 256 pixels square). JPG textures in a different form may not compile or may not match up properly during gameplay. There is also the issue of dimension. A texture map of 1024 ×512 might work with a game engine, but consume more video RAM than is available without swapping out other textures.

Another common reason for using textures of dimension 2^n is that this form simplifies the creation of mipmaps, which are precalculated, optimized collections of bitmap images that accompany a main texture. Mipmapping (MIP stands for *multim in parvum* or "many in few") helps a

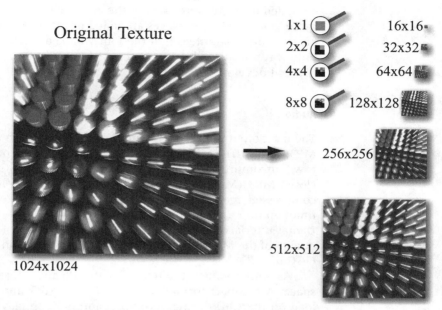

FIGURE 4.17   Mipmapping an original image (left) into consecutively smaller, interpolated images (right) that can be used at runtime for viewing objects at a distance.

texture retain its overall image at different distances or sizes, increases rendering speed, and reduces pixilation artifacts. The process involves taking a texture and breaking it down into pieces half the size of the previous image, recursively. Figure 4.17 illustrates how a 1024 × 1024 pixel image is mipmapped to create versions at 512 × 512, 256 × 256, and so on, to a single pixel.

Instead of interpolating what a texture might look like from a distance at runtime, the game engine can select the appropriate, precomputed mipmap for an object in the game. A higher resolution texture map is used for objects close to the player, and a smaller, lower resolution map is used for the same object viewed at a distance. The goal is to use the smallest texture map possible given the distance that the object is from the viewer. The smaller the texture map, the lower the processing load. Mipmaps are space conservative, in that they increase image storage requirements by only a third.

Fonts

Truetype fonts are standard on the Windows platform, but for fonts to display correctly in a game, they must be either installed in the system or compiled into a resource within the game. This second approach requires more video RAM and places an added burden on the programming and art staff, but guarantees that the font will be available. It may also be the only way a font can be distributed without infringing on the copyright of the font developer.

Audio

The most often used sound formats in game development are WAV, OGG, MP3, and MIDI. Microsoft's Windows Waveform, or WAV, format is a raw, uncompressed format. The open format OGG (Ogg Vorbis) and closed MP3 (Motion Picture Expert Group-1 audio layer 3) formats are compressed, meaning more audio can be crammed on a CD-ROM—sometimes an important factor in game design. The MIDI (Musical Instrument Digital Interface) format is even more space-efficient than MP3, but the quality of the MIDI audio is also significantly less than can be delivered by OGG or MP3.

As with graphics, the tradeoff with the audio formats is speed versus space. A compact format such as OGG or MP3 imposes a considerable load on the CPU during decompression prior to playback. WAV files, in comparison, require ten times more space than an MP3 on a CD-ROM or hard drive, but minimal intervention from the CPU during playback. The length of the audio file is an obvious issue when it comes to space available on a CD-ROM. In addition, the time required to load an audio file into memory and the density of sound data, in terms of the number of channels, resolution, and sampling rate, all contribute to the computational load on the CPU. All of these variables affect audio quality.

Figure 4.18 shows the standard sample rates and resolutions used with mono and stereo audio. Common WAV audio forms are 11 KHz, 8-bit mono; 22 KHz, 16-bit stereo; and 44 KHz, 16-bit stereo. The difference in quality or fidelity of 11 KHz, 8-bit audio versus 44 KHz, 16-bit audio is comparable to going from AM radio to CD sound. The relative cost in memory requirement is significant as well. One second of 8-bit mono WAV audio sampled at 11 KHz requires about 11 KB of space compared with 172 KB for one second of 16-bit stereo audio captured at 44 KHz. One second of near-CD quality stereo MP3 requires only about 16 KB.

The optimum form and format for a serious game depends on the type of audio, the use environment, codec (coder-decoder) license issues, and space limitations. Technically, the sample rate should be about twice the highest frequency of the audio signal sampled. For example, the bandwidth of ordinary (land line) telephone conversations is limited to about 3 KHz, meaning that the standard 11 KHz sampling rate is sufficient to capture most of the information in speech. Furthermore, if the context of the voice is that of a submarine captain yelling out orders to

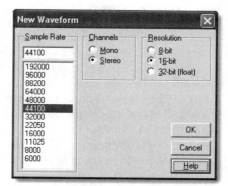

FIGURE 4.18   Dialog box within *Adobe Audition* showing standard audio sample rates, channels, and resolutions.

his crew through the sub's intercom, the added fidelity of a sampling rate above 11 KHz might take away from the realism.

However, sometimes what a game environment brings to the learning process is the surrealistic presentation of ordinary phenomena to enhance learning. The bandwidth of heart sounds as heard through a stethoscope, for example, is only a few hundred Hz. However, to teach medical students how to recognize murmurs and other abnormal heart sounds, realistic sounds aren't necessarily the best teaching materials. Training students with high-fidelity 3D heart sounds created by using digital signal processing techniques on low frequency, monophonic sounds has been shown to enhance a student's ability to discriminate normal from abnormal heart sounds when they're presented without processing [Bergeron91].

The codec licensing issue is significant only if the game engine doesn't support MP3, OGG, or another codec and a third-party DLL or other system add-on must be used to extend the engine. Codecs are not created equal, and while there are many free MP3 and OGG codecs on the Web, the better ones cost money.

COMMUNICATIONS STANDARDS

With the increased prominence of networked gaming, both wired and wireless communications standards are increasingly important in the serious games development arena. The main issues in entertainment game communications are bandwidth and connection quality. Serious games add the constraints of security and privacy, because performance during gameplay may be used to assess the player's knowledge, skills, and attitudes.

Wired Standards

The most important wired communications standards are the various versions of Ethernet. Standard Ethernet provides about 10 Mbps bandwidth. Many users of the Internet approach about one tenth of Ethernet speeds at their desktops through cable modems, DSL, and direct satellite links. The broadband connections that most consumers use to access Xbox live and the Sony network operate at 600 Kbps. More compelling for future multiplayer games are the Fast Ethernet (100 Mbps), Gigabit Ethernet (1 Gbps), and 10 Gigabit Ethernet (10 Gbps) standards, which are available in academia, industry, and the military.

Wireless Standards

The key wireless standards that affect serious games developers are WiFi, Bluetooth, and Cellular communications. However, there are many other wireless standards that may affect opportunities for serious games developers.

Stationary and Mobile Wireless

WiFi: The Wireless Fidelity protocol has three main flavors, referred to as IEEE 802.11a/b/g. The most pervasive is 802.11b, which is popular for fixed wireless systems in homes, airports, hotels, and corner coffee shops. It provides 11 Mbps bandwidth over a 150 foot radius. 802.11a is a higher frequency version of WiFi that provides speeds of up to 54 Mbps over a 100 foot radius. The third protocol, 802.11g, provides the same 54 Mbps bandwidth over the frequency used by 802.11b. The lower frequency of 802.11g means that the range is the same as 802.1b—about 150 feet without a directional antenna system. With a high-gain antenna, a WiFi access point can cover several kilometers [Bergeron01b].

Bluetooth: A short-range (30 feet), low bandwidth (720 Kbps), low-power wireless standard. Bluetooth is used in wireless controllers, handhelds, and some cell phones.

Short-Range PDA

Fast IR: The infrared (IR) standard that supports point-to-point, 1 to 4 Mbps short range (3-6 feet) communications. The Fast IR standard is commonly used with laptops, PDAs, desktop systems, and peripheral devices such as cameras.

Standard IR: Low-speed (75 Kbps), short-range (18 feet) communications for keyboards, mice, multimedia, and game controls.

Cellular First Generation

AMPS (Advanced Mobile Phone System):   The first-generation analog cellular network used throughout the U.S. It supports a data rate of about 2 Kbps—unbearably slow when downloading a game.

Cellular Second Generation

GSM (Global System for Mobile Communications):   The cellular protocol used in over 130 countries, representing over 70 percent of the wireless subscribers worldwide, especially in the EU. GSM has a data throughput of about 16 Kbps.

CDMA (Code Division Multiple Access):   The second-generation communications service in the U.S. that supports a data rate of 14.4 Kbps. The CDMA network, which is used by Sprint and Verizon, has the widest coverage in the U.S.

TDMA (Time Division Multiple Access):   A second-generation wireless standard used with bandwidth up to 19.2 Kbps. Used by Cingular and Nextel.

EVDO (Evolution Data Optimized):   High-speed (400 Kbps) wireless Internet access that rides on top of cellular CDMA service (*www.evdoinfo.com*).

iDEN: The U.S. network built by Nextel and dismantled by Sprint after it acquired Nextel [Strohmeyer05].

D-AMPS (Digital-AMPS or Digital Cellular):   One of the main types of second-generation digital wireless service in the U.S. Bandwidth is about 9.6 Kbps.

iMODE (Interactive Mode):   Nippon Telephone and Telegraph's DoCoMo's second-generation wireless communications protocol that is popular throughout Japan. I-Mode has a maximum speed of 28.8 Kbps.

The naming convention used in some of the above standards is potentially confusing because the network, technology, and standard can be synonymous. For example, CDMA is a standard way of generating a communications signal, and it's also the network used by Sprint and Verizon [Polito05].

Wireless Alliances

Following are examples of the many wireless alliances that have formed in the volatile wireless space that may affect serious games development. Most important are the alliances built around smart phones—phones that can run games and other multimedia.

Bluetooth Alliance: More than 2000 companies that adhere to the Bluetooth wireless standard (*www.bluetooth.org*)

Ericsson/Sony: A joint program between wireless handset designer Ericsson and consumer electronics designer and developer Sony (*www.sonyericsson.com*)

Symbian Alliance: The partnership of Ericsson, Motorola, Nokia, Matsushita Communication Industries, and Psion Symbian that supplies the operating system for 87 percent of the smart phone market [Strohmeyer05] (*www.symbian.org*)

Sony/NTT DoCoMo: An alliance that provides video games over wireless Internet phones through a link-up to the PlayStation 2 (*www.nttdocomo.com*)

Wireless alliances may prove central to cell phone game distribution in the U.S. if the pattern set by NTT DoCoMo is followed. For now, independent cell phone game publishers such as Yahoo Mobile, Jamdat, and Gameloft provide the majority of cell phone games.

INTEROPERABILITY

Developing simulations, serious games, and other forms of training in a way that enables interoperability is one means of increasing the depth and scope of instructional materials available to learners while reducing overall development costs and time. Interoperability, the ability of computers and applications to communicate and share resources in a heterogeneous environment, is dependent on standards.

In the mid-1990s, the Defense Modeling and Simulation Office (DMSO) introduced High Level Architecture (HLA), an architecture standard for simulation reuse and interoperability [DMSO05]. The standard was developed in response to the large numbers of different types of simulations developed and maintained by the DOD. DARWARS, a more recent initiative, is an interoperability standard for training systems that is designed to leverage the connectivity of the Internet [DARWARS05]. These and several other interoperability standards—some overlapping and others independent—often affect design and development of serious games for the military.

Just as numerous standards complicate the development of serious games on cell phones, the lack of a universal interoperability standard for simulations and serious games often hampers development of serious games for the military. The problem extends to other disciplines as well. For example, there have been several failed attempts at defining standards for the interoperability of simulations in biology and medicine [Wastney99]. One of the most recent interoperability initiatives in medicine is the work by MedBiquitous (*www.MedBiq.org*) a standards organization dedicated to advancing healthcare education.

To appreciate the potential of a cross-discipline, universal standard for the interoperability of simulations and simulation-based serious games, consider the following scenario. A medical physiologist at Stanford develops a detailed, verified model of the endocrine system. Another physiologist at the University of Michigan develops a serious game around a simulation of energy depletion in skeletal muscle with exertion. Later, a psychiatrist skilled in simulation technology connects to both systems over the Internet and uses the output from both systems to create a simulation of fatigue due to mental and physical stress. A developer in Florida who is working on a serious military game needs to factor in fatigue in simulating a soldier's speed and agility, aiming accuracy, and decision making. While there is more to repurposing models and simulations than interoperability, such as validating the models for the new use, the potential benefits are enormous.

Examples of organizations working on interoperability standards relevant to serious games development include the following:

- Advanced Distributed Learning (ADL) Initiative
- Aviation Industry CBT Committee (AICC)
- Coalition for Networked Information (CNI)
- Institute of Electrical and Electronics Engineers (IEEE)
- Instructional Management System (IMS) Global Learning Consortium
- International Organization for Standardization (ISO)
- Multimedia Educational Resource for Learning and Online Teaching (MERLOT)
- Schools Interoperability Framework (SIF)

These organizations and coalitions vary in focus and degree of formality. Most suggest standards that might be used by their membership community, although some, like the ADL Initiative, might be mandated by a military contractor. The organizations are described briefly in the following sections.

Advanced Distributed Learning (ADL) Initiative

The U.S. military's latest foray into interoperability standards, the Advanced Distributed Learning (ADL) Initiative, was launched by the Department of Defense and the White House Office of Science and Technology Policy [Thropp04]. The most significant standards that have been generated by the ADL initiative relevant to serious games development are SCORM and OPEL.

The SCORM (Sharable Content Object Reference Model) standard is intended to provide interoperability and repurposeability of Web-based learning content. The standard defines sharable content objects (SCOs) that can be assembled from across the Web in real-time, on demand, to provide learning anytime, anywhere [Thropp04]. Content that is SCORM-compliant can be plugged in to other SCORM-compliant applications with the aid of a Learning Management Systems (LMS). In this way, the ADL attempts to address the common problem of disposable, insular course-ware that is impossible to repurpose, modify, or maintain.

The SCORM is significant to the serious games development community in that eLearning content developed for the military often must be SCORM compliant. Because the military represents a huge market for eLearning, many vendors of generic Web development tools, such as Macromedia, offer products that can generate SCORM-compliant course-ware. In addition, because of the momentum of the military eLearning establishment, developers are frequently required to develop online material in compliance with SCORM in other industries, including healthcare [Cohen05].

The SCORM, first introduced in 2000, is updated periodically. However, the latest official standard, SCORM 2004, doesn't address gaming technologies. Interoperability of games is addressed in the evolving OPEL (Open Platform for ELearning) standard. OPEL, which was unveiled at the 2005 Games Developers Conference [ReganBray05], handles the integration of games with SCORM and Learning Management Systems.

Referring to the functional architecture of OPEL in Figure 4.19, a learner is involved in didactic training using courseware assembled from sharable content objects by a Learning Management System (LMS). At some point in the training, the courseware requests a game-based learning experience to supplement the didactic content. The LMS identifies the most appropriate game and presents it to the learner. At the end of the learner's experience with the game, the game reports the assessment of the player to the LMS.

This seamless integration of a game with didactic content is possible because the games available on the Internet first register with the brokering LMS, which stores information about the objectives, activities, and tasks associated with each game. The *objective* of one game may be to learn skeletal anatomy, through first-person shooter *activities*, with *tasks* such as shooting bones according to a point system. The LMS can differentiate between multiple games associated with the same objectives, activities, and tasks by evaluating the numerical values associated with each of the three variables. For example, the objective of one game may be to learn skeletal anatomy, while that of another might be to learn skeletal and muscular anatomy. The first game would have a higher objective score in the area of skeletal anatomy.

In theory, OPEL will make it possible for a learner to retrieve and interact with a serious game designed to cover a given topic, regardless of

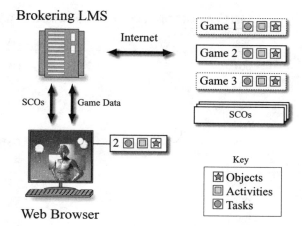

FIGURE 4.19   OPEL functional architecture for integrating games with SCORM and Learning Management Systems.

the game's location, underlying language, or authorship. For more information on the evolving OPEL standard, SCORM, and related initiatives, see the ADL Web site (*www.adlnet.org*).

Aviation Industry CBT Committee (AICC)

The AICC was one of the first organizations to recognize and promote the need for standards in the development, delivery, and evaluation of computer-based teaching (CBT) and related training technologies. Although not specifically created to support serious games standards, the AICC's guidelines for CBT development are broad enough and industry-independent enough to encompass games development. In this regard, the AICC should be considered an integral component of other standards organizations discussed here, including the ADL, IEEE, and IMS.

The AICC maintains a set of nine technical guidelines known as AGR's (AICC Guidelines & Recommendations), in the form of white papers and technical documents on their Web site, *www.aicc.org*. The AGR's, listed in Table 4.6, pertain to any form of computer-mediated instruction, including serious games. For example, AGR-002 describes delivery platform standards in terms of video RAM, operating system, clock speed, and audio capabilities, and AGR-003 provides guidelines for interoperability of digital audio on various hardware platforms. Some of the recommendations are dated, and refer to technologies such as videodisk players and video overlay cards.

TABLE 4.6   AICC Guidelines and Recommendations Topics

AGR	DESCRIPTION
001	Listing of AGR's
002	Courseware Delivery Stations
003	Digital Audio
004	Operating/Windowing Systems
005	CBT Peripheral Devices
006	File-Based CMI Systems
007	Courseware Interchange
008	Digital Video
009	Icon Standards: User Interface
010	Web-Based CMI Systems

From the serious games development perspective, the two most important AGRs deal with computer-managed instruction (CMI) over networks. AGR-006 addresses interoperability of LAN-based CBT courseware from multiple vendors. The goal is to enable a given CMI system to manage CBT lessons from different origins. It also includes the ability for a given CBT lesson to exchange data with different CMI systems. AGR-010 addresses the interoperability of Web-based CBT courseware and CMI systems.

A game can be self-tested and marketed as "Designed to AICC Guidelines," which suggests that it adheres to the full list of AGR's. The only official measure of AGR compliance, "AICC Certified," requires testing by an AICC-authorized Independent Test Lab, such as the U.S. Naval Undersea Warfare Center at Keyport, Washington, or the University of New Mexico, College of Education. AICC Certification addresses only AGR-006 and AGR-010, which define the communications between CMI systems and CBT courseware.

Coalition for Networked Information (CNI)

The Coalition for Networked Information (CNI) is focused on promoting the use of networked information technology in higher education. Universities and libraries make up the bulk of membership, with representatives from publishing, network and telecommunications, and information technology organizations. In addition to developing and managing networked information content, CNI is engaged in the development and deployment of standards and infrastructure components in order to enable the discovery, use, and management of networked information. For more information on architectural and standards frameworks under development to facilitate integration and interoperation, see the CNI Web site, *www.cni.org.*

Institute of Electrical and Electronics Engineers (IEEE)

The IEEE Learning Technology Standards Committee (LTSC), also referred to as the IEEE P1484, is chartered by the IEEE Computer Society Standards Activity Board to develop accredited technical standards, recommended practices, and guides for learning technology of all types. The LTSC coordinates with other organizations that produce specifications and standards for learning technology.

In addition, the LTSC includes working groups in several areas applicable to serious games development, including software architecture and reference models, digital rights, computer managed instruction, learning-object metadata, and competency definitions. For example, the purpose of the competency definitions working group is to define a universally acceptable Competency Definition model to allow the creation, exchange, and reuse of Competency Definition in Learning Management Systems. The standard is needed because of the many definitions of the term *learning objective* and the lack of agreement about how those definitions can be used to define reusable data models. More information on the working groups is available through the LTSC Web site (*ltsc.ieee.org*).

Instructional Management System (IMS) Global Learning Consortium

The IMS Global Learning Consortium, Inc., is nonprofit consortium of hardware and software vendors, educational institutions, publishers, government agencies, systems integrators, and multimedia content providers concerned with interoperability and reuse of eLearning materials. IMS develops and promotes the adoption of open technical specifications for interoperable learning technology and makes the specifications available to the public at no charge.

Some specifications, such as the *IMS Question and Test Interoperability Implementation Guide*, directly address the challenges of using games in learning environment. This and dozens of other freely downloadable specifications documents, on topics ranging from competency definitions to learning design, are available through the IMS Web site (*www.imsglobal.org*).

International Organization for Standardization (ISO)

The International Organization for Standardization (ISO), in conjunction with the International Electrotechnical Commission (IEC), develops international standards for information technology for learning, education, and training (ITLET). The subcommittee of the two organizations that is formally referred to as ISO/IEC JTC1 SC36 is concerned with standardization in the field of information technologies for learning, education, and training to support individuals, groups, or organizations, and to enable interoperability and reusability of resources and tools.

Under the umbrella of SC 36 are seven working groups, including WG2—Collaborative Technology, WG3—Learner Information, and WG4—Management and Delivery of Learning, Education, and Training. The standards from these working groups address serious games development on platforms from stand-alone PCs to networked workstations running high-fidelity simulators and trainers (serious games). For more information, see the JTC1 Web site (*jtc1sc36.org*).

Multimedia Educational Resource for Learning and Online Teaching (MERLOT)

The Multimedia Educational Resource for Learning and Online Teaching (MERLOT) is a membership organization of educators involved in several initiatives focused on online learning materials in higher education. The most relevant to serious games developers is a technology initiative with infrastructure standards, technology tools, and software development policies. The technology infrastructure standards on the software development process, which emphasize the traditional software development pipeline, are available for free download at *www.merlot.org*.

Schools Interoperability Framework (SIF)

The Schools Interoperability Framework (SIF) is a nonprofit industry initiative to develop an open specification for ensuring that K–12 instructional and administrative software applications from different companies can share information. The primary standards publication of the SIF, the *SIF Implementation Specification*, covers interoperability in areas ranging from food services and financial management to instructional services. The specifications for instructional services may be of use to serious games developers focusing on the K–12 market. For more information on the specification, see the SIF Web site, *www.sifinfo.org*.

SUMMARY

Game development is feasible largely because of the standards that temporarily stabilize hardware platforms, development tools, and asset formats, and that provide for communications and interoperability. Platform standards for consoles, PCs, and handhelds, while constantly evolving, are more universally accepted than are the myriad cell phone standards. As a result, even though the base of cell phone platforms is expanding, developing for multiple standards is prohibitively expensive for many developers.

Game standards, including genre definitions and the ESRB rating system, are useful for marketing purposes for big-budget serious games destined for commercial distribution. Game design notation standards are useful in managing the complexity of game design by establishing an unambiguous means of communications. Data Flow diagrams are useful in defining a game in terms of processes that act on input data and produce output data. The Use Case model, which shows the interaction between a player and a game and is commonly expressed as a Unified Modeling Language (UML) diagram, is useful in designing the user interface, in defining a requirements specification, and in overall software design.

Asset standards support the economical repurposing and sharing of graphics, sounds, 3D models, fonts, and other multimedia. Communications standards, both wired and wireless, are especially important in increasingly popular networked gaming.

Interoperability standards initiatives, such as DARWARS and SCORM, Although not universally accepted, can have a serious impact serious games development when compliance is mandatory. Eventually, these and other interoperability standards should evolve to a level that enables developers to create serious games more quickly and easily and reduce needless duplication of effort.

REFERENCES

[Aktas87] Aktas, A. Z., *Structured Analysis and Design of Information Systems*. Prentice-Hall, Inc., 1987.

[Baer98] Baer, Rebecca, "Sun Announces Key Consumer Technology to Bring the Power of the JAVA platform to Auto, TV and Phone Markets." Sun Microsystems. 1998. *www.sun.com/smi/Press/sunflash/1998-03/sunflash.980324.14.html*, accessed September 16, 2005.

[Bapco04] "BAPCo® Releases SYSmark® 2004." BAPCo. 2004. *www.bapco.com*, accessed May 30, 2005.

[Bell04] Bell, Ian, "Windows CE Surpassed Palm OS Shipments." Designtechnica News. 2004. *news.designtechnica.com/article5920.html*, accessed June 12, 2005.

[Bergeron91] Bergeron, B., The Effects of Stereophonic Priming on the Development of Auscultatory Pattern Recognition Skills. *Collegiate Microcomputer* (January 1991): pp. 25–35.

[Bergeron01a] Bergeron, B., *The Wireless Web: How to Develop a Winning Wireless Strategy*. McGraw-Hill, 2001.

[Bergeron01b] Bergeron, B., *The Hitchhikers Guide to the Wireless Web*. McGraw-Hill, 2001.

[Bergeron02] Bergeron, B., *Bioinformatics Computing*. Prentice-Hall, 2003.

[BergeronBlander02] Bergeron, B., and Jeff Blander, *Business Expectations: Are You Using Technology to its Fullest?* John Wiley & Sons, 2002.

[CNET05] CNET, CNET Reviews. CNET. 2005. *reviews.cnet.com.*, accessed May 26, 2005.

[CoadYourdon90] Coad, Peter, and Edward Yourdon, *Object Oriented Analysis*. Prentice Hall PTR, 1990.

[Cockburn00] Cockburn, Alistare, *Writing Effective Use Cases*. Addison-Wesley, 2000.

[Cogley05] Cogley, V., Clash of the Titans: ATI & NVIDIA Put Their Newest Horses on the Track. PC Modder. Reference Series 2(2005): pp. 99–105.

[Cohen05] Cohen, Cheryl, SCORM Unplugged. 2005. *meld.medbiq.org/primers/SCORM_primer_cohen.htm*, accessed June 9, 2005.

[DARWARS05] DARWARS, Frequently Asked Questions. DARWARS. 2005. *www.darwars.com*, accessed September 16, 2005.

[DMSO05] DMSO, High Level Architecture. Defense Modeling and Simulation Office. 2005. *www.dmso.mil/public/transition/hla*, accessed September 17, 2005.

[ESRB05] ESRB, ESRB Rating System. 2005. *www.esrb.org*, accessed April 9, 2005.

[GaneSarson77] Gane, Christopher, and Trish, Sarson, *Structured Systems Analysis: Tools and Techniques*. IST, Inc., 1977.

[Gelperin04] Gelperin, David, *Methods & Tools* (Spring 2004): pp. 8–24.

[Greenes94] Greenes, Robert, Bryan Bergeron, et al., The American Board of Radiology's Self-Evaluation Workstation Project. *SCAR '94* (1994): pp. 424–29.

[Goldberger00] Goldberger, A., L. Amaral, et al., PhysioBank, PhysioToolkit, and PhysioNet: Components of a New Research Resource for Complex Physiologic Signals. "*Circulation* 23(2000): pp. e215–220.

[Harris05] Harris, Will, "Graphics Card Workshop." *PCExtreme* (May 2005).

[ICRA05] ICRA, ICRA Rating System. 2005. *www.icra.org*, accessed September 16, 2005.

[Jacobson92] Jacobson, Ivar, Christenson, M., et al., *Object-Oriented Software Engineering: A Use Case Driven Approach*. Addison-Wesley, 1992.

[Machrone01] Machrone, Bill, Dell Dimension 4100. 2001. *www.pcmag.com/article2/0, 1759,69000,00.asp*, accessed January 13, 2005.

[MaximumPC03] MaximumPC, Maximum PC Benchmarks Effective December 2003. 2003. *www.maximumpc.com/features/reprint_2001-08-16.html*, accessed May 30, 2005.

[Microsoft05] Microsoft, Xbox 360 Fact Sheet. Microsoft. 2005, accessed September 10, 2005.

[NVIDIA05] NVIDIA, NVIDIA GeForce 6 Series. 2005. *www.nzone.com/page/nzone_section_hardware.html*, accessed May 30, 2005.

[PalmSource05] PalmSource, Licensees. PalmSource. 2005. *www.palmsource.com*, accessed June 4, 2005.

[Pender03] Pender, Tom, *UML Bible*. John Wiley, 2003.

[Polito05] Polito, Julie, "Will The Real Verizon Guy Please Stand Up? *Cell Phone Handbook* (Spring 2005): p. 10.

[ReganBray05] Regan, Damon, and Christopher Bray, OPEL: Integrating Games with SCORM and Learning Management Systems. 2005 Game Developers Conference (2005).

[Strohmeyer05] Strohmeyer, Robert, "Merge and Purge: The Spring and Nextel Combination Spell Doom for Nextel's Old Wireless Network. *Cell Phone Handbook* (Spring 2005): p. 13.

[StrohmeyerGinther05] Strohmeyer, Robert, and Lisa Ginther, "Battle of the Phone Operating System." *Cell Phone Handbook* (Spring 2005): p. 12.

[Tapwave05] Tapwave, Zodiac—The Palm Powered Multimedia Handheld. 2005. *www.tapwave.com*, accessed July 30, 2005.

[Thacker05] Thacker, Jim, "Winning the Next Generation Game." *3D World* (June 2005): pp. 16–17.

[Thropp04] Author, Sharable Content Object Reference Model (SCORM®) Sequencing and Navigation Version 1.3, edited by S./E. Thropp, Advanced Distributed Learning (ADL), 2004.

[UngSmith05] Ung, Gordon, Will Smith, "Xbox 360s Hardware Horsepower." *Official Xbox Magazine* (July 2005): pp. 18–20.

[Wastney99] Wastney, Meryl, Patterson Blossom, et al., *Investigating Biological Systems Using Modeling.* Academic Press, 1999.

[WingfieldClark05] Wingfield, Nick, and Don Clark, "With Intel Inside Apple, Macs May Be Faster, Smaller." *The Wall Street Journal* (June 7, 2005): pp. B1–7.

BEST PRACTICES

In This Chapter

- User interface design
- Programming
- Working with assets
- Actors and level design
- Archiving
- Assessment

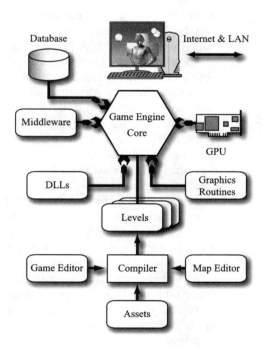

INTRODUCTION

Anyone who reads the regular postmortems section in *Game Developer* magazine comes to appreciate the risks inherent in the art of game development. Best practices, the process equivalents of standards, have evolved from the written and oral accounts of the successes and failures of game developers. Following best practices—heuristics of what has been shown to work in the past—won't guarantee success. However, developers who ignore them are destined to repeat the failures of those who have gone before them.

This chapter provides an overview of best practices that apply to serious games development, from how to approach user interface design and game programming to the best methods of defining the logic of a level. Best practices should be reflected in the game design document, which is discussed in Chapter 8, "Serious Games Design."

USER INTERFACE

The user interface is the boundary at which form and function either coalesce to provide phenomenal gameplay or collide and create confusion. When teamed with exceptional graphics, sounds, physics, and AI, a great user interface can propel an entertainment game to AAA status or a serious game designed as an employee training tool to a favorite pastime. Conversely, a game with the best middleware and engaging plotline that runs on a hot platform but with a poor interface will languish on the shelves.

A popular misconception is that serious games are little more than veneer glued over the mathematical models, images, and text that constitute the serious content. Although lesser serious games have been created using this cosmetic approach to development, the most successful games feature user interfaces that are created with the user as well as the serious content in mind [BergeronRouse92]. As illustrated by the game development pipeline, solution design normally precedes the coding and implementation phase of development. Furthermore, coding and implementation (including interface design) typically occur in parallel.

Game user interface design is an art and science rooted in military aviation and missile systems. The first commercial computer to use a graphical user interface (GUI) with the familiar desktop-with-icons metaphor and a mouse, the Xerox Star, was a workhorse of the U.S. Military for missile testing in the Pacific in the mid-1980s. Instead of plotting missile trajectory with a series of X's on a character-based display, the Star could plot flight paths as continuous arcs with a resolution based on individual pixels. Although the Star was a commercial failure, it inspired the GUI used on the Apple Lisa, the predecessor of the Macintosh OS and Windows.

In designing the Lisa interface, Apple Computer relied on the best interface experts in Silicon Valley at the time—military avionics interface designers [Idbias05]. Thanks to efforts by Apple's Human Interface Group and the initially closed "Certified Apple Developer" program, developers were strongly encouraged to follow best practice interface designs, as dictated by Apple. The constraints were arduous to game developers and others used to working in a free, open environment. From the user perspective, the constraints resulted in applications that acted very much the same, regardless of the application area. Once users learned one application, they could pick up any other Macintosh program and within minutes begin work.

Although there are no formal regulations on game interface designs, game developers have heuristics about what works, and what doesn't, thanks to a body of knowledge built up over the past two decades through organizations such as CHI and events such as Siggraph. It doesn't take a user interface guru to recognize when a physical or graphical interface design element doesn't work—but it usually requires a professional to know exactly how to fix a poorly designed interface.

One of the major challenges of designing good user interfaces is addressing differences in player cognitive styles, preconceptions, and gaming experiences. Whereas the typical 18-year-old college student will likely pick up a game controller and begin working with a new game in a few seconds, a 55-year-old business executive might never get the hang of a controller.

Another challenge is overcoming the interface biases that different members of the game development team bring to the interface design process. This difference in perspectives is illustrated in Figure 5.1, which shows the type of interface typically used by programmers, artists, and players. Programmers design and manipulate the AI, physics, and other behaviors of a game through a dry text-based interface, typified by the *Microsoft C++.net* environment. In this world, the addition of colored fonts or a new menu bar is a major change worthy of a news release. Artists, in contrast, work with graphical environments, such as *GameSpace or 3DStudio*, adjusting variables such as color, texture, and polygon count. What the user sees and interacts with, in this example a screen from *Microsoft Flight Simulator*, reflects choices made by programmers and artists.

Because the interfaces used by artists tend to be highly graphical, it might seem that user interface design should be left to the artists in the development group. However, the user interface is much more than the graphics on a screen. The principles of good game user interface design are embodied in the concept of an interface hierarchy between the CPU and the player, as shown in Figure 5.2. In this model, the simplest, most primitive interface is the physical interface, and the most advanced is an emotionally intelligent interface, in which the interface not only establishes an emotional bond with the player, but does so in a way that respects the

FIGURE 5.1 The *Microsoft Visual C++.net* interface for programmers (left), *GameSpace 3D* modeler interface for artists (right), and *Microsoft Flight Simulator* interface for players (center).

player's intelligence, time and needs [Bergeron01]. The six tiers of the interface hierarchy are described below.

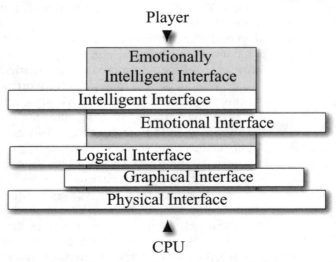

FIGURE 5.2 User interface hierarchy. Auditory and tactile interfaces are considered part of the physical interface.

Physical Interface

The physical interface is the hardware communications channel that carries the player's physical actions and the game's feedback. The most common hardware configuration is a keyboard and mouse, often supplemented with a controller, but the possibilities range from a keypad, trackball, stylus, or microphone, to a variety of sensors, a touch screen or pad, or a video camera (see Table 5.1). Game feedback can come from LEDs, LCD panels, haptic or vibration-equipped controllers, and the hardware platform's audio system. The physical interface defines the form, and therefore limits the functionality, of a gaming system. For example, the pressure-sensitive pad that provides the main physical interface to the exergame *Dance Dance Revolution* defines the range of moves available to players. A cumbersome, overly complex physical interface will ruin gameplay, regardless of the functionality it provides.

TABLE 5.1   Physical Interface Input and Output Devices and Interface Design Issues

INPUT/OUTPUT DEVICE	PHYSICAL INTERFACE ISSUE
Controller	Configuration, responsiveness, and provision for vibration feedback
Haptics	Calibration and software drivers
Indicators (e.g., LEDs)	Clarity of meaning, resolution, visibility
Keyboard	Alternative layouts, integrated trackball, function keys
Monitor	Resolution, color accuracy, and latency
Mouse/Trackball	Ergonomics, configuration, handedness
Pressure Sensitive Tablets or Pads	Ergonomics and configuration
Sensors (e.g., Temperature, Direction)	Sensitivity, accuracy, repeatability, and resolution
Speakers/Headphones	Accuracy and fidelity of sound reproduction
Video Camera	Resolution, sensitivity

Each of the physical input/output devices noted in Table 5.1 is associated with issues that may affect gameplay. As noted in the discussion of the heart auscultation game HeartLab, the fidelity and accuracy of speakers and headphones may be critical if a game is dependent on players differentiating between subtle sounds. With keyboards, the primary interface issue is mapping to support both left and right handed gameplay.

The most common challenge at the physical interface level of game design is controller mapping (see Figure 5.3), because players often have a favorite layout and model of controller and are averse to playing games that don't support their mapping. However, sometimes a particular mapping is impossible, given differences in controller design. For example, some controllers have two thumb-operated analog sticks and other models have only one, and some models have extra buttons.

Because the controller mapping can adversely affect gameplay, a best practice for developers is to offer players a means of customizing the mapping to suit their needs. Testing a game with a variety of controllers before it ships can pinpoint ergonomic issues related to different interaction styles, such as "sloppy thumbs," that might require changes in the game code [West05]. Furthermore, because some gamepads lack vibration feedback, the user interface should never rely on vibration feedback alone to signal an event to the player.

FIGURE 5.3   The challenge of game controller mapping is compounded by the wide range of controllers available for the PC.

For game developers who work with embedded computer systems, such as mannequins or military equipment instrumented with microcontrollers or handheld PCs, input sensors are a major focus. Off-the-shelf sensors for temperature, humidity, direction, acceleration, light, sound, distance, vibration, pressure, and magnetic flux vary in sensitivity, accuracy, repeatability, and resolution. Furthermore, communicating the sensor values to the player is often a challenge, especially if the physical interface is used to communicate directly with the player. The use of sounds, light, and vibration feedback has to be thought through carefully and mapped to the player's expectations. For example, in an instrumented mannequin used to teach the placement of a laryngoscope—an illuminated, stainless steel blade used to open the airway for insertion of a breathing tube prior to surgery—a sound warning of excessive pressure on the dentures is more appropriate and useful than a flashing light because the operator's eyes should be focused on the mannequin's throat.

Graphical Interface

The graphical interface—what some developers consider *the* interface—is the collections of indicators, menus, gauges, and controls drawn on the screen that map the player's actions to the physical interface. Text is also considered an element of a graphical interface.

A common metaphor used in military serious games is the heads up display (HUD), as shown in Figure 5.4. Heads up displays have obvious applicability in first person shooters, where there isn't time to click on icons or on-screen buttons to uncover information. All information necessary for the player's survival must be visible at all times. Heads up displays can be used with any game genre. Some game designs call for a different HUD with each level, while other designs rely on a single HUD throughout the game.

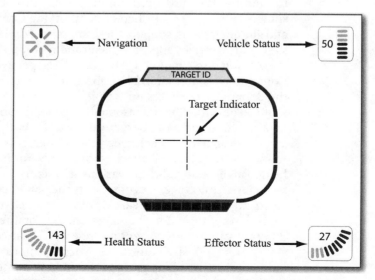

FIGURE 5.4   Heads Up Display (HUD) with navigation aid, status information, and targeting crosshairs.

The definition of a heads up display for a game design document is more than a sketch of an oval with cross hairs in the center. A complete description of a HUD includes the following:

Worldview: The player's perspective in various modes of travel, such as first person in walk mode and first or third person in flight mode.

Status information: Indicators such as status of player health, fuel level for vehicles, ammunition supply for weapons, or time remaining to complete the level.

Effector selection: An indication of the weapons, instruments, and other effectors selected by the player. The selection might be highlighted by an audible signal, changes in the target indicator, part of the effector protruding into the visual field, or the appearance/disappearance of an icon in the heads up display.

Navigation aids: Information such as compass heading, radio beacon, locator radar, and proximity maps.

Target indicators: Crosshairs and other target indicators associated with effectors. Target indicators may signify the point of entry of a hypodermic needle, the location of an item on a map, or the focal point of a weapon.

The parameters used to define a HUD, as well as their location and form on the screen, are game dependent. One of the best examples of a context-specific HUD in a serious game is provided by *Ben's Game*, from the Greater Bay Area Make-A-Wish Foundation (*www.makewish.org*). The status information for ammunition level, attitude, and health—which is shown in Figure 2.9 of Chapter 2, "Working Context"—is age-appropriate and the metaphors support the gameplay. For example, the ammunition supply for weapons appear as medications, as opposed to bullets or missiles.

As noted in Chapter 1, "Historical Perspective," a characteristic of serious games is that alternative interfaces are common. A best practice in the design of interfaces for serious games is to emphasize mental models that learners may have reasonably developed on their own or have been exposed to in the past [BergeronRouse92]. For example, an interface for a game designed to teach mechanical engineers the biomechanics of the human heart might use mechanical pumps for heart chambers, valves for heart valves, and tubes of various diameters to represent differences in peripheral resistance. In contrast, if the same game were earmarked for electrical engineer, the heart would be modeled from current or voltage sources, capacitors for chambers, diodes for the valves, and resistors of different values to represent peripheral resistance.

Custom physical interfaces, such as mock surgical instruments or mannequins, are obvious examples of how unique interfaces can be used to create engaging serious games. More challenging is devising interfaces that effectively transform abstract logical concepts into concrete spatial relationships or numerical quantities.

Shown if Figure 5.5 is a close-up of an on-screen control for ordering tests within a patient simulator designed for medical students. Instead of presenting plain check box or radio button options for test, information is provided on the relative value of each test in terms of sensitivity and specificity.

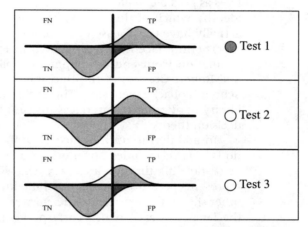

FIGURE 5.5   Selection box that quantifies the abstract concepts of sensitivity and specificity associated with available clinical tests within a patient simulation. Test result distributions are for diseased (top) and normal (bottom) patients are shown for each test. FN—False Negative; TP—True Positive; TN—True Negative; FP—False Positive.

For each test, the distribution of diseased patients is along the top and that of the normal patients is along the bottom. The decision threshold is represented by the vertical bar that cuts through both distributions. The location of the two distributions relative to each other and to the decision threshold is test-dependent.

It's important to note that this interface design assumes students have been exposed to the concepts of test sensitivity, specificity, false positives and false negatives in their classes in biostatistics. The sensitivity of a test is defined by the number of true positives (TP) divided by the number of true positives plus true negatives (TN). The more sensitive the test, the more patients with a disease test positive. Test 1 in Figure 5.5 is the most sensitive, because the area under the true positive (TP) part of the graph is larger than that of the false negative (FN), relative to the other tests.

The specificity of a test is defined by the number of true negatives (TN) divided by the number of true negative plus the number of false positives (FP). According to Figure 5.5, the specificity for each test is identical. Assuming costs, side effects, turn-around time, and other factors are equal, Test 1 is the superior test because it has the greatest sensitivity. In practice, clinical tests vary considerably in selectivity, specificity, and cost. Inexpensive tests with high sensitivity and low specificity are used for screening purposes because it's important to identify as many true positives as possible. Follow-up tests typically have much greater specificity to identify which of the patients that tested positive for the screening test actually have the disease or condition.

The interface metaphor shown in Figure 5.5 is based on the *SimKit* simulation front-end development toolbox developed by Mike Pollack and Robert Greenes of the Decision Systems Group at Harvard Medical School [PollackGreenes85]. The goal in developing *SimKit* was to create a library of alternative interfaces for simulations that relied concepts from decision theory.

In addition to an interface metaphor based on population distributions, *SimKit* includes an interface metaphor based on a ray tracing of light traveling through a convex lens. An object on one side of the lens represents pretest probability and the inverted image of the object on the other side of the lens represents posttest probability. Students can change the lens geometry, which corresponds to test sensitivity and specificity, and observe the size of the projected image, which corresponds to posttest probability [PollackGreenes86]. SimKit can be used to display the same concepts as a ladder diagram or as a flowchart.

Logical Interface

The logical interface level deals with the rules, guidelines, and standards of interface behavior, such as how a game responds to a button pressed on the controller in different contexts. Because the logical interface helps define player expectations, it is critical in minimizing possible player frustration. As shown in Figure 5.2, the logical interface of a game may communicate directly with the physical interface without going through a graphical interface. A game based on music and sound, but without a graphical component, or one that uses a string of LEDs instead of a bitmapped display, may have a logical interface.

A spreadsheet or word processing program may have a perfectly logical interface, but without higher-level interface components, it would be difficult to engage the player or support a fun interaction. Similarly, mathematical models and simulations that are simply outfitted with a graphical interface often fail to constitute a game.

Emotional Interface

The emotional interface, which is intended to elicit emotions in the player, marks the transition from simulations and simple quizzes to full-fledged games. All good games include the basic components of an emotional interface. There must be some element of risk—something unlikely in a pure simulation or spreadsheet. Furthermore, there must be a prospect, but not necessarily certainty, of a physical or virtual reward. Moreover, the process of interaction and/or the end point of the game must elicit some form of emotion in the player. For example, consider the backstory to *Tetris Worlds* (THQ), in which one of the goals is to rescue a species called Minos. The storyline is at least an attempt to motivate players with the prospect of reward beyond the personal satisfaction of winning a level.

Referring to the interface layers in Figure 5.2, an emotional interface can build on logical and/or graphical interfaces, or communicate directly with the physical layer. In addition, the degree to which graphics are incorporated into a game with an emotional interface can vary considerably. The original online role playing game *Dungeons and Dragons* is an example of a successful game with an emotional interface composed of simple text on an otherwise blank screen. An instrumented mannequin used to train medics and other first responders may have an emotional interface by virtue of its lifelike features.

Intelligent Interface

The intelligent interface level is primarily concerned with providing the game with adaptability through a variety of pattern recognition techniques. Intelligence, after all, is simply the ability to adapt or change with experience. A game with an intelligent or adaptive interface necessarily incorporates elements of an emotional interface. However, a nongame application with an intelligent interface needn't have emotional interface components, but may communicate directly to a logical interface. In other words, providing nonplayer characters with behaviors through an AI engine doesn't guarantee players will respond emotionally the characters or find the interaction engaging.

One of the most important intelligent interfaces in serious games design is one that relies on an Intelligent Tutoring System for progression and content selection. The interface may be character-oriented, as in a patient simulation in which nonplayer characters are injured and must be cared for. The intelligence can also be directed at dynamically altering the difficulty of the challenges presented to the player through the game environment.

An example of an intelligent interface for serious game is the interface to the DARWARS Tactical Language Training System, designed to train soldiers in the Arabic language [Johnson04]. In addition to realistic context-specific scenarios, such as meeting a Lebanese man at a cafe, the system provides individualized language coaching. The American Association of Artificial Intelligence (AAAI) also maintains a list of military AI projects, including those that make use of intelligent tutoring at *www.aaai.org/AITopics/html/military.html*.

Emotionally Intelligent Interface

An emotionally intelligent game interface is designed to modify player behavior by forming a bond, such as trust, between the game and the player. A player may learn to trust a nonplayer character, for example, whether that character is computer-generated or an avatar of another online player.

A game with a fully emotionally intelligent interface would not only express emotions, but it would know how to manage those expressions and how to use its emotions to modify player behavior. Since emotionally intelligent games are concerned with influencing the emotions of players, some form of intelligence or pattern recognition is required to recognize what emotions are likely to be generated in a given situation. As its name suggests, an emotionally intelligent interface incorporates elements of both intelligent and emotional game interfaces.

Interface Dialogues

In designing the user interface for a game, it's often helpful to consider the interface hierarchy in the context of dialogues between the player and the game. As illustrated in Figure 5.6, even a straightforward logical interface supports a dialogue or communications channel between the player and an application such as a simulation. At the logical interface level, the dialogue is in the form of data as input and answers as output. There is no emotional bond (the *fun factor*), and the underlying pedagogy, if any, is typically obvious to the user.

Ascending to the emotional interface level, the dialogue is more stimulus-response than simple data and answer. Furthermore, the bond fostered by the interchange is emotive. The pedagogy can be hidden from the player, or at least incorporated in a serious game in a way that allows the player to focus on the fun aspects of gameplay while simultaneously acquiring the knowledge, skills, and attitudes related to the serious content.

At the intelligent interface level, the dialogue between player and game is more interactive, with queries and stimulus supplied by the player and a response provided by the game. The bond is emotive, and the pedagogy is available for inspection by the user, but hidden from

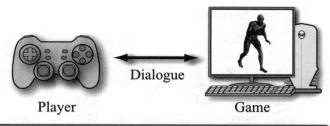

FIGURE 5.6 Serious games interface dialogues.

Dialogue	Input	Output	Bond	Application	Pedagogy
Emotionally Intelligent	Query & Stimulus	Response & Suggestion	Emotive	MMP Game	May Be Hidden
Intelligent	Query & Stimulus	Response	Emotive	Online Game	May Be Hidden
Emotional	Stimulus	Response	Emotive	SP Game	May Be Hidden
Logical	Data	Answer	None	Simulation	Explicit

view. The richness of dialogue supported by an intelligent interface most obvious in online gaming, where players engage in a dialogue with each other within the context of a game.

The interface dialogue at the level of an emotionally intelligent interface is characterized by query and stimulus on the input or player side and response and suggestion on the game side. As with the intelligent and emotional interfaces, the bond between player and game is emotive. Many massively multiplayer games and limited multiplayer online games are capable of emotionally intelligent dialogue. A standalone game in which a mentor avatar guides the learner through challenges can also support an emotionally intelligent dialogue.

PROGRAMMING

There are two types of programming in typical serious games development. The first is the entertaining or gaming elements, such as 3D graphics, the AI behind the ultimate bad character or boss, and the player interaction. The second type is focused on the serious content underlying the game. It's often a good idea to keep the two programming tasks separate because different tools and techniques can be used to optimize each task. It's also a good idea to consider prototyping languages and other tools separate from the deliverables.

Languages

Most professional game shells for the PC and consoles support ISO-standard C and C++. Similarly, C++, C#, JAVA, and BREW are popular programming environments for cellphones. Qualcomm's mobile development environment BREW (Binary Runtime Environment for Wireless) is a compiled alternative to interpreted languages such as Java. The environment, which is backed by mobile developers such as Electronic Arts, allows developers to work in C and C++ and then compile the code for specific handsets [Jenkins05].

The problem with traditional C and C++ is the cumbersome and time-consuming write-compile-run cycle. Many developers avoid this routine by using a scripting language. Because scripting languages are often implemented with interpreters rather than multipass, optimizing compilers, they trade efficiency of execution for rapid development.

One of the most well known scripting languages is Python, which is essentially an interpreted version of C++. Many programmers report increased efficiency over compiled C++. Like C++, Python can be integrated with other languages. See *www.python.org* for more information. A popular alternative to Python is Lua, (*www.lua.org*), which is compiled either at run-time or beforehand to increase performance.

Some game engines support limited scripting languages to connect preexisting components, and provide developers with hooks for DLLs and other means of adding low-level routines written in compiled C++. For example, Conitec's *GameStudio* uses a C-like scripting language, *CScript*. Although the language is compiled prior to run-time, it doesn't offer the execution efficiency possible with code written for an optimized C compiler. It's also limited in the number of ISO C functions supported.

As with many other game engines, *GameStudio* can be extended with add-on products. Dynamic Linked Libraries (DLLs), which are compiled functions and routines, usually written in C, are a powerful way of extending the functionality of a game engine that doesn't support native optimized compiled code. DLLs are also a popular way of hiding proprietary routines from curious eyes. Instead of writing code in a game editor that might be read by someone with the same editor, routines are in a neat binary package. DLLs are also an easy way of extending a proprietary game engine in which the developer doesn't want to let the source code out in the community. Instead, the game engine vendor releases the specifications for the DLL API. A routine written in optimized C or hand-tuned Assembler and then compiled as a DLL can often speed game execution by replacing poorly optimized native code with more efficient code. However, there is no standard DLL format that works across all game engines.

It's possible to write entire levels in compiled C++ attached to a game through DLLs and dispense with the native game editor, but most developers use DLLs to overcome performance bottlenecks and add functionality such as support for vibration feedback to a game engine. DLLs communicate with a game engine through a standard Application Programming Interface or (API).

DLLs are also a good place to put formulas, models, and other serious content. The benefits of enhanced execution speed and security aside, storing the serious content separately from the other game code enables updates to the content without having to recompile the game. Furthermore, although there is no universal game engine API for DLLs, the serious content can be maintained in optimized C++ or C and the API segment of the DLL can be rewritten to suit the needs of a particular game engine or game environment. The alternative, rewriting the physiology or mechanics equations anew for a handheld or cellphone, typically requires much greater effort because of the need to validate and debug the new code.

Data Structures and Algorithms

To appreciate the contribution of programming best practices to the overall game development process, consider the functional architecture of a game based on the game engine shown in Figure 5.7. Starting from the bottom of the figure and working up, assets are assembled and, together with output from the game editor and map editor, compiled into the levels that will constitute the game. Assets include textures that will be applied to wall and other objects, 3D models that form the basis for the playable character and non-playable characters (NPCs), Sprites, Decals, Terrains, video segments, sounds, and music.

The game editor is used to create and modify code written in BASIC or some variant of C. The game editor is where the game designer defines the gameplay, including the fun and challenging moments of the game. The map editor is used by the game designer to define the map of the game world. Using a graphical map editor, the developer can design a sandstone castle in the middle of a desert, or a navy ship on an intercept course with a submarine in the Atlantic.

The code, map definitions, and assets are compiled or otherwise assembled into a readily accessible form so they can be used by the game engine. Regardless of how the levels are created, the game engine incorporates the data and, using graphic routines included in the operating system or add-ons, calculates the 2D image that will be displayed on the computer monitor. If the PC platform includes a video card with a Graphical Processor Unit (GPU) that supports the graphics routines, then the performance of the graphic renderings should be enhanced.

Middleware, in the form of a bundled or third-party AI or physics engine, can provide the base game engine with added functionality. A database, also connected to the game engine via an API, can be used to provide

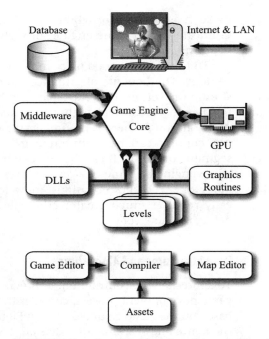

FIGURE 5.7   Functional architecture of a game based on a game engine showing components involved in game creation and play. Black ball and socket connectors representing standard Application Program Interfaces (APIs).

long- and short-term memory for profiling the player and keeping track of score and game state. During gameplay, the game engine may interface with the Internet and local area network (LAN) to receive updates and support multiplayer interaction, and to share content and interoperate with other game systems. This latter feature is increasingly important in serious games for the military.

While scripting may be sufficient to connect the disparate systems in a game, low-level programming will probably be required to create engaging gameplay. Successful game developers don't rely on custom code at this level of detail, but use standard algorithms and data structures whenever possible. Algorithms are the specific instructions that tell the computer what specific steps to perform and in what specific order. Data structures are ways of storing data so that they can be used efficiently.

The standard data structures used in game programming include arrays, lists, queues, stacks, tables, graphs, and trees [Dalmau04]. Trees are especially useful in game programming because they are useful for classifying and accessing large amounts of information. Many game engines rely on BSP trees and Octrees for rendering and working with 3D data sets.

Data structures can be depicted graphically, but are usually defined in C or another high-level language used to code the game engine. The description of a binary tree, a data structure commonly used in game development, is illustrated in Listing 5.1.

LISTING 5.1   Binary Data Structure.

```
/* Binary tree data structure */

struct t_node {
    void *item;
    struct t_node *left;
    struct t_node *right;
    };

typedef struct t_node *Node;

struct t_collection {
    int size;
    Node root;
    };
```

The best online resource for searching, sorting, and other bread-and-butter algorithms and the data structures that support them, is the National Institute of Standards and Technology (NIST) [NIST05]. This government agency provides a variety of resources for game developers, including the Dictionary of Algorithms and Data Structures for programmers (*www.nist.gov/dads/*). Another source for proven data structures is the Standard Template Library (STL) [Meyers01]. Microsoft's proprietary data structure library, .NET, is another option.

NIST is an excellent source for proven algorithms, as are any of the numerous algorithm titles by Robert Sedgewick, including *Algorithms in C++*. One of the problems with algorithms is determining when they break down. Even published algorithms suffer from lack of proof that they work under all conditions. For example, even though the shortsort algorithm is simpler than other sorting algorithms, it is avoided because it can't be proven to work for all unsorted lists.

Program Flow Diagrams

While programming a sorting algorithm, it's easy to forget about the bigger picture of creating a fantastic game. For this reason, seasoned game designers create a roadmap, initially as part of the game design document, and later as part of a working document shared by the development staff. The high-level flow diagram in Figure 5.8 illustrates one of these roadmaps. In this example, players begin by selecting a profile and then a difficulty level. The main menu provides players with access to a utility to manage their profiles, play the game, get help, and select game options such as keyboard and gamepad mapping. Upon exit, players are presented with their scores.

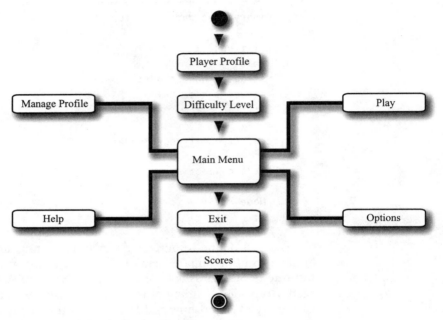

FIGURE 5.8   High-level program flow diagram.

In addition to diagramming the high-level program flow, subordinate-level program flow should be documented until each subcomponent of program flow is decomposed to its logical endpoint—down to the level of pseudocode, if possible. As shown in Figure 5.8, program flow at the Play node of the high-level diagram starts with Level Select, and continues to a cutscene and mission briefing before the level is open to the player for play. After the level has been played, the score is presented to the player, followed by a debriefing. If the level was completed successfully, the player may opt to advance to the next level. Each node in Figure 5.9 should be decomposed in turn. Simple nodes such as Level Select might require only one additional diagram. Others such as Play might require considerably more diagramming.

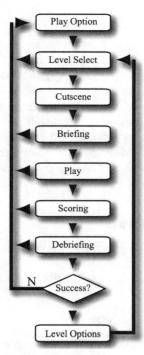

FIGURE 5.9   Program flow
diagram illustrating the flow
of data during game play.

Code Review

Successful game developers do the things that unsuccessful developers
avoid. One of these tasks is code review, the peer review of source code
throughout the coding process that is intended to improve code quality
and circumvent potential problems in the game [McConnell04]. Simply
because a game compiles and runs doesn't guarantee there are no security vulnerabilities, potentially unstable conditions, or unnecessary memory consumption in the executable code.

Code review is typically performed by peer programmers, either formally or informally, with the help of established guidelines. There are
tools intended to shorten or automate the review process. For example,
Microsoft's C++ complier for the .Net environment has a built-in optimization feature that is supposed to result in faster, cleaner code. However, there is no substitute for careful, focused peer review of source
code, even if some programmers cringe at the thought of allowing a co-
worker to snip away at another programmer's prized algorithm.

WORKING WITH ASSETS

Programming is often an improvisational activity, especially when a development team is working with new hardware or third-party software. Players will never know that a particular data structure or algorithm was chosen over another unless the decision negatively impacts gameplay. Graphics, sounds, and other assets, in contrast, are out in front of players. Artwork that is acquired or developed in-house must be indistinguishable from one artist to the next and consistent throughout the game. For this reason, successful development shops create an *Art Bible*, which shows example artwork as a guide for asset development and acquisition. Moreover, the Art Bible is created during the design stage, before assets have been developed.

Asset Types

Even a simple game may have thousands of assets, and each asset must be tracked through the development pipeline. The types of assets included in the Art Bible may include any or all of the following:

Graphic Arts Assets

Textures: Environment, object, and equipment textures
Fonts: System and embedded fonts used in the game and marketing materials
Terrain: Mountains, hills, grasslands, and other outdoor textures
Sprites: 2D pre-rendered figures
Animations: Individual images intended to be shown in rapid sequences
Wallpaper: Desktop patters used in marketing
Vehicle models: Land, sea, air, and space vehicle models
Level maps: Models of game levels
Special effects: Gun firing, grenade explosions, blood, fog, rain, snow, lightning, smoke, and fire
Interface art: Screens, buttons, menus, fields, and other interface widgets
Power-ups and Easter eggs: Artwork associated with power-ups and Easter eggs
Motion capture data: Preproduction data used for animation
Video: Cutscenes and other video content

Models

Effector models: Weapon, projectiles, spent casings, medical instruments, equipment

Environmental models: Object models in the environment, such crates, trees, rocks, and buildings

Character Models: Player and nonplayer character models

Sound Assets

Music: Tunes keyed to action, victory, and defeat

Special effects: Explosions, weapons discharges, warning buzzers

Voices: Recorded and synthesized voices

NPC sounds: Footsteps, sneezes, breath sounds

Environmental sounds: Wind, rain, birds, or traffic

Interface sounds: Mouse clicks, joystick, and keyboard feedback

Programmed Assets

Bones models for NPCs

An example of an Art Bible entry for fonts is shown in Figure 5.10. The font entries in the Art Bible should include the actual font faces as well as the standard title. It's important to distinguish between fonts provided by the operating system and those embedded in the game.

Embedded fonts, which are usually compiled and encrypted in the game, are used for nonstandard fonts, such as the FutureKillBold Skew font in Figure 5.10. Standard system fonts, such as Times New Roman, may be specified for help screens and other applications in the game where a substitution will not adversely affect the look and feel of the game.

FIGURE 5.10   Example Art Bible exhibit showing fonts assets.

Master Asset List

As a result of the asset development process, the relatively small sample of art assets in the Art Bible will be dwarfed by the media that will actually be used in the game. This collection of assets, known as the master asset list, should be continually updated and maintained as a resource for the art, programming, maintenance, and quality assurance staff. Entries in the master asset list should include the following:

Name: Based on a standardized naming convention
Unique ID: Supports asset management with a database
Format: File format
Size: File size, with polygon count for 3D models
Author/source: The author and source
Creation date: For tracking and archiving purposes
Version: Supports asset management and the ability to repurpose earlier versions and formats
Level(s) used: Index assets by level to identify potential conflicts that could result from a global replacement of an asset

The most critical feature of the master asset list is the naming convention, which should be defined in the design document before thousands of assets have been created. Some asset management programs supplement file name with additional data fields, but these tools and options don't obviate the need to identify one or more naming conventions.

In addition to obvious local naming convention options that include level name, type of asset, and source, domain specific naming conventions should be used whenever they are applicable. For example, in medicine, the Medical Subject Heading or MeSH is used by every major medical library and by the major medical search engines. MeSH is the National Library of Medicine's (NLM's) controlled vocabulary thesaurus, which is arranged alphabetically and hierarchically. For example, in a medical game that presents pathology images of the heart, MeSH terms are an obvious component of a naming convention and/or file structure. The MeSH entry for the sinoatrial node, the part of the heart responsible for initiating the normal heartbeat, is shown in Table 5.2.

TABLE 5.2   MeSH Entry for the Sinoatrial Node

	MeSH DESCRIPTOR DATA
MeSH Heading	Sinoatrial Node
Tree Number	A07.541.409.819
Scope Note	The small mass of modified cardiac muscle fibers located at the junction of the superior vena cava (VENA CAVA, SUPERIOR) and right atrium. Contraction impulses probably start in this node, spread over the atrium (HEART ATRIUM) and are then transmitted by the atrioventricular bundle (BUNDLE OF HIS) to the ventricle (HEART VENTRICLE).

Entry Term	Sinuatrial Node
Entry Term	Sino-Atrial Node
Entry Term	Sinu-Atrial Node
Allowable Qualifiers	AB AH CH CY DE EM EN GD IM IN IR ME MI PA PH PP PS RA RE RI SE SU TR UL US VI
Online Note	use SINOATRIAL NODE to search SINO-ATRIAL NODE 1966-77 (as Prov 1966-69)
History Note	78; was SINO-ATRIAL NODE 1964-77 (Prov 1964-69)
Unique ID	D012849

MeSH Tree Structures

Anatomy

    Cardiovascular System

      Heart

        Heart Conduction System

          Sinoatrial Node

Top of Form

Bottom of Form

Several components of the MeSH entry could be used in naming assets. The most obvious is `Sinoatrial Node`, which could be stored under a file system patterned after the MeSH tree structure shown near the bottom of Table 5.2. Another, less human-readable, option is to use the Unique ID, in this case `D012849`.

At first glance, using a naming convention based on MeSH may seem like overkill. However, several months into development, with several hundred images of the heart in the Master Asset List, MeSH, or something like it, is a welcome tool for reducing complexity and ambiguity. In addition to providing public access to an online MeSH browser, the NLM makes MeSH available for free download from the library's Web site, *www.nlm.nih.gov/mesh*. It's a good idea to download the MeSH files for a standard, in-house reference because the NLM updates the thesaurus annually.

There are alternatives to MeSH within medicine, such as the International Classification of Diseases (ICD-10) vocabulary, the standard endorsed by the World Health Organization (WHO) [WHO05]. The latest version of ICD can be accessed and downloaded for free from the WHO Web site (*www.who.int/classifications/icd/en*).

Examples of controlled vocabularies in other field include the Thesaurus for Graphic Materials I (TGM I) [LOC05], the Getty Vocabularies [Getty05], and the NASA Thesaurus [NASA05]. TGM I, which contains 6,300 terms for indexing visual materials, is used by the Library of Congress to catalogue images. The Getty Vocabularies include The Art & Architecture Thesaurus® (AAT), the Union List of Artists Names® (ULAN), and the Getty Thesaurus of Geographic Names® (TGN).

The AAT encompasses more than 133,000 terms relating to fine art, architecture, decorative arts, archival materials, and material culture. The ULAN contains more than 225,000 names and biographical and bibliographic information about artists and architects, including variant names, pseudonyms, and language variants. TGN contains 1.3 million names, including vernacular and historical names, geographical coordinates, and place types related to art and architecture. The NASA Thesaurus, which is available on CD-ROM and free download, contains over 18,000 terms and 4,000 definitions. For additional controlled vocabularies, see the Web site of the American Society of Indexers, *www.asindexing.org*.

ACTOR DESCRIPTIONS

Actors are the emotional hooks that pull players into a game. The primary actors in most games are the player character(s), nonplayer character(s), vehicles, and effectors. Actors should be defined completely and precisely, as early in the design process as possible. Character definitions for RPGs typically emphasize behavior traits, such as aggressiveness, over physical characteristics.

Player Character

The range of descriptions applicable to a player character (PC) depends on the game's genre and the nature of the character, including whether the character is human or takes some other form. The following example is taken from a serious medical game, *Military Malaria* (Archetype Technologies), designed to teach army medics effective malaria countermeasures. The player character in the RPG assumes the role of a female *Anopheles gambiae* mosquito, one of the best-known vectors of the *Plasmodium* parasite that is responsible for malaria.

During gameplay, players must avoid and overcome the manmade and natural deterrents that could thwart their ability to spread the parasite to human hosts. Players of the PC-based game begin the game as an adult mosquito seeking human hosts. Successful players find hosts and live inside the human bloodstream, only to be picked up by another Anopheles mosquito, and the cycle continues until thwarted by technology or the environment. The main categories for the player character, Anopheles, are defined here:

Bite rate: Number of bites per second. The more bites per second, the more quickly the player character can escape possible harm.

Capacity: Bite capacity.

Damage per second: Reflects the probability of infection per bite.

Effector: The weapon or cause of change, in this case, the *Plasmodium* parasite.

Energy: Source of energy, in this case, human blood.

Levels: Levels in which the adult player character may appear.

Lifespan: Normal lifespan without technological intervention.

Modes of combat: Player may simply bite or attempt to infect the host.

Olfactory range: Distance within which the player can sense the odor of a host.

Resistance: Resistance to insecticides, common in areas where spraying is practiced.

Sex: Female in this example, because male *Anopheles* aren't vectors or malaria.

Speed: Speed of travel.

Sound: Sound made during flight.

Special: Special capabilities, including means of evading enemies.

Stage: Which of four stages, Egg, Larva, Pupa, or Adult.

Travel: Mode of travel, primarily flying, with some walking.

Visual range: Range player is capable of observing during gameplay.

Weaknesses: Limitations that the player character must consider during gameplay.

The key player character descriptions are usually incorporated in a character profile that includes graphics of the character and descriptive graphics that supplement text descriptions, as in Figure 5.11. The profile shows 3D rendering of Anopheles, including a perspective view and a smaller side view. The spatial coverage of visual and olfactory fields is shown, with 360-degree olfactory coverage and 230 degree visual field coverage

Nonplayer Character

The descriptions of nonplayer characters (NPCs) are usually richer than player character descriptions because NPC actions are defined in software. Characteristics such as aggressiveness and tendency to use defensive maneuvers aren't provided by the player, but must be explicitly defined in the AI engine or other component of the game.

The following NPC example is taken from a first-person medical sniper game, *Achilles* (Archetype Technologies), which is designed to

Player Character: Anopheles

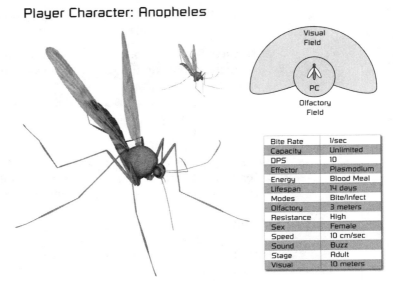

Bite Rate	1/sec
Capacity	Unlimited
DPS	10
Effector	Plasmodium
Energy	Blood Meal
Lifespan	14 days
Modes	Bite/Infect
Olfactory	3 meters
Resistance	High
Sex	Female
Speed	10 cm/sec
Sound	Buzz
Stage	Adult
Visual	10 meters

FIGURE 5.11   Player character profile from *Military Malaria* showing 3D renderings, olfactory and visual fields, and abbreviated character descriptions.

teach military medics basic musculoskeletal and skeletal anatomy. During gameplay, the player character faces mutants in an off-world outpost. These mutants can be stopped only by shooting them in their weak spot, which varies from one mutant to the next. Fortunately, the player's weapon system can identify the weak spot—by name. It's up to the player to locate the anatomical site and go in for the kill. Note the larger number of descriptors related to combat and survival compared with the RPG *Military Malaria*.

Auditory range: Range within auditory field for player sounds, such as walking. The range for other sounds, such as gunshots, is normally calculated as a function of the sound source and distance between the source and NPC.

Combat: Combat capabilities, such as frontal assault, hand grenade toss, or sniper capabilities.

Decision making: Decision-making skill set, such as evasion and pathfinding.

Defense: Defensive moves, such as the ability to construct barriers from blocks, tables, and other items in the environment.

Goal: Goal of NPC, which typically ranges from aiding and following to harming the player character.

Head health: Head health value, used to calculate the effect of weapons on a head shot.

Leg health: Leg health value. Leg health is diminished when the leg is hit by weapons fire.

Torso health: Torso health value. Torso health, which is diminished when the torso is hit by weapons fire, is usually less than leg health, signifying greater susceptibility to injury.

Levels: Levels in which the NPC may appear.

Offense: NPC offensive moves and weaponry.

Shooting accuracy: Relative accuracy out of 100 percent. A relative accuracy of 90 percent means that an NPC shooter makes nine out of every 10 shots.

Special: Character-specific special capabilities, such as speed, power, agility, and defensive systems.

Strengths: Particular strengths of the NPC, which may be physical or psychological.

Travel: Mode of travel, which may be on foot, running, or hang-gliding.

Visual range: Range in the visual field for which NPC will respond to the player character or another NPC.

Weaknesses: Behavioral or physical weaknesses that an opponent could exploit.

Weapons used: Types of weapons the NPC can use against the other characters.

The nonplayer character profile, shown in Figure 5.12, includes values for the key descriptors. The profile indicates that mutants use a fighting style that combines frontal assault with a duck-and-cover defense. The strengths, weaknesses, and weaponry relative to the player character's descriptors define the chemistry of gameplay.

Vehicles

Operating a wheeled or flying vehicle is fun for many players. However, creating a believable vehicle is a major stressor of physics engines and processor power. The following description is taken the vehicle Stinger in the *Achilles* game. This flying vehicle, which is designed to operate realistically in the atmosphere, is defined in operational terms normally used for aircraft [Bourg02; Conger04]:

Attack angle: The angle between the wing's chord (the line between the leading and trailing edges of a wing) and the relative direction of the wind

Capacity: Payload capacity, in mass or volume

Center of mass: The point at which the vehicle's mass can be assumed, for computational purposes, to be concentrated

Control surfaces: Placement and size of ailerons and rudders

Drive: Propulsion mechanism

NPC: Mutant

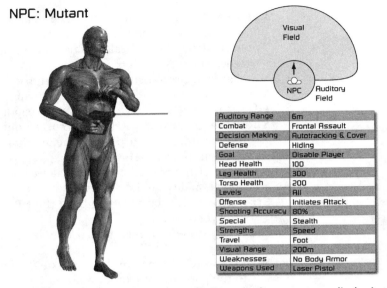

Auditory Range	6m
Combat	Frontal Assault
Decision Making	Autotracking & Cover
Defense	Hiding
Goal	Disable Player
Head Health	100
Leg Health	300
Torso Health	200
Levels	All
Offense	Initiates Attack
Shooting Accuracy	80%
Special	Stealth
Strengths	Speed
Travel	Foot
Visual Range	200m
Weaknesses	No Body Armor
Weapons Used	Laser Pistol

FIGURE 5.12   Nonplayer character profile from the first-person medical sniper game *Achilles*.

Environmental factors: Air viscosity, temperature, humidity, and other factors that affect performance

Geometry: The overall geometry of the craft

Mass: The mass of the vehicle, with and without fuel

Maximum pitch: Maximum angle along the axis parallel to the wings of a flying vehicle

Maximum roll: Maximum rotation about the axis from nose to tail of a flying vehicle

Maximum velocity: Maximum velocity of a vehicle

Maximum yaw: Maximum extent to the degree a vehicle is pointing away from its direction of travel due to rotation about its vertical axis

Power source: Source of the vehicle's power

Precision: For vehicles with weapons systems, the precision of the weapon

Range: Maximum distance the vehicle can travel without refueling or repairs

Size: Absolute size of the vehicle

Surface area: The surface area of the vehicle

Weapon system: Relevant to the extent the system affects flight and handling characteristics

The game physics for a variety of cars, trucks, boats, hovercraft, and aircraft have been extensively defined [Bourg02]. However, most of the physical parameters can be approximated if the vehicles serve as filler or backdrop material in a level, as long as the approximation doesn't diminish the entertainment value of the vehicle. Conversely, if the operation of the vehicle is part of the serious content to illustrate the contribution of Robbin's Effect and Bernoulli's Principle to handling and maneuverability, for example, then the Stinger's geometry and surface area increase in relative importance. Robbins Effect describes how lift is created by a spinning cylinder. Bernoulli's Principle states that in fluid flow, an increase in velocity occurs simultaneously with decrease in pressure.

The Stinger's profile, shown in Figure 5.13, incorporates a subset of the descriptors defined earlier, as well as graphics that provide a dynamic view of vehicle operation. For example, the plot of flight time versus air speed indicates that the relationship between the two variables is non-linear. Conversely, lift increases linearly and then, at some angle, drops precipitously (stalls). Because the Stinger isn't the focus of serious content in the game, only a handful of parameters are used to model flight characteristics.

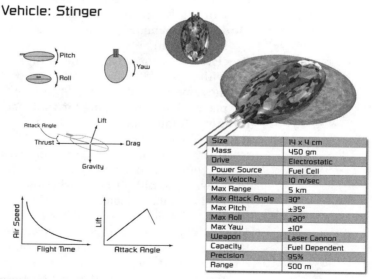

Size	14 x 4 cm
Mass	450 gm
Drive	Electrostatic
Power Source	Fuel Cell
Max Velocity	10 m/sec
Max Range	5 km
Max Attack Angle	30°
Max Pitch	±35°
Max Roll	±20°
Max Yaw	±10°
Weapon	Laser Cannon
Capacity	Fuel Dependent
Precision	95%
Range	500 m

FIGURE 5.13   Profile of the flying vehicle Stinger, from *Achilles*. Vehicle parameters are supplemented with graphics and graphs that illustrate the dynamic interrelationships of variables such as lift and attack angle.

Effectors

Effectors are the devices, forces, and technologies that empower player and nonplayer characters to make progress toward their respective goals. The purest, unambiguous effectors are weapons used to kill or subdue an opponent. In a serious game, the weapons may be antibiotics and the opponents may be bacteria. Regardless of their form, effectors are usually handled by the game's AI engine [Champandard04]. The following effector descriptions are based on a plasma carbine weapon from the *Achilles* game described earlier.

Ammunition: The nature of the projectile or beam emitted by the weapon.

Capacity: Number of rounds the weapon is capable of delivering before reloading.

Damage: Damage caused by the weapon, which negatively impacts character head, leg, or torso health.

Damage per second (DPS): The amount of damage delivered by the weapon per second of operation. DPS is especially relevant with beam weapons that may require one or two seconds of continuous damage to kill or stun the target.

Kill radius: The radius, in specified units from the weapon, in which it is capable of mortally wounding the targeted victim.

Modes: The modes of operation available to the operator, such as kill and stun.

Precision: A measure of the clustering of projectiles from a gun with repeated firing. Precision may be defined as a function of movement, with different precision values associated with the player character moving forward, backward, and laterally.

Range: Total range of the weapon.

Rate: Fire rate, per second.

Recoil: Recoil of the weapon with each shot. Larger recoil should be reflected in changes in the scenery (normally an upward movement with firing), in the sound played, and in the vibration feedback, if available.

Sound: Sound emitted by the weapon when fired.

Speed: Speed of the projectile generated by the gun.

Splash: Size of the area of damage on the target, which is normally reflected in the artwork. A cannon projectile normally produces more splash (a larger damage area) than a bullet fired from a pistol, for example.

Spread: The opposite of precision. Spread typically increases with increasing distance from the weapon.

Plasma Carbine

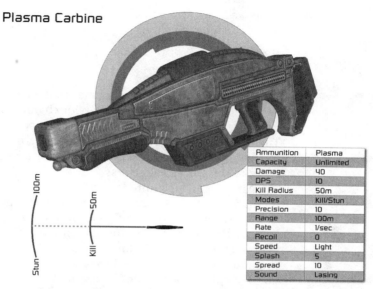

Ammunition	Plasma
Capacity	Unlimited
Damage	40
DPS	10
Kill Radius	50m
Modes	Kill/Stun
Precision	10
Range	100m
Rate	1/sec
Recoil	0
Speed	Light
Splash	5
Spread	10
Sound	Lasing

FIGURE 5.14 Plasma carbine effector profile. Kill and stun ranges are depicted graphically and appear in the summary characteristic table.

The plasma carbine profile shown in Figure 5.14 is typical of a hand-held weapon in first person shooters and sneakers. A more powerful weapon is associated with a larger damage score, a greater damage per second score, or both. However, increasing the rate of fire and the kill radius could provide a more lethal weapon, especially for rapidly moving targets. The plasma carbine profile includes a kill radius of 50 m, which is indicated graphically in the range profile adjacent to the table of profile values.

The plasma carbine profile takes on special meaning when compared with the profile of the nonplayer character in Figure 5.12. Comparing the two profiles reveals that the laser carbine weapon would have to be discharged three times at the head of the mutant to bring Head Health from 100 down to zero (40 points/blast × 3). A kill could also result from one discharge from the laser carbine weapon if Head Health was 60 and the Desert Mutant was simultaneously hit by a grenade with a damage score of 30. What isn't clear from a simple comparison of profiles is the status of a mutant simultaneously hit with a grenade and the stun beams from two plasma carbine weapons.

Even though the complex interplay of weapon and target properties is normally handled by the game's AI engine, the weapon properties and interactions with player characters and objects in the environment must be specified by the developer. This can be done in pseudocode, as a list of if-then clauses, or as an effector matrix. Of these options, the effector matrix is the most effective.

Effector Matrices

Figure 5.15 shows an effector matrix developed for the *Military Malaria* game. The matrix compares behavior characteristics of the adult Anopheles with technologies or effectors that can be used to thwart the mosquito. The behavior patterns associated with the Anopheles, namely the activity, feeding, and resting profiles are, associated with susceptibility and resistance to the various effectors.

Anopheles mosquitoes tend to be active at dawn and dusk, or at night. Some tend to feed indoors, and others feed outdoors. Similarly, some rest indoors, while others rest outdoors. As shown in the matrix, a bed net (first column) is effective on mosquitoes that are active at night, feed indoors, and rest indoors. This relationship should be obvious, given that mosquitoes that sleep through the night, feed outdoors, and rest outdoors wouldn't pose much of a threat to someone sleeping indoors. The matrix also shows that a repellent, such as DEET (*N, N-diethly-3-methyl-benzamide*), works best with mosquitoes that are active at dawn/dusk, and that feed and rest outdoors. According to the matrix, chemoprophylaxis (medication) is the best technology to thwart the Anopheles, regardless of behavior. The simplified matrix is incomplete in that it doesn't reveal more subtle details, such as potential side effects from the medication and mosquito resistance to it.

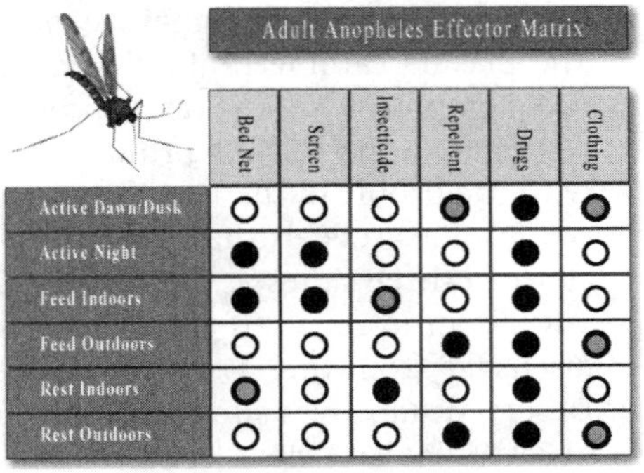

FIGURE 5.15 Adult Anopheles effector matrix relates mosquito behavior patterns to effector susceptibility. Susceptibility values are none (open circle), moderate (grayed circle), and complete (closed circle).

The effector matrix for the adult Anopheles is only one of several matrices developed for the *Military Malaria* game. Not only is there an effector matrix associated with each of the other three stages of the mosquito—egg, larvae, and pupa—but there are matrices that consider effectors over time and with different environmental factors. For example, not shown in the adult Anopheles effector matrix are the numerous preventative measures such as draining swamps that involve modifying or destroying the breeding habitat, .

Having a domain expert on hand is one way to avoid missing crucial details in an effector matrix. Technologies can also be used to ensure that every possible combination of effector has been considered and that the logic is sound. Decision tables, one such technology, are compact, precise methods of modeling complex logic [Hurley83]. Decision tables were originally developed to construct the logic of computer programs in a clearly arranged manner [McCarthy86] and were used to verify the completeness of simulations as early as the 1960s [Ludwig68].

A decision table is traditionally divided into four sections (see Figure 5.16). The upper-left quadrant contains conditions, the upper-right contains the condition rules, the lower-left contains actions to be taken, and the lower-right contains action rules. The condition and action entries can have the values "true," "false," or "not important." If the situation matches the pattern of conditions given in a specified row, then the actions in the row should be performed. Decision tables support the construction of AND and OR relationships within rules, as well as AND/OR/ELSE relationships between rules.

Condition Stub	Condition Entry
Action Stub	Action Entry

FIGURE 5.16   The four decision table sections.

An example of a partially populated decision table that considers only two behaviors is shown in Figure 5.17. Like the effector matrix, the tabular format of the decision table allows domain experts to check for invalid rules, completeness, redundancies, contradiction, and impossible situations [Suwa84]. Programmatically, a decision table can be manipulated as a simple trinary array (i.e., −1, 0, 1 or N, −, Y) [Bergeron91].

Adult Anopheles Effector Decision Table

Active Dawn/Dusk	-	-	-
Active Night	Y	-	N
Feed Indoors	-	Y	N
Feed Outdoors	-	-	-
Rest Indoors	-	-	Y
Rest Outdoors	-	-	-

Bed Net	●	●	●
Screen	●	●	○

FIGURE 5.17 Adult Anopheles effector decision table. "Y" = positive; "N" = negative; "–" = irrelevant or doesn't matter. The filled in circles in the lower right quadrant indicate relevant action entries.

The decision table in Figure 5.17 shows a subset of conditions considered in the Anopheles effector matrix. For clarity, the decision table is limited to the bed net and screen actions, although in practice every element in the effector matrix would be considered. The condition stub is populated with the Anopheles behaviors and the action stub shows the options of bed nets and screens. The condition entries have been condensed to a trinary array with only three columns, and these three columns are mapped to the six action entries.

The power of decision tables, and of decision table software, is that complex logic can be condensed into human readable and verifiable form. For example, the decision table in Figure 5.17 has six condition stubs, each of which may be positive (Y) or negative (N) before being processed into the condensed, trinary form. There are 2^n permutations of Y and N,, where n is the number of condition stubs. By quickly examining each of the possible permutations, domain experts may identify a condition that the programmers hadn't considered. Furthermore, the task can be simplified because the condensed state can be automatically computed with decision table software.

Given the complexity of interactions and the number of variables involved in a typical effector matrix, the time to create the effector matrices is during the design phase of game development. Arbitrarily changing an effector attribute later in the development pipeline could have a ripple effect that changes the dynamics of every other effector in the game in unpredictable ways. As such, effector matrices should be an integral part of the game design document.

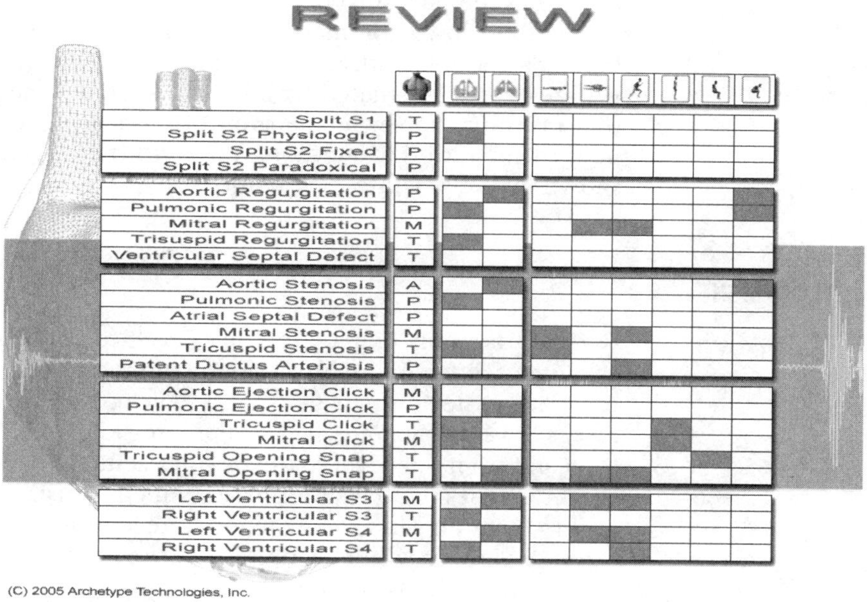

FIGURE 5.18   Simplified effector matrix used as a review screen within *Augmented Reality Medical Simulator—Auscultation*, a serious game designed to teach cardiac auscultation skills.

An effector matrix often has value beyond the design phase of a serious game. For example, it can be simplified and presented to the player in the form of a review of help screen. Figure 5.18 shows the effector matrix used as the basis for *Augmented Reality Medical Simulator—Auscultation*, repurposed as a review screen for players. The numerical values in the original matrix have been simplified to binary relationships, as indicated by grayed (1) or white (0) areas in the matrix. Along the top of the image, from left to right, are icons representing the chest wall and the eight maneuvers that players can use within the game: inhalation, exhalation, assuming the prone position, lying on the left side, exercising, quickly standing, sitting, and sitting, leaning forward. Similar sounds are grouped in rows.

As an example, the aortic regurgitation murmur, shown in the fifth row, is heard best in the pulmonic (P) area of the chest wall. The murmur is accentuated by exhalation and by sitting forward. The effector matrix shows that murmurs of aortic regurgitation and pulmonic regurgitation are similar sounding and that they can be heard best at the same point on the chest wall. The differentiating factor is the intensity change associated with inhalation and exhalation. Inhalation, depicted by the filled lungs, accentuates the pulmonic regurgitation murmur but has no effect on the aortic regurgitation murmur. Exhalation, represented by the deflated lungs, has the opposite effect.

Farther down the matrix, the pulmonic stenosis murmur, another finding associated with the pulmonic valve, is heard best at the pulmonic (P) area and accentuated by inhalation. Unlike the pulmonic regurgitation murmur, however, the sound isn't accentuated by having the patient sit forward. Furthermore, the sounds are significantly different, as shown by the separate groupings.

LEVEL DESIGN

Games commonly employ multiple levels to provide players with an escalation of difficulty, to break up the monotony of a single level, and because it's easier to manage from a development perspective. Successful games have a deliberate, planned progression of challenge, both within a level and from one level to the next. In addition, given the complexity of modern games, it's easier for programmers, artists, and the development staff to focus on game development one level at a time. The practice is so commonplace that level design is a recognized specialty in the game development business [Byrne05].

For maximum entertainment value, game progression should be accompanied by increasing challenge, both within levels and from one level to the next [Csikszentmihalyi91]. The use of a controlled increase in challenge or tension with progression of the story is a staple in theater and literature that dates back at least to Aristotle's time [RayNorris05]. In games, challenge can be increased by introducing time pressure, new travel modes, new or more ferocious enemies, new weapons, or map changes, depending on the game genre and nature of the serious content. For example, multiple attackers and end-level boss fights can be used to increase the challenge in an FPS game. Increasingly complex puzzles can be used in a puzzler or RPG to increase the challenge with each new level.

As illustrated in Figure 5.19, the increase in challenge with game progression perceived by players typically differs from the intended progression. Individual differences in how players navigate through and interact within a game account for the differences between the intended and perceived increases in challenge that accompany game progression. If the progression in challenge perceived by the player is markedly different from what the designer intended, then the player will likely be either bored (game too easy) or frustrated (game too difficult) [Bergeron88; Bergeron-Rouse92].

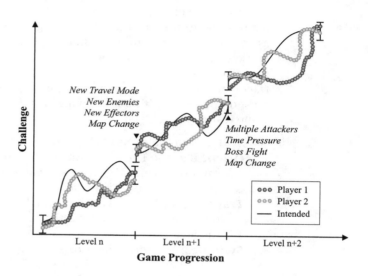

FIGURE 5.19   Game flow diagram showing intended versus perceived increase in challenge with game progression through three game levels.

Controlling the progression of challenge is part art and part science. Experience and natural talent can improve the art, as can the study of progression methods perfected in other media. Orson Scott Card's *Characters & Viewpoint* [Card88] and *How to Write Science Fiction* [Card90] and Noah Lukeman's *The Plot Thickens* [Lukeman02] are three excellent places to start. From a scientific perspective, creating detailed level maps and explicitly defining level logic are two methods that experienced developers rely on to control progression and communicate their vision to the development team.

Level Maps

Most levels are based on physical space that can be depicted as a graphical map. A map may describe a space as small as an operating room table or as expansive as the known universe. A game can use a single map or a different map for each level. Many games load relatively small maps with each level instead of maintaining one huge map in active memory because of the lower RAM and processor requirements associated with small maps.

Just as driving maps indicate railroads, interstate on ramps, and service roads, level maps identify the major operational features of a game. It's possible to play a game without a geographical or physical map, but, as in driving, they can be invaluable. For this reason, there is lucrative market in game maps for entertainment titles. In addition to books of game maps dedicated to a single game, many of the gaming magazines attract readers by offering maps to popular games. Regardless of the source, most of the geographical level maps include information on the following game features:

Scale: An indicator of absolute or relative scale.

Orientation: The direction of true or magnetic north (terrestrial games), up and down (space games), or dorsal, ventral, cranial, and caudal (surgical games).

Traps: Objects or player locations that can trigger an attack or initiate a sequence of events that increases the level of challenge in the level.

Switches: Devices that open passages or in some other way allow the player to progress through a level by virtue of the player reaching a location or checkpoint. A switch with a negative consequence is a form of trap.

Conditional switches: Switches that require the player to satisfy several conditions before a switch will operate. Satisfying a condition could involve accumulating a minimum number of points or visiting a particular location in the level.

Easter eggs: Bonus material used to add to the "fun factor" of the level. An Easter egg can be as simple as a developer's name written on a wall. They usually have nothing to do with gameplay.

Boss: The ultimate nonplayer character that must be overcome by the player to complete the level. In levels that don't involve characters, the boss and associated boss fight can be represented by a final challenge of some type that is harder or more complex than the other challenges in the level. Like Easter eggs, the boss or final challenge adds to the "fun factor" of a level.

The level map in Figure 5.20, developed for the Achilles game, shows the scale, start, and goal areas of the level, as well as the locations of traps, switches, Easter eggs, and the boss in an off-world outpost. The switches are linked to doors that allow the player character to explore areas of the level. An indicator of direction isn't included in the map because absolute direction isn't important in the game associated with this level.

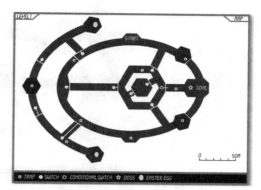

FIGURE 5.20   Level map showing locations of traps, switches, boss, and Easter eggs in the outpost used in level 1 of *Achilles*.

Note the placement of switches relative to the doors they operate. With the longer switch-to-door distances, such as in the lower left of the map, the player character may have to run to reach the door opening before it closes. Also, note that the switch leading to the goal area in the right hand side of the map is conditional, in that the door to the goal area won't open simply by virtue of the player's presence at the switch location.

Level Logic

The conditional logic for switches, the logic for traversing a map, and the relationship between map traversal and serious content are defined in level logic maps. The representation of level logic should reflect the complexity of the level as well as the type of logic involved. For example, the simplest method of defining map traversal logic is with a graphic overlay on the level map, as shown in Figure 5.21. In this example, the switch icons in the original level map have been replaced with directional logic arrows, and each branch point is labeled.

Following the logic path in the level logic map, one possible map traversal path, labeled 1 through 21, is darkened. The player begins at point 1, moves to point 2 and then moves through a one-way doorway or portal. From point 3, the player must proceed to point 4, and then decide whether to move right, to point A, or left, to point 5. Note the multiple possibilities that exist for the player at point 15, which include moving to point 16, C, or G.

Although a graphic overlay is a quick and simple way of defining traversal logic, the method breaks down with complex traversal logic. For example, it may not be obvious from the level logic map, but there are hundreds of possible player traversal paths for the relatively simple map

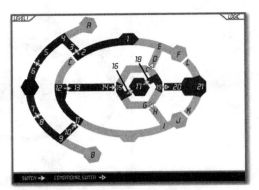

FIGURE 5.21   Level logic map, in the form of a
graphic overlay of the level map shown in Figure
5.20. Traversal logic, shown superimposed on the
level map, with one possible traversal path
darkened and labeled from 1 to 21.

shown in Figure 5.21. Furthermore, each traversal path is associated with
different combinations of challenge positions, points where sound or
music should be played, and locations of serious content.

With a simple level map, it's possible to keep track of traversal logic,
serious content, and gameplay elements with a set of overlays. However,
a more powerful method of mapping level logic is to create a single logic
tree keyed to the original level map. Figure 5.22 shows the logic tree that
represents the level logic map shown in Figure 5.21, as well as every
other possible map traversal.

The logic tree clearly shows dead-end paths in the level map, such as
nodes F and A, as well as circular traversal paths, such as the path including nodes C, D, E, and the starting node, 1. In addition to the map traversal information, the logic tree can be used to indicate where particular
music or sound should be played and where in the logic sequence challenges should appear.

A logic tree is particularly valuable in arranging and tracking knowledge (K), skills (S), and attitudes (A) associated with specific logic paths
in a level. As illustrated in Figure 5.22, the logic tree includes several islands of serious content. Knowledge island K1 encompasses nodes 1–4,
and skills island S1 includes nodes 5–7. More important, the logic tree
highlights how skills island S3 can be bypassed by players who opt to pass
through node G, which exposes players to skill island S2. The logic tree
highlights the level designer's option of insuring that the skills associated
with nodes 16–19 (S3) are covered in S2.

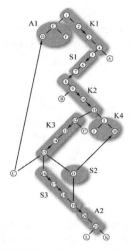

FIGURE 5.22   Logic tree illustrating all possible level map traversals for the level map shown in Figure 5.20. In addition, islands of serious content knowledge (K), skills (S), and attitudes (A) associated with specific logic paths are identified.

Entertainment levels are typically complex logic trees in which many nodes are never traversed. This structure adds to the illusion of a level with infinite possibilities of uncertain paths, and often adds to the entertainment appeal of the level. Two players with different play tactics might progress through a level, and each might have a different experience, depending on the sequence of the particular nodes of the level they visited. Although this approach adds to the fun factor, it can be at odds with ensuring players are exposed to the full range of serious content.

The approach used in traditional computer-aided instruction to ensure content exposure is to present every player with the same sequence of information, regardless of their performance or choice at particular points in the instruction. An enhanced version of this strategy can be used in a level design as well, as in the level illustrated in Figure 5.23. The level map (left) shows a simple sequence of map traversal steps, from start cell to goal cell—with one exception. Depending on the choice made at cell A, players are either forced to repeat the rooms filled in gray at the top right of the logic map or allowed to progress toward the goal cell. The downside of this form of logic is that there can be a marked decrease in the fun factor associated with the level, since the player is forced from one cell to the next, as in a traditional CAI program. In the "forced march" scenario, an overlay logic map should be sufficient because of the simplicity of the traversal logic.

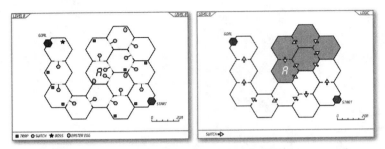

FIGURE 5.23   Level map (left) and traversal logic (right). The player's choice at cell A determines whether cells in gray are repeated. Players must traverse every cell in the level to reach the goal.

ARCHIVING

Asset management is a cornerstone of game development, and at the heart of asset management is archiving. As noted in Chapter 3, "Technology Trends," formal asset management, otherwise known as knowledge management, is practiced by the best companies in every industry. All it takes is one server crash to ruin a development shop—unless the server has been properly backed up.

Anyone with a music or movie collection knows that the best practice for extending the longevity of data on DVD and CD-ROM is to store the media in a constant, low humidity and low temperature environment, away from direct sunlight. An extreme example of this practice is the Bettmann Archive, which is housed in a 10,000 square foot limestone mine just northeast of Pittsburgh [Boxer01]. Underground caves aside, when it comes to best practices for archiving, the National Archives and Records Administration (NARA) sets the standard [Bergeron02]. NARA offers free publications on digital data archiving at *www.archives.gov/electronic_records_archives*.

According to NARA guidelines, data on CD-ROM are stored in standard ISO 9660 format, without compression, in plain ASCII or EBCDIC form. Similarly, data files and databases are stored as simple text arrays, lists, or tables. Images are acquired and saved as uncompressed Windows TIFFs. These TIFFs serve as master documents that are used to generate smaller GIF and JPEG files for daily use. In other works, NARA maintains all originals in the highest resolution available. For serious game developers, this practice translates to archiving WAVs for sound, TIFFs for graphics, and 3D Studio Max, Maya, or other native format for 3D models.

NARA's proactive stance against potential disasters is also worth noting. Their disaster prevention process includes monitoring temperature and humidity control equipment, providing guidelines for storing media, and encouraging fire prevention. The Archives also mandates periodic transfer of data to new storage media formats to avoid data loss because of changing technology or deterioration. Backups are created on a regular basis and backup media is stored in a separate location from the originals. Moreover, instead of the typical practice of labeling the backups "Backup—Date," the NARA specifies label contents, which are listed in Table 5.3.

TABLE 5.3   NARA Archive Media Labeling Best Practices

TAPES AND REMOVABLE MEDIA	TEMPORARY STORAGE MEDIA
Dates of coverage	Date of creation
Date of creation	Hardware platform
File titles	Organization responsible for the records
Number of tracks	Security classification
Organization responsible for the records	Software used to create the data
Record formats and lengths	Title of contents
Recording density	
Security classification	
Title of contents	
Type of internal labels	

In addition to the practice of the NARA, the best practices for archiving and data management in other industries are relevant to game development shops. Mission-critical computing departments in healthcare, banking and the military use uninterruptible power supply (UPS) hardware for filtering the power mains as well as for providing several minutes to several hours of backup power in the event of power outage. They ensure that ambient temperature and humidity are controlled to within a narrow range and that the air flow on the computer equipment is maintained above a minimum number of cubic feet per minute.

The best installations use name-brand hardware, with separate servers for archiving, testing, and deployment. In addition, the archive server discs are configured as redundant arrays that minimize the chances of data loss in the event of a disc crash. These shops have trained technicians who verify that archive media has data on it before it is labeled and stored offsite and who simulate disasters and document their ability to recover data [Avrin00].

ASSESSMENT

Serious games differ from entertainment games in the degree to which they are assessed for efficacy, whether expressed in terms of purchase behavior, academic test scores, or performance on the job. The best practices in assessment include the use of an established nomenclature for defining behavior change, effective, validated protocols, and the use of reporting standards.

Nomenclature

Assessment involves comparing the goals established during the requirements specification stage of development with measurable behavior changes in players after gameplay. Successful assessment depends on the care with which the list of measurable behavior change is constructed, especially when the game is in the form of an open-ended simulation in which players control the duration and extent of exploration and learning.

One way to assure desired behavior changes are measurable is to describe them in using a standard nomenclature designed for testing. Bloom's taxonomy, developed by Benjamin Bloom, is used throughout academia for curriculum development and testing [Bloom84]. It defines six levels of competence:

Evaluation: The ability to compare and discriminate between ideas and make choices based on reasoned argument
Synthesis: The ability to create new ideas from old ones
Analysis: The ability to see patterns and recognize hidden meanings
Application: The ability to use information
Comprehension: The ability to grasp meaning and understand information
Knowledge: The ability to observe and recall information

Each level of competence is associated with a specific taxonomy that serious games developers can use to describe the behaviors associated with a competence addressed by the game. For example, knowledge is described in terms such as "tell," "show," and "identify," whereas synthesis is described in terms such as "design," "combine," and "integrate." An online listing of the taxonomy is available through the University of Washington's Faculty Web server, *faculty.washington.edu/krumme/guides/bloom1.html*.

As an example of Bloom's Taxonomy in use, consider the following excerpts from the serious games design documents developed for the *Achilles* and *Augmented Reality Training Simulation* programs.

After playing *Achilles*, medics will be able to do the following:

- *List* the major surface muscle groups, cardiovascular structures, and skeletal structures
- *Explain* the relationship between blood loss rate and injury location
- *Show* the location of the major organ systems on a mannequin or another medic
- *Demonstrate* the ability to estimate survival time based on injury site
- *Classify* the muscle groups and organ systems in anatomical terms

After playing *ARTS*, students will be able to do the following:

- *Identify* the location of the primary cardiac auscultation points
- *Describe* the different maneuvers and their effect on heart sounds
- *Identify* heart sounds based on sound, maneuvers, and location on the patient's chest wall
- *Describe* the character of the major heart sounds, in terms of tempo, envelope, and timing
- *Classify* murmurs and sounds as systolic, diastolic, or pansystolic
- *Identify* the type of abnormal sound a simulated patient in less than three minutes

In each case, Bloom's Taxonomy is used to specify concrete, measurable behaviors. After playing *Achilles*, students will be able to *list*, *explain*, *show*, *demonstrate*, and *classify* specific structures and relationships. In other words, the effectiveness of *Achilles* or any other serious game defined in terms of behavior change can be tested, either by directly observing players or by administering a test.

Protocols

Assessment guidelines or protocols are dictated by best practices as well as the constraints imposed by organizations, typically in the form of clearance by an Institution Review Board or IRB. Clearance by the Institution Review Board (IRB) is a major milestone in developing a study. Although every organization's IRB guidelines are unique, most cover the same general topics: the subjects, the investigator, and study design.

The most significant guidelines deal with subjects, including the number of subjects, how they are recruited, provisions for privacy protection, and details on payments that will be made to subjects. The investigator must also disclose the level and type of risk subjects might be subject to, whether physical, social, psychological, legal, or economic. The investigator must provide evidence of expertise in the field and disclose any potential conflict of interest issues, such as a financial interest in the outcome of the study. Finally, the investigator must submit a study design to the IRB for approval. The design should provide details of the research protocol, including the objectives and specific aims of the study, research design and methods, and data collection and statistical considerations. Most of the conditions imposed by the IRB are obvious, such as taking measures to guarantee that students could not be identified individually, and that their participation or lack of participation in no way affects their grades.

As an example of an assessment protocol, consider the approach that we used in one of several studies conducted on *HeartLab*, an open-ended, simulation-based game designed to teach cardiac auscultation skills. In assessing the effectiveness of the game, we first enlisted the support of an educational psychologist who specialized in psychometrics. Based on our discussions, we formulated a protocol that defined the assessment process, from the manner in which student volunteers would be selected and assigned to different study groups to statistical methods that would be used to interpret the significance of the results. The plan was submitted to the IRB for approval, which was granted.

Because the game was open-ended, we devised a two-stage evaluation process. The first, a formative evaluation, made extensive use of feedback from physicians and medical student users in a variety of clinical and nonclinical settings. Results of this formative evaluation were then used in the formulation of the summative evaluation, which involved a number of extensive studies on users. The formative evaluation process relied heavily on feedback provided by domain experts, as to the validity of the underlying simulation, and medical students, as to whether the game was perceived as being useful in their medical training. This feedback was obtained online from systems in clinical settings and in a library setting.

Evaluation of the open-ended strategy included determining whether students viewed the game as efficient means of acquiring knowledge, as manifested by a willingness of students to use and reuse the game. More strenuous criteria, assessed by the summative evaluation, included demonstrating that learning had occurred, and that this new knowledge was carried over into clinical practice.

Feedback from students included data recorded by the program at run time, and questionnaires administered after program use. Questions answered during the formative evaluation included the following:

- Was the instructional strategy utilized the most efficient? Student feedback, in terms of boredom and frustration measures, was used to help answer this question.
- Did the interface promote or hinder the user's activities? Student responses to otherwise identical simulation applications with various user interface designs were recorded.
- Was the game useful? Usage measures and data from questionnaires were used to gain insight into this question.
- Did students learn from the game? The formative evaluation used questionnaires, whereas the summative evaluation employed pre- and post-test studies.

- What was the relative efficiency of the simulated patient cases? The relative perceived efficiency of simulated versus actual patient contact time was recorded. A summative evaluation that made use of comparative trials was used to determine this relative efficiency measure.

In the study, second-year medical students were given the opportunity to participate in the study designed to test the hypothesis that use of the game would enhance auscultatory skills, and that this improvement could be correlated with time spent in gameplay. In measurable behavior terms, we postulated that who used the game would be able to do the following:

- *Identify* the location of the primary cardiac auscultation points.
- *Describe* the effect of maneuvers on heart sounds.
- *Identify* abnormal heart sounds
- *Describe* the character of abnormal heart sounds.
- *Classify* murmurs and sounds according to their timing in the cardiac cycle.

Student volunteers took a 15-minute pre-test at the beginning of the semester and agreed to take a post-test at the end of the semester. The results were not used in any way to evaluate the students, and students could withdraw from the study at any time. During the study, student time and activity within the game was recorded. The results of the post-test were compared with the pre-test to each student. The results of the post-test were also analyzed in relationship to the number of hours spent in gameplay.

This high-level summary illustrates some of the basic issues that must be addressed during a formal evaluation of a game. An actual study protocol includes detailed information on the size and nature of the study and control groups, including basic demographics, and details on the statistical analysis, including how data on subjects who drop out of the study are treated.

There are myriad protocols that can be used to evaluate serious games. The above example focused on learning, but it could have examined, for example, clinical performance on the hospital wards. A popular model for the evaluation of computer-based instruction that recognizes the multiple layers of evaluation is described by Kirkpatrick [Kirkpatick96]. The model recognizes four levels of evaluation:

1. *Response.* Did learners like the training and did they complete it?
2. *Learning.* What skills and knowledge did they acquire?
3. *Performance.* How much is job performance improved? What can learners apply to their jobs?
4. *Results.* How well did the organization meet its business goals? Was the return on investment positive and significant?

The evaluation of performance and results are often more valuable, but also more problematic, to perform. For example, evaluating computer-based instruction from a business or Return on Investment (ROI) perspective is historically problematic. The traditional ROI calculation for classroom instruction versus computer instruction is the return on immediacy, such as when untrained first responders must be trained immediately for an ongoing biological event [Hartley01]. When there is an ongoing disaster, the return on immediacy climbs exponentially and may overshadow initial investment considerations.

In general, the higher the level of evaluation, the longer one has to wait to collect data because time must be allowed for the effects on knowledge and proficiency to reach equilibrium. For example, knowledge typically peaks at the end of training, and then declines exponentially until it reaches a plateau, as illustrated in Figure 5.24. Performance, in contrast, begins to increase during training, and reaches a plateau only much later—long after knowledge has dropped to a steady state.

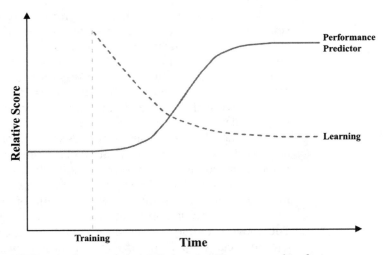

FIGURE 5.24   Expected change in learning measures and performance predictors following training.

Reporting

Assessment requires data, and much of the best data comes from user tracking through program instrumentation. Ideally, several key performance indicators are collected and stored centrally for analysis [Bergeron90]. Although user tracking adds a modest overhead burden on the serious games developer when one game is involved, the challenge becomes exponentially complex as the number of games involved increases.

Consider the case where a medical school learning laboratory has a library of serious games that teach a variety of medical concepts using the case-based approach. Each patient case game teaches medical students some subset of anatomy, physiology, biochemistry, and other clinical sciences. In order for an instructor to monitor student progress in the core sciences, he must compile use statistics from each game and come up with a composite score. However, if each game is stand-alone, with incompatible student tracking data formats, then the task may be practically impossible. One option is to write every game in-house and implement a unified reporting system. The other option is to purchase games that write reports in the same format.

In either case, the tracking data must be written to a standard format. Of the available standards, the most likely candidate is the eXtensible Markup Language, or XML. The name is a misnomer because XML isn't a language in itself, but a protocol for containing and managing information [Ray01].

The genesis of XML as a reporting language dates back to the earliest digital computers. To increase the readability of text displayed on computer consoles, a variety of computer-specific control codes were developed. To facilitate the sharing of electronic documents, these proprietary markup codes were replaced with standard codes. The term "markup" came from the printing industry, where proofreaders mark formatting and correction codes on page proofs that are then typeset.

The first widely recognized standard was the Generalized Markup Language (GML), introduced in the late 1960s. In 1978 the American National Standards Institute (ANSI) defined the Special Generalized Markup Language (SGML) specification based on GML. By the mid-1980s, SGML was recognized by the U.S. DOD, the International Organization for Standardization (ISO), and the Office of Official Publications of the European Community. SGML gave rise to XML in 1998 to fill the need for interactive Web pages that could be used to process transactions and as a means of sharing data between applications.

XML doesn't have a predefined vocabulary or taxonomy. Instead, the vocabulary and the relationship of the vocabulary words to one another and the document (the taxonomy) are defined as declarations are made. To appreciate the utility of XML as a means of defining data for use in game reporting, consider the learner performance report in XML, shown in Listing 52.

LISTING 5.2   Learner Game Performance Tracking Data in XML

```
<learner>
    <surface_anatomy>
        <score >87% </score>
        <anatomy >landmarks </ anatomy >
```

```
    </ surface_anatomy >
    < skeletal_anatomy >
        <score >73% </score>
        <anatomy >bony prominences </ anatomy >
    </ skeletal_anatomy >
</learner>
```

The report in Listing 5.2 indicates that the learner scored 87 percent in recognizing surface anatomy landmarks, but only 73 percent in recognizing bony prominences in skeletal anatomy. By virtue of the hierarchical structure of the report, XML can be used to store data in a way that lends itself to searching and other forms of automatic computer processing. A graph that includes the hierarchical structure described in Listing 5.2 is shown in Figure 5.25.

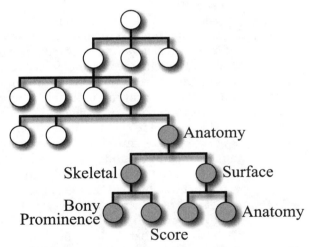

FIGURE 5.25 Hierarchical structure of an XML document. The darkened nodes correspond to Listing 5.2.

The taxonomy drawn in Figure 5.25 lends contextual meaning to the tags used to define the XML document. Consider the *score* tag under surface anatomy, indicating learner score in the area of surface anatomy (specifically landmarks). Alone and out of context, *score* could refer to any item in the report. However, with the tags, a computer program written in a procedural language can also infer context from the structure. As a result, a search for "anatomy score" shouldn't return "87%" in any context other than surface anatomy.

In addition to providing a context for the vocabulary used to tag data, the use of a specific schema for a particular report greatly facilitates the ease with which it can be communicated from one learning management system or independent game to the next. When the schema is known, mapping one schema onto another is straightforward, as in Figure 5.26.

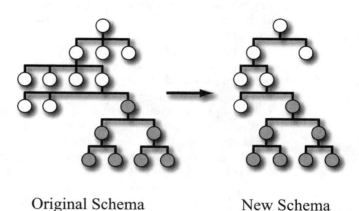

Original Schema   New Schema

FIGURE 5.26   Schema mapping of original XML document (left) and new schema (right).

Schema remapping may simply involve shuffling the expected structure of an XML document from one format to another, without any loss of data. For example, if several games teach anatomy, but the format of tracking data are different for each game, it's a simple matter to unify the XML into one hierarchy. This transformation from one schema to another may also involve filtering unwanted or unnecessary data. In the figure, the darkened components of the XML document are retained in the new schema, but several of the other components of the original schema (in white) don't appear in the new schema. For the latest information on XML and reporting, see *www.w3.org/xml*.

SUMMARY

Best practices come from experience. Serious game developers can benefit from the experiences of entertainment game developers, the modeling and simulation community, educational courseware designers, and the general software industry to the extent that a serious game makes use of elements defined by each discipline. Many of the best practices in the entertainment games industry are directly applicable to serious games development because both groups of developers engage in programming, asset development, level design, creating actor descriptions, and archiving.

In the design of a user interface, it helps to consider the interface not as a monolithic whole, but as a multitiered model with the physical interface as its base. Upon this base are built the graphical, logical, emotional, intelligent, and emotionally intelligent components. A given serious game may not have an entire complement of layers from physical to emotionally intelligent, but all games have at least the first four tiers, from physical to emotional.

Programming best practices include a consideration of the languages used to construct the game and the quality and sources of the specific data structures and algorithms used to perform basic operations. Program flow diagrams are useful in documenting high-level program flow. Code review, a practice common in the programming industry, is an important quality assurance practice that attempts to identify programming problems early in the programming process.

The best practices of working with assets include developing an Art Bible that details the various asset types and a constantly updated Master Asset List that contains an exhaustive list of the assets used in a game. Detailed actor descriptions, including a description of the player character, nonplayer character, vehicles, and effectors leave little room for error or misunderstanding during the design and implementation of actors. Effector matrices and decision tables are useful in fully defining the possible character states.

Level maps and logic maps are components of level logic best practices that help ensure a deliberate, planned progression of challenge while simplifying the development process. Best practices archiving methodologies, such as the proactive methods advanced by the NARA, help guarantee the survival of the development shop's intellectual properties. Assessment, often emphasized in serious games work, is best addressed by starting out with goals expressed as measurable behavior changes using a standard nomenclature, following proven protocols, and reporting user activity with standards such as XML.

REFERENCES

[Avrin00] Avrin, D. E., K. P. Andriole, et al., "Simulation of Disaster Recovery of a Picture Archiving and Communications System Using Off-site Hierarchal Storage Management." *Journal of Digital Imaging* 2(2000): pp. 168–70.

[Bergeron88] Bergeron, B. P., "Toward more effective learning environments: strategies for computer simulation design." *Collegiate Microcomputer* 4(1988): pp. 289–309.

[Bergeron91] Bergeron, B. P., R. N. Shiffman, et al., Composing User Models through Logic Analysis. *Fifteenth Symposium on Computer Applications in Medical Care* (1991): pp. 681–85.

[Bergeron90] Bergeron, Bryan, "Program instrumentation: A Technique for Evaluating Educational Software." *Collegiate Microcomputer* 1(1990): pp. 34–46.

[Bergeron01] Bergeron, B., *The Eternal E-Customer: How Emotionally Intelligent Interfaces Can Create Long-Lasting Customer Relationships.* McGraw-Hill, 2001.

[Bergeron02] Bergeron, B., *Dark Ages II: When The Digital Data Die.* Prentice Hall PTR, 2002.

[BergeronRouse92] Bergeron, Bryan and Ron Rouse, Cognitive aspects of modeling and simulating complex biological systems, in *Structuring Biological Systems: A Computer Modeling Approach.* CRC Press, 1992.

[Bloom84] Bloom, Benjamin, *Taxonomy of Educational Objectives.* Pearson Education, 1984.

[Bourg02] Bourg, David, *Physics for Game Developers.* O'Reilly & Associates, 2002.

[Boxer01] Boxer, S., "A Century's Photo History Destined for Life in a Mine. *The New York Times* (April 15, 2001): p. B1.

[Byrne05] Byrne, Ed, *Game Level Design.* Charles River Media, 2005.

[Card88] Card, Orson, *Characters and Viewpoint.* Wriger's Digest Books, 1988.

[Card90] Card, Orson, *How To Write Science Fiction & Fantasy.* Wriger's Digest Books, 1990.

[Champandard04] Champandard, A. J., "Scripting Tactical Decisions," in *AI Game Development: Synthetic Creatures with Learning and Reactive Behaviors.* New Riders Publishing, 2004.

[Conger04] Conger, D., *Physics Modeling for Game Programmers.* Thomson Course Technology, 2004.

[Csikszentmihalyi91] Csikszentmihalyi, Mihaly, *Flow: The Psychology of Optimal Experience.* Perennial, 1991.

[Dalmau04] Dalmau, D., *Core Techniques and Algorithms in Game Programming.* New Riders, 2004.

[Getty05] Getty, *Learn about the Getty Vocabularies.* 2005. *www.getty.edu/research/conducting_research/vocabularies/*, accessed June 15, 2005.

[Hartley01] Hartley, D. E., *Return on Investment, in Selling e-Learning.* ASTD, 2001.

[Hurley83] Hurley, R. B., *Decision Tables in Software Engineering.* Van Nostrand Co., 1983.

[Idbias05] Idbias, S. *Joy Mountford.* 2005. *www.idbias.com/people.html*, accessed June 13, 2005.

[Jenkins05] Jenkins, David, E.A. Fathammer, "Bandai Announce BREW Support." *Game Developer.* 2005. *www.gamasutra.com/php-bin/news_index.php?story=5614*, accessed June 14, 2005.

[Johnson04] Johnson, W., Tactical Language Training System: An Interim Report. *Interservice/Industry Training, Simulation, and Education Conference (I/ITSEC)* (2004): pp. 1–11.

[Kirkpatick96] Kirkpatick, D. L., *Evaluating Training Programs: The Four Levels.* Berrett-Koehler, 1996.

[LOC05] LOC, *Thesaurus of Graphic Materials I (TGM-I).* Library of Congress. 2005. *www.loc.gov/lexico/servlet/lexico?usr=pub&op=sessioncheck&db=TGM_I*, accessed June 16, 2005.

[Ludwig68] Ludwig, HR, Simulation with Decision Tables. *Journal of Data Management* (January 1968): pp. 20–27.

[Lukeman02] Lukeman, Noah, *The Plot Thickens.* St. Martin's Griffin, 2002.

[McCarthy86] McCarthy, J., Decision Tables and Logic Processing. *Computer Language* (November 1986): pp. 73–80.

[McConnell04] McConnell, Steve, *Code Complete.* Microsoft Press, 2004.

[Meyers01] Meyers, Scott, *Effective STL.* Addison-Wesley, 2001.

[NASA05] NASA, *Scientific and Technical Information*. NASA. 2005. *www.sti.nasa.gov/thesfrm1.htm*, accessed June 15, 2005.

[NIST05] NIST, *Dictionary of Algorithms and Data Structures*. National Institute of Standards and Technology. 2005. *www.nist.gov/dads/*, accessed May 8, 2005.

[PollackGreenes85] Pollack, Mike, and Robert Greenes, Computer-Based Educational and Analytic Support through Linking of Pictorial Simulations and Spreadsheets. *Proc Society for Medical Decision Making Seventh Annual Meeting* (1985): pp. 18.

[PollackGreenes86] Pollack, Mike, Robert Greenes, A pictorial Simulation Construction Kit for Enhancing Knowledge-Based Learning. *MedInfo '86* 1986): pp. 887–90.

[Ray01] Ray, Erik, *Learning XML*. O'Reilly & Associates, 2001.

[RayNorris05] Ray, Robert, Bret Norris, *The Weekend Novelist*. Watson-Guptill Publications, 2005.

[Suwa84] Suwa, M., A. C. Scott, et al., "Completeness and consistency in a rule-based system," in *Rule-Based Expert Systems*. Addison Wesley, 1984.

[West05] West, Mick, "Pushing Buttons: Intelligent Solutions for Ambiguous Player Controls. *Game Developer* (May 2005): pp. 19–26.

[WHO05] WHO, *International Classification of Diseases (ICD)*. WHO. 2005. *www.who.int/classifications/icd/en*, accessed June 15, 2005.

TOOLS

In This Chapter

- Software and hardware tools for serious game development
- Example development suites

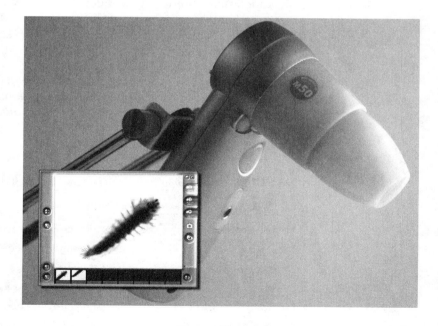

INTRODUCTION

Walking through the vendor area during the annual Game Developers Conference, it's difficult to imagine a time when game development tools were in short supply. When the game development industry was in its infancy, there were no conferences with aisle after aisle of game engines, middleware, and 3D rendering packages. Instead, developers had no choice but to write directly to blitters, sound mixers, and shaders, and create graphics with in-house editors.

Given the availability of off-the-shelf tools, most serious games developers are tool users as opposed to tool builders. Commercial game engines, programming languages, and 3D modeling packages are too accessible for developers to have reason to build home-grown applications. No longer do real developers necessarily create applications from scratch. Even game developers working with embedded hardware avail themselves of microprocessor kits and libraries of proven routines. Game development is now about integration—selecting tools that not only work together to fulfill the needs of the game design, but that are affordable, easy to learn and use, and that provide the greatest return on investment. This is no mean task, given the complexity of the technologies that feed the game development pipeline.

Table 6.1 provides an inventory of the major hardware and software tools applicable to serious games development. With the exception of digitizers and audio equipment, most hardware used in game development is similar to that used in any modern business. The major difference between the laptops, workstations, and monitors that can be found in the typical game development shop and those in, say, an automated meat packing plant, is raw processing power and video capabilities. Companies such as Alienware®, which offer bleeding-edge hardware at a premium, enjoy a brisk business because of the extreme demands developers place on computer hardware when compiling a level, rendering a complex 3D scene, or encoding a video file.

TABLE 6.1   Hardware and Software Tools for Serious Games Development

HARDWARE	SOFTWARE
Audio Equipment	2D Art/Image Manipulation
Data Storage	3D Rendering/Modeling/Animation
Deployment Platform	Asset Management
Desktops	Audio Utilities (Composition, Editing, Codecs)
Digitizing Equipment	Game Engines/Development Environments
Graphics Accelerator Cards	Middleware (AI, Physics, Networking, User Interface)
Laptops	Programming (Languages, Compilers, Debuggers)

→

HARDWARE	SOFTWARE
Monitors	Assessment (Statistical Analysis, User Tracking)
Servers	Utilities (Installers, Security)
Workstations	Video (Editing, Codecs)

SPECIALIZED HARDWARE	SPECIALIZED SOFTWARE
Electronic Test Equipment	Electronic Distribution
Embedded Microprocessors	Hardware Emulators & Cross Compilers
Prototyping Boards	Mobile Programming Libraries

Most of the software for serious games development is highly specialized. The modeling and simulation tools used to develop serious content are typically used in academic and commercial research labs and engineering shops. 2D and 3D rendering packages are popular in the hobby and graphic arts communities, but the high-end packages are limited to professional development shops.

Middleware and game engines are even more specialized. Although there are hundreds of enthusiast-level engines and development environments for hobby and educational users, there are at best a few dozen engines worth considering for serious games development. While many of the game engines and middleware products can be differentiated according to price, the software product or license price isn't necessarily a reflection of capability or quality. Often the price is a function of the market size and the amount and type of hand-holding provided by the vendor.

This chapter explores the range of practical and affordable hardware and software tools available to serious games developers, with an emphasis on tools likely to be used by a smaller, resource constrained shop. The challenge in providing an all-inclusive overview of tools are that applicable to every serious games developer is the vast difference between high- and low-complexity games.

As illustrated in the first two chapters, a serious game might take the form of a Web-based, 2D game written in Macromedia® Flash™, a custom hardware device, or a full 3D underwater environment with haptic feedback and 3D sound running on the Unreal Engine 3. A lone developer working on the Flash-based game might use a bitmap editor, such as Adobe® Photoshop®, to create the visual assets, and purchase any sound effects form one of the many sites on the Web. The developer working on the hardware device might spend more time with a multimeter and soldering iron than coding the game logic. The team of developers working on the 3D program would likely use every software and hardware tool listed in Figure 6.1—and then some. Furthermore, the artist of the team might consider a program like Photoshop suitable for creating a button or texture, but not for creating real content—something requiring the power and versatility of a 3D modeling program like 3ds Max.

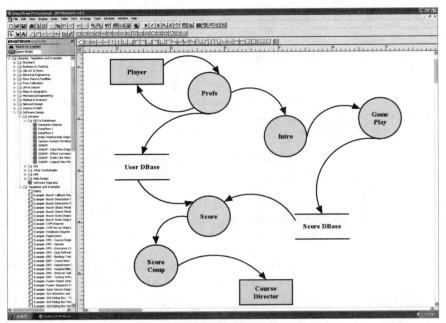

FIGURE 6.1   SmartDraw 6, showing a UML data flow document of the *Augmented Reality Medical Simulator* game. The list of templates and symbols is visible along the left side of the document.

A discussion of tools is also complicated by the volatility of the game tool market, with its seemingly constant mergers and acquisitions, the particular products introduced here will likely change in name and capability. However, more important than a particular tool is the types of tools that are available, and the criteria by which they are judged as suitable for serious games development. Although it's tempting to use a criteria such as the speed with which a given tool can be used to propel a game down the development pipeline, to do so would be myopic.

The gold standard in serious games is measurable behavior change. Moreover, although serious games might take numerous forms, there are no studies that show 3D games are inherently better at eliciting measurable behavior changes in players than 2D games, or that a particular game engine creates longer lasting behavior change in players than another engine. In the proper hands, the tools listed here, admittedly a small sample of what is available in the industry, can be used to create a game that succeeds by the gold standard.

DESIGN SOFTWARE

The fist step in developing a serious game to create a serious games design document that defines every detail of the development pipeline, from the creating the requirements specification and technical architecture to assessment and maintenance (see Appendix D, "Serious Games Design Document Outline"). Defining the purpose of the project, knowledge, skills, the attitude requirements that will serve as the basis for analysis, and other requirements can be facilitated with any number of tools, from Microsoft® Word and a business plan template from the Microsoft Web site (*office.microsoft.com/en-us/templates*) to specialized graphics packages.

One of the easiest to use graphics packages available for illustrating a game design document is SmartDraw™ (*www.smartdraw.com*), in part because of the vast library of symbols and templates that can be downloaded for free from the Web. The UML drawing in Figure 6.1 was created to illustrate the high-level technical architecture of the PC-based *Augmented Reality Medical Simulator* game introduced in Chapter 2, "Working Context." The diagram shows that when players enter their preferences, such as environmental sound level, an entry is made in the user database. Players can enter the game environment after passing through the introduction screen. Activity within the game is stored in a score database, which servers as the basis of the score display after gameplay. A score comparison feature (Score Comp) ranks scores from other sessions and other players and reports the gaming activity to the course director. SmartDraw is easy to learn because of the abundance of free online tutorials. Completed drawings can be embedded in Microsoft Word or exported in a variety of standard formats, from JPG and TIFF to DXF.

An alternative to SmartDraw is Microsoft Visio (*www.mvps.org/visio*), another comprehensive design package. Although *Visio* ships with fewer symbols and templates than SmartDraw, Microsoft also offers an extensive library of online templates and icons. Like SmartDraw, Viso can incorporate symbols from third parties.

As an illustration program, Visio is slightly more difficult to use than SmartDraw. However, where Visio shines is in its ability to integrate with and automate the development pipeline. Programmers can use Visio to create database diagrams automatically from SQL Server or Access, and UML diagrams from Microsoft Visual Studio™ .NET projects. Management can use Visio to create timelines from Microsoft Excel™ or Microsoft Project™, calendars from Microsoft Outlook, and organizational charts from Excel or Microsoft Exchange Server. In addition to creating diagrams from other Microsoft applications, Visio data can be exported to drive Microsoft Excel, Word, and SQL Server applications in the development pipeline.

In addition to data flow diagrams and other game design graphics, a game design document should contain the summary of a compelling story—normally referred to as the concept. Tools that can help create the story behind a serious game include IdeaFisher (IdeaFisher Systems, Inc.), Dramatica Pro (Write Brothers, Inc.), and Power Structure (Write-Brain. com). IdeaFisher is an outline and synonym generator that can suggest catchy phrases, symbolism, and plot elements. Dramatica Pro is a story-telling and scene creation utility for screenwriters that can help developers create realistic scenes and dialogue.

Power Structure is a general-purpose writing tool that supports character development, dialogue, and scene structure. Power Structure was used to develop the concept and backstory for the *Achilles* game because the program's Conflict View allowed the developers to assess the escalation of tension and conflict with game progress (see Figure 6.2). Another option, the Gestalt View, is useful in viewing the narrative according to Aristotle's three act model, which divides drama into beginning, middle, and end.

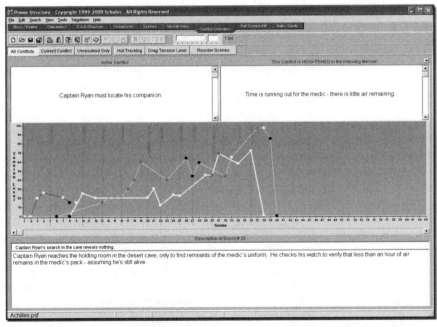

FIGURE 6.2 *Power Structure*, showing Conflict View of the narrative developed for the *Achilles* game.

Writing utilities aren't for everyone or for every serious game, and they won't provide the creativity needed to increase the odds that a serious game is fun or engaging. However, these tools can enable writers to save time and effort that can be invested elsewhere. The Writer's Store (*www.writersstore.com*) offers a wide selection of software for creating and perfecting narratives. See Appendix F, "Resources," for additional writing resources.

HARDWARE

The most appropriate computer hardware for a given game development project depends on the nature of the game, the work habits of the development team, the timeline, and the budget. The development hardware used in a small shop with one programmer and a part-time artist might consist of a desktop PC for the artist, a laptop for the programmer, and a second laptop for testing the game under development. A less economically challenged shop might have two workstations with large LCD displays and a hefty server.

Listed in Table 6.2 are recommendations for high-end to entry-level hardware for development, data acquisition, and embedded hardware games. The brands of the computer, processors, and accessories listed in the table are intended to provide readers with a concrete illustration of the range of hardware capabilities that should be considered by anyone setting up a serious games development shop or team. Computers from mainstream companies such as Compaq, HP, Gateway, and Sony, and performance systems from the likes of Falcon Northwest, VoodooPC, and Killer, are reasonable replacements for the suggested Alienware and Dell systems. Also, note that in the context of this discussion, *high-end* refers to affordable high-end solutions and not the massive rendering farms and other stratospheric hardware found in the larger entertainment studios.

TABLE 6.2   High-end, Mid-level, and Entry-level Hardware Recommendations for Serious Games Development

	HIGH-END	MID-LEVEL	ENTRY-LEVEL
DEVELOPMENT			
Programming Workstation	Alienware MJ12® 7550i with Intel EM65T 3.6 GHz, 2 GB RAM, 400 GB HD, DVD R/W, 20" LCD monitor	Dell Precision 670 with Intel Xeon 3.2 GHz, 2GB RAM, 250 GB HD, DVD R/W. 20" LCD monitor	Dell Precision 670 with Intel Xeon 2.8 GHz, 1GB RAM, 40 GB HD, CD R/W. 19" CRT monitor
Art Workstation	Alienware MJ12® 7550i with Intel EM65T 3.6 GHz, 3 GB RAM, 400 GB HD, DVD R/W, Dual NVIDIA® Quadro™ FX 4400 PCI Express 512MB, dual 20" LCD monitors	Dell Precision 670 with Intel Xeon 3.2 GHz, 2GB RAM, 250 GB HD, DVD R/W. 20" LCD monitor	Dell Precision 670 with Intel Xeon 2.8 GHz, 2GB RAM, 160 GB HD, CD R/W. 19" CRT monitor

→

	HIGH-END	MID-LEVEL	ENTRY-LEVEL
Testing Platform	Dell Dimension 667r configured per minimum system requirements	Dell Dimension 667r configured per minimum system requirements	Generic desktop PC configured per minimum system requirements
Server	Dell PowerEdge 2800, Raid 10 4x300 GB, 4GB RAM	Dell PowerEdge 800, 160 GB, 1 GB RAM.	Dell PowerEdge SC420, 160 GB, 512K RAM.
Network	Linksys Wireless-G Broadband Router with SpeedBooster and EtherFast 10/100 switch	Linksys Wireless-G Broadband Router	Linksys Wireless-G Broadband Router
DATA ACQUISITION			
Images	Canon EOS 20D camera Proscope USB microscope HP Scanjet 8290 flatbed scanner	Canon Digital Rebel XT Proscope USB microscope HP Scanjet 8200 scanner	Nikon Coolpix 5600 Canon CanoScan LiDE 500F scanner
Video	Canon XL-2 Creative Sound Blaster® Audigy® 2 ZS Platinum Pro	Sony HDR-FX1 Creative Sound Blaster® Audigy® 2 ZS	Canon ZR300 Camcorder
Sound	Creative Sound Blaster® Audigy® 4 Pro and analog source Marantz PMD670 digital recorder Sennheiser HD600 headphones	Creative Sound Blaster® Audigy® 4 Pro and analog source Marantz PMD660 digital recorder Sennheiser HD580 headphones	Olympus VN-240 PC Digital PC Link Voice Recorder Laptop with audio digitizer Sennheiser HD457 headphones
Physiologic Signals	CleveMed BioRadio 150 wireless monitor	BioBench virtual instrument	Parallax USB Oscilloscope
EMBEDDED HARDWARE SYSTEMS			
Microcontroller Prototyping	Parallax BASIC Stamp Discovery Kit Repurposed controller	Parallax BASIC Stamp Professional Starter Kit Repurposed controller	Parallax BASIC Stamp 1 Starter Kit Repurposed controller
Test Equipment	Fluke digital multimeter B&K signal generator B&K regulated power supply Tektronix TDS1000 oscilloscope	Fluke digital multimeter Parallax USB oscilloscope	Radio Shack digital multimeter

Development Hardware

Because of development demand on hardware, even the entry-level computer systems listed in Table 6.2 for programming and art development are high-performance. However, the difference in price between high-end and entry-level workstations is considerable. In 2005 an NVIDIA® Quadro™ FX 4400 PCI Express 512 MB video card for an Alienware MJ12 workstation sells for as much as the entry-level Dell Precision 670 computer. The added cost of high-end hardware can be inconsequential if the development team can leverage the hardware to create better graphics and gameplay more quickly.

Some hardware options are so inexpensive that there is no significant difference between high- and low-end configurations, such as the network router options listed in Table 6.2. At less than $100, routers are an inexpensive component of the development infrastructure—as long as they're installed properly. Servers should accommodate the daily volume of data generated and archived daily and provide reasonable insurance against catastrophic loss of data.

Of particular importance is the testing platform, which should be configured at minimum system requirement level, as specified in the serious games design document. Furthermore, the testing platform is of value only if it's used frequently to check the status of builds, and not simply dusted off when development is theoretically near completion. For example, Alienware MJ12 with 256 MB of video RAM was used to develop the *Achilles* program, which was destined for a platform with only 32 megabytes of video RAM. At one point in development, we went two weeks without checking for compatibility on the test machine, only to spend the good part of the following week trying to determine the source of multiple problems on the test machine. It turned out that seemingly random freezes were due to exceeding the capacity of the 32 MB video card. The fix required reworking the game environment graphics so that video card wouldn't spend time paging textures in and out of memory.

Not listed in the development hardware section of Table 6.2 are the standard infrastructure technologies that are assumed, such as uninterruptible power supplies (UPS) for the servers, a temperature controlled environment for equipment longevity and developer productivity, and ergonomically correct keyboards, trackballs, and mice.

Data Acquisition Hardware

Ideally, all of the images, video, and sound required for a game can be purchased from one of the many suppliers on the Web. However, it's often the case that the desired style, resolution, or topic isn't available. In this situation, it's up to the development shop to acquire the content so that the art staff can work it as-is or with modification into the game design. The basic hardware for data acquisition is described here.

Images

One of the most difficult tasks in designing and developing a 3D video game is coming up with the assets required to create consistent and appropriate themes of color, lighting, and texture. Consider the assets required for a serious game intended to teach surgical procedures to residents through a simulated hospital operating room (OR) environment. The blue surgical drapes can't be just any shade of blue and the finish can't resemble shiny silk or crinkled paper. If the drapes don't appear to be made of traditional blue fabric, the surgical residents might not know that the color and texture are off, but they will know that something isn't right. Lacking off-the-shelf assets, the best way to present realistic settings in a game is to capture the colors, textures, and lighting of the real thing.

Digital cameras offer the quickest, most versatile solution to image acquisition. An entire OR can be filmed in a few minutes, and then the images can be transferred directly to a workstation for processing. For textures, a camera with a good macro lens is essential, as are the usual accessories, including a stable tripod or monopod. Flash should usually be avoided because it changes the color and apparent texture of surfaces. The latter can be minimized by using an off-camera flash that exposes the surface off-axis.

A digital SLR that supports data capture and storage in RAW format, such as the current equivalents of the Canon EOS 20D, Digital Rebel XT, or the Nikon D70, is ideal. Most digital cameras for the consumer market store images as JPGs to save space on the storage media. Because the compression process that results in JPGs involves throwing out data, there is less data to work with after the images have been downloaded into a computer for processing. The advantage of working with RAW images over JPGs is that the art staff has more leeway in manipulating RAW images with Photoshop or other image editor.

When working inside without a flash, a fast or large aperture lens (for example, f/2.8) is essential. Accelerated compact flash memory cards, such as the Lexar Media 2 GB 80x Pro Series Compact Flash Card or equivalent Type I cards from ScanDisk, provide storage capacity for dozens of RAW format images. RAW images require between 10 and 15 MB of space per image, depending on the camera resolution.

A fast lens and a good digital camera body can cover most image acquisition needs for games that use textures of walls, floors, and objects that will be viewed from a normal distance. However, when the operational scale approaches the microscopic then even a good macro lens won't do. In medicine, details of moles and other skin lesions, insects and insect bites, or blood and tissue samples require a microscope for visualization and image capture. Similarly, in manufacturing, defects in weld joints, paint finish quality, oxidation of metal, and surface damage from weather or abuse require microscope optics and a means of digitizing the images.

One solution to capturing microscopic images is to attach a 35 mm camera to a microscope, expose a roll of film, and then scan the resulting slides. A better solution for modest magnifications is to use a digital microscope. The ProScope USB microscope (*www.theproscope.com*) is the least expensive and most versatile of the professional-class digital microscopes on the market (see Figure 6.3). The complete system, with adjustable stand, set of detachable lighted lenses, and case sells for around $1,000. The handheld unit and 50× lens is a more affordable option, at about $300.

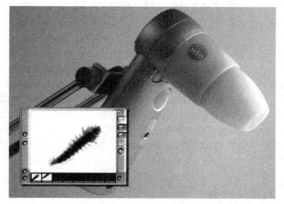

FIGURE 6.3   ProScope USB microscope with insert of the accompanying software illustrating an image of a mosquito larva at 200×.

In addition to the dedicated lens system, an adapter provides compatibility with standard c-mount camera lenses, telescopes, and microscopes. The microscope with the 200× lens was used to capture microscopic images of mosquito adults and larva for the *Medical Malaria* game described in Chapter 5, "Best Practices." The software that accompanies the USB-powered microscope captures individual JPG images, triggered either by the software or from the handheld unit.

The main limitation of the ProScope, which also captures movies, is that the image resolution is only 640 × 480. In developing textures for the mosquito and larva in *Medical Malaria*, this resolution limit was problematic. The images of scaling on the mosquito thorax and hairs on the larva body proper were only a dozen pixels square. Creating a 128 × 128 texture entailed the use of Adobe Photoshop to replicate the small samples and create a larger texture that could be applied to the models.

An often overlooked image acquisition device is the flatbed scanner. Even inexpensive units, such as the Canon CanoScan LiDE 500F, which sells for about $100, captures 48-bit color images at over thousand pixels per inch. The resolution and pixel depth are more than adequate for capturing textures and small 3D objects. An advantage of lightweight, USB-power units such as the CanoScan is mobility. When used with a laptop, the scanner can be placed against material and objects that need to be scanned. The major difference between the CanoScan and a high-end unit such as the HP Scanjet 8290 is scanning time, which can be up to a minute for the CanoScan versus a few seconds for the more expensive Scanjet. As noted earlier, the specific models and brands are irrelevant—the important take-away is the relative capabilities of each technology.

Video

Video cutscenes are one way to provide a game with an instant backstory and working context. Often, cutscenes are made from gameplay composites, but they can also come from external sources. External cutscenes have the benefit of sparing the programming staff from scripting gameplay. Video is also used in serious and entertainment games to document character movement, complex procedures, the details of how a vehicle handles a curve, or how an attack chopper kicks up dust as it lands.

Options for video capture range from inexpensive consumer camcorders, such as the equivalents of the Canon ZR300, to the Sony HDR-FX1 and the professional/consumer Canon XL-2. As with digital still cameras, the more and better quality the glass in front of the charge-coupled device (CCD) and the greater the resolution, the more capable and expensive the camcorder. Video capture is at least as much about the reflectors, backdrops, and lighting equipment as it is about the camera.

The most appropriate camera hardware for game development depends on the capture requirements. For documentation purposes, a small, unobtrusive, lightweight camcorder is ideal. However, for textures and image capture for asset development, the better camera systems provide noticeably better results. Both the Canon XL-2 and Sony HDR-FXI provide macro image capture with their standard lenses. The Canon has the advantage of compatibility with the line of Canon still image lenses.

In addition to acquiring assets, video cameras are useful in the testing stage of development, to record player interaction with a particular user interface or mechanism on a hardware-based serious game. In video tracking, there are usually two or three cameras in the test area, one on the player and one on the keyboard and display. In this configuration, facial expressions and eye movement can be tracked in parallel with what's happening on the screen.

Sound

Thanks to the popularity of PC-based digital music synthesizers, MP3 players, and the emphasis on 3D sound in entertainment games, there are dozens of hardware options for sound capture. Although even basic PCs have reasonable sound capture hardware, the best sound capture option for recording voice and special effects is to use specialized hardware in a soundproof sound studio. However, at $5,000 or more for a day at a recording studio, a studio might not be an option.

Simply plugging a microphone into the sound card of a desktop PC will often result in keyboard, mouse, and fan noises in the recording. A quiet laptop with a quality, noise-canceling microphone is a better solution, assuming the built-in sound capture hardware is adequate. Better results can usually be achieved with a low-noise analog or high-end digital recorder and post-processing with a PC.

The standard audio capture hardware that ships with a laptop or desktop PC is easier to use with an audio capture utility, such as the Advanced MP3/WMA Recorder, from XaudioTools.com (*www.xaudiotools.com*). The utility, shown in Figure 6.4, can capture streaming audio from any source—from the Internet, a video game, or DVD, to iTunes—and store it as a WAV, MP3, or WMA file. In addition to original audio capture, the utility is useful for converting sounds from MP3 to WAV when the originals have been lost or are unavailable. An alternative to the simple and easy to use Advanced MP3 is Total Recorder Pro, from High Criteria

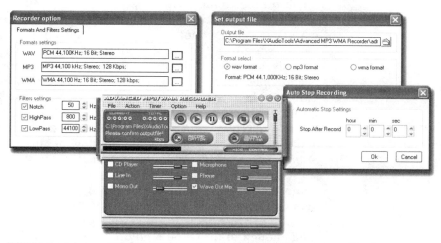

FIGURE 6.4 *Advanced MP3/WMA Recorder*, a low-cost audio capture utility for capturing sound using native PC hardware.

(*www.highcriteria.com*). The shareware utility has more features than Advanced MP3, including optional add-ons and basic editing capabilities.

The hardware solutions to sound capture listed in Table 6.2 assume on-site recording of sounds, from natural environmental sounds to the percussion of grenade launchers. Low-end solutions, such as the Olympus VN-240 PC Digital PC Link Voice Recorder, can be used to capture sounds for prototype development. The problems with digital *voice* recorders include limited bandwidth and low signal-to-noise figures. The handheld recorders are capable of 30 hours or more of recording because of heavy onboard compression and filtering out the higher frequencies. The more expensive recorders that are designed for music recording, such as the Marantz series of portable digital recorders, have greater bandwidth and typically significantly better noise figures.

Even low-end, digital voice recorders are easier to work with than cassette recorders because they obviate the need to digitize the analog audio from tape. However, there are many affordable audiophile-quality cassette tape decks still in circulation. Creative Sound Blaster offers a line of consumer cards that can be used to capture audio from analog sources, including cassette and VCR tapes.

A number of digital stethoscopes are available for capturing physiological sounds and well as sounds from engines or other mechanical devices, such as the ticking of a watch or the trigger action of a gun. One of the best recording stethoscopes for physiologic sound recording is the 3M Littmann Electronic Stethoscope–Model 4000. At about $425, it's an expensive sound acquisition device, but sounds can be quickly and easily downloaded to a PC via an IR link. The similarly priced Welch Allyn Meditron Electronic Stethoscope–Model 5079-400 is another viable option. Both stethoscopes differ from most electronic stethoscopes on the market in that they not only electronically amplify, filter, record sounds, but the sounds can be transferred to a PC for use in a game.

Developers who choose to work with audio should consider quality headphones, such as the Sennheiser line (*www.sennheiserusa.com*). A common mistake is to work with computer speakers, which can hide or muffle hum, clicks, and pops that may be noticeable to players who use headphones, play games in a quiet room, or crank up the volume of their audio system. For example, in developing the sound routines for the *Augmented Reality Medical Simulator*, a major hurdle was identifying the sources of occasional snaps and pops in the heart sounds. When the audio files were examined through Adobe® Audition™, the sound envelopes were free of spikes and the sound was clean. However, when the sound files were played through the game environment, the pops were loud enough to throw off a physician or student listening closely for the opening snaps characteristic of some cardiac diseases. The low-level noises probably wouldn't have been noticeable to a casual player listening to an explosion or other special effects, and they weren't noticeable to students when the heart sounds were played through the computer speakers. The work-around involved bypassing the game development environment's built-in sound handling routines with those of a custom DLL.

As a final note on sound capture hardware, players are much less forgiving of sound anomalies than blemishes on a texture or problems with color palates. Postprocessing can address issues such as compression, equalization, and normalizing levels, but it can't remove the rumbling from traffic, conversations picked up from the office next door, or other noise without degrading the desired audio. Investing in quality audio capture up front can save time and headaches in the postprocessing phase of development.

Physiologic Signals

Virtual instruments—signal acquisition and analysis instruments that use the PC for back-end signal processing and display—are a viable option for game developers who need to collect data for the serious component of a game that makes extensive use of physiologic data. Parallax offers an inexpensive USB oscilloscope (about $130) that uses the CPU in a laptop or desktop PC to analyze and display data from the hardware module. More capable but more expensive virtual instruments are available from National Instruments (*www.ni.com*), which has been a leader in the virtual instrument industry for years. Its icon-based LabVIEW software (*www.ni.com/labview*) can emulate dozens of virtual instruments, from frequency counters to digital oscilloscopes. In addition to this general-purpose, extensible virtual instrument interface, National Instruments offers specialty-specific instrument interfaces to its line of data acquisition hardware.

BioBench, shown in Figure 6.5, is designed specifically for data acquisition in the life sciences. The advantage of *BioBench* over a general-purpose oscilloscope or other virtual instrument is that the interface is familiar to clinicians and physiologists who have worked with EKGs, pulse oxymetry, blood pressure, and other physiological signals.

A more expensive but portable and less obtrusive signal monitoring device, the *BioRadio 150*, is available from CleveMed (*www.clevemed.com*). The $6,000 wireless unit can be used to monitor EEG, EMG, EKGs, pulse, respiration, blood oxymetry, and even eye movement during gameplay.

In addition to providing a useful data acquisition platform for asset development, both the *BioBench* and *BioRadio 150* can be use in the testing and assessment phases of game development. Measures such as EKG signals, pulse, jaw muscle activity, and depth of breathing can be captured and used to infer the player's state of stress during gameplay. EEG data, such as detection of 40-Hz oscillations in the thalamocortical neuronal circuits of the brain, can be used to infer learning is occurring [Vlessides04].

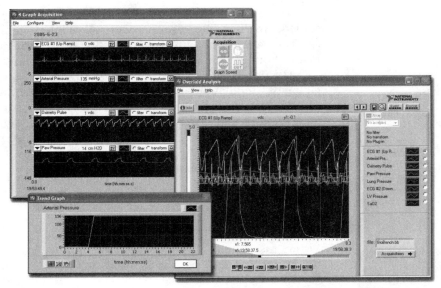

FIGURE 6.5 National Instruments *BioBench* virtual instrument for biomedical data acquisition and analysis.

Embedded Hardware

Embedded hardware, whether used as an alternative to game controllers, a basis for stand-alone games, or to collect data used to construct a game, is a familiar serious gaming paradigm. As noted in Chapter 1, "Historical Perspective," and Chapter 2, "Working Context," many serious games have an embedded hardware component. Flight simulators outfitted with realistic cockpit controls and mannequins with heart and lung sounds are examples of embedded hardware systems that extend the functionality and pedagogical value of stand-alone and PC-based serious games.

Repurposed Controllers

There are several approaches to providing alternative hardware interfaces to PC-based games. The easiest and least expensive approach is to harvest the main circuit board from a wireless or wired game controller and use the circuitry to instrument an appropriate device or object.

Figure 6.6 shows the main board of a Wireless Kensington RumblePad 2. The original unit, shown in the lower right corner of the figure, was disassembled by removing five retaining screws. Next, the two joystick mechanisms were unsoldered from the motherboard, and the connection to the vibration motors and two external switching pads were set aside. The board supports 16 digital (on-off) and four analog inputs. The two output connections can be used with the original vibration feedback mechanism to provide proprioceptive feedback or to energize other circuitry.

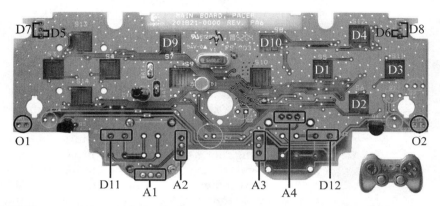

FIGURE 6.6   Main board of a wireless Kensington RumblePad 2, showing the 12 standard digital (D1–D12) inputs as well as the 4 analog (A1–A4) input ports and two analog output (O1 and O2) ports. An assembled RumblePad 2 is shown in the lower right.

The beauty of embedding a repurposed controller in, say, a mannequin used to teach medical students or medics, is that the interface protocols and software support have been taken care of by the controller manufacturer. The control panel used to calibrate the RumblePad 2, for example, works just as well with the controller rewired and embedded in the chest cavity of mannequin. Furthermore, from a programming perspective, all that programming staff has to do is reference the controller buttons and joystick states as usual.

The meaning of button on-off events or position of the joystick is determined by software. Listing 6.1 shows the CScript code required to access the state of the first controller button from the 3D GameStudio game shell.

LISTING 6.1   Accessing Status of Controller Button 1 with *3D GameStudio* CScript

```
// Access controller buttons to play cardiac auscultation
// sounds, according to button and patient_condition global
// ————————————————————————————
action play_heartsound ( )
{
```

```
while (1) // wait for system events
   {
   If (joy_1 == on) // controller button 1 pressed
      {
         play_aortic_area (patient_condition);
}
wait (1);
}
      }
```

The code in Listing 6.1 is from the serious medical game *Augmented Reality Medical Simulator™—Auscultation*. The game was developed using 3D GameStudio, a repurposed RumblePad 2 wireless controller, a Capeline vest, and about $50 in sensors and miscellaneous parts.

The listing shows the ease with which controller events can be evaluated from within a game engine. When the circuit associated with button 1 is closed, whether from a thumb on button 1 of an intact game controller or a stethoscope head placed over a proximity sensor, the game plays the heart, lung, or abdominal sound appropriate for the patient's condition and the location of the stethoscope.

A portable version of the game, named *Mixed Reality Auscultation Trainer*, was developed using an iPAQ PocketPC and a Bluetooth link to transfer stethoscope position information from the sensors to the handheld. The handheld version, shown in Chapter 1, "Historical Perspective," was designed to address the problem of transporting full-sized, instrumented mannequins to remote areas for training army medics and first responders.

The sensors for laptop and PocketPC versions of the auscultation game are embedded in a vest worn by an instructor or another trainee to provide the player with the tactile response and emotional interchange of a real patient encounter. The augmented reality system can double as an ordinary instrumented mannequin by placing the vest on an inexpensive mannequin (see Figure 6.7).

Thanks to the availability of off-the-shelf hardware, most of the development work was associated with determining how to present cases in a fun and engaging manner. This included developing an intelligent tutoring system to enable the game to select cases appropriate for the player's level of expertise and to provide constructive criticism. Evaluation of the system, the greatest challenge in the serious games space, is ongoing.

A repurposed game controller can be used to create much richer interfaces than the simple application demonstrated by *Augmented Reality Medical Simulator™—Auscultation*. For example, when the hardware is used with a flexible mannequin, whether that of a child or adult, embedded switches can be used to signal players when they are applying exces-

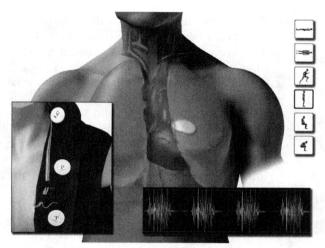

FIGURE 6.7 *Augmented Reality Medical Simulator—Auscultation*,
showing the on-screen game interface and the sensor vest (insert)
and several of the proximity sensors. © Archetype Technologies, Inc.

sive pressure or palpating the wrong area during an exam. The analog inputs to the controller provide even more flexibility, because they can be used to assess, for example, the degree to which a plastic knee joint is bent during an orthopedic examination or the force applied to a mannequin's chest wall during CPR training.

Considering most PC game engines support at least two game controllers, the number of input channels shouldn't be the limiting factor in an embedded controller game design. Furthermore, because the intensity, duration, and pattern of the vibration feedback can be manipulated programmatically, the output channels of a controller can be used to create a wide range of feedback options. For example, by intermittently compressing a water-filled sac connected to rubber tubes under a latex mannequin's skin, the controller output can be used to simulate normal and abnormal pulses. In addition, the pattern and number of output pulses can be interpreted by other embedded hardware to provide feedback ranging from haptics to synthesized speech and robotic movement.

Hardware Mods

An inexpensive approach can be used to develop exergames by modifying the miniature, battery-powered consoles, such as the *Plug It In And Play TV Games*, available from Radio Shack. With four mercury tilt switches, a few feet of ribbon cable, a momentary-on switch, and a balance board, playing

PacMan become a physically demanding exercise that develops the player's balance and body awareness. A balance board is simply a plastic or wooden disc, typically 18 inches in diameter, with a three- or four-inch dome mounted in the center of one side. Physical therapists and sports trainers use balance boards with their clients for rehabilitation of ankle injuries, to enhance range of motion, and for motor skill training. See OPTP for affordable models starting at around $30 (*www.optp.com*).

Modding a TV game involves disassembling the plastic case and soldering two wires of the ribbon cable in parallel with the main or reset switch and the remaining four pairs of wires in parallel with each of the four switches normally activated by the joystick. Notch out a small segment the seam of the plastic case to allow the ribbon cable to pass through without being crimped and reseal the case.

Next, glue or tape the four mercury tilt switches to small piece of plastic or inside a small plastic project box, with the four switches arranged so that they are 90 degrees apart (See Figure 6.8). That is, one points north, one points south, one points east, and one points west. Tilt each switch a few degrees so that the ball of mercury in each switch is normally not touching the electrodes when the plastic or project box is perfectly horizontal. Resistors or other spacers can be used to help angle the switches so that the mercury is near the tip of each glass envelope when the cluster is horizontal, as shown in Figure 6.8. Wire the mercury switches in parallel with the switches in the joystick corresponding to the same position. For example, the switch at 0 degrees in the joystick unit is connected to the mercury switch at 0 degrees. Mark the mercury switch at 0 degrees so that the orientation of the cluster can be determined later.

FIGURE 6.8 Mercury switch assembly, momentary-on switch, and ribbon cable used to convert a miniature console game into an exergame. © Archetype Technologies, Inc.

In operation, the mercury switch cluster is attached by Velcro to the bottom or top of the balance board with the marked mercury tilt switch facing forward. The joystick unit is placed on the floor, between the TV monitor and the balance board, and the player holds the reset switch in one hand. Instead of pressing the joystick forward to move the *PacMan* character forward, the player presses her toes down and adjusts her body to maintain balance. The ball of mercury in the marked tilt switch rolls forward and closes the circuit—equivalent to pushing the joystick forward.

To move the character left, she shifts her body weight to the left, with the right foot higher than the left foot, and so on. More advanced players stand on the board with one foot. Balance-challenged players start by sitting on the board and progress to standing when they're ready. In addition, some boards can be adjusted to provide different levels of instability to suit the player's skill level. The handheld switch is used to advance from one level to the next and to reset the game. The exact function might vary, depending on the model of TV game used. At a minimum, it should control firing or other main action.

For the average player without injury or balance issues, game selection is based on personal preference. However, for a player coming off of an injury, game selection should reflect the rehab requirements. For example, if the player has an ankle injury that requires predominantly lateral or side-to-side exercise, then a game that emphasizes left and right movement, such as *Centipede*, is more appropriate than *PacMan*. The mercury switches (about 60 cents each), cable, and momentary-on switch are available from Electronix Express, *www.elexp.co*m.

Microcontrollers

One method of interpreting game controller output signals is to embed a microcontroller along with the game controller hardware. Microcontrollers are self-contained computer systems on a chip, with a CPU, RAM, input/output circuitry, and a low-level operating system, optimized to control electronic devices. Several of the exergames discussed in Chapter 2, "Working Context," make use of microcontrollers to convert motion and impact into data that can provide the basis for gameplay on a PC or as a standalone gaming system. Standalone, microcontroller-based gaming systems are attractive when then is a need to leave the PC behind because of expense, need for portability or extended battery life, or because the environment is too rough for a laptop.

Figure 6.9 shows *Reflex Trainer*, a microcontroller-based serious game developed to train martial artists to respond faster to visual stimuli in preparation for sparring. In operation, the unit is strapped to a heavy bag as close to the level of the intended kick or punch as practical. With everything set, the player presses the button in the center of the unit.

Within a random period of time from one to five seconds, the two rings of LEDs flash, signaling the player to kick or punch the bag. A sensor in the unit measures the time and g-force of the blow and computes the player's reflex time. The time is displayed in milliseconds by illuminating the appropriate number of LEDs in the outer ring. The inner ring of LEDs shows the impact force, in g's.

BASIC Stamp
Microcontroller

FIGURE 6.9   Cutaway view of *Reflex Trainer* and the BASIC stamp microcontroller at the heart of the game. © Archetype Technologies, Inc.

Five seconds later, both rings of LEDs dim, and after a random delay of between one and five seconds, the LEDs flash, and the process is repeated until the player has made 10 attempts. The best time and impact force of the 10 rounds is displayed by the LEDs until the unit is reset for the next round or next player.

The electronics in the game can withstand the impact from gameplay, and the plastic case and LEDs can survive rough handling that would destroy an LCD screen. In addition, the LEDs can be easily read at a distance by a trainer and other players working on heavy bags in the same room. The unit can run continuously for days on a 9-volt battery.

Reflex Trainer is an example of a standalone game based on an inexpensive microcontroller, the BASIC stamp from Parallax (*www.parallax. com*). The BASIC stamp, which has been popular with hobbyists since the early 1990s, is a complete computer system and light BASIC interpreter on a surface mount chip. Games or other programs are written in PBASIC (Parallax BASIC) on Windows, Linux, or Macintosh, and then downloaded through a USB or serial cable to the EPROM on the stamp. After the program is downloaded, there is no need for the PC unless the program on the nonvolatile EPROM must be modified. Like other microcontrollers, the BASIC Stamp provides multiple input and output channels and isn't limited to driving strings of LEDs. The chip can interface with alpha-numeric LCD displays, WiFi and Bluetooth networks, video systems, and robots.

Parallax offers several microcontroller models, with processor speeds from 20–50 MHz and from 6 to 12 input/output channels. In addition to microcontrollers based on PBASIC, Parallax offers a JAVA-based microcontroller, the Javelin Stamp. The company also offers a wide variety of input transducers, from strain gauges to accelerometers (see Figure 6.10). The microcontroller can also drive a variety of output transducers, including one of several LCD screens offered by Parallax. Furthermore, the BASIC stamp or other microcontroller can be used to condition input transducers so that they appear as simple button presses or joystick movements in the controller. In this way, light, sound, humidity, sound, pressure, or change in direction can be used to trigger events in a PC game.

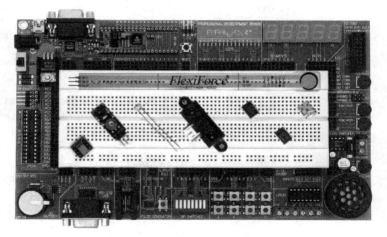

FIGURE 6.10   *Parallax Prototyping Board* showing a BASIC stamp microcontroller (top left). On the white prototyping area are sensors for force (top) and (left to right) orientation and g-force, vibration, light (analog output), distance, proximity, magnetic flux, and light (digital output).

Thanks to economic pressure from the consumer and military electronics industries, sensor technology has kept pace with advances in general purpose microcomputer technology. Sensors are smaller, provide more functionality, and have more onboard processing than ever before, reducing component count and making interfacing to microcontrollers simple electronically and programmatically. For example, the Memsic MX2125 accelerometer chip—first chip to the left on the prototyping area in Figure 6.10—can detect acceleration, vibration, impact, tilt, and rotation [Memsic05]. Inside the 1×1 cm chip, a heating element in the center of a gas filled chamber causes a pocket of hotter gas to rise to the top. Temperature sensors around the outside of the chamber determine the position of the pocket and onboard processing converts this data to digital information that can be read by a microcontroller.

Prototyping boards, such as the one in Figure 6.10, are the hardware equivalents of game engines, in that most of the work is in connecting predefined components. Creating a circuit involves inserting pre-trimmed wires and components into the perforated prototyping area. Input and output interfaces to the external world, including the PC used to program the microprocessor, are on the board. As a result, the developer is free to focus on coding the microcontroller.

Interfacing the accelerometer to the BASIC stamp on the prototyping board is as simple as inserting the accelerometer chip, two resistors, and two wires into the board. Programmatically, the accelerometer can be accessed by the BASIC Stamp chip with a dozen lines of PBASIC code, shown in Listing 6.2.

LISTING 6.2   Measuring Acceleration with the MX2125 Accelerometer with PBASIC and a BASIC Stamp Microcontroller

```
' Read the pulse outputs from a Memsic 2125 accelerometer
' and convert to G-force, according to the formula:
' milli-g = ((t1 / 10 ms) - 0.5) / 12.5%
'

' ———— I/O Definition ————-
' Use Pin 8 of the BASIC Stamp for input
'

Xin PIN 8
'

' ————- Constants ————-
' Scale constant is defined by the BASIC Stamp BS2P
'

Scale CON $0C0
'

' Use the high-going pulse of the accelerometer's output
'

HiPulse CON 1
'

' ————Variables ————-
' Raw data and milli-g variables
'
```

```
xRaw VAR Word
xmGForce VAR Word
'

'  —————————-Program Code  —————————-


Main:
DO
GOSUB Read_G_Force
/ Put subsequent GOSUB's here
            LOOP
          END


'  —————————Subroutine  —————————-
'

        Read_G_Force
PULSIN Xin, HiPulse, xRaw
xRaw = xRaw */ Scale
xmGForce = ((xRaw / 10) - 500) * 8
RETURN
```

The PBASIC code in Listing 6.2 reads the force on the MX2125 accelerometer chip and converts it to milli-g's (1/1000th of a g). The code is used with timer and randomization routines in the *Reflex Trainer* game.

Once the sensor data have been read into a microcontroller, the game and content acquisition applications are limited only by the developer's imagination. For example, the data from an accelerometer chip can be used with the repurposed game controller discussed earlier to control navigation and other movement in any game. Alternatively, the g-force data could serve as the basis for a musical exergame in which the player's running pace is used to select and play music of the same tempo.

Attaching the accelerometer to a balance board, such as the Reebok Core Trainer, can be used to covert any PC or console game into a sports game. The advantage of using a relatively expensive accelerometer in place of simple on-off mercury tilt switches is that the speed and direction of movement can be used to control a game. Although not applicable to a simple *PacMan* character, the difference in speed could be used to signal a player character in a modern game to walk, jog, or run in a particular direction.

The initial version of the *Augmented Reality Medical Simulator* system, introduced in Chapter 2, "Working Context," was developed with a repurposed game controller interface. In porting the system to a pocket PC for added mobility, the controller was replaced with a custom Bluetooth communications system compatible with the handheld. In the second-generation game, sensor processing and interpretation are handled by a BASIC stamp microcontroller that communicates with the handheld via

Bluetooth. Sound, gameplay, and ITS-based mentoring are provided by the handheld.

The bottom line is that serious games aren't limited to the confines of the PC or console box. For example, the hardware developer Gizmondo (*www.gizmondo.com*) has demonstrated several augmented reality interfaces to its handheld unit that might have application in serious games [Mott05]. Academia is also involved in augmented reality and wearable sensors research at institutions worldwide. The information available on augmented reality from MIT [MIT05], CMU [CMU05], and Columbia University [Columbia05] is particularly worth reading.

Readers interested in using microcontrollers and sensors for acquiring serious content or developing embedded hardware games should consider one of the many educational kits offered by Parallax. A BASIC Stamp starter kit, complete with prototyping board, microcontroller, parts, and book, is available from RadioShack for about $80. Documentation and tutorials on microcontrollers are available for free download from the Parallax Web site, and the company frequently offers reconditioned kits on eBay. See Appendix F, "Resources," for information on vendors and reference books.

Test Equipment

The minimum toolset for working with microcontroller hardware is a multimeter, primarily to verify that power is applied to the circuit and that there is continuity in the connections between the microcontroller and sensors. Developers working on complex circuit designs will benefit from a graphical means of tracing the chip logic, such as the inexpensive Parallax USB oscilloscope or high-end equipment from Fluke and Tektronix.

PROTOTYPING SOFTWARE

With rare exception, the journey down the game development pipeline includes a period of prototyping to address the uncertainties inherent in game design, whether related to serious content or gameplay. For example, as described in this chapter, software tools are readily available to support prototyping in both areas.

Serious Content

Deriving the equations that describe the orbit of a satellite or the survivability of a child in an area with endemic malaria are major steps in developing serious content. Regardless of the field, the data necessary to derive the equations necessary for a serious game are often unavailable, out of date, or inaccurate. In the instances when the data are available, game developers are usually faced with the need to simplify the math to free up computer resources for gameplay. For example, replacing trigonometric functions with computationally light, but less accurate, lookup tables is a common simplification technique. At issue is how much simplification is possible without invalidating the serious content.

Mathematical Modeling and Simulation

One way to verify that a simplified equation is good enough to serve as the basis for a serious game is to create a model with the equation, run it in a simulation, and then compare the output with actual data. There are two classes of mathematical modeling and simulation packages available to develop and test the equations associated with serious content. The first is low-level tools, such as Microsoft Excel, Mathcad Professional from Mathsoft (*www.mathsoft.com*), and MATLAB/Simulink from The Mathworks (*www.mathworks.com*).

In the proper hands, *Excel* can model anything that the other two packages can handle. However, it's most useful with relatively simple models and analysis because of the time involved in setting up a model. Mathsoft and MATLAB, in contrast, have predefined input and output screens that enable developers to quickly import data, manipulate the equations, run the simulation, analyze the data, manipulate the equations, and so on, until the domain expert (subject matter expert) working with the development shop is satisfied with the output.

The second class of modeling packages enable developers to work at a high system level to assess and develop computationally efficient equations. This category of tool is exemplified by Extend, from ImagineThat! (*www.imaginethatinc.com*), an interactive, icon-based modeling and simulation environment. Extend uses a hierarchical graphical interface in which a model is built by dragging blocks from a library onto a worksheet, connecting the blocks, and then entering the appropriate equations.

Figure 6.11 illustrates a pharmacology model of drug absorption developed with Extend. The main variables, dosage and dosages per day, can be changed by moving the two slider controls along the left side of the main panel. The model can be rerun to display the dynamic change in blood sugar with different doses of insulin and dietary changes over time.

The power of Extend and programs like it is that only the high-level view of the model is visible during the simulation runs, which allows domain experts and others to focus on systemwide effects of equation changes. The low-level details are easily accessed for manipulation, however. For example, clicking on the Absorption icon in the upper right of the main window of Figure 6.11 brings up a subwindow that shows absorption is modeled as a function of an absorption constant (absorption

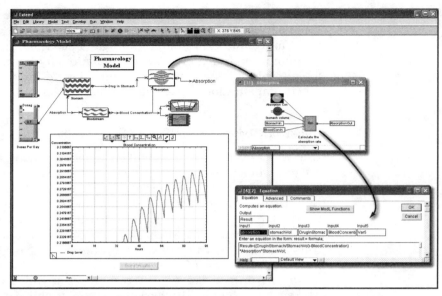

FIGURE 6.11 *Extend 6* from ImagineThat!, exploded to show the hierarchical encapsulation of modeling blocks and the underlying equation.

con), stomach volume, stomach input (stomachIn), and blood concentration (bloodConIn). Similarly, clicking on the Eqn icon in the absorption window brings up the equation editor that shows the equation relating the output to the four variables. Each of the other icons in the main window encapsulate lower-level icon models that eventually lead to numerical equations. An advantage of an icon-based interface of tools like *Extend* is that it facilitates ease of use and understanding by domain experts who must validate the models and underlying assumptions.

Gameplay

A storyboard—a graphical sketch of gameplay—is a good place to start a game design. However, defining the dynamics of gameplay usually requires an interactive prototype. Among the inexpensive game prototyping tools are lightweight compilers and click-together game development utilities by TheGameCreators (*www.thegamecreators.com*). The British company, known for its DarkBasic Pro development environment, offers a series of game development options for prototyping to simple game development.

The operational term in game prototyping is speed, and a novice can use the no-programming, click-together environment of FPSCreator (See Figure 6.12) and The 3D Gamemaker to create a game in less than ten minutes. As the name implies, FPSCreator is designed to develop first-person shooter games. In creating a game or prototype, developers first define a map for each level, using pre-fab corridors and rooms. Next, marker zones are added to define player start and goal locations, player checkpoints, healing areas, and other triggers. The game is then populated with non-player characters and props. Programming AI scripts and other elements of gameplay is optional. With the click of a button, the game compiles into an executable (.exe), which can be distributed, license-free.

FIGURE 6.12   *FPSCreator*, showing the click-together development environment (left) and the resulting 3D game (right). Note the overlay on the game showing CPU usage, frames per second, and other performance indicators.

In the hands of creative developer, FPSCreator can be used to create interesting games that have a retro look and feel. As a serious games prototyping tool, FPSCreator excels at interactive map design, especially in determining the best location for triggers, ambushes, and challenging goal locations. An early prereleased version of FPSCreator was used to prototype the levels used in *Achilles*, which was eventually coded in *3D GameStudio Pro* (Conitec) and Microsoft C++ for the DLLs. Although *3D GameStudio Pro* is more capable than FPSCreator, in terms such as lighting, character control, scripting options, and raw performance, its graphic editor is no match for the authoring environment provided by FPSCreator. Over the course of only a few hours, the developers were able to build a half-dozen levels and test them for playability. The maps were then reproduced in the 3D GameStudio Pro editor.

Another inexpensive game development environment from The GameCreators is The 3D Gamemaker, which supports first-person shooters, driving games, and third-person walkthroughs, among other genres. Like

FPSCreator, the program is good for prototyping level maps, and can import 3D models, sounds, and images. As a result, the prototype can approximate the look and feel of the final game. However, The 3D Gamemaker doesn't have a scripting language for fine-tuning the nonplayer character AI or other gameplay elements. Also, there is no export utility to use the maps in other game development environments.

The most powerful prototype development option from TheGameCreators, DarkBasic Pro (See Figure 6.13), is a full-fledged game development environment, complete with support for DirectX 9, particles, bone animation, and control over lighting. DarkBasic Pro is a good prototyping option for developers who are familiar with BASIC and DirectX. However, the resulting code and assets can be used as the basis for the full game.

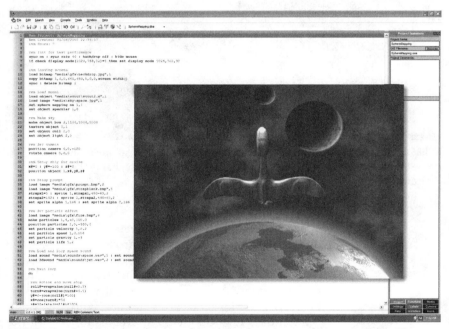

FIGURE 6.13 *DarkBasic Pro* character-based development environment with a 3D game executing in the foreground.

Developers considering Dark Basic or DarkBasic Pro for prototyping should pick up the *Beginner's Guide to DarkBasic Game Programming*, by Jonathan Harbour and Joshua Smith [HarbourSmith03]. The book comes with a CD-ROM that features trial versions of DarkBasic and DarkBasic Pro and several utilities for prototyping or developing games.

GAME ENGINES AND DEVELOPMENT ENVIRONMENTS

Choosing a game engine for production should take into account the design document, the collective experience of the development team with game engines, development tools, and the prototypes, and criteria such as the popularity and cost of the engine.

Table 6.3 lists the top ten commercial and open source 3D game engines, based on statistics compiled by DevMaster.net, a hobbyist game makers site, as of July 1, 2005. The commercial and open source game engines differ in cost, availability of source code, and the nature and amount of support from the developer. Not surprisingly, the most popular commercial game engines are also the least expensive. The license for the Torque Engine, the top-ranked commercial engine, is $100, including source code. There are no royalty strings attached.

TABLE 6.3   Top Ten Commercial and Open-Source 3D Game Engines, in Order of Popularity

ENGINE	DEVELOPER	GRAPHICS API	LANGUAGE	OS
Commercial				
Torque Engine	GarageGames	OpenGL, DirectX	C/C++	Windows, Linux, MacOS
TV3D SDK 6	Truevision3D	DirectX	C/C++, C#, Delphi, Visual Basic 6, VB.NET	Windows
3DGameStudio	Conitec DataSystems	DirectX	C/C++, Delphi	Windows
Deep Creator	Right Hemisphere	DirectX	C/C++	Windows
Reality Engine	Artificial Studios	DirectX	C/C++	Windows, XBox
Cipher	RH Systems	OpenGL	C/C++	Windows
Agent FX	Agency 9 AB	OpenGL	Java	Windows, Linux, MacOS, Solaris
3D Rad	3D Rad	DirectX	BASIC	Windows
Quest 3D	Act-3D B.V.	DirectX	C/C++	Windows
AMP 3D	Slam Software and 4D Rulers	OpenGL	C/C++	Windows
Open Source				
OGRE	Steve Streeting	OpenGL, DirectX	C/C++	Windows, Linux, MacOS
Crystal Space	Jorrit Tyberghein	OpenGL	C/C++	Windows, Linux, MacOS
Irrlicht	Nikolaus Gebhardt	OpenGL, DirectX	C/C++, C#, VB.NET	Windows, Linux

→

ENGINE	DEVELOPER	GRAPHICS API	LANGUAGE	OS
jME	Mark Powell and Others	OpenGL	Java	Windows, Linux
Reality Factory	Gekido Design Group	OpenGL, DirectX	C/C++	Windows
RealmForge GDK	Dan Moorehead	OpenGL, DirectX	C/C++, C#, D, Delphi, Ada, Fortran, Perl, Python, VB.NET	Windows, Linux, MacOS, Solaris, HP/UX, FreeBSD
The Nebula Device 2	Radon Labs	DirectX	C/C++	Windows
Axiom	Axiom	OpenGL, DirectX	C#, VB.NET	Windows
OpenSceneGraph	Robert Osfield and Don Burns	OpenGL	C/C++	Windows, Linux, MacOS, Solaris, SunOS, FreeBSD, Irix, Playstation
Genesis 3D	Eclipse Entertainment	DirectX	C/C++, Delphi, Visual Basic 6	Windows

Source: DevMaster.net. Accessed July 1, 2005.

The Torque Engine, by GarageGames, is a convenient focal point for a discussion of evaluating game engine options. A visit to the GarageGames Web site (*www.garagegames.com*) reveals that the Torque Engine

Has been used in several commercial games: There is proof that the game engine is complete and capable of generating a game solid enough to withstand the rigors of the commercial market.

Has an active and significant developer community: The odds are high that someone will be online to help solve a particular problem.

Provides access to source code: There is no need for a legal software escrow account. If the company behind the game engine folds, developers who have invested in the engine can continue on their own.

Is royalty-free: There are no additional legal or other hidden costs to contend with after a serious game is ready for publication and distribution.

Is well documented: The developer or the development community invested resources into developing documentation that can reduce the learning curve.

Offers a vast library of free online tutorials: The engine should be easier to learn, and the game developer isn't using the game engine as a means of selling training.

Is run by named staff with full contact information, including an address: A game engine might be developed in someone's garage, but the names, addresses, and photos of the management and development team on the Web site usually means that the team is committed to the engine.

Uses standard asset formats: Game engines that use proprietary asset formats and that can't export assets to standard formats lock developers into the engine.

Has a variety of reasonably priced add-ons: The business model isn't built around expensive add-ons. For example, in addition to the FPS and racing kits included in the base Torque Engine package, an RTS kit is available for about $50.

Has modest development hardware requirements: Extravagant development hardware requirements usually mean sloppy, bloated code.

Provides a free, full-function demo: The try-before-you-buy option underscores the developer's belief in the product.

Even though the Torque Engine (see Figure 6.14) fulfills the preceding criteria, it might not be appropriate for a particular serious game project or a developer. For example, compared with engines like Unreal or Gamebryo, Torque is clearly less powerful and less capable on several fronts. On the other extreme, the engine requires a C++ compiler on the development platform—a stipulation that might turn away prospective developers in a small shop who don't want to work in the Microsoft Visual C++ environment.

FIGURE 6.14 *Torque Engine* showing the terrain editor tool in operation.

The Torque Engine has been used to create network-aware multi-player games, but the game engine must be running locally on each player's PC. However, in some cases the immediacy of a Web-based game is preferable to a lengthy download and installation process. Macromedia Director™ (see Figure 6.15) and Authorware are popular authoring tools that can be used to create Web-based games. Unlike Torque Engine and many other large-footprint 3D game engines, Macromedia's shockwave player supports the development of 3D games that can be played over the Internet in a local Web browser.

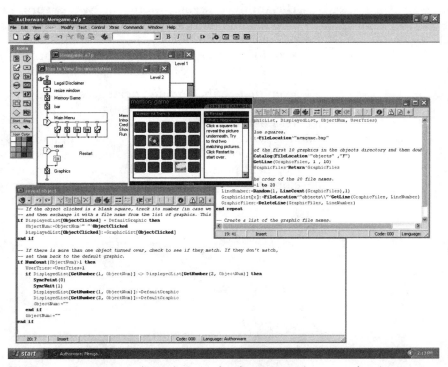

FIGURE 6.15 The Macromedia *Authorware* development environment showing a memory game under development.

The icon-driven Authorware is designed to integrate tightly with Learning Management Systems, whereas Director has much more flexibility and power when it comes to rendering 3D scenes. For example, Director supports bones, keyframe animation, a shader, and the other features commonly provide by 3D game engines. Furthermore, a game can be developed for the Web or and then delivered on CD-ROM with little or no recoding. Another advantage of Director is that multimedia shops familiar with the toolset can get up to speed in game design and development without learning a completely new suite of tools. While not as flexible Director, Authorware ships with a utility that enables developers to create SCORM-compliant simple games. This can be a critical feature, especially if the client is the U.S. military.

A notable game engine that doesn't appear in the top ten game engines list is Delta3D, from the Moves Institute Naval Postgraduate School (*www.delta3d.org*). Delta3D is an effort by the U.S. military to commoditize the game-based training, especially low-profile, low-budget games that can benefit from gaming technology but don't have the funds to support licensing a commercial game engine. Delta3D is an open source game engine in version 0.9 as of July 1, 2005. When the full version is released, it should become a major development environment for the military serious games development community because of its support for simulation industry standards.

The nature of the serious content, intended platform, experience, budget, and other internal factors will narrow the choices down to a handful of game engines. In the end, it's a popularity contest of sorts, because there's safety in numbers. A game engine that's otherwise perfect for a particular game design but has a small user base is a risky investment. Most engine developers don't have the resources to hand-hold individual developers, but instead facilitate a self-help game developer community by hosting online forums and generating newsletters.

Compared with PCs, there are fewer game engines for handhelds and cell phones. As noted in Chapter 5, "Best Practices," there are three major development standards: J2ME, BREW, and Symbian. J2ME, from Sun Microsystems, is free, and development shells that simplify J2ME programming, such as Omega Basic, are inexpensive and license-free. The proprietary Brew software development kit can be downloaded directly from Qualcomm (*brew.qualcomm.com*). Licensing and testing fees have to be paid to verify Brew-compatibility testing by a Qualcomm-certified shop. Developers who want to work with Symbian-compatible phones can download the free CodeWarrior for Symbian OS from the Symbian Web site (*www.symbian.com*). See Appendix F, "Resources," for additional cell phone and handheld development resources.

CODE CREATION AND MANAGEMENT

The livelihood and mental health of programmers often depend on having the most reliable, efficient, and effective tools on hand when they're needed. There are hundreds of tools available for every operating system and every conceivable task associated with creating and managing code. The most useful address the challenges common to any type of games development, such as how to address errors efficiently, how to increase programmer efficiency, and how to increase game performance.

Editors

Because of the popularity of Microsoft's Visual C/C++™, many programmers are comfortable with the standard Microsoft text editor. However, game editor developers frequently don't follow the Microsoft interface guidelines in their products. Programmers who want to work in multiple environments, but don't want to learn multiple editors, can use third-party game editors that provide the look and feel of the Visual C++ editor. For example, Brain Editor Pro (Twinno Software) is an alternative to the native editors that ship with Blitz 3D, DarkBasic Pro, 3D GameStudio, RAD, and the Torque Engine.

In the example shown in Figure 6.16, Brain Editor Pro is configured for 3D GameStudio. Help, dictionary functions, and legal-vocabulary highlighting and color are specific to 3D GameStudio, but the general layout parallels that of Microsoft Visual C/C++. With *Brain Editor Pro*, switching from CScript in 3D GameStudio to Visual C++ to code a DLL doesn't require the programmer to adjust to a new menu system or list of keyboard commands. Similarly, Brain Edit Pro enables a programmer to develop a prototype in Dark Basic Pro and then code the final version in the Torque Engine, all within the same editor.

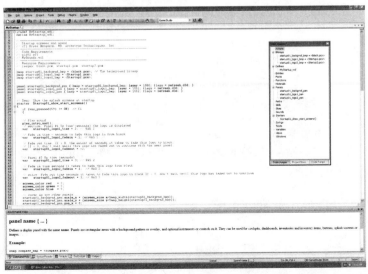

FIGURE 6.16   Brain Editor Pro provides a standard editor environment for programmers familiar with the Microsoft Visual C/C++ interface. By Twinno Software, *www.Twinno.com*.

Another advantage of using Brain Editor Pro over a native editor is the existence of advanced utilities for syntax checking, code completion, and highlighting. There is also a commands database, a project backup function, automatic indenting, a code jumper, function folding, and dynamic bracket matching. A modest project management utility, in the form of an integrated to-do list, is also included.

Brain Editor Pro is one of many alternative editors available for programmers. A search on Programmer's Paradise (*www.programmersparadise.com*), an excellent source of programming tools, reveals roughly 100 editor products. Readers interested in alternative editors should also consider the small, independent developers that offer inexpensive editors over the Web.

Compilers and Scripting Languages

The compilers and scripting languages that programmers can use for game development are usually dictated by the game engine. As depicted in Table 6.2, the languages supported by the top 10 commercial and open source game engines include C/C++, C#, D, Borland Delphi, Ada, FORTRAN, Perl, Python, VB.NET, and JAVA. In some cases, it isn't a question of which compiler or scripting language will work, but what the game engine developer is capable of supporting, in terms of skills. For example, in creating DLLs for 3D GameStudio, Conitec officially supports Microsoft C++ version 6, but states that game developers have used other compilers, including Borland Delphi. As noted earlier, this is where the size and depth of the development community come into play. There are also the practical limitations of funding, and the performance requirements, as specified in the requirements specification.

An advantage of using standard compiler environments is the availability of tools that support distributed compiling, such as IncrediBuild, by Xoreax (*www.xoreax.com*). IncrediBuild accelerates Microsoft C++ builds by distributing compilation tasks to other PCs running the network. Xoreax claims distributed compiling can reduce build times on the order of 90 percent. As with all distributed computing applications, the time savings depends on the performance of the network and the availability of idle hardware on the network. Xoreax licenses IncrediBuild on a per-seat basis.

Utilities

Utilities is a catch-all phase for the hundreds of add-ons that can make a programmer's life more pleasant and more productive. Some of the more important utilities for game development include Software Configuration Management (SCM) systems, code cleanup utilities, and profilers.

SCM systems are for organizing and tracking game program development, through activities such as version control, merging and tracking files, resolving differences between different revisions of the same file, and setting up incremental builds. Commercial SCM systems include Perforce, from Perforce Software (*www.perforce.com*), and IBM Rational ClearCase (*www-306.ibm.com/software/rational*). Tigris.org (*www.tigris.org*) offers an extensive list of open source versions of SCM systems.

Code cleanup, the programmer's equivalent of the grammar and spell check utilities in Microsoft *Word*, is practically synonymous with PC-Lint from Gimpel Software (*www.gimpel.com*). *PC-Lint*, one of the longest-lived utilities in the desktop computing industry, checks C/C++ code for bugs, glitches, inconsistencies, and other common coding errors.

As described in Chapter 4, "Standards," profilers help programmers identify which routines should be optimized for better gameplay. Programmers who use game engines with proprietary scripting languages usually have to rely on the profiling tools that ship with the engine. However, a variety of profiling utilities are available for game and DLL development in industry-standard C/C++. There are also profiling utilities available for Java development, including Borland Optimizeit (*www.borland.com/optimizeit*).

In addition to commercial profilers, there are several noncommercial utilities available to anyone as part of the DOE Advanced Computational Software Collection (*acts.nersc.gov*). For example, TAU (Tuning and Analysis Utilities), developed at the University of Oregon and the Advanced Computing Laboratory at Los Alamos National Laboratory, is available as part of the collection.

MIDDLEWARE

Middleware, whether for enhanced physics, AI, or fighting, tends to be game engine-specific. Of course, high-end middleware products are compatible with the engines used by the entertainment community because it can support hefty license fees. The middleware made for the game engines serious games developers use are generally affordable tools created by small shops. Even so, selecting the best middleware for a serious game involves attention to the same selection criteria used by developers of the AAA titles. There are obvious criteria, such as cost and availability of source code, as well as the feature set and proof of successful integration with specific game engines and other middleware. Evaluating the feature set of middleware packages can be daunting, especially at the beginning of a game development project, when there may be uncertainties in the game design.

Table 6.4 lists a subset of the features supported by Mythic AI (*www. saknet.com/ai/*), a third-party AI middleware solution for 3D GameStudio.

The feature set, which includes provision for following, hiding, and using weapons, limits the middleware to shooter games.

TABLE 6.4   Example of AI Middleware Feature Set

FEATURE	NOTE
Animations	User defined animations
Attack mode	Attack while in motion
Bot communications	Bots communicate when target spotted
Bot on Bot	Bot confrontations
Follow bots	Follow and helper bots
Health state	Bot reaction based on health state
Hiding spot events	Modifiable behavior when hiding
Hiding spots	Attack from an area of cover
Hit boxes	Site definable response to injury
Hit reactions	Response when hit
Injury response	Definable injury behavior
Investigate mode	Bots automatically investigate area
Models	User defined models
Patrol mode	Bots patrol specified area
Pursue	Shortest path pursuit
Real-time path finding	Custom pathfinding
Skill level	Accuracy and skill definable
Sleep mode	Sleep with fatigue
Sound sensitivity	Bots respond to noise
Sounds for events	Response to sounds definable
Visual sensitivity	Definable visual acuity
Wait	Bots stand and wait while scanning environment
Weapons	User defined weapons

Physics and AI middleware that target the general entertainment market is often offered in a form that can be called by DLL or accessed through a static library linkage. However, connectivity doesn't address issues such as memory management and integration with other middleware and tools. It's one thing to get a physics or AI middleware package working with a game engine, and another to get all three to work together. Developers considering a middleware package should demand evidence from the vendor that demonstrates compatibility with a specific engine and middleware combination.

ASSET CREATION AND MANIPULATION SOFTWARE

A game can have serious content validated by Nobel laureates and use the top-selling game engine and middleware, but without compelling assets, no one will bother playing it. The easiest and least expensive option for obtaining quality assets is to make use of the wide variety of affordable textures, terrain maps, sound tracks, and 3D models available through sites such as those listed in Table 6.5 and in Appendix F, "Resources."

TABLE 6.5   Sources of Game Assets on the Web

SOURCE	3D MODELS	TEXTURES	MUSIC	SOUND EFFECTS
3-D-Models.com				
www.3-d-models.com	X			
3DRT.com				
www.3drt.com	X			
DAZ Productions				
www.3dlinks.com	X			
Leonardo Software				
www.leonardosoft.com				X
Neo Sounds				
www.neosounds.com			X	X
Opuzz				
www.opuzz.com			X	
Renderosity				
www.renderosity.com	X			
Sounddogs.com				
www.sounddogs.com				X
SoundRangers				
www.soundrangers.com			X	X
The 3D Studio				
www.the3dstudio.com	X			
TurboSquid				
turbosquid.com	X	X		
Ultimate 3D Links				
www.3dlinks.com	X	X		

Thanks to a large amateur game development community, there is an abundance of content for almost every conceivable project and budget. Most of the assets available from the sources in Table 6.5 are royalty-free, and the typical price for a model is under $20. However, some highly accurate anatomical models of single organs sell for as much as $500. For most assets, the issues are quality and appropriateness. Lacking ready-made or custom assets, developers can turn to the wide variety of tools available for asset creation and manipulation.

2D Image Tools

Adobe Photoshop is a popular tool for 2D image work, from drawing 2D characters and scenery to shifting the color balance of a texture. The companion drawing tool for vector art, Adobe Illustrator, is useful for creating organization charts and documentation, but not as easy to use as tools such as SmartDraw. Developers with an academic affiliation can purchase the Adobe Creative Suite CS2, which contains Illustrator, Photoshop, InDesign, GoLive, and Acrobat at heavily discounted prices through one of the academic software portals, such as the Academic Superstore (*www.academicsuperstore.com*). Of course, the academic products are not for commercial development.

3D Image Tools

3ds Max, Maya, and Lightwave 3D dominate the high-end 3D modeling and animation market. Electronic Arts and other major entertainment game developers pay several thousand dollars per seat for 3ds Max because it's the standard. 3ds Max is also available to students and faculty through an affordable academic year license plan. As such, there is a thriving market in third-party hardware, software add-ons, books, and training videos for 3ds Max. The same types of add-ons are available for Maya and Lightwave 3D, but not in the same number or variety.

Some developers can't afford the industry standards. For these developers, there is a second tier of 3D modeling and animation tools, such as Caligari GameSpace, shown in Figure 6.17. Although the very compact menu system takes time to master, the program is capable of producing quality content for about a tenth of the price of 3ds Max. The downside, of course, is that a developer may invest months of effort learning a second-tier program instead of developing a more saleable skill with one of the top three standards.

One of the best deals on a 3D editing package is MilkShape (*www.swissquake.ch*), which was originally designed to create 3D artwork for *HalfLife*. Aside from its graphic capabilities, MilkShape is used by many game designers as an import-export utility because it can read and write

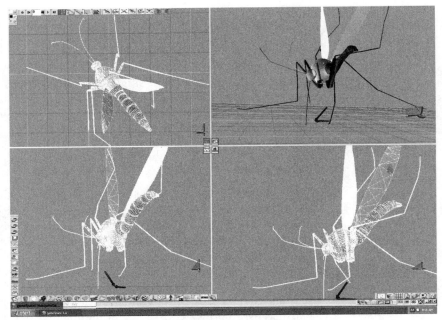

FIGURE 6.17 Calgari GameSpace showing multiple perspectives of an Anopheles mosquito model.

virtually every major file format. A commercial option for 3D file conversion is Polytrans from Okino Software Products (*www.okino.com*).

In addition to general-purpose 3D authoring and editing tools, there are niche tools optimized for specific tasks. For example, when the scale of 3D objects in a game is critical, a tool like PhotoModeler Pro (Eos Systems Inc.) can help. PhotoModeler enables developers to create accurate, to-scale 3D models of real-world objects from multiple photographs, as shown in Figure 6.18. The program enables developers to capture the 3D geometry of the object, which can then be output as a model. Typical objects that are well suited to PhotoModeler's capabilities include houses, buildings, bridges and other structures, as well as vehicles, machinery, or mechanical components. Modeling complex organic features such as faces is challenging for anything other than low-poly output.

PhotoModeler is capable of high accuracy for applications where correct geometry and dimensions are important for realism. In addition, the program can also be employed in a quicker fashion to generate basic, textured 3D models for situations where high dimensional accuracy is not a priority. PhotoModeler can also be used for perspective-matching to help the developer with camera position and orientation. A demo version is available for download at *www.photomodeler.com*.

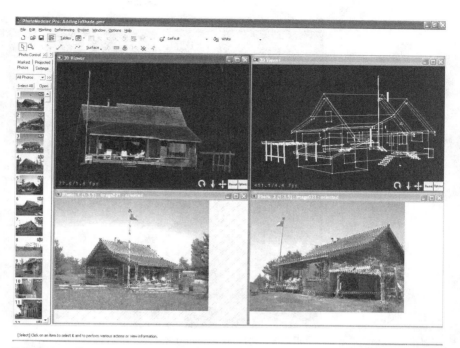

FIGURE 6.18   *PhotoModeler Pro* showing 3D source images (bottom), 3D wireframe model (top right), and final textured 3D model (top left). © Eos Systems, Inc. Used with permission.

When it comes to creating humanoid characters, Poser 6®, from e-frontier (*www.e-frontier.com*), stands alone. The program, shown in Figure 6.19, can be used to modify Poser-compatible models, and can export modified models and character poses in a variety of formats, including those compatible with 3ds Max, Maya, and LightWave 3D.

Poser 6 is specialized for rendering human forms and does it well. However, it lacks the toolset of a generic 3D authoring or editing tool. Furthermore, release 6 is incompatible with previous versions, meaning that thousands of Poser-compatible models on the Web must be used with Poser 5. Apparently, in an attempt to fill the immediate vacuum, e-frontier created an online repository of models, called Content Paradise.

When it comes to creating terrains for games that take place outdoors, options include Terrex, by Terrain Experts (*www.terrex.com*), Bryce, by DAZ Productions (*www.daz3d.com*), and *Terragen*, by Planetside Software (*www.planetside.co.uk*). Both Terrex and Bryce are flexible tools, in that they can be used to render a variety of objects. Terrex is commonly used for real-time 3D image generation, especially for military applications.

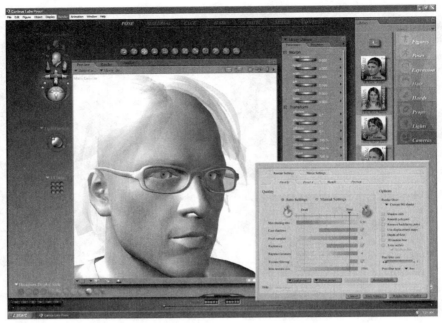

FIGURE 6.19   Poser 6, showing setup prior to rendering.

The interface to Bryce, shown in Figure 6.20, is clever and visually appealing, but often nonintuitive. Even so, the program can be used to create lifelike terrains and background images. Bryce is particularly good at combining photographs and other images with rendered content. DAZ Productions offers a plug-in that enables Bryce to import, edit, and render any of the objects in its gallery of 3D models.

Terragen, a work in progress, is great at one thing—generating photorealistic terrains (see Figure 6.21). The program, which is stable and full-featured, despite its prerelease status, is free for noncommercial use. According to the official Web site, the core technology behind Terragen was developed for the film industry. It has been used to render scenes in *Star Trek* and other titles.

In addition to this small sampling of 3D tools, there are myriad utilities and specialized applications that range from freeware to thousands of dollars in price. Some of the more useful of the inexpensive utilities include a series of programs available through The GameCreators (*www.thegamecreators.com*). These include Canvas 3D Pro, a 3D modeling and animation tool, Action 3D, a polygon reduction tool, and Character Shop, a 3D animation package for designing humanoid characters.

FIGURE 6.20   Bryce, showing the main rendering screen (rear), sky lab (center), and materials lab (front).

FIGURE 6.21   Terragen, showing a rendered scene in the foreground.

Canvas 3D Pro is a light but very easy to learn and use package for creating 3D models. One of the features of the program is its ability to import 13 standard file formats and export to 17 formats. Like MilkShape, it's a good tool to have around for converting content found on the Web to a format that can be used by the game engine.

Action 3D is a particularly useful utility because it enables a developer to reduce the polygon count of a 3D object and thereby improve game performance. The same processing is available through more comprehensive graphics packages.

Motion Capture

Motion capture-based animation is an expensive proposition. Companies such as ViconPeak (*www.vicon.com*) offer motion capture hardware and software solutions that can be used to create characters that run and walk naturally. Another motion capture vendor that caters to the entertainment industry is NaturalMotion (*www.naturalmotion.com*), which offers the Endorphin motion capture application. While *Endorphin* may be appropriate for high-end entertainment titles, a small shop is more likely to benefit from a $50 library of motion capture files, such as those provided by Character Shop. The program can be used to convert a character mesh created by a 3D modeling program into a rigged, animated character model. The program loads a character mesh, attaches it to a skeleton with a set of premade animations, and outputs an animated model.

Distributed 3D Rendering

Rendering large 3D scenes can bring any workstation to its knees. The least expensive way to speed up rendering time is to distribute the rendering to a network of PCs strung together as a dedicated rendering farm or to the other PCs in the development shop. The idea is to parallelize the rendering process as much as possible. For example, nine 1 GHz PCs rendering in parallel will render a 3D scene more quickly than three 3 GHz PCs rendering in parallel [Tait05].

Commercial distributed rendering products include Smedge (*www.uberware.net/smedge2*), Qube! (*www.pipelinefx.com*), *Rush* (*www.seriss.com/rush*), and Muster (*www.wertex.com*). A free, open-source product worth considering is DrQueue (*www.drqueue.org*). Readers interested in advances in distributed rendering should review the work on the open source Chromium project (*chromium.sourceforge.net*) at Lawrence Livermore National Laboratories and Stanford University. Additional information on distributed processing products can be found on Gamasutra (*www.gamasutra.com*) and other game development sites listed in Appendix F, "Resources."

Video Software Tools

A source for industry-standard solutions for cutscenes and other game video is Avid Technologies (*www.avid.com*). In addition to several video editing and finishing products, Avid offers a complete line of video products for the asset development pipeline.

At the other end of the spectrum is Adobe Premiere Pro, which supports a subset of the features provided by Avid's products. Unfortunately, Premiere Pro's ease of use isn't up to the level achieved by Adobe Photoshop or Adobe Illustrator.

A video application worth considering is Camtasia Studio, from Tech-Smith (*www.techsmith.com*). The suite of utilities enables video-naive developers to create cutscenes by recording gameplay, editing the scenes, and saving the output. Camtasia Studio supports a variety of file formats, including Flash, Windows Media, and RealMedia.

Audio Tools

Audio is frequently contracted out because of the level of expertise required to produce professional results. There are at least as many software options in the world of audio synthesis, editing, and processing as there are in the graphics world, and more people work with music than work with digital images and 3D models.

Developers who want to create placeholder music or create simple background tunes have several options. The easiest to use is Apple's Garage-Band (See Figure 6.22). The Mac program enables someone with modest musical abilities to use the array of virtual instruments and a keyboard interface to the Mac to create tunes. Features include an 8-track digital recorder, a real-time mixer, and a library of Jam Packs from Apple. A large user community and the availability of inexpensive sample tracks adds to the attraction of GarageBand for creating custom tunes. GarageBand won't make a developer with a tin ear a musician, but with a library of tracks, it's possible for anyone to pull together background music as a placeholder for game prototypes.

A PC-based equivalent of GarageBand is MusicCreator Pro, from CakeWalk (*www.cakewalk.com*). This digital audio tool, which also targets the home musician, enables the musically inclined to create, mix, and deliver music. It features a console similar to that of the easier-to-use *Garage-Band*, with a multitrack piano view. MusicCreator Pro can also incorporate MIDI tracks into projects and export the compilation to a WAV file for processing. In addition to MusicCreator Pro, CakeWalk offers a comprehensive line of more advance home and professional synthesizer and recording tools. At the high end is Sonar 4 Producer, which transforms a high-end PC into a virtual recording and production studio. Although not for the casual user, it can be more economical than studio time.

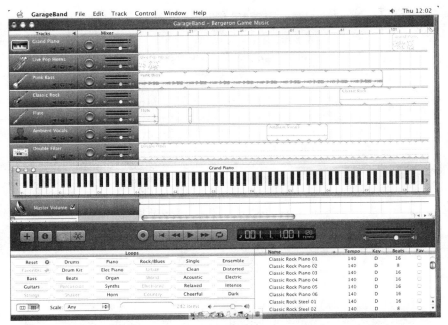

FIGURE 6.22   GarageBand, showing an array of virtual instruments (top left), the keyboard interface (horizontal, center), and instrument timeline (top right).

A GarageBand work-alike for the PC and the Mac is Computer Muzys, a free music composition tool that ships with Computer Music magazine (*www.computermusic.co.uk*). Like many of the UK-based magazines that address the computer and gaming industry, the magazine includes a CD-ROM insert with each issue. In addition to a copy of Computer Muzys, the CD-ROM typically contains several hours of sample tracks and add-ons for their popular Computer Muzys program. The program isn't as graphically crisp as GarageBand, but the functionality is more like that of Cakewalk Pro.

Regardless of whether the game music, voice tracks, and sound effects are downloaded from the Web, recorded and synthesized locally, or purchased from a custom music shop, the sound has to be processed before it can be incorporated into a game. The best of the affordable tools on the market is Adobe Audition, shown in Figure 6.23. The program provides nearly 50 digital signal processing tools and effects, mastering and analysis tools, and audio restoration features.

Audition can handle multiple tracks, provide a wide range of filters and effects, and work with a wide spectrum of audio file formats. One of the most useful utilities is conversion of WAV files to MP3 format to save

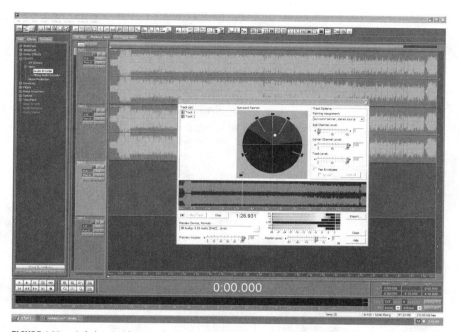

FIGURE 6.23   Adobe Audition, showing the multichannel encoder utility window in the foreground.

disk space. Another is the ability to down-sample files, from high-bandwidth 48-bit samples to 8- or 16-bit audio.

The advantage of using Adobe Audition is the availability of third-party DirectX plug-ins, akin to the plug-in market that has thrived for years around Adobe Photoshop and Illustrator. One of the more useful plug-ins for version 1.0 of Audition is PanHandler, from Kelley Industries (*www.kellyindustries.com*), which provides Audition with the ability to create surround sound panning and encoding for 3D sound effects. The Dolby matrix encoding creates four channels (Left, Center, Right, and Surround) that can be applied to the individual sounds used in cutscenes to enhance the illusion of motion and gameplay. The surround sound effects are not the same as the 5.1 surround sounds available through the native multichannel encoder option, shown in Figure 6.23, which is applied to an entire sound track. Both surround sound encoders require a sound playback system capable of multiple channels. For example, the Adobe 5.1 encoder output requires a sound card capable of at least six analog channels, as well as the amplifier and speakers to go along with it.

In addition to commercial sound editors, there are a number of shareware and freeware options for recording and editing sounds. In particular,

Audacity is worth looking into. It's free (*audacity.sourceforge.net*), open-source, and cross-platform.

MANAGEMENT SOFTWARE

Tools for managing a game development project span the spectrum from project management to data and asset management and testing management.

Project Management

The standard for project management is Microsoft Project. In addition to the Gantt Chart view shown in Figure 6.24, it provides a variety of views, including calendar, network diagram, task usage, and resource graph to help management monitor progress along the development pipeline.

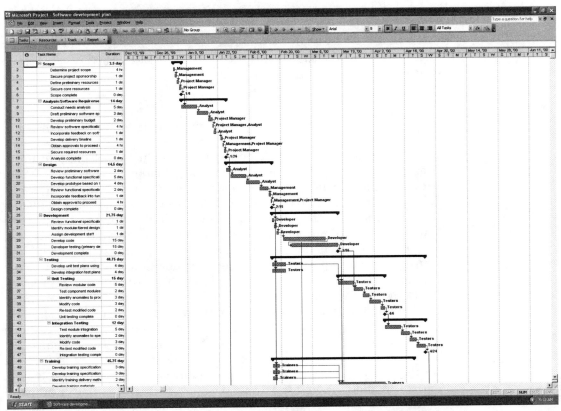

FIGURE 6.24 Microsoft Project, showing the Gantt Chart view of a software development project.

Like the other Microsoft Office packages, Microsoft Project benefits from an extensive online library of templates. For example, the project shown in Figure 6.24 is a software development project template downloaded from the Microsoft Web site. An alternative to Microsoft Project is the general-purpose SmartDraw program, which also benefits from a comprehensive library of templates. The difference is that SmartDraw's project management templates are static and unlinked. Changes made in the Gantt chart in Microsoft Project are automatically reflected in the resource graph. However, SmartDraw's graphs must be updated manually. Even so, for a small development project or for a game design document, a Gantt chart can be made in SmartDraw within a few minutes.

Asset Management

Asset management software for game development ranges from *Version Cue CS2*, by Adobe (*www.Adobe.com*), to Alienbrain Studio 7, by Alienbrain (*www.alienbrain.com*). Alienbrain Studio 7 is an integrated digital asset management and software configuration management (SCM) system. Even though licensing is in the neighborhood of a thousand dollars per seat, the software is designed specifically for game development and is highly regarded by the entertainment game development community.

For small development groups without the finances to license Alienbrain, there are open source SCM systems described earlier, and stand-alone asset management tools. Version Cue CS2, which Adobe bundles with its Creative Suite 2CS, provides image file version tracking that is independent of the file name, the ability to search for images based on a variety of criteria, including keywords, and features such as automated backup. Version Cue CS2 works in conjunction with Adobe Bridge navigational control center, which is also part of Creative Suite 2CS.

Cumulus, from Canto Software (*www.canto.com*) is similar to Version Cue CS2, in that it's optimized for cataloging and searching image files. The single-user product version of Cumulus goes further in that it manages video and audio in addition to image files. Canto also offers a line of server-based products capable of supporting large game development projects.

Testing Management

Testing a serious game destined to be deployed in a university or medical school can take the form of a three- or four-hour pizza session wherein a dozen student volunteers gather in a computer teaching lab and attempt to break or otherwise find fault with a game. More advanced testing might involve a day-long session with multiple players, using video cameras to record every detail of the sessions.

Large-scale testing, such as what might be performed for Web-based simulations and games used throughout a campus or company, may benefit from testing management software packages such as DevText, from TechExcel (*www.techexcel.com*). These packages provide a central repository for creating, managing, and analyzing testing data, scheduling and test assignment utilities, a Web-based interface that supports data entry from remote locations, and workflow tools.

Regardless of how testing is performed, it's important to distinguish testing from assessment. Testing can be used to identify flaws in the user interface or underlying logic. Assessment is the process of determining how closely the measurable behavior changes in players match the expected changes.

Although there are tools that can be used to facilitate assessment, such as statistical analysis packages, the really challenging part of assessment is devising and running a meaningful study. This normally involves the help of a professional educational psychologist or psychomatrician, properly selected volunteers, and strict adherence to scientific methods.

DEPLOYMENT SOFTWARE

Following the continuum of the game development pipeline, after developing and testing a game, it's almost ready for deployment. Almost, because the game has to be packaged for distribution, either on the Web or CD-ROM. There is also the documentation—electronic help files and perhaps a printed manual—that must be included in the final package, and finally the installer and distribution utilities that automatically install the game and proactively address issues such as software piracy.

Packaging

Packaging a game for distribution at a minimum includes creating a unique icon for the game. In addition, some game developers create wallpaper themed after their game. One of easiest-to-use icon development tools is Impact Software's Microangelo Toolset (*www.microangelo.us*), shown in Figure 6.25. The inexpensive utility is a miniature, self-contained paint program that enables a developer to draw or copy and paste an image into the icon editor space. The program also provides a close-up and actual size view of the icon under construction.

After creating a suitable icon, developers can use Microangelo Toolset to associate the icon with the game so that the proper icon will appear on the player's machine. Creating a custom icon isn't strictly necessary, but distributing a game with its own icon is a nice finishing touch that doesn't require much in terms of time or resources.

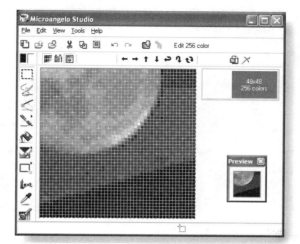

FIGURE 6.25   *Microangelo Toolset* icon editor.

Installation

There are two basic types of installation programs: those that simply create a self-launching installer and those that provide compression. Setup2Go is simple packager that creates automatic installers for Windows games. The freeware is available for download from the publisher, SDS Software (*dev4pc.com/setup2go.html*). The software can be used to create any automatic setup routines, including font installation, shortcut icons on the desktop, and Start Menu changes, in any one of twenty languages. A software wizard, shown in Figure 6.26, simplifies the process of identifying files, fonts, and images that must be included in the setup. The licensed version ($30) is free of the splash screen advertisement.

Installer VISE from MindVision Software (*www.mindvision.com*) is used to build a master installation set for CD-ROM or Internet distribution. In addition to installation, the product includes a compression and decompression engine that saves disk space and decreases the amount of time required to download a game installer from the Internet. Pricing is per seat per year. A one-year subscription for one programmer is about $700.

Documentation and Help

It's easy to forget the dreaded user manual. Even if players never consult the help function, the fact that help is available is a selling point. In the hands of a good technical writer, almost any of the available tools can be used to create functional printed or electronic documentation and online

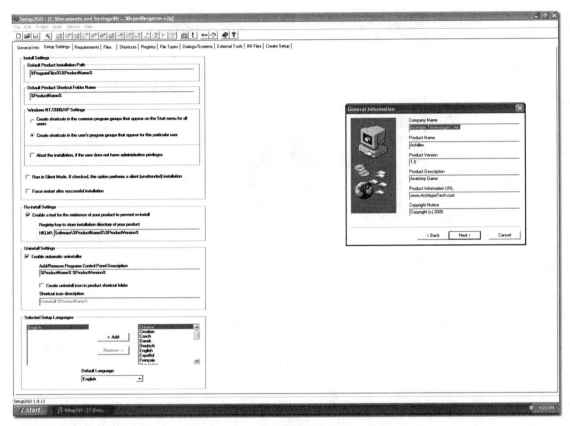

FIGURE 6.26 *Setup2Go* installation tool, showing the setup setting menu (left) and the wizard (insert, right).

help. One of the best commercial tools for developing online help is Adobe Acrobat, which can be used to create PDF documents. More advanced help, such as term lookup and nested layers requires a more capable tool, such as Macromedia's RoboHelp (*www.macromedia.com/robohelp*).

Distribution Software

Distribution software includes utilities for encryption, localization, and copy-protection. Encryption utilities address engine protection so that third parties can't get access to the underlying engine. Similarly, asset encryption keeps licensed music, graphics, and other content bundled with a game out of the public domain.

Aladdin Software (*www.aladdin.com*) offers several products. *HASP* requires players to insert a hardware key in their PC prior to gameplay. *eSAFE* blocks spyware and provides content and asset protection. *eToken* is an authentication and password management system.

More specialized asset management solutions include digital rights management tools from Macrovision (*www.macrovision.com*). SafeDisc Advanced provides content encryption and anti-duplication for CD-ROM and DVD-ROM games. Hawkeye is an anti-piracy service for networks to protect the illegal downloading of games.

ExeQuo (*www.exequo.com*) provides localization services for games sold in markets with different native languages.

DEVELOPMENT SUITES

Listed below are the development suites used to develop to simple serious games: *Achilles,* a 3D FPS anatomy trainer; and *Augmented Reality Medical Simulator*, a hardware-based serious game for teaching cardiac auscultation. These suites are intended to illustrate the hardware and software associated with the development of low-complexity serious games. The suites described do not represent an endorsement of a particular hardware or toolset, but illustrate the resources that a one- or two-person shop could to create low-budget serious games of similar complexity.

Few developers get it right the first time. For example, in developing the *Augmented Reality Medical Simulator* game, subtle problems in the sound generation required the creation of DLL. Another option would have been to try a higher-performance development environment—at a cost of throwing away the BASIC code and rewriting the algorithms in C/C++. However, doing so would have obviated one of the advantages of the development environment—ease of maintenance by relatively naive programmers.

Readers who are new to game development may learn on one game engine or development environment and set of authoring tools, develop a better understanding of their needs, and then move on to more suitable tools. The good news is that the assets and algorithms developed in one environment often transfer to another.

Achilles 3D Anatomy Trainer

This development suite reflects the hardware and software used to create a prototype of the first-person sneaker game *Achilles*. The main challenges were related to limited video RAM on the target hardware platform.

Design Software

- Adobe Photoshop
- Adobe Illustrator
- SmartDraw
- Microsoft Word

Development Hardware

Programming: Alienware MJ12m 7700 laptop, 3.8 GHz, 2 GB RAM, NVIDIA Quadro FX Go 1400/256 MB
Art: Alienware Area 51 3.8 GHz Pentium 4, 2 GB RAM, nVIDIA GeForce 6800 Ultra/256 MB RAM; 20" LCD monitor
Testing: Dell Dimension 4600, 2.8 GHz Pentium 4, 1 GB RAM, Radeon 9000/64 MB RAM
Server Dell PowerEdge 800, 160 GB, 1 GB RAM
Network: Linksys Wireless-G broadband router

Infrastructure:
- APC uninterruptible power supplies
- Networked HP laser printer
- Multiple DVD burners for incremental backups

Data Acquisition Hardware

Images:
- Canon EOS 20D camera with EF 24-70mm f/2.8L USM
- Proscope USB microscope
- HP Scanjet 8290 flatbed scanner

Video:
- Canon XL-2
- Apple eMac 1.4 GHz, 1 GB RAM

Sound:
- Creative Sound Blaster® Audigy
- Marantz PMD 430 professional stereo cassette recorder
- Sennheiser HD600 headphones

Prototyping Software

Serious content: *Poser* for character development
Gameplay:
- FPSCreator Prerelease (level maps)

Game Development Environment

3D GameStudio Pro

Code Creation and Management

Editors:
- Brain Editor Pro for 3D GameStudio Pro
- Microsoft Visual C++ editor for DLL development

Compilers and scripting languages:
- CScript for 3D GameStudio Pro
- Microsoft Visual C++ for DLLs

Utilities:
- Internal profiler
- PC Lint

Middleware:
- Mystic AI
- Twinno Software Force Feedback
- Superfluxus Media Evolution No 9
- Superfluxus Media Tiny Things particle generator

Asset Creation and Manipulation Software

2D image tools:
- Adobe Photoshop
- Neonlite Software A4 Font Generator

3D image tools:
- GameSpace
- Aeon Games Mapper
- Aeon Level Exporter
- Poser
- Bryce
- MilkShape

Video software tool:
- Camtasia

Audio tools:
- GarageBand
- Adobe Audition

Textures: The Game Creators *Dark Matter*
Models:
- DAZ Productions
- Turbo Squid

Management Software

Project management: Microsoft Project
Asset management: Cumulus
Testing management: in-house system

Deployment Software

Packaging: Microangelo Toolset
Installer: Setup2Go
Documentation and help: Adobe Acrobat
Distribution software: proprietary *3D GameStudio* encryption

Augmented Reality Medical Simulator

The following development hardware and software reflect the resources required to develop the *Augmented Reality Medical Simulator*. Note that there are typically two separate efforts involved in developing an embedded system such as this—the PC-based game and the external hardware system.

Design Software

Adobe Photoshop
Adobe Illustrator
SmartDraw
Microsoft Word

Development Hardware

Programming: Alienware MJ12m 7700 laptop, 3.8 GHz, 2 GB RAM, NVIDIA Quadro FX Go 1400/256MB
Art: Alienware Area 51 3.8 GHz Pentium 4, 2 GB RAM, nVIDIA GeForce 6800 Ultra/256 MB RAM; 20″ LCD monitor
Testing: Dell Dimension 4600, 2.8 GHz Pentium 4, 1 GB RAM, Radeon 9000/64 MB RAM
Server: Dell PowerEdge 800, 160 GB, 1 GB RAM
Network: Linksys Wireless-G broadband router
Infrastructure:
- APC uninterruptible power supplies
- Networked HP laser printer
- Multiple DVD burners for incremental backups

Data Acquisition Hardware

Images: Canon EOS 20D camera with EF 24-70mm f/2.8L USM
Sound:
- Proprietary physiological sound synthesizers
- Sennheiser HD600 headphones

Embedded Hardware

Wireless communications: Repurposed Rumblepad 2 controller
Sensors: Custom proximity sensors
Test equipment: Lab-grade digital multimeter
Miscellaneous:
- Regulated, digital power supply
- Cable harness for sensors
- Vest
- Dremel cordless drill
- Soldering equipment
- Plastic for encapsulating sensors

Prototyping Software

Serious content: Extend
Gameplay: DarkBasic Pro

Game Development Environment

DarkBasic Pro

Code Creation and Management

Editor:
- Native DarkBasic Pro
- Native Microsoft Visual C++ editor

Compilers and scripting languages:
- BASIC for DarkBasic Pro
- Microsoft Visual C++ for DLLs
Utilities: Internal profiler
Middleware: Custom DLLs for sound synthesis

Asset Creation and Manipulation Software

2D image tools: Adobe Photoshop
3D image tools:
- GameSpace
- Poser

Audio tools: Audition
Textures: The Game Creators *Dark Matter*

Management Software

Project management: Microsoft Project
Asset management: Cumulus
Testing management: In-house system

Deployment Software

Packaging: Microangelo Toolset
Installer: Setup2Go
Documentation and help: Adobe Acrobat
Distribution software: Proprietary 3D GameStudio encryption

SUMMARY

The wide range of software and hardware tools capable of supporting serious games development is a reflection of the serious games application space. Although it's tempting to view tools in terms of how well they improve developer efficiency and effectiveness, the gold standard is really how well they support specific, measurable behavior changes in players.

Of the tools discussed in this chapter, most have direct application in supporting the traditional games development pipeline that starts with a requirements specification and ends with deployment and maintenance. Key exceptions include tools for serous content development, especially mathematical modeling and simulation. It's also important to note that although there are statistical packages to help analyze the data from an assessment study, the most difficult part of assessment is defining and running the studies that generate the data.

REFERENCES

[CMU05] CMU, ZKEY. 2005. *www-2.cs.cmu.edu/afs/cs/project/stereo-machine/www/z-key.html*, accessed July 1, 2005.

[Columbia05] Columbia, MARS — Mobile Augmented Reality Systems. Columbia University. 2005. *www1.cs.columbia.edu/graphics/projects/mars/mars.html,* accessed July 1, 2005.

[HarbourSmith03] Harbour, Jonathan, and Joshua Smith, *Beginner's Guide to DarkBasic Game Programming.* Premier Press a division of Course Technology, 2003.

[Memsic05] Memsic, Accelerometer Basics. Memsic. 2005. *www.memsic.com/memsic/pdfs/Accel%20Primer.pdf,* accessed June 23, 2005.

[MIT05] MIT, *Wearable Computing.* MIT. 2005. *www.media.mit/wearables,* accessed July 1, 2005.

[Mott05b] Mott, Tony, "Gizmondo Finds Second Gear." *EDGE* (June 2005): pp. 16–8.

[Tait05] Tait, Matthew, "Build Your Own Render Farm." *ExtremeTech* (Spring 2005): pp. 77–81.

[Vlessides04] Vlessides, Michael, "New WAV Index Monitor Appears to Measure Depth of Hypnosis."*Technology in Anesthesia* (December 2004): pp. 14–66.

SERIOUS BUSINESS

In This Chapter

- The entertainment and serious games markets
- Understanding the customer base
- Legal issues
- Managing risk and locating sources of funding

Traditional Learning

Old Technology   New Technology

Substitution   Diffusion

Reinforcement   Reinforcement

Disuse   Disappropriation   Appropriation   Use

Serious Games

INTRODUCTION

Game development—serious or otherwise—requires more than simply filling a room with talented artists and high-end workstations and arranging frequent pizza deliveries. Some artists, programmers, and level designers primarily want to practice their art while working toward a worthwhile goal. Others aspire to develop the next AAA entertainment title, as well as the fame and fortune that would accompany the achievement.

Whatever the motivation, game development involves business. It costs real money to equip and staff a development shop. Moreover, the payment for a serious game is often based on deliverables, meaning that until delivery, some or most of the financial risk is borne by the developer.

As discussed in Chapter 4, "Best Practices," there is a considerable body of best practices associated with game development. However, an even larger body of knowledge exists in business. The management of development shops playing to win in the serious games business should be as familiar with the best practices relevant to the business of serious games as they are with the development pipeline.

An example of a validated body of best practices common to successful businesses is the criteria for the Malcolm Baldrige National Quality Award, which was introduced in Chapter 3, "Technology Trends" [NIST05]. The criteria, which are valuable as guideposts for serious games developers, are described in detail in Table 7.1.

TABLE 7.1   Description of the Malcolm Baldrige National Quality Award Criteria Categories

CATEGORY	EXPLANATION
Leadership	How the senior leaders guide and sustain the business, governance, and how the business addresses its ethical, legal, and community responsibilities.
Strategic Planning	How the business develops strategic objectives and action plans; how they are deployed; how they are modified if necessary; and how progress is measured.
Customer and Market	How the business determines the requirements, expectations, and preferences of customers and markets; how the business builds relationships with customers; factors that lead to customer acquisition, satisfaction, loyalty and retention, and to business expansion.
Measurement, Analysis, manages, and Knowledge Management	How the business selects, gathers, analyzes, and improves its data, information, and knowledge asset, and how it reviews its performance.

$\rightarrow$

CATEGORY	EXPLANATION
Human Resource Focus	How the business motivates employees to develop and utilize their full potential in alignment with the business and personal growth.
Process Management	How the business processes create customer and organizational value.
Business Results	How the business performs in product and service outcomes, customer satisfaction, financially, and in the marketplace, in human resource, and operations, relative to the competition.

Just as there are established tools and processes that games developers use to create assets and code, the business community has its own vernacular and methodologies to help measure and visualize otherwise abstract concepts such as value and strategic planning. For example, under the category of Customer and Market, successful developers offer customers an attractive value proposition—a strategy that differentiates their products from those of the competition.

In determining the best value proposition for a particular game development house, management should consider the market constraints in light of the shop's capabilities. A commonly used model for exploring the value proposition is the value point triangle shown in Figure 7.1. In this model, price, quality, and speed of development are assumed to be orthogonal characteristics of the games offered by development shops.

FIGURE 7.1   The value proposition triangle. The development shop that produces games described by point A offers average price, quality, and speed of development. The shop with products at point B emphasizes speed of development.

The value proposition offered by a shop that produces games described by point A in the model is average quality, price, and speed of development. In contrast, the value proposition offered by the development shop at point B is rapid development time, albeit at a higher price and lower quality than average.

Successful businesses in most industries offer a value proposition that emphasizes quality, price, *or* speed, such as the development shop described by point B in the model [Bergeron02]. Some businesses are successful in two areas, such as quality and speed, typically with a severe penalty in the third area. For example, FedEx emphasizes speed first, with quality a close second. Customers are willing to pay an exorbitant premium over surface mail rates for the service.

The problem with development shops that offer average price, quality and development speed is that they are vulnerable to competition from shops that specialize in one of the three areas. Consider a serious games development shop that specializes in creating game prototypes for the military. Prototypes, by definition, are quick and dirty affairs. The shop's ability to crank out four or five prototypes quickly in coming to a final design may be far more important to the military than the shop's ability to produce one or two high-quality prototypes—none of which will be used. Whether a particular shop offers a value proposition based primarily on price, quality, or speed depends on the local market conditions, demand, and the shop's business model.

This chapter provides an overview of the business of serious games development, including the serious games market, stakeholders, human resources, legal issues, and public relations perspectives. A few business tools, such as the value proposition triangle mentioned previously, are introduced to untangle the complexities of business. In addition, a short primer on business plans is offered in Appendix E, "A Brief Business Plan Primer."

ENTERTAINMENT GAMES INDUSTRY

From a traditional business perspective, the entertainment gaming industry *is* the gaming industry, accounting for 248 million units and $9.9 billion in U.S. sales in 2004 [Lippman05; Wingfield05]. Although the lion's share of video game software sales is linked to the performance of a few dozen entertainment titles on one of four major platforms, niche areas such as mobile games, portable games, and serious games have emerged as significant areas of development. Moreover, thanks to nearly ubiquitous computing power and affordable game engines, employment opportunities for serious games developers are poised for expansion.

Not only does the serious games industry benefits from the affordable, readily available hardware platforms and software tools developed for the mass consumption of entertainment video games, but even the hype surrounding entertainment gaming spills over into the serious games space. For example, the 2005 E3 Conference was dominated by news about the latest game consoles from Microsoft, Sony, and Nintendo. Despite the barriers to entry that may be too great for many small shops to overcome, the graphics and gameplay offered by these consoles set player expectations for gameplay, including that of PC-based serious games. The consoles also forced tools developers who cater to the serious games market to upgrade their offerings or focus on the retro gaming market.

The Numbers

The most important parameters of the entertainment games industry are recent and expected economic performance. Historically, the multi-billion-dollar industry is cyclical, with a peak in economic performance about every six years or so, keyed to a new generation of game consoles [Economist02]. The boom in game sales isn't immediate, because it typically requires software developers at least a year to produce titles that take full advantage of the new hardware features.

Assuming past performance is a predictor of the next boom, the top three console makers have positioned the industry for a boom in 2007 and 2008. Moreover, because the largely untapped but growing cell phone game market is likely to have its boom a few years later, the trough following the boom in console games may not be as low as in previous years. This section examines the predictions of the global market for video games, online gaming, and mobile gaming.

Global Market

According to PricewaterhouseCoopers, the worldwide video game market will reach $55.6 billion by 2008 [WinklerSchooler04]. The largest and most rapid growth will be in the Asia/Pacific region, accounting for 43 percent of the global market. Markets in Europe, the Middle East, and Africa will continue to expand, accounting for 25 percent of the global market in 2008. Within Europe, the top markets for games will remain, in order, the United Kingdom, Germany, France, and Spain [Tait04]. Growth in the U.S. market is expected to come in third, ahead of the small South American market [WinklerSchooler04].

The message is that entertainment game developers are increasingly competing in a global market, and one in which the greatest opportunities are not in the English-speaking cultures. Developers who want to compete in the global market, whether in entertainment or serious games, must consider issues such as localization and differences in best practices.

Content differences are also important for serious games; for example, the drugs used to treat various diseases differ widely from one region of the world to the next.

Online Gaming

The domestic market for online gaming—gameplay over the Internet, usually through a browser—is projected at nearly $3 billion by 2008 [WinklerSchooler04], in part because of rapid expansion of online gaming portals. This trend in expansion is evident today in portals such as Yahoo! and RealNetworks.

Yahoo!, a major player in the online gaming market, expanded its business beyond that of America Online, Electronic Arts, and Microsoft by forming partnerships with media-rich companies such as GameSpot (*www.gamespot.com*) [RCR05]. People are willing to buy games, but it's the advertising revenue that supports Yahoo!. RealNetworks followed Yahoo's example by buying up game developers such as GameHouse [RealNetworks04].

Mobile Gaming

Mobile or wireless gameplay through cell phones is viewed by the general media industry as the next big area of growth [Bergeron01]. In addition to cell phone-based TV, music, and gambling, games alone will account for over $3 billion by 2008 [WinklerSchooler04]. In Japan, the epicenter of mobile computing and gaming, the cell phone game market was valued at $280 million in 2005 [Dvorak05]. The Asia/Pacific region as a whole is projected to continue to dominate the mobile gaming market, in part because it has more wireless subscribers than any other region in the world [WinklerSchooler04].

Europe, the Middle East, and Africa have the second largest pool of mobile subscribers, with a corresponding market potential for mobile games. Wireless gaming in the region is projected to become the largest source of wireless data revenue, with $1.5 billion in sales by 2008 [Linsalata04]. Tools such as J2ME and BREW are making it easy for developers in these countries to exploit the potential market by creating games for multiple mobile devices [Kushner02].

Some of the key players in the mobile gaming market include InfoSpace, Jamdat, Jamba, Gameloft, Sorrent, Digital Chocolate, and I-play. Jamdat, which launched its mobile game line in 2004, had 200,000 registered users and a total of 22 million multiplayer sessions logged as of May 2005 [Brown05]. Digital Chocolate (*www.digitalchocolate.com*), founded by Trip Hawkins of Electronic Arts, launched *Mobile League Sports Network*, a fantasy league that enables baseball and football fans to swap players and create their own virtual teams. Disney uses cell phone games as marketing tools to promote its films. In marketing the animated film *The Incredibles*, Disney released ring tones, images, and games.

Sports and advergames may be gaining in popularity on cell phones, but the most innovative cell phone games cater to a very different market. Just as sex videos accelerated the rate of adoption of VCRs and the Internet, wireless operators have found that racy cell phone videos and games are driving a surge in cell phone use [Bryan-LowPringle05].

An example of an adult cell phone game is *virtual girlfriends* by Artificial Life (*www.v-girl.com*). The Hong Kong product is strikingly similar to the talking bot (software robot) technology developed by companies for customer relationship management (CRM) purposes prior to the dot-com crash [Bergeron01]. Interactive bots and avatars directed at adult entertainment have a direct bearing on the mobile serious games market to the degree that standard tools for creating and editing the bots become available for serious games development. Bots have been used as the basis for serious games and patients in medical simulations on Web and PC platforms [Bergeron01; Plantec04].

Another example of adult game content for cell phones is a strip poker game by ThumbPlay (*www.thumbplay.com*), a relatively tame game for domestic Cingular subscribers. Cherry Sauce (*www.cherrysauce.com*) offers more explicit strip poker, an adult memory game, and an adult adventure game.

Trends

Several trends in the entertainment gaming industry are redefining the evolving serious games industry, from the increased expense of bringing a game to market and the use of new business models to genre blending and a renewed interest in in-game advertising.

Increased Expenses

The cost of bringing a full-featured entertainment game to market is increasing [Godinez05]. Launching an average entertainment game in 2004 required about $10 million, with half going to development costs and the other half going to marketing [Snider04]. In 2005 development cost alone for the average video game was about $7.5 million [Lippman05].

The increasing production cost is reflected in the prices of the latest titles. Even with the prospect of in-game advertising and a lucrative online Xbox live infrastructure, the cost of the first games for the Xbox 360 is $60, up 20 percent from the cost of games for the original Xbox [EBGames05].

Console and Wireless Dominance

Console games are projected to continue their dominance, eroding the PC-gaming market worldwide [WinklerSchooler04]. The only exception is Latin America, where PC-games are increasing in popularity because of lack of competition from other gaming platforms [Pricewaterhouse Coopers05]. Wireless and online gaming are projected to increase significantly through 2008, with wireless outstripping PC-gaming by the end of 2005 [Lawrence05].

The serious games industry could be hurt by the pullout if the manufacturers of high-end but affordable PC hardware and game tool developers abandon the PC in favor of the console market. One of the reasons the military pursued PC-based serious games development is off-the-shelf $900 video cards outperformed custom systems that cost hundreds of thousands of dollars and required years to design and build [Herz02]. Of course, the console manufacturers might eventually open their platforms to small shops with $20,000 to $30,000 projects.

New Business Models

The entertainment video game industry is increasingly experimenting with joint ventures with the video industry [Marr05; Tourtellotte05]. The interest in this new business model is fueled in part by the erosion of the male 18–34 TV-viewing market, a change attributed to the increasing popularity of video games [Molineaux04]. Although joint ventures have been tried in the past, the lucrative young male audience wasn't at stake, suggesting that there is more pressure on at least the video industry to devise viable business models for these joint ventures.

The morphing of the traditional entertainment games business model into something that resembles a model used in the video industry is evident in some of the new game pricing models. The traditional video media company Turner Broadcasting has experimented with offering video games on a subscription model through its broadband site GameTap (*www.gametap.com*). This alternative to purchasing increasingly expensive games follows the pay-per-view model pioneered by the TV cable industry.

Better Characters

Although *PacMan* was a phenomenal success, not much can be said for the character's personality. Fast-forward to games like *Psychonauts* (Double Fine Productions) and even *Halo 2* (Bungie) and the characters display at least a semblance of emotional intelligence. With the introduction of the latest generation of consoles, the entertainment game development industry is focused on building more lifelike characters [Mott05]. This includes not only more photorealism, but characters endowed with emotion, passion, and intelligence.

Part of the motivation for developing realistic characters is that it's possible, thanks to the multi-core processors capable of handling AI with one core while another handles rendering. Another factor is simply competition for market share. The Xbox failed to usurp Sony as the dominant force in the video game market. Of the top video games that sold the most units in the United States as of July, 2005, three were for the Playstation consoles (*Grant Theft Auto*: *Vice City*; *Grand Theft Auto*; and *Grand Theft Auto 3*) and two were for the Nintendo (*Super Mario 64* and *Pokemon Yello*) [Lippman05]. It's only through offering must-play games with better gameplay that Microsoft, Sony, or Nintendo will increase or at least sustain market share.

More Domestic Wireless Games

As the capabilities of U.S. carriers and handsets approach those of the more technologically advanced systems in Europe and Asia, game developers and carriers are positioning themselves to exploit the domestic mobile games market [Nelson05]. Enabling technologies, including easy-to-use toolsets that make developing for hundreds of cell phone and wireless PDA models feasible, are a major force behind this trend [Barbagallo04; 03]. Projections from PricewaterhouseCoopers suggest that in the United States, wireless games will experience the fastest growth rate, from $281 million in 2004 to $2.1 billion in 2009 [PricewaterhouseCoopers05].

Genre Blending

Innovative developers are mixing genres—combining first-person shooters and role playing games, for example, to provide more variety in gameplay and to differentiate their products in the marketplace. Examples of successful commercial games with nontraditional genres include *Full Spectrum Warrior*, *Mercenaries*, and *Destroy All Humans* from Pandemic, and *Deus Ex* from Ion Storm.

Digital Distribution

Developers are experimenting with direct-to-consumer digital distribution as an alternative to publisher-controlled shrink-wrapped distribution [PricewaterhouseCoopers05]. This move has been facilitated by the increased adoption of broadband Internet, which has increased demand for online gaming [WinklerSchooler04]. Of course, digital distribution is the norm with mobile games.

In-Game Advertising

Taking a lead from the TV industry, in-game advertising is being used to offset game development costs. In 2004, companies paid $200 million to place ads in games, and the market is expected to reach $1 billion by 2008 [Hershman05]. The projected increase reflects the availability of dynamic localization tools from sources such as Massive (*www.massiveincorporated. com*), inGamePartners (*www.ingameads.com*), Bidamic (*www.bidamic.com*), and DoubleFusion (*doublefusion.com*) that enable advertisers to customize adds within a game. These tools require the game developer to use an SDK that handles communications with a server that feeds content to games connected to the Internet. In exchange for this modest overhead, advertisers can insert and retire advertisements at will. Previously, advertisement was restricted to ads inserted into games as they were developed, sometimes years before the game was released.

Massive, the creator of the first video game advertising network, enables advertisers to reach large, aggregated audiences through real-time delivery of full-motion video advertising, akin to the system used with cable TV subscribers [PRNewswire05]. Massive partnered with Nielsen Interactive Entertainment, which will provide third-party accountability and measurement of advertising.

Game adds, like pop-ups and spam, may ultimately alienate many gamers. Even so, the technology behind in-game full-motion video is significant for serious game developers because of the potential for using the technique with serious content. For example, the video could range from current events to details of a new surgical procedure, depending on the game. Furthermore, because the video could be defined at will and without programming, the shelf life of the serious game could be extended by several months to years.

Shifting Demographics

Entertainment games are no longer the sole purview of 17- to 34-year-old males. According to the 2004 demographic figures from Entertainment Software Association, 35 percent of game players in the United States are under 18. The majority of players (43 percent) are between 18 and 49, and 19 percent are 50 years or older [ESA05]. The ESA also reports that 43 percent of players are female, but this figure doesn't reveal volume of gameplay.

The top-selling *Sims* franchise attracts as many female players as male players [Croal02; Oser 04]. In the casual games market, mature adults have emerged as a significant source of revenue [Kushner04]. Seeking to broaden the market base, developers of console games are designing games to appeal to older audiences [Wingfield05].

SERIOUS GAMES MARKET

Quantifying the potential of the serious games market is challenging because most of the statistics available for the games industry don't consider serious games as a distinct category. There are some exceptions. For example, the market for online advergames was $77 million in 2002, with projections of $230 by 2007 [Mack04]. More important than backward-looking statistics are the forward-looking predictors of success in the serious games market, including innovative business models and market data.

Business Models

A distinguishing feature of most serious games is that the business models—that is, how a developer can make money from making and marketing games—often bear little resemblance to those used in the entertainment industry, where developers receive some percentage of publisher's profits after publisher expense. There's a significant potential upside for developers of a successful entertainment title that brings in $10 million over three or four years.

The business models in the serious games development industry are often less compelling, primarily because the business models for most serious games fit the domain of the serious content, and not the game industry. Many, if not most, serious games are never sold commercially, but are used internally. A pharmaceutical company that is used to paying $100,000 for a training game for its sales reps isn't going to offer the developer the equivalent of a royalty for copies of the game given to physicians.

Games with an agenda, realistic games, core competency games, and mods developed for training and education are often built around cost-plus business model. Serious games developers often receive a fixed percentage of development costs, because this is the model used by multimedia developers that work in the same space.

The lack of a major upside limits the attractiveness of a serious games development project to venture capital firms. VCs work with multipliers of 5 to 10 and more, which limits their interest to serious games destined for the retail shelves. However, even without the potential upside of a AAA hit, game developers can develop and maintain a solid business in several key markets, whether working on the inside of a large corporation or as an independent development shop.

Markets

Among the most promising markets for serious games developers are the civilian and military components of the U.S. government, medicine, academia, and industry. Serious game developers should be aware of the opportunities afforded by the massive spending for defense and homeland security in each of these areas. The Homeland Security Advanced Research Project Agency (HSARPA) alone had a $1 billion budgeted for late stage technologies [OSTP05].

U.S. Government

Most of the funding available for serious games development from the U.S. government is associated with R&D, with funding for defense spending consistently greater than nondefense spending. According to the U.S. general accounting office, in fiscal year 2005, the federal R&D budget was $132.2 billion, with more than half—$75 billion—devoted to defense research [OSTP05]. As shown in Figure 7.2, this disparity in spending is long-standing, peaking in 1986, with a difference in funding between defense and nondefense spending of approximately $30 billion. The most recent figures of actual spending, which are from 2003, show the difference in spending was still significant at nearly $8 billion [NSB04]. The additional defense funding translates to increased odds of finding a source of funding for a serious game in the defense sector.

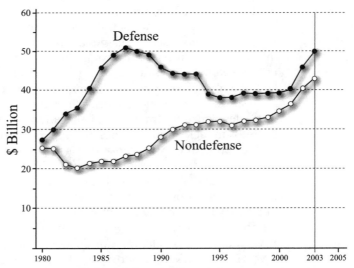

FIGURE 7.2   U.S. federal defense and nondefense research and development expenditures, based on 1996 dollars. *Source:* National Science Foundation.

In France, the government hands out tax subsidies to the top video game developers to promote the industry [Gumbel05]. Although the U.S. government isn't as supportive of the gaming industry, it does provide a multitude of funding opportunities. As illustrated in Table 7.2, civilian government funding agencies include the Centers for Disease Control, Environmental Protection Agency (EPA), and U.S. Department of Justice.

TABLE 7.2   U.S. Government Funding Agencies

CIVILIAN GOVERNMENT FUNDING AGENCIES

Center for Disease Control (CDC)

Department of Energy (DOE)

Department of Homeland Security (DHS)

Environmental Protection Agency (EPA)

National Institute of Allergy and Infectious Diseases (NIAID)

National Institutes of Health (NIH)

U.S. Department of Justice (DOJ)

The owner of an independent serious games development shop doesn't simply contact the head of the Centers for Disease Control or Department of Energy with an idea for a serious game. These and other government agencies are accessible through special programs established to announce funds for specific projects and to accept proposals for projects—including serious games. Many of these special programs are administered through the Small Business Association (SBA). Of particular relevance to serious games developers, the SBA provides oversight of funding for Small Business Innovation Research (SBIR) and Small Business Technology Transfer (STTR) for the government agencies shown in Table 7.3.

TABLE 7.3   Sources of SBA-Administered SBIR/STTR Programs

SBA-ADMINISTERED SBIR/STTR AGENCIES

Department of Agriculture

Department of Commerce

Department of Defense*

Department of Education

Department of Energy*

Department of Health and Human Services *

Department of Transportation

Environmental Protection Agency

National Aeronautics and Space Administration *

National Science Foundation*

* =

The SBIR Program provides up to $800,000 in early-stage research and development funding directly to small technology businesses or individual entrepreneurs who form a business. The money is available in phases, with Phase I funding limited to $70,000 for a six-month effort to prove feasibility. Those who successfully complete Phase I can compete for more significant Phase II R&D funding of up to $730,000 for a two-year effort.

Obtaining SBIR funding starts with searching the periodic SBIR announcements posted to the SBA's Web site (*www.sba.gov/sbir*). Announcements are posted for each of the SBA-administered agencies once or twice a year, according to the schedule posted on the site (see Figure 7.3). Response deadlines are generally two months from the initial posting date. For example, the DOD 2005.2 SBIR Solicitation was issued to the public on May 2, 2005 and the deadline for receipt of proposals was July 15, 2005.

The most effective method of identifying game-related SBIR topics is to use the search engines available for each agency, such as the DOD SBIR search engine, TOPICS (*www.dodsbir.net/Topics*). To illustrate the opportunities for game development funding, searching for "games" in the DOD 2005.2 solicitation revealed nine opportunities for serious games developers, seven within the army and two within DARPA. Topics ranged from "Adaptive Role-play Exercises for a Leader Development Center" to "Haptic Health Care Specialist Training Environment."

Responding to an SBIR is as straightforward as uploading a proposal to the SBIR site and filling out a short form. Successful applications receive funding within about nine months of the solicitation closing date. Developers interested in pursuing SBIR or STTR funding should verify eligibility by reviewing requirements on the SBA or agency SBIR/STTR Web site.

The STTR program provides up to $850,000 in early-stage research and development funding directly to small companies working cooperatively with researchers at universities and other research institutions. Like the SBIR program, funding is in phases; Phase I provides for up to $100,000 for a one-year effort, and Phase II provides up to $750,000. The main operational difference between the two programs is that a small business can compete for SBIR funding on its own. The business must partner with a research institution, such as a university, to compete for the funding. There are also rules about relative effort—the business must perform at least 40 percent of the work, for example—as explained on the SBA Web site. The same sites that cater to the SBIR program support the STTR program.

The STTR is similar in structure to SBIR but it funds cooperative research and development projects involving a small business and research institutions, such as universities, federally funded research and development centers, and nonprofit research institutions. The purpose of STTR is to create a vehicle for moving ideas from research institutions to the market, where they can benefit civilian and military customers. As a point of reference, DOD's STTR program was funded at $42 million in fiscal year 2002 [NSB04].

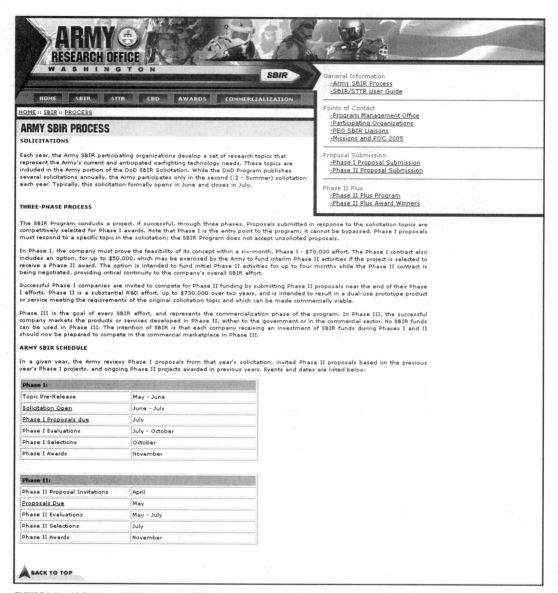

FIGURE 7.3   U.S. Army SBIR 2005.2 solicitation.

A form of government-industry partnership, the Cooperative Research and Development Agreements (CRADA), may be useful for serious games development shops that work with the government. A CRADA is an agreement that defines the scope and terms of collaborative relationships between government scientists and outside collaborators in industry or academia. The collaborator usually shares research, funding, and staffing costs with the government. The government owns patents on inventions that arise from work conducted under a CRADA, but the collaborator obtains an option to negotiate an exclusive license to these inventions.

The largest participant in the CRADA technology transfer program is the DOD, which accounted for nearly half of all CRADAs in 2000. The Department of Energy is the second largest participant, at nearly a quarter of all CRADAs in the same year. The majority of CRADAs for the DOD are from the army [NSB04].

While the DOD does solicit help from the private sector through SBIR and STTR grants, it also has internal resources. In 1999 the military created the Institute of Creative Technology (ICT) in Marina Del Ray, which has produced titles such as *Full Spectrum Command*, *Full Spectrum Warrior*, and *Full Spectrum Board Game* [Bonk05].

Medicine

Medicine, whether academic, private, or military, is another promising area for serious games. As noted in Chapter 2, "Working Context," serious medical games are useful for training clinicians, educating patients, and providing therapeutic adjuncts. The most immediate business need is in the military, where clinicians spend most of their careers waiting for a war to break out and then realize that they haven't adequately maintained their skills in combat trauma. The systems—some games and some pure simulations—that have been developed to address this shortcoming are in five general areas: PC-based multimedia, digital mannequins, virtual workbenches, total immersion virtual reality, and augmented reality. Each of these areas is amenable to serious games techniques. However, with the exception of PC-based multimedia and some forms of augmented reality, developing serious games that make use of these technologies can be a complicated, expensive affair. Even so, there is federal funding available through SBIR/STTR mechanisms to offset the initial investment.

Many medical institutions offer funding for technological innovations—including serious games—that can help in the teaching and practice of clinical medicine. For example, the Center for Integration of Medicine and Innovative Technology (CIMIT) offers funding for innovative projects, with awards ranging from $20,000 to $250,000 (*cimit.org/awards_categories.html*). The National Institutes of Health (NIH), in addition to participating in the SBIR program, administers a separate funding mechanism through its Web site (*grants1.nih.gov/grants/guide/index.html*). As of July 6, 2005, the NIH site listed funding opportunities for two game-related topics, one related to violence and traumatic stress and the other on environmental approaches to treating obesity. Clearly, there is funding for serious games development in medicine—it just takes a bit of digging to locate the sources.

Academia

The internal academic market is ripe for serious games developers who are fortunate enough to land grant support from the government and/or industry. Virtually every university-level institution has a computer lab or in some way integrates computer-based learning into its curriculum. Developers outside academia can use the government's STTR program to achieve significant financial leverage for serious game development, regardless of whether the games are intended for internal academic use or commercial application.

Industry

Every large commercial organization has a budget for training and development. As shown in Table 7.4, the categories of topics offered through training organizations such as the American Management Association range from administrative support to strategic planning. Tapping into industries through the various training and development providers or internal multimedia development shops are valid avenues to securing funds for serious games development.

TABLE 7.4   Categories of Training Courses Offered by the American Management Association

CATEGORIES OF TRAINING COURSES OFFERED BY THE AMA
Administrative Support
Business Writing and Presentation Skills
Communications and Interpersonal Skills
Finance and Accounting
Human Resources and Training
Information Technology
Leadership
Management and Supervisory Skills
Marketing
Project Management
Purchasing/Supply Management
Sales
Senior Management
Strategic Planning

Source: AMA Seminars, March–December 2006.

The challenge in working with industry in the area of training and development is finding an appropriate business model. Whereas developers of advergames might be able to arrange a contract in which residuals (royalties) are paid for a certain number of viewers over a predefined minimum, educational games are more likely to be treated as commodities. It's up to the game developer to convince the head of training and development of the added value of having game-based learning as one component of a complete curriculum—a task facilitated by solid assessment figures.

STAKEHOLDERS

Stakeholders in the serious games industry are the individuals and organizations that have something to gain or lose, depending on the success or failure of the industry. The primary stakeholders, listed in Table 7.5, include those involved directly in the industry. Secondary stakeholders are affiliated with related industries.

TABLE 7.5   Stakeholders in the Serious Games and Related Industries

STAKEHOLDERS
Game Industry
1st-Party Platform Developers/Publishers
3rd-Party Game Developers
Contract Game Developers
Game Publishers
Publisher-Owned Internal Developers
Related Industries
Animation and Graphics
Business Services
Education
Government Agencies
Hardware Developers
Marketing and Communications
Middleware Developers
Military
Research
Tool Developers
Video and Film

Primary stakeholders include game developers, traditional game publishers, and publisher-owned internal development shops. For a shop that uses direct digital distribution, the organization that supports the game server is an important stakeholder. Secondary stakeholders in the serious games industry include the vast array of support services, hardware developers and manufacturers, and tool developers that are either served by the industry or served it.

The identity of the specific stakeholders associated with a given development shop is important in developing a business plan and in assessing the risks of potential business strategies. Knowledge of the external business environment, including the competition, tool suppliers, and other stakeholders, can be invaluable in developing a winning business strategy.

CUSTOMER BASE

Supply is of no value without demand, and with a perishable commodity such as serious games, the timing of that demand is critical in assessing the viability of a product. The timing and nature of demand for serious games can be understood and modeled in terms of technology adoption rate and the phenomenon of rising expectations.

Technology Adoption

Growth in the serious games industry is dependent on a growing customer base, which translates to bridging the gap between geeks and mainstream players. In the business vernacular, this is equivalent to "crossing the chasm" between the early adopters and the early majority in the technology adoption curve shown in Figure 7.4 [Moore99]. According to the model, as soon as a product is introduced, a small number of technology-focused Innovators go to great lengths to acquire it. Often the Innovators are price insensitive and are willing to pay unreasonable sums to be the first in their peer group with the technology. Later, the educated but less technologically aware Early Adopters follow the Innovator's lead and invest in the technology. The major influx of customers constitutes the Early Majority, followed by the Late Majority. Finally, the Laggards, who tend to be less educated and less economically able buy into the product. Assuming that serious game adoption follows the traditional technology adoption curve, understanding this model can help game developers time rollouts and decide when to push a technology and when to wait for the market to catch up.

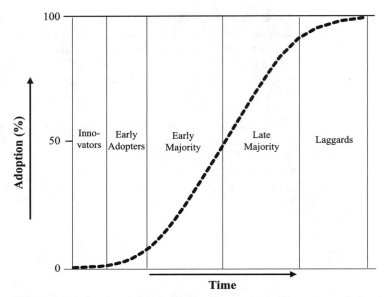

FIGURE 7.4   Technology adoption curve. The curve applies to group behavior.

Progress along the technology adoption curve depends on a variety of factors, including the risk aversion of the potential customer base. All else being equal, low risk aversion translates to a rapid rate of adoption. Of course, other factors that affect the adoption rate include cost, the maturity of the technology, the immediacy of demand, and whether adoption is directed or volitional. However, even if the end users are directed to use a serious game in training, the technology adoption curve still applies to those who make the purchase decision.

Rising Expectations

The genesis of customer expectations is important to understand because expectations define the market potential of the serious games industry. As shown in Figure 7.5, expectations are dynamic, in that as technologies such as video games mature, the difference between the expectations of the most demanding and least demanding customers narrows.

The significance for serious games developers is that customer expectations are rising. Even though entertainment gamers have traditionally been the most demanding customers in the gaming industry, the expectations of the serious games community is approaching those of the entertainment community. The practical implication of this trend is that serious games developers must continue to evolve their craft toward that of the entertainment market, or risk losing market share to traditional forms of technology used to transfer knowledge, skills, and attitudes.

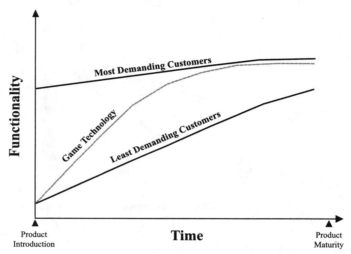

FIGURE 7.5   Time versus functionality expectations. With the maturation of game technology, there is increasingly less difference between demands of entertainment games customers and serious games customers.

The coevolution model is another tool management that a serious games development shop can use to view the evolution of customer expectations. The model, shown in Figure 7.6, illustrates how the wants and needs of customers coevolve with advances in game hardware and software. Serious games replace traditional learning as serious games are substituted for other technologies, such as PowerPoint slides and multimedia presentations. Because the new technologies change users, expectations rise, and the old technologies are abandoned.

In this coevolution model, old technologies, such as the previous model of a video game console, are replaced by new technologies (the new model) through the processes of substitution and diffusion. Substitution occurs when a new technology is substituted for an older technology. Diffusion describes the adoption or appropriation of the newly introduced technology into the customer's life. Diffusion is a function of the rate of appropriation, which is in turn a function of the positive reinforcement that the customer receives from working with the technology. The central theme of this model is the interaction between the customer and the technology. As the technology evolves, the customer's expectations of what a game—serious or otherwise—can and should deliver are permanently altered.

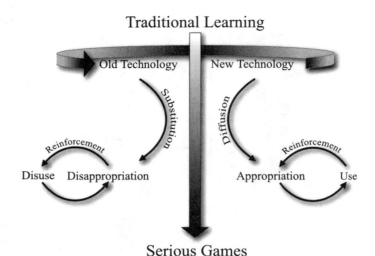

FIGURE 7.6   Coevolution of serious games technology and customers.

The coevolution model explains how a serious games technology suddenly becomes old to customers when they are exposed to faster, easier to use, more feature-laden entertainment games and game consoles. In this way, the cycle continues, with the technology modifying the user as he interacts with the latest technology. What's more, not only is this cycle continually progressing, but as aptly described by James Gleick in his book *Faster*, the pace of technological innovation is accelerating. As such, the process of appropriation and then disappropriation of "new" technology is accelerating.

HUMAN RESOURCES

The business of game development is about attracting, retaining, and managing talented, skilled people. The typical organizational structure of this talent pool in a moderate-sized (10- to 20- person) development shop is shown in Figure 7.7. There are employees dedicated to centralized processes such as game design, programming, art, modeling, and deployment, as well as internal and outsourced domain expertise. Overseeing development is the project manager, who is responsible for the development pipeline, and the producer, who is responsible for the success of the overall project.

The domain expertise can be a significant in terms of cost and headcount. For example, we were the chief scientists for a 20-person shop that focused on developing simulation-based serious games for the pharmaceutical and medical education industries. The head of sales had a PhD in pharmacology and the head of business development had worked as a nurse for many years. One of the four programmers had a PhD in physics, and the head of marketing had managed a department in a major medical journal. In addition, we had a cadre of about a dozen medical students, physiologists, and practicing physicians who worked on an as-needed basis. Most of the time, the number of on-staff and consultants working in the capacity of domain (subject matter) experts was at least half of the total headcount.

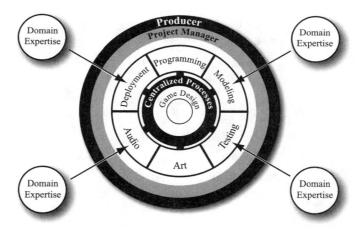

FIGURE 7.7 Organizational structure of a moderate-sized development shop. The areas of domain expertise serviced by outside consultants, shown outside of the main diagram, are project dependent.

The staffing of each area of expertise within the shop depends on the nature and number of games under development and the total number of employees and contract workers. A moderate-sized shop might have 18 to 20 employees and three or four contractors, distributed over management, office support, programming, artwork, marketing, internal IT, and customer support. The entertainment games industry giant, Electronic Arts (EA), has about 4,800 employees [Hoovers05]. Even with 100 employees on a team, entertainment games require 18–24 months of development time [Ramshaw05].

Whereas a small 3- to 5-person shop necessarily has employees who each perform multiple functions, the larger shops use highly specialized staff. As shown in Table 7.6, game developer job categories include a range of programming and engineering specialists, visual arts professionals, design, audio, and production specialists. Within the area of visual arts alone, there are 2D and 3D artists, texturers, modelers, animators, art directors, lead artists, and video editors. In addition to hands-on developers, the business side of operations includes a typical management team, with a CEO/president and heads of marketing and sales.

TABLE 7.6   Job Categories

GAME DEVELOPER JOB CATEGORIES

Audio

Audio Engineer

Composer/Musician

Sound Designer

Business

Analyst/Lawyer/Consultant

CEO/President

Content Acquisition/Licensing

Educator

HR/Training Manager/Recruiter

IT Manager

Marketing/PR/Sales

Program Manager

Student/Intern

VP/Executive Manager

Game Design

Creative Director/Lead Designer

Game Designer

Level Designer

Writer

Production

Executive Producer

Producer/Project Lead

QA/Tester

Programming/Engineering

Art Technician

Hardware Engineer

Lead Programmer

$\rightarrow$

GAME DEVELOPER JOB CATEGORIES

Network Engineer

Programmer

Technical Director

Visual Arts

2D Artist/Texturer

3D Artist/Modeler

Animator

Art Director

Lead Artist

Video Editor

Even the largest serious games development shops have to reach outside of their organization occasionally for special talent. Aside from domain experts, the representative services that are commonly outsourced range from business services, art, and music production, to motion capture (see Table 7.7).

TABLE 7.7   Commonly Outsourced Serious Games Development Services

SERIOUS GAMES DEVELOPMENT SERVICES

Business (legal, accounting, licensing)

Contract art/animation/video

Contract music/sound

Contract programming

Contract testing Q&A

Disc replication

Internet service providers/web hosting

Internet/networking infrastructure

Localization

Motion Capture Services

Professional representation (recruiters, agents)

Marketing/PR

Many production tasks, such as disk replication, are simply less expensive and/or of better quality when outsourced. A key service that is commonly outsourced regardless of the internal expertise is the testing related to the serious content. For example, in the 20-person shop noted previously, we routinely sent models and other content out for third-party review, even if the original development was performed by a contractor. Invariably, the second reviewer found some detail that had to be addressed before release.

LEGAL ISSUES

Legal issues abound in the serious game industry, from securing intellectual property rights and managing the red tape associated with government contracts to dealing with generic business concerns such as human resources. For example, at the 2005 E3 in Los Angeles, voice actors picketed for a larger share of game profits [Gentile05]. The American Federation of Television and Radio Artists reached a deal with video game makers in June of 2005. Actors accepted a 36 percent raise over three years instead of the residual payments or profit sharing that they had demanded [Reuters05]. In contrast, the Screen Actors Guild vetoed the offer [AP05]. The negotiations and contractual arrangements obviously involved considerable legal assistance and expense.

Although a limited number of serious games developers will have to negotiate a labor contract with the Screen Actors Guild—the majority of voiceover work for video games is performed by nonunionized artists [Lippman05]—all development shops work with intellectual property, and many aspire to work with the government or perhaps develop a serious game in health care. The main legal issues associated with these areas are discussed later in this chapter.

Intellectual Property

Game development is synonymous with intellectual property development. Programmers create code and artists create assets that can be copyrighted. Marketing creates a brand name that can be trademarked. An outside contractor designs a new hardware interface that can be patented. Although the terms copyright, trademark, and patent are often bandied about in the game development industry, many developers fail to protect their intellectual property because they don't understand the various forms of protection.

Copyright

Copyright is a form of protection provided to the authors of original works of authorship, including C++ code, level designs, and 3D models, both published and unpublished. U.S. Copyright law, as defined by the

Copyright Act of 1976, gives the owner of copyright the exclusive right to reproduce the work, to prepare derivative works, to distribute copies of the work, and to display or perform the work publicly. Copyright law is relevant to virtually all aspects of game development, from the game design document to the artwork on the CD-ROM and jewel case.

Copyright protection begins with the first line of code, regardless of whether it is published [Bruk01]. For personally authored works, the copyright lasts the life of the author plus 50 years. However, for corporate work created in the course of employment, copyright belongs to the employer and lasts 100 years from creation, or 75 years from publication, whichever comes first. Once a copyright expires, the work enters the public domain, and it might be freely copied and distributed. A copyright can be sold (assigned), or the rights can be temporarily granted, to second parties through exclusive or nonexclusive licenses.

As with other forms of intellectual property protection, copyright law doesn't provide for automatic enforcement—or pay the legal fees. It's up to the copyright holder to bring the infringing party to court. In the United States, copyright infringements are normally dealt with in civil lawsuits in federal court. There is no international copyright, but several international treaties recognize copyrighted materials. Most countries, including the United States, recognize the Berne Convention, which grants copyright protection to works of authors who are citizens of any member country [Copyright05].

A copyright protects the *form* of expression rather than the subject matter of the writing. For example, a game design document could be copyrighted, but this would only prevent others from copying the design document. It wouldn't prevent others from developing the game described in the original document. Copyrights are registered by the Copyright Office of the Library of Congress for a nominal filing fee.

Trademark

Trademarks apply to words, short sentences, and symbols that developers use to identify and distinguish their games from those of others. Service marks are the same as trademarks, except that they identify and distinguish the source of a service rather than a product. Trademark protection applies to most serious games development projects, although not to the degree of copyright protection.

In the United States, trademark law is defined by the Lanham Act of 1946 and administered by the U.S. Patent and Trademark Office (*www.uspto.gov*). Trademarks are granted for renewable 10-year terms. As with copyrights, trademarks may be assigned or licensed. The Trade-Related Aspects of Intellectual Property Rights agreement of 1994 (TRIPS) defines the international protection of trademarks [WHO05].

Acquiring trademark protection is considerably more complex, expensive, and time consuming than the automatic protection afforded by copyright law. Even so, anyone can obtain trademark protection through the U.S. Patent and Trademark Office (USPTO) portal at *www.uspto.gov*.

Consider the steps we went through to trademark the phrase "Augmented Reality Medical Simulation." The first step was to search the USPTO's online database for a previously filed trademark of the same name. When no match was found, we completed an electronic form in the Trademark Electronic Application System (TEAS), also at *www.uspto.gov*. The most difficult part of the form was determining the most appropriate class of service. If no class of service is assigned, someone in the USPTO will assign a class, based on the phrase to be trademarked. However, the best approach is to spend a few minutes scanning the list of classes in the online Goods and Service Manual. In this example, the closest match was "009—Virtual reality software for medicine."

A few seconds after submitting credit card information for the $325 processing fee, an email acknowledgment of the application appeared in our inbox. Six months later, we were contacted by an examining attorney for clarification. Finally, nine months after the initial filing, the trademark was assigned. Because of the lag time, it's important to choose the class(es) of service carefully with the initial application. Corrections and updates are possible, but there is a charge for each change and, more importantly, significant lag time between interactions with the USPTO.

Patents

Patents, which are used to protect inventions, are the most complex, costly, and, fortunately, least often used form of intellectual property protection for serious games developers. Furthermore, despite a number of books that profess otherwise, filling out a patent application without the help of a qualified attorney is shortsighted.

A patent is a legal document granting the inventor the right to exclude others from making, using, offering for sale, or importing the invention. There are three types of patents: utility, design, and plant. The most important to game developers is the utility patent, which applies to any new and useful process, machine, article of manufacture, or composition of matter, or any new and useful improvement.

An invention must meet three criteria before it can be patented: it must be novel; involve an inventive step; and have demonstrated utility or a clear industrial application [Pressman02]. There is nothing in the criteria that suggests an invention must be physical or mechanical, and patents apply equally to a better mousetrap and a better computer algorithm for, say, handling game physics. The term of a patent is 20 years from the date on which the application for the patent was filed with the

U.S. Patent and Trademark Office. The exact time of filing is important, because if the patent office receives several identical patents on the same day, only the first one filed is recognized.

Patents are expensive, and really useful only as leverage in court to collect monies from a company that infringes on the patent. A patent also has value as an asset that can be sold. It takes about two years and $10,000 to $100,000 for the average patent application to be granted. Simply holding on to a patent is expensive. All utility patents are subject to maintenance fees that must be paid to maintain the patent in force.

Two of the many intricate twists and turns of patent law are Provisional Patent Applications (PPAs) and Reach-Through Patents. PPAs are placeholders for formal patent claims. PPAs provide a means of filing without disclosing the exact nature of the patent while establishing an early effective filing date. The downside of PPAs is that, unlike regular patent applications, they can't be extended past 12 months.

Reach-Through Patents potentially apply to serious games development that relies on third-party game engines, middleware, and utilities. Reach-through patents were popularized in the mid-1980s, when it was common practice for software tool developers to charge a royalty or license for products made with their tools. For example, if a compiler was purchased or licensed by a developer that went on to develop a commercial application, the compiler company often demanded some percentage of the retail value of the application.

Because computer tools were rare in the 1980s and there was a race to develop real applications, many software developers agreed to relatively egregious terms, including reach-through licensing. In time, when competitive products appeared on the market, the tools were dropped in favor of royalty-free tools. A parallel situation exists today. While many game development utilities and tools are available to individuals for personal use, some of the high-end game engines charge reach-through fees for commercial games developed with the tools. Developers who fail to pay what are often significant fees when they have a blockbuster hit can be sued on the basis of reach-through patent rights.

Trade Secrets

Trade secrets are another form of intellectual property, but there are no fees and no forms to fill out. A secure safe, or better still, a good memory with no written evidence for anyone to stumble upon, makes for a good trade secret. One of the greatest threats to trade secrets is estranged former employees who might go to a competing developer, despite having a nondisclosure agreement (NDA) with the former employer. There is also the potential that a competing company will discover a developer's trade secret on its own, leaving the original company with no advantage in the marketplace.

Defense

Intellectual property protection provides developers and artists with leverage they can use to fight intentional and unintentional infringement. For example, a high-profile case involving Sony Corp and Immersion Corp came to a head in March of 2005, when Sony was ordered to pay $90.7 million in damages to Immersion over a patent infringement lawsuit related to the Dual Shock controller for Sony's PlayStation consoles [Kageyama05].

The rights of a business to maintain trade secrets can also be held up in court. In 2003, Electronic Arts sued 23 former employees who, it alleged, took materials from the Medal of Honor games when they left to form Sparks Entertainment. EA received damages and legal costs [Parker03].

The key word in intellectual property rights work is enforceability. Despite copyright laws, game piracy is rampant in China and other parts of Asia [Gibson05]. Piracy is also an issue in the United States, where some game engine developers claim as many as one in five console gamers are pirating software [Fahey05].

Government Contracts

Landing a government contract is a difficult but typically worthwhile endeavor. However, a serious games developer working with the government has to contend with legal overhead often referred to as interface management. For example, a developer working through a government contractor is usually required to sign an NDA and/or an Associate Contractor Agreement (ACA). An ACA defines the relationship between the developer and the contractor and forms the basis for sharing information, data, technical knowledge, expertise, and/or resources essential to the project.

In addition to an ACA, the game developer may be required to provide the government agency with Government Purpose Rights (GPR) for all technical data and noncommercial software developed under government contract. An unrestricted GPR allows the government to do whatever it wants to with the data and/or software, as long as they are used for U.S. government purposes.

The game developer may add significant restrictions to the GPR to protect its intellectual property, including reinstating copyright protection lost to the government. For example, the developer could stipulate that prior to releasing data to third parties, the government must advise the developer in writing. Furthermore, the developer could require third parties to agree in writing to obtain the written permission of the developer before releasing the data.

Medical Devices

One of the potentially problematic legal areas of civilian serious games development is related to medical games. A serious game developed in the medical area is just like other game as far as the law is concerned—unless it can be classified as a medical device. Medical devices must be approved by the FDA before they can be sold.

According to section 201(h) of the Federal Food Drug & Cosmetic Act (FD&C), the definition of a medical device includes an instrument, apparatus, or machine that is intended for use in the diagnosis, cure, treatment, or prevention of disease [FDA05]. Key in this definition is the intended use. For example, a tongue depressor is a medical device, but the same stick could be used to hold a popsicle.

As with the previously discussed forms of intellectual property, the key factors in acquiring FDA approval for a medical device are time and money. For a serious game to receive approval, it must undergo extensive studies to prove efficacy and freedom from side effects. The fees for an FDA product review are significant, even with the heavy discounts afforded small businesses. Gaining FDA approval for a serious medical game can cost several hundred thousand dollars and take many months.

To illustrate the numerous intellectual property and potential medical device issues associated with a medical serious game, consider the *Posture-Perfect* game, shown in Figure 7.8. The system consists of sensors that respond to rotation and flexion that are held in place over the player's spine by a snugly fitting athletic shirt and a wireless, battery-powered link to a game running on a PC. The link is based on the same repurposed controller technology discussed earlier, and the sensors are connected to the analog joystick connections on the repurposed controller board.

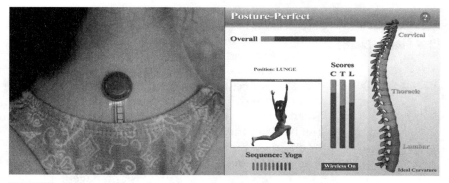

FIGURE 7.8 *Posture-Perfect*, showing the tip of the spine sensor array over the cervical spine of a player (left panel) and the game interface (right). © Archetype Technologies, Inc. Used with permission.

The flex sensors used in this game are paper-thin strips about five inches long and a quarter inch wide. Unbent, the sensors have a nominal resistance of a few thousand ohms. When bent, however, the resistance increases several fold. The flex sensors are held against the player's spine, and flexion in the spine is reflected by a change of resistance in the flex sensors, which is read by the game as a new joystick position. Rotation of the spine is similarly tracked with rotation sensors.

During gameplay, which is a modified version of Simon Says, the wearer assumes a standard yoga position, as directed by the game. The player has 10 seconds to assume the proper position and then the game reads the curvature of the spine. The curvatures in the cervical, thoracic, and lumbar vertebrae are computed by the PC and compared with the ideal for the given position. The closer the player's curvature measurements to the ideal, the higher the score in each area, and the greater the total score for each run of ten poses.

Feedback on spinal alignment is given in the form of audio signals so that the player can experiment with his or her spine position without having to look at a computer monitor. *Posture-Perfect* was developed as a training aid for fitness clients, not as a medical device. Although the system could potentially be used as a medical device to mitigate lower back pain, it was determined that the investment required to patent the technology and apply for FDA approval was prohibitive, given the market potential of the device. However, patent protection was sought for the spine sensor array.

Readers of the microcontroller section in Chapter 6, "Tools"—will recognize the simplicity of the PC-based serious game—a half-dozen sensors, a repurposed game controller, and a game engine provide the bulk of raw materials. However, simplicity in design doesn't simplify the developer's task of securing the intellectual property rights to a system.

RISK MANAGEMENT

Serious games development is a risky business. There are myriad risks related to project management, the selection and use of development tools and other technologies, the development pipeline, and the fate of the finished game. Consider that, as in the entertainment games industry, it may not be clear until the feedback from customers arrives that a game is a dud as an entertainment vehicle. Fun isn't something that can be engineered into a game, even when a development shop follows best practices.

In the software industry, risk management is a science that involves concepts such as risk exposure, probability theory, and decision theory [Hall98]. From a pragmatic perspective, the primary business risks associated with serious games development are related to timing, business strategy, and knowledge management.

Timing

Game development requires an investment of time and energy, with the expectation that there will be a payoff at some point after delivery of the game. Few serious game development projects have the luxury of a flexible timeline or of full payment upfront. Even academic grants have fixed deliverables and disbursement schedules.

The traditional plot of cash flow over time for a game development project is shown in Figure 7.9. Cash flow is negative by the time of solution design, and this trend accelerates as programmers and artists come online during the code/implement phase of the development pipeline. Negative cash flow begins to abate during the test/debug phase, and even more so when the game is deployed.

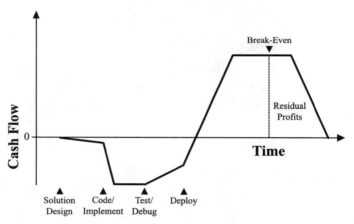

FIGURE 7.9   Cash flow for a game development shop, assuming a royalty-based business model. Cash flow from external funding is not shown.

If the game is well received, cash flow swings positive at some point after deployment. If the game is a hit, break-even occurs relatively soon after deployment. In a royalty-based business model, subsequent cash flow is profit for the development shop. Eventually, the cash flow resulting from the game diminishes toward zero.

In a cost-plus business model, the timing of payments to the development shop are typically tied to milestones, such as a third at the time of contract signing, another third upon the delivery of an alpha or beta version, and a final third at sign-off of the production version of the game. Regardless of the payback timing, a self-sustaining development shop has to manage production so that profits from one title provide the cash flow for ongoing operations and startup costs for the following title. Delays in bringing a serious game to market can devastate the bottom line because of the extended period of expenses, a missed marketing window, or loss of market share because of competitors [Gaynor96]. All three factors may affect cash flow independently or together.

Entertainment games are increasingly designed for maximum shelf life by adding features such as on-line gameplay. Serious games can be designed to maximize longevity through gameplay options as well. However, regardless of the novelty of gameplay, serious games are at risk for premature death because of the volatility of the underlying serious content. For example, if three weeks after the release of a medical game for medical students, the drug used to treat the condition in the game is recalled by the FDA, then the game may have to be recalled. Development shops that work on a cost-plus basis could benefit from the situation, in terms of additional work. However, shops working for residual profits might not even break even.

Strategy

In the serious games development business, strategy includes identifying the best operational methods, determining how to fight the competition, and identifying which opportunities to pursue.

Operations

Operational methods focus on maximizing the effectiveness and efficiency of the development pipeline. Management has to consider factors such as the capacity of the shop, scheduling employees and contract workers, inventory control, production quality standards, and overall control of the development pipeline. For example, in considering the production capacity of the shop, management may have to decide whether to buy middleware from a vendor or divert production capacity to create AI and physics in-house.

Competition

Strategies for fighting the competition address issues such as how to preserve or grow market share or profitability. Management must assess the value propositions of the major competitors and, if appropriate, adjust the development shop's value proposition accordingly. For example, if the major competition is a large development shop that competes on the basis of price, then management should consider offering either high-quality, high-margin games or quick turnaround.

Opportunities

Determining which business opportunities to pursue—that is, how the development shop should expand—requires an assessment of the economy, trends in the industry, and the agility of the shop's management and employees. The most common expansion option, simply growing the shop to handle more of the same kind of business so that it can benefit from economies of scale and the stability of a larger, regular staff, isn't necessarily the best course of action.

A tool often used to assess expansion options is the Ansoff Matrix, a strategic diagram developed by H. I. Ansoff [Silbiger99]. The matrix, shown in Figure 7.10, relates new and existing products to new and existing markets. Newness relates to the shop's experience, not to the absolute age of the product or market. Furthermore, although the options theoretically aren't mutually exclusive, in practice, few development shops have the money or human resources to pursue expansion opportunities in more than one dimension at a time. Following the matrix, there are four alternative expansion strategies for a serious games development business:

- *An old or existing product in an existing market.* This calls for a market penetration strategy in which the shop attempts to consolidate the market. For example, a shop catering to the military industry could expand by increasing its marketing and lobbying efforts toward the military and expanding its offerings of military serious games.
- *An old or existing product and new market.* This expansion strategy involves market development, also termed related diversification. For example, a shop experienced in developing games to train army medics could expand into the serious medical games market.
- *A new product in an existing market.* This expansion strategy calls for product development. For example, a shop experienced in developing combat training games for the military could expand by incorporating realistic medical cases within its games and attempt to find buyers within the military.
- *A new product in a new market.* This expansion strategy calls for unrelated diversification. An example would be for a serious games development shop that is skilled in creating warfare games for the military to expand by offering advergames to the athletic shoe industry.

Each expansion strategy is associated with risk. The riskiest expansion strategy is to develop a new product for a new market. Conversely, the expansion strategy with the least risk is increasing the market penetration of an old product in an old market.

Businesses often use tools to evaluate the risk of each expansion option. For example, in assessing the risk of expanding product development, a useful tool is the Technology Continuum matrix. This decision support tool, shown in Figure 7.11, is based on internal technology maturity and

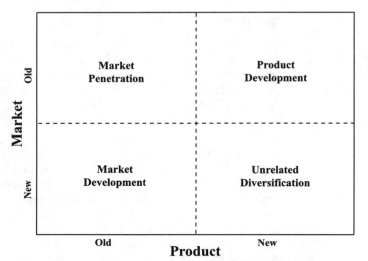

FIGURE 7.10   Ansoff Matrix for assessing expansion strategies.

external market maturity [BergeronBlander02]. As a predictive model, it encourages management to look ahead of the current challenges and consider the underlying processes that are involved in bringing a new game or other product to market.

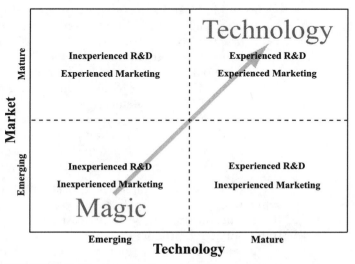

FIGURE 7.11   Technology Continuum matrix.

For example, product development that involves an emerging technology in an emerging market is risky because both the R&D staff and the marketing staff are usually inexperienced. As a result, the risk of failure is high, and the game likely has the characteristics of magic—context dependency, results that can't be replicated, and instability—rather than those of a solid technology.

The product development scenario with the least amount of risk is to use a mature technology in a mature market. The R&D staff should know or have access to information on the strengths and limitations of the technology, and the marketing staff should be familiar with the market. The other two product development options, involving either emerging technologies or new markets, are associated with risks somewhere between the two extremes.

In addition to the Ansoff Matrix and the Technology Continuum models, there are strategy assessment tools that can be used to understand and mitigate the risks associated with business decisions. Among the most notable is Michael Porter's Five Forces model, which is useful in developing a survival strategy. The model is described in the context of a business plan in Appendix E, "A Brief Business Plan Primer."

Knowledge Management

Small, independent shops that rely on contract labor for development are at risk for losing—or never owning—the core intellectual assets they need to design, develop, and deliver serious games in a consistent manner. Consider the staffing model for a small development shop illustrated in Figure 7.12. Management, programming, artwork, and game design are core competencies of full-time staff, while audio, testing, deployment, and domain expertise are outsourced.

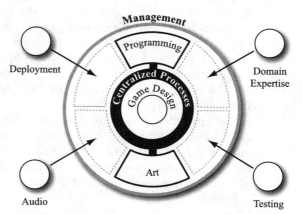

FIGURE 7.12   A staffing model for a small serious games development shop.

As noted earlier, the advantages of outsourcing certain processes include cost savings and flexibility. For example, even if the development shop plans to specialize in a particular domain, it usually doesn't make economic sense to hire a full-time domain expert. A retainer or other arrangement is usually more mutually beneficial. However, when it comes to competencies such as deployment or testing, the choice of a consultant versus a hire is often less clear. The risk of a consultant divulging a trade secret or of simply being unavailable for an unexpected or rush project has to be weighed against the likelihood of enough future business to risk taking on more full-time staff.

Employment status doesn't resolve the risk of losing a core competency of the business. For example, if the employee responsible for the artwork—from textures to 3D models—decides to leave, then the business may not recover. The smaller the shop, the more devastating the effect of a departure.

Mitigating the risk of losing a core competency requires the implementation of basic knowledge management practices, such as documenting procedures, rewarding employees for sharing, not hoarding knowledge, and codifying the development process with computer-based tools whenever feasible [Bergeron03]. For example, encouraging a programmer to take the time to document his code on a daily basis may be difficult in the middle of game development crunch. However, the long-term survival of the business may depend on the documentation. It's up to management to decide how to best ensure that employees contribute to building a process that can outlive them as they build a game.

PUBLIC RELATIONS

Serious games have inherited a marketing and public relations headache from the entertainment games industry in the form of an overall negative perception of games, gamers, and the ethics of some game designers [Takahashi04]. This blemished perception is fostered by the occasional case in which a creative lawyer blames a crime committed by their client on crime-theme video games [Bishop05], and by the convenient examples of obviously negative behavior in popular video games.

The scene with a prostitute in the AAA game *Grand Theft Auto* (Take Two Interactive) was a frequently cited example of negative behavior models in video games until it was temporarily replaced as the poster child for bad games by *NARC* (Midway Games). In *NARC*, the player can assume the role of a bad cop who can use the drugs he seizes from dealers. A hit of crack makes the cop a great shot, speed transforms him into an Olympic-class sprinter, and a toke of marijuana slows things down to a slow-motion replay.

Grand Theft Auto returned to the center of the debate when it was revealed that the "Hot Coffee" mod unlocked content that allowed players to make characters engage in sexually explicit acts [Baertlein05]. After Senator Hilary Clinton asked the Federal Trade Commission to investigate the game as well the industry's rating-enforcement practices, the ESRB changed the rating of the game from M (Mature 17+) to AO (Adults Only). Moreover, other senators challenged the ESRB's effectiveness at self-policing the industry.

Laws have been enacted to protect children from video games. Despite effort by the International Game Developers Association (IGDA), The Safe Games Illinois Act was signed into law in 2005 [Klepek05]. The law bans the rental and sale of violent and sexually explicit video games to children younger than 18 and imposes an additional rating system on video games. Retailers who fail to properly label games or place proper signs face a $500 fine for the first three violations and a $1,000 fine for every subsequent violation. Retailers who violate the ban face an additional fine of $1,000. A dedicated Web site, *www.safegamesillinois.org*, explains the act and provides parents with an automated system they can use to report violators.

The medical community has come down hard on video games, especially regarding overuse by children and adolescents. The ill effects of gameplay reported in the medical literature include video game addiction [Griffiths98], increased aggressiveness [Anderson01], epileptic seizures [Maeda90], auditory hallucinations [Spence93], bed wetting [Schink91], repetitive strain injuries, and obesity [Shimai93]. Players suffering from video game addiction can be treated in clinics in the United States as well as China [Ang05].

The negative perception of excessive play isn't universal. In Korea, for example, high-scorers in the online game *Lineage* aren't addicts—they're pop-stars with thousands of followers. There are also outspoken supporters of the medium whose messages sometimes break through the negative noise of the popular press. James Gee, author of *What Video Games Have to Teach Us about Learning and Literacy*, highlights the potential educational benefits of video games [Carlson03; Gee04]. Similarly, in his book *Killing Monsters: Why Children Need Fantasy, Super Heroes and Make-Believe Violence*, Gerald Jones promotes the concept that make-believe violence is a therapeutic outlet for children [Jones02]. In their book *Got Game: How the Gamer Generation Is Reshaping Business Forever*, John Beck and Mitchell Wade promote the positive influence of video games on the workforce [BeckWade04].

The medical community has even recognized some redeeming value in playing video games. In a 2005 editorial in the *British Medical Journal*, Mark Griffiths, a professor of gambling studies at Nottingham Trent University, concludes that video gaming is safe for most players and can be useful in health care [Griffiths05]. Griffiths highlights the use of video games in pain management, exemplified by the work of Dr. Hunter Hoffman and Virtual Reality Therapy described in Chapter 2, "Working Context" [Hoffman04]. The editorial also points out that video games have been used as a form of occupational therapy for hand injuries [King93] and spinal cord injuries [O'Connor00], and in developing skills in children with learning disabilities [Sedlak82], and that the adverse effects of gameplay resolve spontaneously with decreased frequency of play.

How the psychosocial evolution of entertainment games will eventually affect serious games is unclear. However, legislation for additional labeling or anything else that raises production costs or extends the development time of serious games would be detrimental to the genre. Perhaps a new term for "serious games," such as "mixed-reality training," would give marketing groups the leverage they need to distance the genre from entertainment games in the minds of consumers.

SUMMARY

Successful developers offer customers an attractive value proposition, which is a strategy that differentiates their products from those of the competition. The value is normally considered in terms of price, quality, and speed of development.

From a traditional business perspective, the entertainment gaming industry *is* the gaming industry. Most entertainment games sales are linked to the performance of a few dozen titles on one of four major platforms. In addition, niche areas such as mobile games, portable games, and serious games have emerged as significant areas of development.

Historically, the multi-billion-dollar industry is cyclical, with a peak in economic performance about every six years or so, keyed to a new generation of game consoles. Globally, the most rapid gains in sales are projected for the Asia/Pacific region. Domestically, the online gaming and mobile/wireless market is expected to expands significantly. These trends will necessarily affect serious games developers, as will the entertainment industry trends of increased development expenses, console and wireless dominance over the PC, new business models, better characters and other engines that result in enhanced gameplay, and in-game advertising. The shifting demographics of gamers are also significant.

Quantifying the potential of the serious games market is challenging because most of the statistics available for the games industry don't consider serious games as a separate category. A distinguishing feature of most serious games is that the business models for internally distributed games often bear little resemblance to those used in the retail entertainment industry. Of the markets available for serious games, the most promising are the U.S. government, medicine, academia, and industry.

The primary stakeholders in the serious games industry include game developers, traditional game publishers, and publisher-owned internal development shops. In addition, the customer base can be modeled in term of technology adoption rate and the phenomenon of rising expectations.

Human resource issues related to serious games development are primarily related to the heavy dependence of serious games developers on outsourced domain expertise. It's not unusual for a significant percentage of the development shop to be fluent in the subject area of a serious game. The most important legal issues in the serious game industry involve securing intellectual property rights and managing the red tape associated with government contracts.

Serious games development is associated with myriad risks related to project management, the selection and use of development tools and other technologies, the development pipeline, and the fate of the finished game. Most of these risks are related to timing, business strategy, and knowledge management.

A major challenge inherited by the serious games industry is overcoming the public's overall negative perception of games and gamers. Despite the bad press, there is a growing body of literature that highlights the potential benefits of gameplay, from enhanced mental health to better productivity on the job.

REFERENCES

[AndersonBushman01] Anderson, C. A. and B. J. Bushman, "Effects of Violent Video Games on Aggressive Behavior, Aggressive Cognition, Aggressive Affect, Physiological Arousal, and Prosocial Behavior: A Meta-analytic Review of the Scientific Literature." *Psychol Sci* 12 (2001): pp. 353–9.

[Ang05] Ang, Audra, "China Treats Addicted Video-Game Players." Associated Press. 2005. *news.yahoo.com/s/ap/20050704/ap_on_hi_te/china_kicking_the_net*, accessed July 4, 2005.

[AP05] AP, "Actors Guild Vetoes Deal for Video Games: Tentative Contract Had 36 Percent Pay Hike over 3 Years." MSNBC. 2005. *www.msnbc.msn.com/id/8317834*, accessed July 8, 2005.

[Baertlein05] Baertlein, Lisa, "Games Ratings Board Probing Grand Theft Auto: SA." Reuters. 2005. *news.yahoo.com*, accessed July 9, 2005.

[Barbagallo03] Barbagallo, Ralph, Wireless Game Development in C/C++ with BREW. Wordware Pub., 2003.

[Barbagallo04] Barbagallo, Ralph, *Wireless Game Development in Java with MIDP 2.0*. Wordware Pub., 2004.

[BeckWade04b] Beck, John and Mitchell Wade, *Got Game: How the Gamer Generation Is Reshaping Business Forever*. 2004.

[Bergeron01] Bergeron, B., *The Eternal E-Customer: How Emotionally Intelligent Interfaces Can Create Long-Lasting Customer Relationships*. McGraw-Hill, 2001.

[Bergeron01] Bergeron, B., *The Wireless Web: How to Develop a Winning Wireless Strategy*. McGraw-Hill, 2001.

[Bergeron03] Bergeron, B., *Essentials of Knowledge Management*. John Wiley & Sons, 2003.

[BergeronBlander02] Bergeron, Bryan, and Jeff Blander, *Business Expectations: Are You Using Technology to its Fullest?* John Wiley & Sons, 2002.

[Bishop05] Bishop, Bill, "Boys' Plea Deal Shelves 12-year Prison Terms: Defense Lawyers Link Robberies Committed by Three Eugene Teens to Violent Rap Lyrics and Crime-Theme Video Games." *The Register-Guard* (Feb 12 2005).

[BonkDennen05] Bonk, Curtis and Vanessa Dennen, *Massive Multiplayer Online Gaming: A Research Framework for Military Training and Education*. Advanced Distributed Learning, 2005.

[Brown05] Brown, Erika, "Coming Soon to a Tiny Screen Near You." *Forbes* 11 (2005): pp. 64–76.

[Bruk01] Bruk, D.L., "Copyrightable Functions and Patentable Speech." *Communications of the ACM* 2 (2001): pp. 69–75.

[Bryan-LowPringle05] Bryan-Low and David Pringle, "Sex Cells." *The Wall Street Journal* (May 12, 2005): p. B1.

[Carlson03] Carlson, Scott, "Can Grand Theft Auto Inspire Professors?" *The Chronicle of Higher Education*. 2003. *chronicle.com/free/v49/i49/49a03101.htm*, accessed July 6, 2005.

[Copyright05] Copyright, *Copyright Law of the United States of America and Related Laws Contained in Title 17 of the United States Code*. U.S. Copyright Office. 2005. *www.copyright. gov/title17/92appii.html*, accessed July 5, 2004.

[Croal02] Croal, N'Gai, "Sims Family Values" *Newsweek*. 2002. *msnbc.msn.com/id/3070145*, accessed July 8, 2005.

[Dvorak05] Dvorak, Phred, "Game Makers Bet That Playing on the Go Will Be Hot." *The Wall Street Journal* (May 17, 2005): pp. B1–5.

[EBGames05] EBGames, *XBox 360*. 2005. *www.ebgames.com/ebx/ads/shops/xbox360/*, accessed July 5, 2005.

[Economist02] Economist, "Console Wars." Economist.com. 2002. *www.economist.com/ business/displayStory.cfm?story_id=1189352*, accessed July 4, 2005.

[ESA05] ESA, *2005 Sales, Demographics and Usage Data*. Entertainment Software Association. 2005. *www.theesa.com/files/2005EssentialFacts.pdf*, accessed September 18, 2005.

[Fahey05] Fahey, Rob, "One in Five Console Gamers is a Pirate, Claims Macrovision." gamesindustry. biz. 2005. *www.gamesindustry.biz/news.php?aid=7419*, accessed July 5, 2005.

[FDA05] FDA, *Device Advice: Is the Product a Medical Device?* FDA. 2005. *www.fda.gov/cdrh/ devadvice/312.html*, accessed July 5, 2005.

[Gaynor96] Gaynor, G. H., *Handbook of Technology Management*. McGraw-Hill, 1996.

[Gee04] Gee, James, *What Video Games Have to Teach Us about Learning and Literacy*. Palgrave Macmillan, 2004.

[Gentile05] Gentile, Gary, "Actors Weigh Strike over Video Game Voices." Associated Press. 2005. *news.yahoo.com/s/ap/20050525/ap_on_bi_ge/video_games_labor*, accessed May 25, 2005.

[Gibson05] Gibson, Ellie, "Games Market in China Booms Despite Piracy." gamesindustry.biz. 2005. *www.gamesindustry.biz/news.php?aid=7540*, accessed July 5, 2005.

[Godinez05] Godinez, Victor, "Video Game Software Production Costs Rise, Experts Say." *The Dallas Morning News* (April 30, 2005).

[GriffithsHunt98] Griffiths, M. D., Hunt, N., "Dependence on Computer Game Playing by Adolescents." *Psychol Rep* 82 (1998): pp. 475–80.

[Griffiths05] Griffiths, Mark, "Video games and Health." *BMJ* 331 (2005): pp. 122–23.

[Gumbel05] Gumbel, Peter, "Losing the Controls." *Time International (Europe Edition)* (January 24, 2005).

[Hall98] Hall, E. M., *Managing Risk: Methods for Software Systems Development.* Addison-Wesley, 1998.

[Hershman05] Hershman, Tania, "Advertisers: Game On." *Technology Review.com* (May 2005).

[HerzMacedonia02] Herz, J. C. and M. Macedonia, *Computer Games and the Military: Two Views.* Defense Horizons 11, Center for Technology and National Security Policy, National Defense University, 2002.

[Hoffman04] Hoffman, Hunter, "Virtual-Reality Therapy." *Scientific American* 12 (2004): pp. 58–65.

[Hoovers05] Hoovers, *Electronic Arts, Inc.* Hoovers. 2005. *www.hoovers.com,* accessed July 5, 2005.

[Jones02] Jones, Gerald, *Killing Monsters: Why Children Need Fantasy, Super Heroes and Make-Believe Violence.* Basic Books, 2002.

[Kageyama05] Kageyama, Yuri, "Sony Ordered to Pay in Playstation Case." Associated Press, 2005. *sfgate.com/cgi-bin/article.cgi?file=/n/a/2005/03/28/financial/f053454S84.DTL,* accessed July 5, 2005.

[King93] King, T. I., "Hand Strengthening with a Computer for Purposeful Activity." *American Journal of Occupational Therapy* 47 (1993): pp. 635–7.

[Klepek05] Klepek, Patrick, *IGDA Fights Legislation.* 1up.Com. 2005. *www.1up.com,* accessed March 22, 2005.

[Kushner02] Kushner, David, "The Wireless Arcade." *Technology Review* (July/August 2002): pp. 56–52.

[Kushner04] Kushner, David, "The Wrinkled Future of Online Gaming." *Wired* (June 2004): pp. 98–101.

[Lawrence05] Lawrence, Stacy, "Digital Media Make Their Mark." *Technology Review* (July 2005): p. 31.

[Linsalata04] Linsalata, David and Schelley Olhava, et al., *U.S. Wireless Gaming 2004–2008 Forecast and Analysis: Gaming . . . Together* IDC, 2004.

[Lippman05] Lippman, John, "Players in a New Game." *The Wall Street Journal* (July 8, 2005): pp. W11C.

[Mack04] Mack, Ann, "Game On: Advertisers Embrace Gaming and the Audience it Attracts." *MediaWeek* 26 (2004): pp. 18–20.

[Maeda90] Maeda, Y, T. Kurokawa, et al., "Electroclinical Study of Video-Game Epilepsy." *Develop Med Child Neurol* 32 (1990): pp. 493–500.

[Marr05] Marr, Merissa, "Videogames Grow Up." *The Wall Street Journal* (April 10, 2005): pp. B1–10.

[Molineaux04] Molineaux, Sam, "Playing to Win: After 25 years, Content is King and Activision is Getting the Royal Treatment." *Hollywood Reporter* (May 12, 2004).

[Moore99] Moore, Geoffrey, *Crossing the Chasm: Marketing and Selling High-Tech Products to Mainstream Customers.* HarperBusiness, 1999.

[Mott05] Mott, Tony, "360 Sparks a Revolution." *Edge* (June 2005): pp. 8–15.

[Nelson05] Nelson, Jeffrey, "Verizon Wireless Builds on Commanding Lead in Multimedia Services With 3D Games On V Cast." Verizon. 2005. *news.vzw.com/news/2005/06/pr2005-06-01p.html*, accessed July 8, 2005.

[NIST05] NIST, *2005 Baldrige National Quality Program: Criteria for Performance Excellence.* National Institute of Standards and Technology, 2005.

[NSB04] NSB, *Science and Engineering Indicators—2004.* National Science Foundation, 2004.

[O'Connor00] O'Connor, T. J. and R. A. Cooper, et al., Evaluation of a manual wheelchair interface to computer games. *Neurorehabil Neural Repair* 14 (2000): pp. 21–31.

[Oser04] Oser, Kris, "EA Seeks Partners for Sims Sequel." *Advertising Age* (October 11, 2004).

[OSTP05] OSTP, *Budget 2005.* Office of Science and Technology Policy, Executive Office of the President. 2005. *www.ostp.gov/html/budget05.html*, accessed July 8, 2005.

[Parker03] Parker, Sam, "EA Settles Suit with Former Developers." *Gamespot*, 2003. *www.gamespot.com/news/2003/04/10/news_6024928.html*, accessed July 5, 2005.

[Plantec04] Plantec, P., *Virtual Humans*. AMACOM, 2004.

[Pressman02] Pressman, D., *Patent it Yourself*. NOLO Press, 2002.

[PricewaterhouseCoopers05] PricewaterhouseCoopers, *Global Entertainment and Media Outlook: 2005–2009*. PricewaterhouseCoopers, 2005.

[PRNewswire05] PRNewswire, *From just a virtual idea, advertising in video games is now a massive reality*. PRNewswire. 2005. *www.prnewswire.com*, accessed July 4, 2005.

[Ramshaw05] Ramshaw, Mark, "Evolve or Die." *GameState* (Spring 2005): pp. 4–9.

[RCR05] RCR, *Yahoo! buys gaming firm to boost wireless effort*. RCR Wireless News. 2005. accessed July 4, 2005.

[RealNetworks04] RealNetworks, *RealNetworks to Acquire GameHouse, Inc: Acquisition Creates Powerhouse in Downloadable PC Game Market*. RealNetworks. 2004. *www.realnetworks.com/company/press/releases/2004/gamehouse.html*, accessed July 4, 2005.

[Reuters05] Reuters, "Hollywood Unions Reach Deal with Video Game Makers." *The Washington Post*, 2005. *www.washingtonpost.com/wp-dyn/content/article/2005/06/09/AR2005060900117.html*, accessed June 9, 2005.

[Schink91] Schink, J. C., "Nintendo Enuresis." *American Journal of Diseases in Children* 145 (1991): p. 1094.

[Sedlak82] Sedlak, R. A. and M. Doyle, et al., Video Games — A training and Generalization Demonstration with Severely Retarded Adolescents, Education and Training in Mental Retardation and Developmental Disabilities. 17 (1982): pp. 332–36.

[Shimai93] Shimai, S., Yamada, F., et al., "TV Game Play and Obesity in Japanese School Children." *Perceptual and Motor Skills* 76 (1993): pp. 1121–22.

[Silbiger99] Silbiger, Steven, *The Ten Day MBA*. William Morrow and Company, 1999.

[Snider04] Snider, Mike, "Hollywood at the Controls: Video Games Feed Off Each Other." *USA Today* (May 10, 2004): pp. 1D–2D.

[Spence93] Spence, S. A., Nintendo "Hallucinations: A New Phenomenological Entity." *Irish Journal of Psychological Medicine* 10 (1993): pp. 98–99.

[Tait04] Tait, Leonie, "UK: Europe's Leading Video Game Market—01 Aug 2004." Euromonitor International. 2004. *www.euromonitor.com/article.asp?id=3621*, accessed July 4, 2005.

[Takahashi04] Takahashi, Dean, "Ethics of Game Design." *Game Developer* (December 2004).

[Tourtellotte05] Tourtellotte, Bob, "Microsoft Nears Movie Deal for 'Halo' Videogame." Reuters, 2005. *news.yahoo.com/s/nm/20050610/film_nm/media_halo_dc*, accessed June 6, 2005.

[WHO05] WHO, *TRIPS: Agreement on Trade-Related Aspects of Intellectual Property Rights Part II—Standards concerning the availability, scope and use of Intellectual Property Rights.* World Health Organization. 2005. *www.wto.org/english/tratop_e/trips_e/t_agm3_e.htm*, accessed July 5, 2005.

[Wingfield05] Wingfield, Nick, "A Battle Breaks Out Over Sports Rights In Videogame World: Software Titan Electronic Arts, Blindsided by Upstart, Nails Exclusive NFL Deal." *The Wall Street Journal* (July 11, 2005): pp. 1.

[Wingfield05] Wingfield, Nick, "The New Wave of Videogames." *The Wall Street Journal* (May 12, 2005): pp. D1–D4.

[WingfieldMarr05] Wingfield, Nick and Merissa Marr, "Games Players Can't Refuse?" *The Wall Street Journal* (April 10, 2005): pp. B1–10.

[WinklerSchooler04] Winkler, Peter and Laura Schooler, *Global Entertainment and Media Outlook: 2004–2008.* PricewaterhouseCoopers, 2004.

8

SERIOUS GAME DESIGN

In This Chapter

- The Serious Game Design Document
- Mapping the design document to the development pipeline

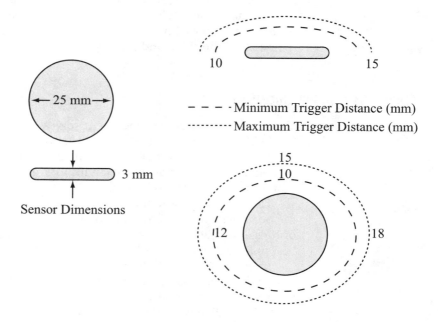

25 mm

3 mm

Sensor Dimensions

10   15

– – – Minimum Trigger Distance (mm)
········· Maximum Trigger Distance (mm)

15
10

12   18

INTRODUCTION

The idea for a serious game may spring from any number of sources—a science fiction novel, a movie, playing other games, or the explicit needs of an organization—and then percolate in a designer's head until it's ready for the real world. The transition from concept to concrete, actionable plan is marked by the creation of the serious game design document (SGDD).

Creating a serious game design document requires a developer to think and plan in terms of a definite goal, with timelines and resource requirements. The document should provide enough detail for a development shop to create the game with little or no hand-holding.

Serious games design documents are unique in that they not only define an entertaining setting and storyline, but they use characters, themes, and synthetic environments to impart specific knowledge, skills, and attitudes (KSAs) to players. This duality of purpose is fundamental to the design of serious games and adds a level of complexity that should be reflected in the design document. For example, an object added to a game to increase its entertainment value could have a detrimental effect on the KSA transfer, and vice versa. There may also be differences in how intellectual property is acquired and incorporated in a serious game. Instead of being handed the intellectual property, developers of serious games may be tasked to work with domain experts and to develop content that fulfills the needs of the client and the target audience.

SERIOUS GAME DESIGN DOCUMENT

The serious game design document serves as a communications vehicle for the development staff, as the basis for fund raising, and as a marketing and sales tool. For example, one of the core uses of a design document in academia is to use it as an appendix in a grant request to validate the monies requested and the timeline.

The complexity and focus of the game will determine which areas of the document require more thorough treatment. Regardless of the depth of focus, the serious game design document should reflect the industry best practices and standards upheld by the developer.

In some cases, a serious game design document may be indistinguishable from a design document for an entertainment title. However, even in these cases, there may be significant process differences that aren't immediately obvious from reading the document. For example, in the entertainment game design documents are usually developed in-house because of the commercial intellectual property and the need for the writer to have intimate knowledge of the shop's game development pipeline. In contrast, the design document for a serious game might be written in part by an outside consultant working closely with a domain (subject matter) expert.

For example, we (the authors) were a consultant to developers who were working on a serious game for a major pharmaceutical firm. The firm wanted the game to use as a promotional tool for the rollout of a new drug for diabetics. Furthermore, the pharmaceutical firm had retained the services of one of the world's foremost physician-scientists in the field of diabetes to serve as the content expert for all promotional and educational material related to the rollout of the drug. However, the pharmaceutical firm, the development shop, and the expert were located in different parts of the country, and the expert was too busy with patients and research to travel to the development shop.

We developed the components of the design document that had to be vetted by the expert at his location, where he was accessible throughout the day. These components required drug-specific information about how the drug worked in the body, the side effects, the profiles of laboratory results, and how the drug compared with other drugs on the market.

Most of the data were the results of clinical trials that showed patient responses to different doses of the drug over different periods of time. The data, which would have been worth millions of dollars to the competition, were unpublished and under the strict control of the pharmaceutical firm. In addition, only aggregate data were released by the firm, meaning that data from individuals were not available. This complicated the design of the underlying model because the game was supposed to feature individual patients, not groups. Average responses of several patients did not show the range of individual variability in response to the drug. However, with the assistance of the domain expert we were able to develop a rough model that applied to individuals without access to the individual data.

This model was important in estimating resources required to build a more precise model and the serious game. After two weeks of working with the domain expert, we were able to agree on the serious content. The documents that we authored regarding the serious content were merged with the content for the balance of the design document, which was prepared in conjunction with the developer's in-house staff.

TABLE 8.1   Mapping of the Serious Game Development Document to the Development Pipeline

PIPELINE	OVERVIEW	REQUIREMENTS SPECIFICATIONS	TECHNICAL ARCHITECTURE	GAME DESIGN	PROGRAMMING	ASSET ACQUISITION & DEVELOPMENT	TRAINING & DEBUGGING	DEPLOYMENT	MAINTAINANCE & TROUBLESHOOTING	PROJECT MGMT	LEGAL
Requirements	x	x								x	x
Technical Architecture	x		x							x	x
Solution Design	x			x						x	x
Code/Implement	x				x	x				x	x
Test/Debug	x						x			x	x
Deploy	x							x		x	x
Maintain/ Troubleshoot	x								x	x	x

There is no universal format for a serious game design document, or an entertainment game design document, for that matter. Even so, every well-formulated serious game design document addresses every phase of the game development pipeline. Table 8.1 illustrates the mapping of the game development pipeline to the various sections of the SGDD template offered below. If the game is the basis for a new business venture, then the document should include elements of the business plan outlined in Appendix E, "A Brief Business Plan Primer." An outline of the SGDD is provided in Appendix D, "Serious Games Design Document Outline."

What follows represents instructions for developing a serious games design document, based on the author's experience developing serious games in academic medicine, for the pharmaceutical industry, and the military. Because of the wide range of application areas, target areas, and business models, the categories discussed below will have to be expanded or removed to reflect specific projects. For example, many serious games are developed as internal projects in academia or for internal use within a business. If so, the business model may be centered on securing a grant from a particular government agency or a local fund. The length of a typical design document is also highly variable. A game design document for a game of the complexity of *Full Spectrum Warrior* could easily run three hundred pages. In contrast, a simple 2D game in a well-defined domain might require less than a hundred pages.

Overview

Provide an overview of the game development project, from a synopsis of the history of the project and the needs identified in the requirements specification section to the risks listed in the legal section. Readers of the document should know what they can expect to gain by reading through the document. If the SGDD will be placed on a server as a dynamic or living document, then add version tracking information here, including the date of creation and subsequent updates.

Requirements Specification

The Requirements Specification component of the SGDD acknowledges the needs of the players, financial backers, and other major stakeholders, as well as the nature of the content and pedagogical objectives. Requirements specifications drive the remainder of the game design document. Often, the requirements specification component of the SGDD must be signed off by a decision maker before work on the remainder of the game design document is begun.

Purpose of Game

Outline the purpose of the game, define how it will be used, and address how knowledge, skills, and attitudes will be imparted to the player.

Scope

Define the scope of the game development project. This could range from developing a prototype for market testing an advergame to creating a full game as part of a national medical study in pain control. Many serious games are developed for limited distribution.

Goals

Define the goals of the requirements specification section of the document, as it relates to the complete game design. As noted earlier, the requirements specification is the driving force behind the subsequent work in the game development pipeline. Without a solid requirements specification, the product could end up as either an entertaining game with insufficient pedagogical value or as dry educational courseware.

Background

Provide an overview of the challenge the game will address. For example, if the challenge is somehow enticing busy maintenance workers in a hospital to take twenty minutes out of their lunchtime every week to review biohazard disposal safety procedures, a serious game might be the ideal vehicle. Even so, this section of the document should identify alternative approaches that may have larger ROIs for the same effort, even if they don't involve game technology. Rewarding every worker who scores well on a paper and pencil test after reading an inexpensive booklet may be a better investment than developing a serious game.

Player Profiles

Define the demographics and habits of the intended players, to a level of detail appropriate to the purpose and intended use of the game. The player profiles for an advergame targeting beef eaters should include dietary habits, for example, but the age or sex of the player may be irrelevant. Typical demographic variables applicable to most games include age, educational level, family size, geographic location, home ownership, income, marital status, nationality, religion, and sex.

Serious games design documents often incorporate more refined profiles, especially in academia. For example, it's obvious that medical students have a college background, but the details of the undergraduate program may be important. Students with an undergraduate background in differential equations and advanced physics courses can be presented with concepts in forms that would be difficult for students with only life sciences courses. The metaphors understood by the two groups of students would likely differ, and the sophistication of a simulation-based serious game might have to be modified to suit both groups of students.

Detailed demographics are often important in determining the most appropriate game genre, style of play, deployment platform, and distribution media. Traditional board games running on a PC may be appropriate for someone who spends a lot of time at home in front of a computer, but a busy resident might only have time to use a game on her iPod to brush up on her cardiac auscultation skills during her bus commute to work.

Needs of the Supporting Organization

Define the underlying needs of the organization supporting game development. A nonprofit organization may have a charter to increase the public awareness of a social issue, whereas the U.S. Navy might want to attract more recruits.

Usability Requirements

List unusual or special usability requirements that should be considered in the game design, such as the following:

- Age (very young or old)
- Cognitive impairment
- Hearing impairment
- Physical disability
- Time constraints
- Stress level
- Psychiatric condition
- Visual impairment (including color blindness)
- Cultural bias
- Handedness

Usability requirements of particular importance to serious games tend to be discipline specific. For example, in the exergame based on repurposed miniature consoles, described in Chapter 6, "Tools," age, physical disability, and visual impairment are all major considerations. Deconditioned men and women in their 60s and 70s often have significant balance issues due to core muscle atrophy and diseases, such as diabetes, that affect their sense of touch in their feet. These people can use the exergame with constant support, such as a chair. Alternatively, they can use the game in a seated position. Visual impairment can also adversely affect balance, and the visually impaired can also use a chair or other support to compensate for their loss of visual acuity.

Time constraints tend to be more relevant in serious games than in entertainment games because playing the latter is typically a leisure time activities. Busy professionals may have only a few minutes a day that could be used for gameplay-based learning. The design should take this into account, as reflected in the choice of platform and the complexity of the game.

Use Environment

Define the use environment, highlighting factors that could influence the effectiveness of the game as a pedagogical vehicle. Some of the key issues include the following:

- Ambient noise level
- Availability of controllers
- Hardware platform
- Operating hours
- Environmental factors
- RF interference potential

- Supervision available
- Security (theft potential)

The interplay of the use environment and game effectiveness may not be obvious. For example, we discovered that track balls should be avoided in games that will be deployed in pediatric hospital settings. Children have a tendency to remove the ball from the trackball, rendering the controller useless.

Some use environment issues, such as the hardware platform, are universal. In developing *Achilles*, the amount of video RAM available on the deployment platform was a constant concern. The delivery platform had 32 MB of video RAM, which limited the resolution of the nonplayer characters—the focus of the game. This constraint often forced a tradeoff in the amount and nature of special effects and the number of textures used to create the game environment. Had the game been designed for entertainment only, the tradeoffs would have been less in favor of the nonplayer character.

Source of Entertainment Content

Identify the source of the entertainment content that will be developed or acquired for the game. Available content should be added to the document in an appendix.

Source of Serious Content

Identify the source of the serious content that provides the basis for the knowledge, skills, and attitudes the game is intended to convey to players. Typical sources of serious content include books and other printed material, validated online content, and domain experts. For example, sources of data for the Achilles game included *Grant's Atlas of Anatomy*, and the images from the National Library of Medicine's *Virtual Human Project*.

The best source for serious subject matter is usually from someone who has experience in the pedagogical domain addressed by the game. The worst is anonymous Web sites, regardless of the ease of access.

KSA Requirements

Define the specific knowledge, skills, and attitudes that players should acquire during gameplay. The definition should be couched in behavioral terms that are measurable, preferably using a standard nomenclature, such as Bloom's Taxonomy, as described in Chapter 5, "Best Practices."

Business Requirements

Discuss the business related constraints that limit the possibilities of the solution design, including the business model. For a serious game designed for commercial distribution, indicate whether the game is shareware, freeware, or standard retail. For other markets, such as internal to a corporation or academic institution, define the external and internal funding sources, the payment schedules, and dependencies.

Technical Requirements

Document the high-level technical requirements, such as the need for the game to fit on a 650 MB CD-ROM or to be compatible with an existing library of games and computer applications in a learning lab. A game designed for the military might require SCORM-compliance so that the game and student performance data can be accessed by multiple Learning Management Systems. Similarly, a university might be tied to a specific Learning Management System for game and courseware distribution.

Conceptual Requirements

Provide a high-level review of the conceptual requirement that will be fulfilled by the game. Expand on the challenge that the game is intended to address, which might include enticing time-constrained military personnel to drill certain procedures, or to enable medical students to review clinical findings during their commuting time.

Game Features and Differentiation

Provide a nontechnical list of game features, including genre, hardware platform, whether the game will be single or multiplayer, special features, and differentiation factors. The task of differentiation serious games depends on the area of distribution and the domain. For example, within a corporation of institution, the competing games and other resources that can be used to achieve the same goals are typically known or easily discovered. Within a discipline such as medicine, there are several online resources for simulations and games, such as games for health (*www.gamesforhealth.org*) and organizations, such as the American Medical Informatics Association (*www.amia.org*).

Identifying serious games developed by the military can be more problematic for those outside of the military. Developers competing for DOD-sponsored SBIR grants and may be at a disadvantage because of the limited distribution of information regarding other projects.

For serious games intended for widespread, commercial distribution, list features that differentiate the planned game from other games on the market that address the same knowledge, skills, and attitudes. For example, a flight simulator game intended to teach the basics of flight might be a questionable investment, given the availability of COTS programs, such as *Microsoft Flight Simulator*.

When the difference between the planned game and commercial equivalents is unclear, create a product comparison table that includes variables such as genre, KSA focus, platform, multiplayer capabilities, target demographics, key features, and price.

A product comparison table is valuable in identifying competing developers and titles, alternatives to developing a title, and approaches that been successful in the marketplace. A top-selling (AAA) entertainment title might prove to be an excellent model for developing a serious game, just as a failed entertainment game can suggest approaches that should be avoided in developing a serious game. The product comparison table is a useful tool in developing a business plan, as outlined in Appendix E, "A Brief Business Plan Primer."

Feasibility

Provide an objective assessment of the feasibility of the game development project, given the need to convey specific KSAs to players, while fulfilling the business, technical, and conceptual requirements. A component of the feasibility assessment is to determine whether the proposed game development project is a good fit for the development shop. In particular, the shop's expertise in the domain addressed by the serious game is critical. Whereas entertainment games developers might easily switch from a first-person shooter to a racing game, serious games developers generally develop or have in their backgrounds domain expertise. Developers in a small shop with medical experience might extend themselves to work with a game that focuses on training combat medics, but not a game on the order of *Full Spectrum Warrior*.

The feasibility assessment of a new title for an established shop minimally includes a competitive analysis. In cases where a development group is formed expressly to develop a title, the feasibility assessment should include a complete business plan, including competitive analysis, stakeholder analysis, and assessment of the business model. The business plan component of the feasibility study should address the following:

Development shop overview: Describe the development group's expertise in the discipline.

Financial plan: Define how the shop will make a profit or at least make use of grant funds.

Market analysis: Describe the potential market for the game. If the game is funded by the government or grant, then the prospect for follow-up funding should be considered.

Marketing plan: For a game planned for commercial distribution, define how the shop will exploit the market.

Product strategy: Describe how the game will be positioned in the marketplace in terms of a value proposition—e.g., moderate cost and quality but fast production.

Vision and mission: Describe how the planned game fits in with the long-range vision of the shop.

Open Issues and Assumptions

List open issues and assumptions that could affect the success of the game development project. Examples of open issues include the following:

- *Unsubstantiated information on competing products, especially when the products aren't marketed commercially.*
- *Incomplete or conditional funding sources.* Continued government funding for serious games development may be conditional and highly uncertain. For example, development funded by the DOD through SBIR is provided in phases. After successfully completing the requirements of Phase I, the developer must compete for Phase II funding. Similarly the likelihood of follow-up congressional funding depends on the political environment at the time of the follow-up request.
- *Ongoing or uncertain intellectual property rights negotiations.* Intellectual property rights to the serious content typically reside with the client if it provided the content. However, when a consultant is contracted by the developer to work with domain experts, then the serious content may be claimed by the developer. In our experience, the cleanest intellectual property arrangement assigns the serious content knowledgebase to the client and the game code and algorithms, including any underlying models and simulations, to the developer.
- *Incomplete staffing.* A single domain expert may be insufficient for the project, and this may not be evident until the after the game development is well underway.
- *Open technology challenges.* Custom hardware interfacing can be problematic when working with tools that assume standard keyboard and mouse interaction.
- *Uncertainties in the player environment.* Serious games targeting widespread distribution face the same platform variability issues confronted by the entertainment games development community. Developers of serious games with a limited, targeted distribution commonly have the luxury of working with a known player environment.

The goal in developing a serious game design document is to minimize uncertainty, identify risk, and formulate a workable plan for game development. Of course, no project ever goes exactly as planned. As with COTS games, there are uncertainties associated with inevitable platform changes, operating system upgrades and patches. Then there are potential changes in the network infrastructure that may adversely affect game development or use. Similarly, an update to the standard used as the basis for serious content midway in the development pipeline could derail the game development project or make the game outdated before it's released.

Developers of simulation-based games often have an added burden of portraying reality to a higher degree of accuracy than a strictly entertainment game. Because of the practical limitations of computer processing power, the mathematical models underlying simulations that drive games are necessarily simplified. The nature and extent of these simplifications and other assumptions should be documented as part of the requirements specification to highlight areas that management should monitor during development. In this way, corrections can be made as soon as deviations from the assumptions are identified.

TECHNICAL ARCHITECTURE

The technical architecture section of the serious game development document defines game technologies that will be used to address the business, entertainment, and pedagogical needs defined in the requirements specifications.

Major Development Tasks

List the major development tasks, from a programming perspective. These tasks will be keyed to resources and time in the Project Management section of the document. Examples of major development tasks include developing, verifying, and validating the underlying models in a simulation-based game, and providing detailed tracking of player actions within the game for intelligent tutoring or later analysis. In addition, there are generic tasks, such as developing a scoring algorithm, integrating middleware with the game engine, and developing 3D model animation scripts.

Technical Analysis

Provide a technical analysis of the game, including experimental features or unknown elements that represent a risk to the project. The technical analysis should address issues such as:

Polygon budget: The maximum number of polygons allowed in a frame or scene. Higher polygon counts require more video RAM and processor power.

Minimum frames per second (FPS): 30 frames per second is generally considered the lower limit for smooth animation.

Fail-safes for dealing with inadequate hardware: Software versions of video firmware and hardware can enable a game to run on an ill-equipped PC.

Known limitations to the current development environment: Issues such as limited animation capabilities, outdated motion capture technology, or an inadequate technical talent pool should be documented and addressed.

Viability of third-party vendors: Because of the volatility of vendors in the game development space, the stability of major third-party vendors should be determined so that backup vendors can be identified.

If possible, identify alternatives that can minimize the risks identified in the technical analysis. For example, if the technical analysis identifies a new, third-party AI engine as a risk for the project because of potential interface problems, the document should identify alternative AI engines known to work with the game environment.

Platform Requirements

Define minimum and suggested platform requirements, including operating system versions, RAM and hard disk memory, playback devices, display capabilities, and graphics extensions. Platform-specific issues, such as support for DirectX 9, should be addressed.

Coding Style

Identify the programming standards and programming style guide to facilitate code review and collaboration. Established standards and style guides should be used over ad-hoc methods, especially in larger shops, where teams of programmers often share code developed by other groups.

Compatibility Standards

List the compatibility standards followed by the development team. A development shop working on a serious game for the U.S. military might be required to maintain compatibility with the latest version of SCORM. There might be additional standards imposed by the game engine, engine editor, and other tools used in development.

External Interfaces

Define the external interfaces required for game operation, evaluation of game results, and real-time monitoring. Examples of external interfaces include the following:

- Connections to a learning management system (LMS)
- Internet connectivity for MMOGs
- LAN connectivity for multiplayer games and pooled high-score tracking
- Wired and wireless connectivity to mannequins and other physical devices

The description of complex interfaces should be supplemented with graphics as needed.

Distribution Media

Define the distribution medium, such as the Internet or CD-ROM (or a mix). The distribution medium can limit the number of assets and features supported by a game because of download time and space constraints.

Multiplayer and Networking

Define the technical architecture that supports networking and, if applicable, multiplayer functionality. The following should be addressed:

Network connection modes: Include wired and wireless LAN, TCP/IP, and modem-to-modem connections.

Network configuration: Massively multiplayer online games typically use a client-server configuration, whereas multiplayer wireless and wired LAN configurations often use peer-to-peer networking.

Server requirements: Including capacity, bandwidth, and fault tolerance requirements.

Maximum player count: Define the maximum number of players for multiplayer and massively multiplayer games.

Customization options: Define player customization options related to network and multiplayer gameplay.

Network quality considerations: Define the technical provision for latency, low bandwidth, and noisy network connections.

Ecommerce: Define provisions for online payment for networked gameplay or to download a stand-alone game.

Saving and Persistence

Define whether a session can be saved and reloaded. If a session can be reloaded, define whether the last state of play is persistent at any point in a level or whether the player is forced to start over at the beginning of a level.

Data Security Plan

Describe the data security plan from the start of development through deployment/maintenance. The plan should address the following:

Onsite backup: Define the procedure for backing up working files as part of an onsite backup program.

Offsite backup: Define the offsite archive, including computer storage capacity, cost, and frequency of moving files to a safe, offsite location.

Network security: Define hardware and software firewalls, bridges, encryption, and other forms of network security.

GAME DESIGN

This section of the SGDD focuses on the solution design stage of the development pipeline. It defines the melding of the computer science described in the technical architecture section with the graphics and other art that addresses the requirements specifications.

Concept

Provide a concise statement of the game concept—that is, the basic idea behind the game. In particular, address how the game will provide for the delivery of KSAs while delivering entertainment value to the player. The concept statement should also differentiate the game from competing titles, if any.

Game Features

Describe the game features that provide the entertainment value and that support the acquisition of KSAs. The feature list should address the following:

Gameplay: Within the scope of the game genre, define the gameplay in terms of the entertainment and educational value of the experience.

Levels: Provide an overview of the levels, the unique features of each level, and the criteria for moving from one level to the next.

Graphic treatment: Consider including a concept screen shot or drawing that captures the flavor of the game.

Pedagogical content: Describe how the game will develop player KSAs. List specific game features that support each of the measurable behaviors defined in the requirements specification. For example, one of the measurable behaviors listed for the *Achilles* program was the ability to explain the relationship between blood loss rate and injury location. In the game, this is supported by a nonplayer character health scoring algorithm that is keyed to specific anatomical locations, in addition to the usual FPS technique of assigning points to head, torso, and legs.

Setting

Describe the setting, emphasizing its role in the game. In particular, note the value of the setting beyond entertainment. For example, it's no accident that the setting for the *DARWARS Tactical Language Training System* is in the Middle East, as opposed to some other Arab-speaking area [Johnson04]. Depending on the game, the setting may include the geographic location, time of day or night, weather, and architecture or terrain style.

Story and Backstory

Provide a narrative of the backstory and story. All good entertainment games have a story and backstory that provides the player with a working context and motivation for solving the challenge presented by game. The backstory, which is the history behind the situation that unfolds in the main story, can add depth and a sense of emotional realism to the story.

Together, the story and backstory can add to the entertainment value of serious games. Consider the puzzler *Smart Bomb* (Eidos) for the Sony PSP, which is, at one level, simply a collection of 3D puzzles. Although the puzzles are challenging and the graphics stunning on the PSP display, there is no innate drama or sense of urgency. The developers add this emotional context in the form of a story and a backstory that begins ten years prior to gameplay, at a time when the world was as the mercy of an unknown assailant who plants sophisticated bombs around the globe. The backstory describes the formation of a global defense network lead by a military leader who suddenly disappears at the start of the story. Now, it's up to the player to save the world from the reign of terror by defusing the various bombs. With the backstory and story, there is more at risk than simply failing to solve a puzzle, assuming players can relate to the story. Even hardcore first-person shooters, such as *DOOM*, are coupled with a story and backstory that provide a rationale for blasting anything that moves.

Characters

Create a character list that includes the player character (PC) and nonplayer characters (NPCs). For each character, provide a graphic and behavior profile, including strengths, weaknesses, mode of travel, decision making, and offensive and defensive moves. If characters support the measurable behaviors listed in the functional specifications section of the SGDD, then describe how each behavior is supported.

Effectors

Define the effectors—the tools that the player and nonplayers use to act on opponents and/or the environment within the game. Describe the relationship of the effectors to the measurable behaviors. In the cardiac auscultation games, the main effector is the player-guided stethoscope. By using the stethoscope, students learn the auscultation points, one of the goals of the program.

Game Flow

Define the game flow, in terms of game challenge and progression, and consider providing a plot of game progression.

Screens and Menus

Provide an inventory of the major screens and menus in the program. If possible, include graphics and screen shots. The major screens in a typical 2D or 3D action or role-play game include startup, main menu, inventory, level, exit, and high-score screens.

In addition to a simple inventory list, use the screens and menus to create the skeleton of a storyboard so that the sequence of screens corresponds to program flow. If the screens support desired behavior changes, then note the change and how it is supported.

Controls

Define the keyboard, mouse, joystick, and any other hardware used with the game. Include any provision for limited-control access, including keyboard-only controls, multiple controller configurations, as well as options for left- and right-handed players. Define the gamepad models and default button mappings, as well as settings for vibration feedback.

Custom controls should be defined mechanically, electronically, and operationally. Include software driver information, power requirements, range of operation, and source. For example, the wireless sensor harness used with the *Mixed Reality Auscultation Trainer* has an operational range of about 30 feet, as defined by the Bluetooth specification. The wireless transmitter uses two AAA batteries that provide power for several weeks of continuous use. Because the sensors are potted in hard plastic, the solder joints are protected from the elements, and the components are protected from any reasonable physical handling.

Options

Define player-controlled options, such as music, voices, and sound effects levels, as well as alternate gamepad mappings and language choices, if applicable.

Sound and Music

Define the various sounds and music used in the game, including NPC and narrator voices. Identify the genre and the overall goal for music in the game, such as conveying tension and excitement, imminent death and destruction, or carefree bliss. If possible, identify the music score for key periods in the game. If licensed music will be used for the game, note license holder and limitations on distribution within the game.

Typical music cues include the introduction, new game and new level, mode change, successful end of level, high score, victory, and defeat. There may be domain-specific sounds as well. For example, the *DARWARS Tactical Language Training System* uses prerecorded Arabic phrases, and the *Mixed Reality Auscultation Trainer* uses physiologic sounds.

Level (*n*) Overview

For games that are designed around levels, provide an overview of the challenges and goals in the level. Include a description of how the level supports the transfer of specific knowledge, skills, and attitudes to the player. The overview should identify what the player can control in the level, in terms of characters, vehicles, weapons, and elements in the environment.

Level (*n*) Environment

Describe the environment for the level, including scale, lighting, the objects in the environment, the player's mode of travel, and the nature of time. Dramatic lighting techniques, such as the use of monochrome surroundings and full-color for NPCs, should be clearly defined. Define whether game time passes faster than normal, slower than normal, or in real time. In defining the objects in the environment, describe how each one contributes to the entertainment and pedagogical value of the level.

Level (*n*) Map

Provide a detailed graphic of the level map. The map should include an indicator of scale, the location of traps, switches, Easter eggs, the boss, and any KSA-related objects.

Level (*n*) Fun Elements

Identify the fun elements in the level, including the following:

Combat encounters: Identify the location and/or nature of combat encounters.

Stealth encounters: Define the interplay of stealth encounters, both offensively and defensively.

Puzzles: Define the puzzles, as well as the solution sets.

Boss battles: Define the boss battle(s), including the strategy that must be used by the player character to defeat the boss.

Easter eggs: Define the Easter eggs and how they can be activated.

Traps: Define the location, activation, and consequences of traps.

Power-ups: Define the power-ups in the level, in terms of activation, how the player is alerted to their presence, the nature of the added power or ability, and the duration of the effect.

Describe the contribution of each element in terms of the entertainment and pedagogical value it brings to the level.

Level (*n*) Logic

Define the logic for the level, in terms of map traversal, sounds, enemy or challenge appearance, switches, and the location of serious content. Consider the use of logic trees for complex levels.

Level (*n*) HUD

If applicable, provide a graphic exhibit and a summary of the information available in the heads up display (HUD). When applicable, describe the worldview and details of the status information, effector selection, navigation aids, and crosshairs used in the display. Define the graphics used in the display, especially external elements, such as fonts.

Level (*n*) Player Character

In games where the player character changes from one level to the next, identify the player character associated with the level, referring to the player character(s) previously defined for the game as a whole. Include player mode of travel, starting location in the level, and reason for being there.

Level (*n*) NPCs

Identify the nonplayer characters associated with the level, including all allies, neutrals, and enemies.

Level (*n*) Effectors

List the weapons or other effectors available to the PC and NPCs in the level. Note whether effectors can be lost or stolen by the opposing side.

Level (*n*) Equipment

Define all special equipment or objects associated with the level. Equipment can range from body armor, med kits, and holsters, to airborne reconnaissance devices, lab equipment, and medical gear.

Level (*n*) Vehicles

Define the player and nonplayer vehicles in term of physical and operational characteristics. If the physical properties of the vehicle are significant in the game from a pedagogical or entertainment perspective, then define the properties in detail sufficient to enable a programmer to code the characteristics of the vehicle in a physics engine.

Level (*n*) Cameras

Define the camera positions and perspectives available in the level. Camera position can profoundly affect the player's perception of gameplay. For example, a standard FPS camera perspective is at the player's eye level, behind the weapon. It is more immersive than a modified FPS camera position, in which the camera is above and slightly behind the player character, distinguishing between the player and the character controlled by the player. A zoom camera can highlight details in the game, and an elevated third-person camera can provide a detached perspective of activity in the level.

Level (*n*) Objectives

Define the primary and secondary objectives for the level from entertainment and KSA perspectives. Define how each of the objectives affects the measurable behaviors listed in the functional specifications.

Level (*n*) Introductory Material

Describe the material presented to the player at the start of the level. This may take the form of a briefing in a military game or a review of engine components in a game designed to teach aircraft mechanics how to service turbine blades. As with the other level components, identify intentional support of the desired measurable behaviors.

Level (*n*) Gameplay

Describe gameplay within the level, including how the player scores points, wins, and gets to the next level, and the relationship of the gameplay to the measurable behaviors. Also define the time required to play the level, and the modes of player interaction within the level.

Level (*n*) Closing Material

Describe the materials presented to the player at the close of the level. A strategy used in some serious games is to vary the presentation as a function of player performance in the level, providing the player with feedback that can aid in learning. For example, the PC-based *Augmented Reality Medical Simulator* game provides the player with feedback after each of the five levels, as well as at the termination of the game, as shown in Figure 8.1.

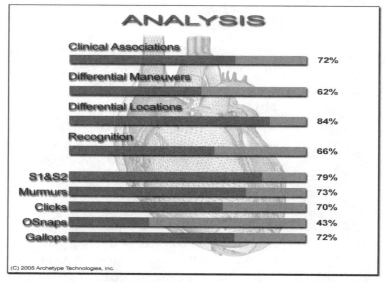

FIGURE 8.1   Level closing material from *Augmented Reality Medical Simulator*.

Level (*n*) Scoring

Define the scoring algorithm used within the level, preferably in a way that shows how the reinforced player behavior within the game is related to the desired measurable behavior changes. Scoring is more than a way of keeping track of a player's performance in a game; it also defines the manner of play and the relative emphasis on entertainment versus learning. If players can accumulate more points in an FPS game by applying their knowledge in a particular area than by shooting opponents, then players will focus on applying knowledge within the level. Conversely, if the same game rewards kills over everything else, players will devote their energy to shooting.

Level (*n*) Cheat Codes

Document the cheat codes that can be used by the development and testing staff to move to specific points within the level or to go to the end of the level. Cheat codes may be left in the final product. For example, in the augmented reality cardiac auscultation games that we have developed, it's impractical to have sensors and cables attached to the development PC at all times. Keyboard equivalents for the activation of each sensor were used to speed development time. The cheat codes were left in to assist in debugging potentially faulty sensors and wireless hardware.

Level (*n*) Assets

Provide a comprehensive list of assets used within the level. Include graphic arts, sound, and programmed assets.

Cutscenes

Define the cutscenes associated with the game. Include the setting, storyboard, script, and logic. Cutscenes can be used to establish context, provide a backstory and story in a few seconds, and help smooth the transition between levels.

Score Tracking

Define the method used for tracking player score. Options include the use of a local database, a file system, or an online repository.

Help

Define the form and location of help, which can range from a local readme file created at startup to an online repository of FAQs that can be accessed while the player is still in the game environment.

Localization

Describe localization plans, including multiple-language options for the help files, multiple-recorded-character voice options, and multi-language fonts, cutscenes, and NPC responses.

PROGRAMMING

This section of the serious game design document extends the information provided in the Technical Specifications section.

Development Hardware

Define hardware requirements for coding, artwork, testing, and asset acquisition. If the game will be networked, then specify a development server.

Development Software

Provide a catalog of the major software titles required to develop the game. Depending on the type of game, the software may include a game engine, game editor, various forms of middleware, databases, a programming environment, code management software, and various utilities. Exclude the tools and utilities used to create and manage assets.

Game Mechanics

Define the game mechanics, in terms of the main program loop, data structures, program flow, dataflow, and use cases. The goal of this component of the SGDD is to define the game explicitly, in terms of a computer application.

ASSET ACQUISITION AND DEVELOPMENT

This section of the SGDD defines the sounds, graphics, models, and other assets must be either developed or acquired.

Art Bible

If available, provide an Art Bible that contains samples of the artwork and other graphical assets that will be incorporated in the game. In many cases, concept art and screen mockups may be all that are available because many of the assets may not have been developed prior to the start of game development. Even when an Art Bible is available, it is usually considered a working document, subject to revision.

Master Asset List

The master asset list contains an exhaustive list of artwork, sounds, models, motion capture files, and any other assets that will appear in the game. The master asset list should include all sounds and music, cutscenes, menus, screens, and all graphics, including marketing and package art. Index each asset by name, ID, format, size, creation date, version, and the levels in which it is used. Furthermore, each asset should be categorized as either a production asset that will be produced in-house or an acquired asset that will be purchased. If the assets will be localized, define the customized assets by territory. Even if specific assets haven't been created or identified, the formats, size, author/source, and the levels in which the assets will be used should be defined.

Software

List the software tools used for asset creation, editing, and management. Include 2D and 3D modeling and rendering packages, motion capture editors, plug-ins and extensions, and asset utilities.

TESTING AND DEBUGGING

Testing and debugging, which begins with the coding and asset development stage and comes to a crescendo with the completion of the initial phase of development, can be a significant component of even the simplest serious game. Because of the frequent need for absolute accuracy, testing and debugging a serious game may require several times the resources typically allocated to the testing of an entertainment game.

For example, even though the actual coding of the PC and PocketPC auscultation games described earlier were developed in a matter of weeks, testing and validation of the sounds and the user interface required months of calendar time. Arranging demonstrations with teaching faculty and running small classes with students was integral to testing ease of use, identifying design issues with the sensors, and assessing the durability of the sensor vest and wireless hardware.

An important component in the validation process was identifying the appropriate experts. The auscultation systems were designed to teach second-year medical students, not cardiology residents. Cardiac specialists often use different techniques in auscultating the heart, such as using the open ended, or bell side, of the stethoscope, stretching the skin over the chest wall, and then creating an airtight seal with the stethoscope. Obviously, the plastic sensors used in the games were not suitable for this type of examination. However, in teaching auscultation, many instructors simply use the diaphragm head of the stethoscope, and focus on correct placement.

Code Review Procedure

Define the procedure for code review, and indicate whether the plan is for an informal review or a structured, scheduled process.

Testing Procedure

Define the game testing procedure, including black-box (user-centric) and white-box (code routine) testing. Staffing should be reflected in the Project Management section of the SGDD. The testing procedure for custom interface hardware and software should be defined explicitly, with acceptable variance in response noted. Often, a description of the jig used for testing hardware is as important as the testing procedure.

For example, in testing the proximity sensors for the auscultation games, the jig was constructed of an $18 \times 12 \times 1$ inch polyethylene cutting board with plastic clips to hold an individual sensor. The jig was in turn placed on a wooden desktop. With the exception of a shielded, battery-powered multimeter and leads, there were no electrical appliances, cords, pens, or other objects within a two foot radius of the sensor under test. Distances were measured with a plastic ruler. Sensors that failed to match the gross sensitivity and sensitivity pattern, within a predetermined range for each variable, were rejected. Figure 8.2 shows an excerpt from the sensor testing procedure description that illustrates the allowable variance for each of the plastic-encased sensor clusters.

Tools

Identify the enabling software tools that will be used in testing and debugging, including tools for profiling and bug tracing.

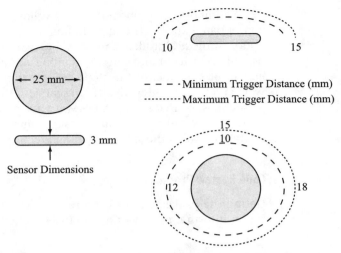

FIGURE 8.2 Testing variance for trigger sensitivity pattern for the sensors used in the interface of the *Augmented Reality Training Simulation* game.

DEPLOYMENT

Deployment often represents a logistical nightmare for developers because of interdependencies, many of which may be outside the control of the developer. This is particularly true of shops that outsource deployment.

Packaging

Define game packaging for deployment, whether electronic or physical. Electronic packaging avoids the costs of replicating and printing CD-ROMs, maintaining inventory, and wasting discs once updates are available.

Documentation

Define the plan for the creation of online and/or print documentation, including whether documentation work will be outsourced. Documentation may be developed for end users, instructors, technical staff, and support staff. Furthermore, documentation may be localized for different cultures and languages.

Setup

Define the encryption and setup software involved in deployment, and identify all third-party applications and drivers required as part of the setup procedure, such as the DirectX Install from Microsoft or the latest OpenGL drivers. Describe in detail the setup procedure.

Distribution

Provide a detailed distribution plan, indicating whether the game will be available through a corporate LAN, Web portal, or retail game stores. The distribution plan for a limited distribution serious game should include a kickoff meeting to raise awareness of availability of the game.

ASSESSMENT

Following the best practices for assessment defined in Chapter 5, "Best Practices," define the assessment protocol that will be used to determine the degree to which the desired changes in player have been achieved. If an IRB is required, include the IRB application in the appendix. Similarly, define the recording standards that will be used to track player activity within the game.

MAINTENANCE AND TROUBLESHOOTING

Maintenance and troubleshooting are part of the cost of doing business in the world of software. Serious games developed through one-time grants and government funding may not have provision for maintenance once the games have been released.

Touch Points

Identify the touch points—avenues for contact—that will be made available for customers, and whether different support will be provided for instructors and players.

Support Software

Identify the support software that will be used to track problems and communicate findings to the development staff.

PROJECT MANAGEMENT

Thus far, the SGDD has identified tasks and challenges that will faced by the development shop. This section identifies the resources and timelines required to handle the tasks.

Development Plan

Using the development pipeline as a point of reference, define the milestones for the game development, including a detailed PERT chart.

Human Resources

Define the resource matrix, including writers, designers, programmers, and the domain (subject matter) experts. The deployment of resources should be keyed to the development plan.

Cost and Revenue Projections

Provide cost and revenue projections throughout the lifespan of the game development project, based on human resource requirements, cost of hardware and software, license fees, and the cost of art and other assets.

LEGAL

In addition to the usual legal issues surround the operation of a business, from payroll to disability insurance, there are typically added issues of intellectual property rights and risk analysis.

Intellectual Property

Document the copyright, trademark, patent, or licensing issues that have or will be dealt with. Include license agreements for third-party software, assets, contractor agreements, serious content, and NDAs. Because the serious content may change unexpectedly over time, provisions for access to updated materials should be addressed.

Risk Analysis

Identify the legal risks associated with the venture, from failure to deliver to funding sources to failure of key suppliers to deliver on time and on spec. Where possible, identify means of minimizing the risk, such as requiring middleware vendors to provide source code escrow in the event of a business failure.

An added risk often associated with serious games is liability for content errors, such as misrepresenting the efficacy of drug or, more likely, the side effects associated with competing drugs. For example, in a medical serious game that we worked with for a pharmaceutical firm, one of the side effects of a competing drug was weight gain. Within the simulation-based game, patients who were placed on the competing drug were shown to gain considerable weight—much more than the typical weight gain associated with the competing drug.

REFERENCES

Provide references to the serious content. When third-party models are used as the basis for simulations, include references to model verification, validation, and underlying assumptions.

APPENDICES

An SGDD is typically more than a hundred pages in length, and much of the space is dedicated to serious content in the appendices. Of particular importance is the inclusion of an acronyms and glossary section for the serious content.

SUMMARY

The SGDD defines how the characters, themes, and gameplay are used to support the development of knowledge, skills, and attitudes in the player. Although there is no universal format for the SGDD, a well-formulated document addresses every phase of the game development pipeline.

Compared with a design document for entertainment gains, the SGDD often incorporates more refined player profiles, discipline specific usability requirements, and a detailed description of the KSA supported by the game. Furthermore, the KSA requirements are preferably expressed in behavioral terms using a standard nomenclature, such as Bloom's Taxonomy.

Other distinguishing features of the SGDD include the emphasis on the development shop's experience in serious subject matter domain, a focus on the intellectual property rights associated with the serious content, and the often extensive testing and debugging phase of development. Finally, the methods for assessing the success of the game in producing the desired, measurable behavior changes in the player should be carefully formulated.

Readers interested in reviewing general game design document templates should read *Game Design*, by Bob Bates [Bates04] and the series on game design by Tim Ryan, hosted on Gamasutra [Ryan99]. For more information on feasibility studies and the business of game development, see *Secrets of The Game Business*, edited by François Laramee [Laramee03].

REFERENCES

[Bates04] Bates, Bob, *Game Design: The Art and Business of Creating Games.* 2nd edition. Premier Press/Course PTR, 2004.

[Johnson04] Johnson, W. and S. Marsella, et al., "The DARWARS Tactical Language Training System." *Interservice/Industry Training, Simulation, and Education Conference (I/ITSEC)* 2004): pp. 1–11.

[Laramee03] Laramee, François, *Secrets of the Game Business.* Charles River Media, 2003.

[Ryan99] Ryan, Tim, *The Anatomy of a Design Document, Part 1: Documentation Guidelines for the Game Concept and Proposal.* Gamasutra. 1999. *www.gamasutra.com/features/19991019/ ryan_01.htm*, accessed May 1, 2005.

CHAPTER

9

OUTLOOK

In This Chapter

- The Serious Games Design Document
- Mapping the design document to the development pipeline

INTRODUCTION

Good science fiction writers create unusual settings that focus the reader's attention on the drama of characters that readers can relate to on an emotional level. Great science fiction writers don't simply place their characters on an arbitrary planet or space ship, but conjure up a plausible, tantalizing future reality. Masters of the art have an uncanny ability to predict the future, not because of a unique ability to see into the future, but because their stories plant seeds that become the shared dreams and aspirations of future entrepreneurs, scientists, and engineers.

Gene Roddenberry, the creative force behind the *Star Trek* franchise, popularized the holodeck, a technology universally recognized as the ultimate video game. As envisioned by Roddenberry, the fully immersive, 3D environment provides seemingly endless gamespace with feedback for all five senses. The holodeck is just what every astronaut of the twenty-third century needs to relax after months of space travel—and what every office worker would love to have after a long day stuck in a cubicle.

A vision of what the future may portend for serious games is described by Orson Scott Card in *Ender's Game*, first published in 1985 [Card91]. Several types of serious military games figure prominently in the book, as does the pervasive computer network that provides the basis for human-human and human-computer discourse. Ender, a child prodigy and computer genius, is recruited by the military to train for one last fight with the Buggers, an alien race that threatens the survival of the human species. The serious military games used to train Ender are so attuned to his psychological state that his real and simulated worlds become indistinguishable.

Science fiction writers have the luxury of exercising their imaginations without the constraints imposed by the practical limitations of current technology or of social inertia. Still, history has shown that dreams precede reality, even if they are directed toward some unforeseen end. For example, in developing the pilot training for the Predator unmanned aerial vehicle, the goal of the contractor is to develop simulators that pilots and sensor operators won't be able to distinguish from the real aircraft [Colucci04]. One can't help wonder whether, in this environment, the military has or will be tempted to blend training and real combat, just as in *Ender's Game*.

Elements of the holodeck and the mind game provide a long-term vision of the state of serious games by 2015 or 2020. However, reasonable predictors of the near-term trajectory of the serious games include the work in academic research laboratories, the request for proposals (RFPs) that deal with gaming and simulation that are being issued by the Department of Defense, and presentations at forward-looking conferences such as D: All Things Digital (*d.wsj.com*), SIGGRAPH (*www.siggraph.org*), and the Wired NextFest (*www.nextfest.net*). Taking these and other data into consideration, the outlook for serious games include:

Increased popularity: Serious games will continue to gain in popularity, especially in academia, the military, private industry, and among individual consumers.

More diversity: The industry will see an explosion in the application of serious games, in both breadth and depth of coverage.

Less emphasis on development tools: Serious games will continue to be defined by content. The availability of more affordable, easier-to-use development tools will highlight the prominence of quality content in serious games development.

More simulation-based serious games: Enabling developments in modeling and simulation, including work to standardize and share models in the biological sciences and other disciplines, will increase the availability of simulations capable of driving games.

More opportunities for developers with domain expertise: Just as developers in the entertainment gaming arena are becoming more specialized to address the increasing complexity of game development, serious games developers with domain experience and development skills will be in demand.

More emphasis on assessment: With more and more varied types of serious games competing for investment dollars from academia, the military, advertisers, and other disciplines, assessment will become as important as the validity of the serious content.

The rationale behind this outlook is provided in the following sections.

SERIOUS GAMES TECHNOLOGY

From a technological perspective, serious games seem destined to expand into at least five different fronts: augmented reality games; personal games; social games; emergent games; and pervasive games. As outlined later in the chapter, the evolution of serious games in these dimensions requires significant technological advances, a favorable economic environment, and a potential user base primed for rapid adoption. In these regards, the continued advances in entertainment gaming act as a catalyst along all five dimensions, enabling serious games developers to focus on serious content and gameplay while the market develops.

Augmented Reality (AR) Games

Augmented reality is the overlaying of computer generated information onto the real world. This is akin to blending the completely synthetic virtual environment created by a virtual reality (VR) system with the images, sounds, smells, and tactile experiences derived from interaction with the real world. The proliferation of serious augmented reality games is an inevitable, evolutionary extension of current gaming technology and practices that attempt to blur the distinction between reality and games.

Unlike virtual reality games, in which players are immersed in a completely synthetic environment, players of augmented reality games simultaneously experience and interact with reality. Sony's *EyeToy* is an example of a commercially viable augmented reality game and a computer-generated world.

Academic experiments into what is possible with large-scale augmented reality games include *Human Pacman*, from the Mixed Reality Lab, National University of Singapore [Sandhana05]. Prior to gameplay, players don a wearable computer, headset and goggles and assume the role of either Pacman or one of several ghosts. The system leverages Bluetooth, WiFi, GPS, IR and sensing technologies to enable players to interact in and with a digitally enhanced version of the real world. There are challenges, such as constantly changing elements in the real world, including cars, buses, and people. The Mixed Reality Lab addresses this and related issues by using augmented reality to create a campus-sized, expansive game space. Through the magic of augmented reality, a large office complex becomes a castle, for example.

A similar augmented reality game, *ARQuake*, has been developed around the *QUAKE* game at the University of Southern Australia [Thomas02]. In this version of the game, monsters attack outdoors, using building and other large, easily mapped structures to anchor virtual objects. A limitation of these AR systems is the need for constantly updated information on the location of objects in the real environment. Outdoors, this task is facilitated by the availability of the GPS system.

Eventually, the need for manual updates could be obviated with the aid of detailed satellite imagery from services such as Microsoft's *VirtualEarth* (*www.virtualearth.com*) or *Google Earth* (*earth.google.com*). For augmented reality gaming indoors, where GPS reception is often blocked by concrete and metal walls and ceilings, WiFi-based location technology, offered by companies such as Pango Networks (*www.pangonetworks.com*), looks promising. The prototype augmented reality interfaces for the Gizmondo and Nintendo have yet to undergo the scrutiny of the mass markets [TigerTelematics05]. They might prove too revolutionary—as opposed to simply evolutionary—to achieve market success.

As discussed in Chapter 6, "Tools," there are numerous academic projects centered on the use of augmented reality and games. Conceptually, it's easy to make the leap from human *PacMan* to large-scale outdoor augmented reality games in which first responders learn to triage hundreds of virtual patients strewn about after a virtual explosion. The same technology could be used at the individual level to give patient stand-ins the appearance of severe trauma—or other actors the appearance of a terrorist clad in a jacket packed with explosives and ball bearings.

Personal Games

Serious games constructed around military weapon systems or physical exam findings may be vital in certain contexts, but to the individual learner, the most important serious games are personal. Not only may they be personalized—designed to suit the player's preferred style of learning and gameplay—but the subject of gameplay is the player. While a personal version of *The Sims* might have entertainment value, when the topic shifts from an arbitrary character to personal health, employment, or mate selection, the stakes are suddenly higher and the gameplay more serious.

The concept of computer-based personal medicine has been around for decades. However, the personal games created to date have focused on one or two organ systems or problem areas, such as cosmetic surgery, nutrition, heart disease, or cancer. Complete, detailed, integrated models of human physiology and biology have not been available.

The lack of models is rapidly succumbing to research and development (R&D) efforts on multiple fronts, despite dozens of false starts [Wastney99]. The pharmaceutical industry alone is spending millions in R&D on computational biology efforts aimed at creating models of organs to test the effects of drugs without placing animal or human subjects at risk [Behar05]. One motivation for this R&D effort is cost savings. The ability to design and test a drug on a PC in a matter of hours could save millions of dollars, compared with the current practice of synthesizing and then testing a drug over several years. Another motivation is the prospect of personalized medicine, where a patient's unique genetic profile is used as the basis for designing a drug that will address the patient's illness without causing side effects [Bergeron04].

Personal models of common diseases such as diabetes are already popular with patients. For example, AIDA, a model of the interaction of diet and insulin, accepts personal values for physiologic parameters and creates a plot of disease progression over time. The model is available as freeware at *www.2aida.net/aida/index.shtml*.

Social Games

In addition to player-centric gameplay, serious gaming will increasingly involve social games. Following the lead of networked, multiplayer entertainment games and high-end military combat trainers, serious games are evolving into team-based learning experiences that emphasize leadership skills, real-time problem solving, and cooperative gameplay. *Full*

Spectrum Warrior (Pandemic Studios) and *First to Fight* (2K Games), online multiplayer entertainment games derived from serious military combat games, illustrate the emphasis on teamwork as well as individual skills.

In addition to military squads, serious social games can address team-based activities in any arena, from the operating room to EMS search and rescue operations. For example, in the operating room, situational awareness and teamwork are at least as important as the surgeon's ability to locate and place a clamp on a bleeder. An affordable medical game in which players could assume the roles of the surgeon, nurses, anesthesiologist, and even the patient could provide the team members with an appreciation of the responsibilities of each role and the need to work as a unit.

High-end room-sized simulations of operating room procedures, such as Harvard's Center for Medical Simulation, discussed in Chapter 2, "Working Context," have shown that this is possible. What remains is for serious games developers to create affordable, standardized, readily available versions of these systems, such as the prototypes that been developed with the support of TATRC.

Emergent Games

The 3d Gamemaker (The GameCreators) is an inexpensive, off-the-shelf game development environment that features an auto-generating function that can produce new, unique games without player or programmer input. Although the gameplay supported by one of these auto-generated games may be unique and sometimes even fun, gameplay is based on internal randomization routines. In contrast, true emergent gameplay—a technology integral to the success of future serious games— reflects the player's past performance, preferred style of interaction, and interests.

The development of practical player-directed emergent gameplay is exemplified by *NERO* (Neuro-Evolving Robotic Operatives). The game, shown in Figure 9.1, is a product of the Digital Media Collaboratory in the IC^2 Institute and the Neuroevaluation group in the Department of Computer Science, all at the University of Texas at Austin. The PC-based program, developed around the *Torque* engine, is available for free download from *nn.cs.utexas.edu/NERO*.

NERO uses an AI scheme based on the real-time evolution of neural network agents that learn through interacting with the player [Stanley05]. The object of the game is to train armies of AI robots to follow a player-defined strategy. After training, the robot team can be deployed in battle against another robot team on the same PC or on another PC on the network. The challenge of the game, and the focus of gameplay, is in devising training regimens that lead to victory in the battlefield. Most of the player interaction is limited to the training component of the game.

FIGURE 9.1   *NERO,* showing a fight between network agents.

After the battles begin, the player assumes the role of a detached observer that can maneuver above the battlefield and monitor the relative performance of the teams from a third-person perspective.

By combining player selection of characteristics, neural networks, and elements of genetic algorithms, *NERO* provides true emergent gameplay. However, player preferences must be keyed in, which falls short of the brain-machine interface in *Ender's Game*. Advances may not be far off, given research into classic psychological theories such as the Yerkes-Dodson law, which states that performance is best when arousal is neither too low nor too high [YerkesDodson08].

Rosalind Picard of the Media Lab at MIT has experimented with physiology signal monitoring to identify the emotional status of players during gameplay in *DOOM* to determine the level of frustration or distress. Players are monitored with EMG (electromyography to measure jaw clenching), GSR (galvanic skin response to measure perspiration), and BVP (blood volume pressure to measure cardiovascular status). Although not quite a brain-computer interface, increases in these parameters correspond to a higher emotional state and, presumably, arousal [Picard97].

Another peek at the future of serious games development in emergent gameplay comes from a project code-named *Spore*, by Will Wright, the creator of *The Sims* [Kosak05]. *Spore* enables players to create custom content that serves as a basis for computer-generated gameplay.

The game starts off simply, with a *PacMan*-like game of 2D microorganisms swimming about in primordial green goop. Through various interactions with the player, the life forms evolve into unique, 3D animated swimming creatures that lay eggs and spawn subsequent generations. Following the evolutionary path onto land, the creatures try to survive in an increasingly harsh environment. This evolutionary process continues, nudged along by the player, until first tribes and then cities are formed. Eventually, cultures, not individuals, compete for survival. The encapsulation of complexity continues to the planet level, and then, with the player at the helm of a UFO, the solar system, galaxy, and universe. The player can deposit life on other planets. If a planet happens to be populated by civilizations of life forms created by other players, multiple players can watch as their artificial life forms coevolve and compete for survival. *Spore* incorporates the 2D gameplay of *PacMan* (Namco), the machine learning of *Black & White* (Lionhead Studios) and *NERO*, the authoring capabilities of *FPSCreator* (The GameCreators), and the player-directed gameplay of *The Sims* and *Sim City* (Electronic Arts).

The significance of *Spore* for the serious games developer, aside from the emergent gameplay, is that the game is based on player content, as opposed to massive teams of artists. The player assumes the role of 3D artist, animator, and to the extent that form defines function, programmer. When the technology behind *Spore* is eventually incorporated into standard development tools directed at developers, small shops currently rate-limited by developer headcount will benefit. They'll be able to do more with less. Similarly, larger shops looking for methods of bringing games to market more quickly will likely embrace the technology. The challenge for the development community is to avoid the mistakes of the past, when edutainment and other eye candy could be produced rapidly, but the quality of data was suspect.

Pervasive Games

Games are riding the wave of pervasive computing and communications that is redefining modern life at home, on the road, and in public and private institutions. Constant access to games, video, communications, and computing power isn't limited to users of cellphones and other wireless handhelds. In the home, the convergence of consumer electronics, computing, and communications has created smart homes, with large-screen entertainment centers, wireless Internet access, music available to download as MP3 files, digital movies, satellite TV, and game feeds. Even the airlines have gotten into the act. Song, a subsidiary of Delta Air Lines, added video games to its high tech in-flight entertainment system. For a $5 fee, passengers have unlimited access to single-user and networked multiplayer games for the duration of the flight.

The integration of game technology into traditional learning environments is illustrated by the digital planetarium at the Chabot Space & Science Center in Oakland, California (*www.chabotspace.org*). The full-dome digital projection system uses 3D gaming technology to enable a program director to take the audience on an interactive flight through a digital universe. The center also uses an online lunar lander advergame to attract patrons to the center, where they can use the full-sized version of the game.

Components of gaming technology are becoming increasingly popular in K–12 and higher education, especially as classrooms move away from traditional book-based learning to more interactive formats. The immediacy of feedback characteristic of games is being introduced into colleges, in the form of interactive clickers. These wireless polling devices, once relegated to business conferences, are now affordable enough to be used by students in U.S. classrooms [AP05].

Grade schools are also following the pervasive computing trend. A public school in Vail, Arizona, was the first to go all-electronic [AP05]. The school administration decided to provide laptops to all 350 students instead of textbooks. This increased reliance on computers and computer technology isn't limited to the United States. In Australia, games are one of the types of media being introduced into the K–12 curriculum [Flak04]. With the infrastructure for all-electronic instruction growing, serious games will no longer be relegated to the computer lab down the hall.

Significance

Technological and market advances in the area such as augmented reality and pervasive games, combined with the proliferation of enabling technologies such as faster processors and more powerful, easier to use authoring tools, promise to lower the barriers to entry for prospective serious games developers. Given the market potential for personal games and other types of serious games that have been incubating in academia and R&D shops, the serious games industry is poised for rapid expansion, both within new disciplines and deeper within disciplines currently using serious games.

As the barriers to authoring diminish and the focus shifts even farther to content acquisition, development, and management, there should be an emphasis on simulation-based serious games. This is likely because of the parallel efforts in the modeling and simulation community to create standards that will facilitate model sharing and communications.

Regardless of the ultimate source of the serious content, the technological trends described above point to more opportunities for serious games developers with specific domain expertise. Developers with specific subject matter expertise who can work as liaisons between experts and the development staff or who can rely directly on their domain expertise will have a distinctive edge over generalists. Similar, developers experienced with IRBs, psychometrics, and implementing assessments will be in demand within every discipline. The demand for specialists and developers skilled in assessment has significant implications for training and career opportunities.

CAREER OPPORTUNITIES

Anyone considering a career in game development—serious or otherwise—should consult the *Game Developer's Market Guide* [Bates03]. In it, Bob Bates not only profiles game development companies, publishers, and schools, but shares insightful interviews with industry insiders. The IGDA forum on breaking into the industry (*www.igda.org/forums*) is a good place to get a flavor for the current job market and the job search process. Other good resources include GameJobs (*www.gamejobs.com*), *Break Into the Game Industry: How to Get a Job Making Video Games* by Ernest Adams, and *Get in the Game: Careers in the Game Industry*, by Marc Mencher. These and other sources of information on career options in the games development industry are listed in Appendix F, "Resources."

In evaluating a career in the serious games development industry, it's also a good idea to review Spencer Johnson's, *Who Moved My Cheese* [Johnson00]. In it, he reminds readers that change is constant, especially in the workforce. Everyone and every industry matures as part of the natural progression of things. For example, the general-purpose computer is now a commodity. Similarly, the software tools industry, once a tide pool of varied and incompatible packages, is consolidating and maturing. Adobe Systems acquired Macromedia to prepare for its battle with Microsoft and Google over who will deliver media-rich content—including games—over the Web [Ricadela05].

Industries related to gaming are also in flux, including the once-bustling movie/DVD industry. Studios once made 60 percent of movie revenue from the sale of DVDs [Marr05]. However, the market for DVD movies has matured, demand is down, and the selling window has been severely shortened. Although no one is certain, it's likely that many of the former DVD clients have turned to gaming as an alternative to passive DVD consumption.

Against this backdrop of questionable or diminishing demand in some major markets, many industries, including gaming, are on the upswing. On-Demand 3D Games, a 3G wireless service introduced into the U.S. in

2005, appears to be taking off [Nelson05]. In addition, most analysts expect the Xbox 360, followed by the Playstation 3 and Nintendo Revolution to create a staggered surge in entertainment game sales through 2007 and perhaps 2008. What happens after that depends on how the cellphone games are received, the rollout dates, and capabilities of the next generation of new video game consoles, and consumer demand.

This projected trajectory for the game industry as a whole bodes well for the serious games industry. The same inexpensive, powerful hardware that runs entertainment games can make an affordable serious games platform. Similarly, the developers of innovative software tools competing for market share in the entertainment game industry will sell the same discounted technology to serious games developers. In short, as companies compete for every stage in the entertainment games value chain, the serious games industry is an incidental beneficiary. Hardware developers that might scoff at developing an augmented reality interface to a handheld console for a serious games project might fight to launch the interface in the potentially lucrative entertainment games market.

Job Market

The games development industry is in a modest upswing, as demonstrated by the advertisements for talent in the print and online developer journals. This situation is good for the serious games development community, even though the entertainment and serious games industries are different in many respects.

The job market for artists, programmers, and other specialists in the entertainment industry is a competitive tournament. Young, talented hopefuls planning to break in to the industry will do just about anything to land a position with one of the big firms. Paradoxically, even though good talent is in demand, psychologically, it's an employer's market. Someone lucky enough to land a job with a top game company isn't likely to balk at 10-hour days and irrational schedules. As long as there's a chance to work up to the top, some artisans will live out of a pizza box to prove they have what it takes to succeed. Some quit when they realize they'll never make it to the top, and the few that do make it keep the pressure up until they land their dream job. Those who fall off the pyramid become part of the ever present pool of local outsourced talent. It sounds bleak, but it's the same model followed in the publishing, movie, and sports industries. At least in the entertainment games industry, developers have the potential to make it—big.

Serious games development shops tend to be small and either part of a larger entity, such as a military institute or university, or independent. Even BreakAway Games, which is responsible for several AAA budgeted serious games, is a mixed shop that caters to the entertainment and serious games industries. See BreakAway Federal Systems at *www.breakawayfederal.com* for information on recent serious games projects.

The pressures and general work environment tend to contrast with those of the large entertainment game shops. A small, independent shop funded by the military to develop a serious game typically doesn't have the same incentive system in many entertainment shops. If an entertainment title is a few weeks late, it could mean a 90 percent cut in bonus pay if the title doesn't make it on the shelves in time for the holiday season. With serious games not destined for the retail shelves, getting the game right is often more important than getting something not quite right out on time.

In looking at the following statistics, it's important to note that the assumption is that serious games developers and game development shops are part of the larger games development community. A shop might be mixed, following the BreakAway games model, or focused solely on serious games development, such as Virtual Heroes (*www.virtualheroes.com*). However, there are multimedia training shops throughout academia and industry staffed by artists, educational designers, programmers, and other specialists involved in serious games development who do not consider themselves games developers. These professionals may never attend the annual Games Developers Conference or belong to the IGDA, but they are nonetheless developing serious games.

These shops are significant for readers trained in game development because they represent employment opportunities. Every major university, medical school, pharmaceutical firm, and major corporation with an internal multimedia training or marketing department represents a job opportunity. The first challenge is locating these shops. The second challenge is fitting in—which is where domain expertise comes in. Given these caveats, the following discussion provides a view of the games development industry from the inside looking out.

The Numbers

Compared with most other skilled professions, game development pays well, as illustrated by the results of the Game Developer's 4th Annual Salary Survey, shown in Table 9.1 [Duffy05]. The figures in the table represent the range of averages reported, from those with less than three years to more than six years of experience. Furthermore, the 2005 survey breaks down the specialty areas into subspecialties. For example, the programming category includes titles of programmer/engineer, lead programmer, and technical director, and the art and animation category includes artist, animator, lead artist/animator titles.

**TABLE 9.1   Summary of Game Developer's Fourth Annual Salary Survey.
(Compiled from 2,091 responses.)**

SPECIALTY	RANGE (K)	AVERAGE BONUS (K)
Programming	54.3–115.1	21,872
Art/Animation	42.5–78.7	19,168
Game Design	43.8–78.9	16,890
Production	52.5–118.4	39,707
Quality Assurance	33.4–69.9	8,534
Audio	64.0–92.3	29,885
Business/Legal	60.5–113.6	45,188

Overall average salary in the industry, by gender, was reported as $70,799 for males and $63,440 for females, with the highest average salaries reported in California, followed, in order, by New York, Washington, Massachusetts, Illinois, and Texas. As in previous surveys, programming is the most lucrative entry-level position in the game development industry.

The Game Developers Survey seems in line with other surveys. According to the 2005 InfoWorld Compensation Survey, the average programming/application managers salary in all fields was $87,180 with an average bonus of $6,764 [InfoWorld05]. This salary falls within the range reported for game programmers. However, the average bonus amount for game programmers is three times the industry average.

Quality of Life

Both the *InfoWorld* and *Game Developer's* surveys revealed that game developers and programmers in all fields are putting in a lot more work than in the past for a little more money. Low job satisfaction among game developers is also commonplace. This finding of dissatisfaction is backed up by the 2004 IGDA Quality of Life White Paper, which was presented at the 2004 Game Developers Conference [Bonds04]. The paper suggests that quality of life, not pay, is the major issue for employees in the industry. According to the paper, game developers tend to be young, career-oriented males who are heavily into games and gaming. A third of the self-selected pool of 994 developers planned to leave the industry within 5 years, and over half expected to leave within 10 years. It is assumed the respondents were largely, if not entirely, from the entertainment gaming community, although no data was collected to corroborate this assumption.

In November of 2004, an anonymous Web log post, "EA: The Human Story," was posted by ea_spouse, a self-described disgruntled spouse (*www.livejournal.com/users/ea_spouse*). The story described the working conditions at Electronic Arts, which included a policy of chronic crunch time with no overtime, no comp time, and no additional sick or vacation leave. The Ea_spouse posting raised the issue of quality of life at work throughout the games development industry.

Quality of life issues have also surfaced in the courts. In a 2004 class-action lawsuit filed against Electronic Art's Redwood City, California, studio, it was alleged that the company drove workers to exhaustion without paying overtime [Takahashi04]. A similar suit was filed against Vivendi Universal Games in Los Angeles around the same time. The suit claimed that the workers in the shop regularly worked 12-hour-plus days without overtime pay and that they were asked to falsify their time sheets [Takahashi04].

Global Competition

Game development of all genres is a worldwide phenomenon. Figure 9.2 shows some of the major global hotspots, based on IGDA chapter locations and Web sites of game development shops. Statistics on regional demographics and economies are based on data from the United States Central Intelligence Agency's (CIA's) *World Factbook 2005* unless otherwise noted [CIA05].

FIGURE 9.2   Game development global hotspots.

Hotspots

In the United States, the major East Coast hotspots for game development are New York, the D.C. metropolitan area, Massachusetts, and North Carolina's research triangle, and on the West Coast, California, Oregon, and Nevada. In between are shops in Texas and Illinois. The undisputed epicenter of entertainment game development is the Los Angeles area, with its pool of movie-industry-trained animators, writers, and sound editors. The San Francisco Bay Area is a close second, with its world-class universities and unparalleled technical talent pool.

The West Coast is also a significant serious games hotspot. The MOVES Institute, one of the largest serious games development shops, is located in Monterey, just south of Silicon Valley. A similar shop, USC's Institute for Creative Technologies (ICT), is in Marina del Rey, ten minutes from the Los Angeles International Airport. Both serious games shops create and evaluate military application of computer games technology. There are many other shops in the area as well.

The U.S. games development workforce is facing increased global competition similar to what transformed the job market in the IT industry. In the game development market, the key variables in assessing the global competition are labor costs, availability of trained, talented workers, and a modern information technology infrastructure. In these regards, the U.S. is well positioned in terms of the talent pool and information technology infrastructure. However, labor costs in the United States are high compared with many other countries that are active in the games development industry.

Figure 9.3 shows the indexes of hourly compensation costs in U.S. dollars for production workers in manufacturing for the year 2003. The data, based on statistics from the U.S. Department of Labor that are compiled every few years, reflects wages within the manufacturing industry [BLS04]. Presumably, hourly costs for technology positions follow the same ratios.

The figure shows that hourly compensation in Canada is about the same as in the United States. With the exception of Japan, the countries in the Pacific Rim have a significant labor cost advantage over the United States and Europe. Moreover, although not shown in the figure, in 2004, the typical salary for a programmer in India was $8,000, compared with $70,000 in the United States [Pink04].

Not surprisingly, India, as well as the other countries with pools of highly educated, relatively inexpensive labor, is a major force in the global game development economy. In 2002 India IT outsourcing accounted for 80 percent of the world's outsourcing [Overby02]. India has almost a thousand software companies and a half million programmers, with major activity in Bangalore (for example, Microsoft and Dhruva Interactive) and Mumbai (for example, Indiagames).

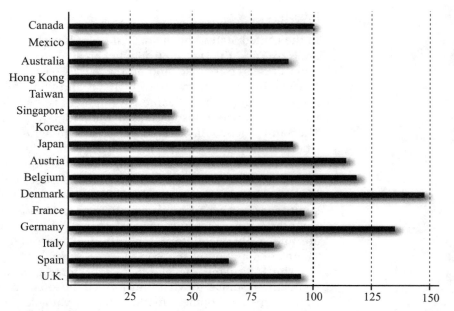

FIGURE 9.3 Compensation index relative to the United States.

Beijing is another up-and-coming game development hotspot, home to Microsoft's Advanced Technology Center, which developed operating system and graphics packages for the Xbox [Buderi05; Huang04]. Other hotspots in and around China include Shanghai, the Pearl River Delta Region, and Hong Kong. China is rapidly expanding, in part because of the large labor pool. Hong Kong is well positioned, with seven universities and nearly 100 percent Internet penetration.

Japan, home of Sony, Nintendo, Namco, and dozens of other game development shops, is an undaunted competitor. The major centers of game development activity are in and around Tokyo, Kobe, Kyoto, and Osaka. Tokyo is home to Tokyo University as well as the National Institute of Advanced Industrial Science and Technology (AIST). Most of the population is online, primarily through their cellphones. Highly trained labor is readily available and is world-class.

Back on the mainland, Seoul is a center of activity. NCsoft, developers of the online multiplayer game *Lineage*, is a national icon. The other hotspots of the Pacific Rim—Taiwan, Thailand, Malaysia, and Singapore—all have solid IT infrastructures. The city-state of Singapore is especially notable for its highly educated work force and its National University of Singapore (*www.nus.edu.sg*), which is known for game-related research and development.

In Australia, game development centers of activity are in the population centers along southern extent of the island—Melbourne, Sydney, Brisbane, and Adelaide. More than half of the population is on the Internet and the talent pool is large. The annual Game Developers Conference is held in Melbourne, also host to Atari, Infinite Interactive, and Blue Tongue, one of the THQ studios.

Much of Europe has an extensive IT infrastructure, a highly skilled labor force, and labor costs that range from below to slightly above the levels in the United States. Virtually every country in Europe is host to game developers, but the U.K., France, and Germany have the largest industries. Microsoft has an offshore R&D shop in Cambridge, England.

Just north of the U.S. border, Montreal is home to developers such as Ubi Soft, Electronic Arts, A2M, Microids, and Strategy First. Toronto is also a major hotspot. South of the border, Latin America represents a modest market for games, but it isn't a contender for game development. There is some activity in Mexico City, which has low wages and one of the best IT infrastructures in Latin America.

Outsourcing Innovation

It is a mistake to think that only rote work is outsourced, leaving the creative R&D work of entertainment games to U.S. designers and programmers. In the global economy, outsourcing is simply a part of doing business. In the entertainment games development industry, the creative components of game development, including R&D, is often outsourced as a means of bringing a game to market faster. In addition to time savings, reasons to outsource are to save money, to have access to intellectual property, to work with a developer who has expertise in a specific area, to attract talent, and to gain an international perspective for a game that will be marketed internationally.

U.S. entertainment games developers routinely outsource to India, China, Japan, the Pacific Rim, the U.K., and France. Notable examples include Electronic Arts, which outsourced some of the art for its *Lord of the Rings* to artists in China [Takahashi04]. Electronic Arts, Microsoft, THQ, UbiSoft, Turbine, and others have used developers in Eastern Europe, China, India, and Taiwan make all or part of their games [Takahashi04].

Although global competition is natural in the modern knowledge economy, jobs in the serious games industry are less exposed to overseas outsourcing than are jobs in the entertainment industry, by virtue of the serious content. Obviously, the R&D components of a game that deals with a U.S. military weapons system aren't going to be outsourced to China or Russia. Artwork and some model building may be outsourced, but the core serious content elements are likely to stay in the hands of the core development group that interfaces with the serious content experts.

The same holds true for serious medical games that revolve around a particular procedure or technology that is embodied in local expertise. How long this last barrier against global competition is uncertain, but the situation underscores the need for developers to offer domain expertise as well as game development skills.

SUMMARY

The outlook for serious games and serious games developers is positive. Serious games should continue to gain in popularity, and the industry should witness an explosion in the application of serious games, in both breadth and depth of coverage. Part of this activity will come from within the games development community, and part will come from the training and development communities within academia, industry, and other disciplines.

Following the current trends, serious games will continue to be defined by quality content, with less emphasis on development tools. In addition, enabling developments in the modeling and simulation community should make more content available for simulation-based games.

The developers who will excel in the serious games industry will have development skills as well as domain expertise in the military, medicine, academia, or some other industry. With the increasing emphasis on assessment to prove efficacy, expertise in assessment will continue to be in demand.

Finally, the ranks of serious games developers includes more than developers moving from the entertainment games industry, but includes the uncounted thousands of professionals involved in serious games development in multimedia, training and development, and education shops worldwide.

REFERENCES

[AP05] AP, "Arizona School Will Not Use Textbooks." 2005. *news.yahoo.com/s/ap/20050711/ap_on_hi_te/no_textbooks*, accessed July 11, 2005.

[AP05b] AP, "Classroom Clickers Make the Grade." *Wired News*. 2005. *www.wired.com/news/technology/0,1282,68086,00.html?tw=rss.TOP*, accessed July 11, 2005.

[Bates03] Bates, Bob, *Game Developer's Market Guide*. Premier Press/Course PTR, 2003.

[Behar05] Behar, M., "The Doctor Will See Your Prototype Now." *WIRED* 2 (2005): p. 38.

[Bergeron04] Bergeron, B, *Case Studies in Genes and Disease: A Primer for Clinicians*. American College of Physicians-American Society of Internal Medicine, 2004.

[BLS04] BLS, International comparison of hourly compensation costs for production workers in manufacturing, 2003. U.S. Department of Labor, Bureau of Labor Statistics. 2004, accessed July 11, 2005.

[Bonds04] Bonds, Scott, Jamie Briant, et al., *Quality of Life in the Game Industry: Challenges and Best Practices*. International Game Developers Association, 2004.

[Buderi05] Buderi, Robert, "Microsoft: Getting from R to D." *Technology Review* (March 2005): pp. 28–30.

[Card91] Card, Orson, *Ender's Game*. Tor Books, 1991.

[CIA05] CIA, *The World Factbook 2005*. U.S. Central Intelligence Agency, 2005.

[Colucci04] Colucci, Frank, "Air Force Refines Training Programs for UAV Operators." *National Defense* (May 1, 2004).

[Duffy05] Duffy, Jill, Game "Developer's 4th Annual Salary Survey." *Game Developer* 4 (2005): pp. 13–17.

[Flak04] Flak, Jo, "Phones, Games and Virtual Worlds: New Media in the Classroom." *Australian Screen Education* (December 22, 2004).

[Huang04] Huang, Gregory, The World's Hottest Computer Lab. *Technology Review* 5 (2004): pp. 32–42.

[InfoWorld05] InfoWorld, 2005 "InfoWorld Compensation Survey." 2005. *www.infoworld.com/reports/24SRcompsurvey05.html*, accessed July 11, 2005.

[Johnson00] Johnson, Spencer, *Who Moved My Cheese?* Penguin Putnam, Inc., 2000.

[Kosak05] Kosak, Dave, "Will Wright Presents Spore and a New Way to Think about Games." *GameSpy*, 2005. *www.gamespy.com/articles/595/595975p1.html*, accessed July 10, 2005.

[Marr05] Marr, Merissa, "In Dream Works Earnings Woes, a Bigger Problem." *The Wall Street Journal* (July 12, 2005): pp. A1–6.

[Nelson05] Nelson, Jeffrey, "Verizon Wireless Vaults over the Bar with V CAST: Customers Embracing V CAST On-demand Video and 3D Games." *PR Newswire* (March 14, 2005).

[Overby02] Overby, S., "A Buyer's Guide to Offshore Outsourcing." CIO (November 2002): pp. 69–72.

[Picard97] Picard, R., *Affective Computing*. MIT Press, 1997.

[Pink04] Pink, Daniel, "The New Face of the Silicon Age." *Wired* (February 2004): pp. 94–138.

[Ricadela05] Ricadela, Aaron, "A New Image." *Information Week* (June 6, 2005): pp. 22–24.

[Sandhana05] Sandhana, Lakshmi, "PacMan Comes to Life Virtually." BBC News. 2005. *news.bbc.co.uk/2/hi/technology/4607449.stm*, accessed June 30, 2005.

[Stanley05] Stanley, Kenneth, Bobby Bryant, et al., "Evolving Neural Network Agents in the NERO Video Game." IEEE 2005 Symposium on Computational Intelligence and Games (CIG 05).

[Takahashi04] Takahashi, Dean, "Our Little Secret: Offshore Outsourcing." *Game Developer* (June 2004).

[Takahashi04] Takahashi, Dean, "Video-Game Workers Sue for Overtime Pay." *Knight Ridder Newspapers* (December 15, 2004).

[Thomas02] Thomas, Bruce, *About the ARQuake Project*. University of Southern Australia. 2002. *wearables.unisa.edu.au/projects/ARQuake/www/index.html*, accessed July 10, 2005.

[TigerTelematics05] TigerTelematics, *Tiger Telematics' Gizmondo Unveils New Gaming Technology*. Tiger Telematics Press Release. 2005. *www.tigertelematics.com/news/Giz_ARand%20 Camera%20Tech_final.pdf*, accessed September 20, 2005.

[Wastney99] Wastney, Meryl, Blossom, Patterson, et al., *Investigating Biological Systems Using Modeling*. Academic Press, 1999.

[YerkesDodson08] Yerkes, R. M. and D. Y. Dodson, "The Relative Strength of Stimulus to Rapidly of Habit Formation." *Journal of Comparative Neurology and Psychology* 18 (1908): pp. 459–82.

GLOSSARY

Serious games development is a multidimensional task that requires in-depth knowledge in several areas. Following is a collection of terms a serious game developer is likely to encounter in the course of financing, developing, and marketing a serious game. Some of these terms are not found in the text. Because the military is a significant source of serious games funding, many of these additional terms relate to ongoing military projects and organizations.

3D Engine: The core program that runs a game and displays the 3D world on the screen.

AAA Game: A game that earns a place among the top 10 in the marketplace.

Abandonware: Games no longer sold or supported by the copyright holder.

Accounts Payable: Total of all monies owed by the organization.

Accounts Receivable: Monies owed to the organization but not yet collected.

Adaptive Learning: An artificial intelligence system that can reprogram itself based on learner performance.

Adaptive System: A system that learns with experience.

Added Value: The additional, tangible, benefit derived by an organization through carrying out a business function or process.

Advanced Distributed Learning (ADL):   A DOD and White House Office of Science and Technology Policy (OSTP) initiative designed to promote universal access to education materials tailored to individual learner needs.

Advanced Distributed Learning Co-Laboratory Network (ADL Co-Lab): A network of facilities and resources designed to foster the collaborative research, development, and assessment of the common tools, standards, content, and guidelines for the ADL Initiative.

Advergame: A game designed primarily to promote a product, service, or organization.

Agent: A software application that performs actions. An agent may be intelligent.

AICC Standards: The Aviation Industry CBT Committee's guidelines and recommendations for Web-based computer managed instruction systems conformance.

American National Standards Institute (ANSI): A nonprofit organization that helps establish electronic data standards.

Amortization: The gradual elimination of a liability in regular payments over a specified period of time. Alternatively, writing off an intangible asset investment over the projected life of the asset.

Application Programming Interface (API): A set of definitions of the ways one piece of computer software communicates with another.

Applied Research: Scientific exploration that is aimed at acquiring specific knowledge that has commercial objectives.

Assets: The multimedia used to make a game.

Asynchronous Collaborative ELearning (ACEL): A collaborative eLearning experience that does not occur in real time.

Asynchronous Learning: When the learner is engaged at a time other than concurrent with the faculty or other learners, usually through the use of email, listservs, audiocassette courses, videotaped courses, correspondence courses and Internet courses.

Augmented Assessment: The innovative use of technologies to increase the efficiency and effectiveness of the technology assessment process.

Augmented Reality: The combination of real-world and computer-generated data.

Authoring System: In the context of game development, a game engine combined with a visual editor for "clicking together" a game prototype.

Backend Process: A process that doesn't represent a game developer's unique skills, knowledge, or processes. Typical backend processes include payroll, billing, and accounts payable.

Bad Debt: Accounts receivable that will likely remain uncollectible and be written off.

Balance Sheet: A statement of the financial position of the organization at a particular time.

Basic Research: Scientific exploration that advances scientific knowledge but that does not have any immediate commercial objective.

Battle Lab: A location where the military uses simulations and prototype equipment to develop strategies.

Battlespace: The environment, forces, and support units in a simulation.

Best of Breed: The service provider that is best in its class of services.

Best Practice: The most effective and desirable method of carrying out a function or process.

Biometrics: A method of verifying the identity of a user based on finger prints, facial features, retinal pattern, voice, or other personal characteristics.

Boss: An enemy character found at the end of a level that is harder to kill than the other enemies in the level.

Broad Area Announcement (BAA):   An announcement of a funding opportunity that covers a broad range of basic R&D opportunities.

Binary Runtime Environment for Wireless (BREW):   Qualcomm's set of software tools for developing wireless games.

Browser: A software program that interprets documents on the Web.

Build: A stage in the development of a game in which independently developed software components are compiled and linked so that they can be tested. A build normally consists of the executable and all of the data files it reads.

Business Game: A serious game that focuses on economics, ownership, operations, or some other aspect of business or investing.

Business Intelligence (BI):   Information technology practices and products concerned with gathering and analyzing financial and operational indicators.

Business Model: The manner in which business generates revenue and profits.

Business Plan: A written explanation of a company's business model.

Business Process Management (BPM):   A business improvement strategy based on documenting, analyzing, and redesigning processes for greater performance.

Capital Budget: A summary of the anticipated purchases for the year.

Capital Expenditure: An expenditure on tangible and intangible assets that will benefit the company for more than one year.

Capitation: A payment structure in which a caregiver is paid a set amount per patient in advance, regardless of how many procedures are performed.

Casual Gamer: Someone who plays games that don't require a huge investment of time.

Central Contractor Registration (CCR):   A process to facilitate registration by a company as a Trading Partner with the Federal Government. This is a necessary process for developers who desire to do business with the DOD.

CLearning: Traditional classroom learning in a classroom at a specific time with a teacher/facilitator.

Client-Server: A computer architecture in which the workload is split between desktop PCs or handheld wireless devices (clients) and more powerful or higher-capacity computers (servers) that are connected via a network such as the Internet.

Cognitive Ergonomics: The applied science of equipment design, as for the workplace, intended to maximize productivity by reducing operator fatigue and discomfort.

Combined Training Exercise (CTX): Training conducted with an allied force.

Command and Control (C2): The basic functions of the military chain of command.

Command Post Exercise (CPX): A training simulation designed for training the commander and staff in which all forces are simulated.

Command, Control, Communications, and Computers (C4): An updated term for Command and Control that reflect the importance of technology.

Command, Control, Communications, Computers, Intelligence, Surveillance, and Reconnaissance (C4ISR): A combination of all information-based roles in military operations.

Commercial Evaluation License Agreement (CELA): A license that allows an organization to evaluate the commercial potential of unpatented, patented, and patent-pending materials or methods.

Computer-Based Training (CBT): Training materials delivered via a computer.

Computer-Managed Instruction (CMI): A system for launching and tracking educational content. Also known as a Learning Management System (LMS).

Concept: The basic idea behind a game.

Confidential Disclosure Agreement (CDA): An agreement that ensures that government employees do not disclose an organization's proprietary information and that an organization does not disclose the government's scientific findings before publication and before the government is able to secure patent rights.

Confidentiality Agreement: A contractual document in which one or both parties agree not to divulge certain information to parties other than the parties involved.

Console: A hardware device, such as the Xbox 360, that connects to a television set for the purpose of playing an electronic game.

Constructive Training: Simulations that rely on simulated people using simulated systems to examine outcomes.

Content Aggregation Model: Within the SCORM standard, a common means for composing learning content from discoverable, reusable, sharable, and interoperable sources.

Content Organization Meta-data: Within the SCORM standard, a description of content organization.

Content Organization: Within the SCORM standard, a map that represents the intended use of the content through structured units of instruction.

Content Packaging: Within the SCORM standard, a way to exchange digital learning resources between different systems or tools.

Contractor: A person or company who does work under a contract.

Controlled Vocabulary: A terminology system unambiguously mapped to concepts.

Convergence: The merging of all data and all media into a single digital form.

Cooperative Research and Development Agreement (CRADA):   An agreement that defines the scope and terms of collaborative relationships between government scientists and outside collaborators.

Copyright: Rights granted by the government for a limited period of time to protect the particular form, way or manner in which an idea or information is expressed.

Critical Design Review (CDR):   The process through which the government approves a design.

Critical Path: The shortest path to the final game product in resource scheduling. The critical path represents the minimum length of time in which development can be completed.

Current Status of Development: The amount of work completed to date relative to the final implementation of a game.

Customer Segment: A homogeneous group of similar game players with similar needs, wants, lifestyles, interaction opportunities, profiles, and purchase cycles.

Cutscene: A noninteractive animation, often accompanied by voice and/or music, designed to advance the plot, portray character, and provide background information, atmosphere, dialogue, and clues.

Cycle Time: The time it takes for a developer to convert an idea into a new game or to improve an existing game.

DARPA: An advanced research arm of the Department of Defense responsible for developing new technology for military.

DARWARS: A DARPA-funded research project to accelerate the development and deployment of next-generation training systems.

Data Collection: The process of capturing raw or primary data from a single source or a number of sources.

Data Maintenance: The efforts required to keep database files and supporting documentation accurate.

Data Mart: An organized, searchable database system, organized according to the user's likely needs.

Data Mining: The process of studying the contents of large databases in order to discover new data relationships.

Data Sources: The primary source documents used for data collection.

Data Structure: A way of storing data in a computer so that it can be used efficiently.

Decals: Textures applied to 2D surfaces in a game.

Decision Support System (DSS):   An application for analyzing large quantities of data and performing a wide variety of calculations and projections.

Decision-Tree Analysis: A graphical process used to select the best course of action in cases of uncertainty.

Defense Contractor: Any person who enters into a contract with the United States for the production of material or for the performance of services for the national defense.

Defense Modeling and Simulation Office (DMSO):   The organization for the DOD that ensures modeling and simulation technology development is consistent with other related initiatives.

Defense Science Board (DSB):   A federal advisory committee established to provide independent advice to the Secretary of Defense.

Defined Allowable Value: The predefined range of alphanumeric values that are valid for a data element in a database.

Defined Measure: A structured measure with defined populations that measure specific events or values.

Deliverables: The products and services specified in a statement of work.

Developer: A company or person that builds games.

Digital Signature: An encrypted digital tag added to an electronic communication to verify the identity of the sender. Also known as an electronic signature.

Direct Cost: That portion of cost that is directly expended in providing a service.

DirectX: A library of APIs for handling tasks related to game programming, proprietary to Microsoft.

Disruptive Technology: A technology that causes a major shift in the normal way of doing things and that improves with time. The PC, digital camera, and cell phones are disruptive technologies.

Distance Learning: Structured learning that takes place when the instructor is not physically present.

Distributed Interactive Simulation (DIS):   A standard for conducting real-time platform-level wargaming across multiple host computers that grew out of SIMNET.

Distributed Learning: Structured learning that takes place anytime, anywhere it is needed or desired.

Distributor: A company that gets games onto the shelves of stores and onto the pages of catalogs.

Domain Expert: Someone experienced in the subject matter relevant to a serious game.

Due Diligence: A thorough effort to intercept potential problems before they occur.

Dynamic Link Library (DLL):   A file containing a library of functions and other information that can be accessed by a Windows program.

Early Adopter: In marketing, a customer who wants the latest and greatest gadget, regardless of cost or inconvenience. Early Adopters follow Innovators in adopting new technologies.

Ease of Use: Regarding a user interface, the ease or efficiency with which the interface can be used.

Easter Egg: Content hidden by the game designers, in hopes that dedicated players will find it.

Economic Darwinism: Survival of the fittest—the most economically successful companies in the marketplace.

Economies of Scale: Reduction in the costs of production due to increasing production capacity.

Educational Game: A game made primarily for the purpose of teaching players.

Edutainment: A game that teaches and entertains. Popular in the '90s, the term has a negative connotation in education.

ELearning: Internet-based learning.

Embedded Training: Training built into equipment so that it is available as the need arises.

Emergent Behavior: Unexpected gameplay that wasn't foreseen or planned for by game developers.

Encryption: The process of encoding data to prevent someone without the proper key from understanding the data, even though they may have access to it.

Enforceability: The conditions under which the terms, conditions, and obligations of the parties under an agreement will be adopted and confirmed by a court.

Entertainment Software Ratings Board (ESRB):   A self-policing body created by the game industry to rate games.

Equity: An accounting term used to describe the net investment of owners or stockholders in a business.

Exergaming: The marriage of physical exercise and video gaming.

Extensible Markup Language (XML):   A specification for Web documents that enables the definition, transmission, validation, and interpretation of data between applications and between organizations.

Federal Acquisition Regulation (FAR):   A regulation regarding the awarding and execution of government contracts.

Federation Object Model (FOM):   The High Level Architecture standard for specifying messages passed between objects during a simulation.

Financial Statement: A written report that quantitatively describes the financial health of a company. This includes an income statement and a balance sheet, and often also includes a cash flow statement.

Forecasting: A mathematical method of extrapolating historical performance data to aid in planning.

Full Time Equivalent (FTE):   Any combination of workers that combines to forty hours per week. FTE does not necessarily equate to headcount. For example, two, half-time (20 hours per week) workers together amount to one FTE.

Game Engine: The core software component of a game that handles rendering, AI, and physics. The term is sometimes applied to large libraries.

Gamebryo: A proprietary, cross-platform 3D rendering engine.

Gantt Chart: A graphical production scheduling method showing lengths of various production stages.

Generation M: The media generation. Persons born immersed in video, music, games, and computer technology.

Government Off-the-Shelf (GOTS):   Software developed by the government or contractors for the government.

Government Purpose Rights (GPR):   If unrestricted, the right of the government to use or disclose the software or documentation developed by a contractor for any U.S. government purposes. Government Purpose Rights are normally restricted by astute developers.

Graphics Pipeline: The sequence of graphics operations involved in transforming a 3D conceptual model into a 2D raster image on a computer screen.

Gross Profit: A financial indicator equal to profit before expenses, interest, and taxes have been deducted.

Gross Revenue: Total revenue less cost of goods sold.

Gross Sales: Total invoice value of sales, before deducting for customer discounts, allowances, or returns.

Hardcore Gamer: A person who spends a high percentage of his time playing action games.

Health and Medicine Game: A game developed to teach some aspect of health or medicine. It might also promote a drug or product.

Heuristic: A rule of thumb.

High Level Architecture (HLA):   A general-purpose architecture for distributed computer simulation systems.

Human Capital: Employee knowledge, skills, and relationships.

Human Factors: The study of the interrelationships between humans, the tools they use, and the environment in which they live and work.

IEEE P1484:   The Institute of Electrical and Electronics Engineering Learning Technology Standards Committee (LTSC).

Indemnification: A method of shifting legal liability from one party to another by contract.

Infrastructure: The system of servers, cables, and other hardware, together with the software that ties it together, for the purpose of supporting the operation of devices on a network.

Insourcing: The transfer of an outsourced function to an internal department of the developer, to be managed entirely by employees.

Institute for Defense Analysis (IDA):   A military think tank.

Instructional Management System (IMS) Project: A global coalition of academic, commercial, and government organizations that work together to define the Internet architecture for learning.

Intangible Asset: Something of value that cannot be physically touched, such as a brand, franchise, trademark, or patent.

Intellectual Property: Know-how, trade secrets, copyrights, patents, trademarks, and service marks.

Intelligent Tutoring System (ITS):   A software system that models the player to provide a more efficient and effective learning experience than would be otherwise possible.

Interface: The procedures, codes, and protocols that enable two systems to interact for a meaningful exchange of information.

Internal Commercial Use Research License Agreement: An agreement that allow companies to use patented or patent-pending technology for internal research purposes with no right to sell or use the technology in a commercial product.

International Organization for Standardization (ISO):   A worldwide federation of national standards bodies that creates standards in a variety of areas, including computer-mediated instruction.

Internet Content Rating Association (ICRA):   The association that rates Web site content, similar to the ESRB rating for COTS software.

Interoperability: The ability of computers to communicate and share resources in a heterogeneous environment.

Interservice/Industry Training, Simulation, and Education Conference (I/ITSEC):   The large military training industry trade show.

Inventory: The stock of goods on hand that is for sale.

Investment Angel: An affluent individual who provides capital for business start-ups in exchange for an equity stake in the business.

ISO 9000:   The family of ISO standards concerned with quality management.

Java 2 Micro Edition (J2ME):   Sun Microsystems's development platform for cell phones and handheld computers.

Joint Forces Command (JFCOM):   The U.S. military laboratory in charge of developing new military concepts and training.

Joint National Training Capability (JNTC):   Facilities for live training in which actors play enemies.

Joint Training Analysis and Simulation Center (JTASC):   A military organization focused on reducing the cost and difficulty of joint exercises and simulations.

Joint Venture: A contractual arrangement between two or more parties forming an unincorporated business.

Knowledge Management: A deliberate, systematic business optimization strategy that selects, distills, stores, organizes, packages, and communicates information essential to the business of an organization in a manner that improves employee performance and organization competitiveness.

Latency: The delay inherent in a system.

Learning Management System (LMS):   A system for launching and tracking learning content. Also known as Computer Managed Instruction (CMI).

Legacy System: An aging computing platform.

Liability: Legal responsibility to do, pay, or suffer something.

License: A legal agreement between an intellectual property owner and a company, for the purpose of using that intellectual property to make products.

Licensed Developer :A developer that makes games under the permission of the hardware manufacturer.

Licensed Game: A game based on a property that isn't owned by the publisher.

Licensed Publisher: A publishing company that has secured permission to publish games on a particular platform.

Localization: The process of adapting a game to a particular country or region.

Lost Opportunity Cost: The cost of not applying resources to toward an alternative investment.

Machinma: Machine- or computer-generated cinema or movies. Also "machinima" or "machinema."

Map: The graphical layout of a level, usually containing location of switches, traps, bosses, and other game elements.

Margin: The difference between the wholesale price and the retail price.

Marginal Cost: The change in cost as the result of one more or fewer unit of output.

Massively Multiplayer Game: A game that can be played by hundreds to thousands of players.

Material Transfer Agreement (MTA):   An agreement that documents and governs the transfer of research materials to and from government laboratories.

Metadata: Data about data.

Metalanguage: A language used to define other languages.

Microcontroller: A computer on a chip optimized to control electronic devices.

Middleware: Software suites containing the elements a developer might need to build a game, such as advanced physics or AI.

Mipmaps: Precalculated collections of bitmapped images that accompany a main texture, intended to increase rendering speed and reduce artifacts.

Mirroring: Two identical files or databases created and updated simultaneously so an exact duplicate exists at all times.

Mobile Game: A game that is played on a wireless, handheld device, especially a cell phone. Also called wireless game.

Mod: A modification to a computer game, usually by someone other than the original developer, which can include new items, weapons, characters, enemies, models, modes, textures, levels, and story lines.

Modding: The process of modifying computer hardware for beauty and/or performance. For gamers, the process typically involves overclocking, which is adjusting processor settings and memory timings to enhance gameplay.

Modified Off-the-Shelf (MOTS):   Commercial off-the-shelf applications in which the source code is modified for military use.

Moulage: The art of applying mock injuries to people or mannequins for the purpose of training medical personnel.

Multi-Learning: Simultaneously learning an abundance of knowledge and skills.

Naval Postgraduate School Network (NPSNET):   A real-time, interactive distributed simulation system that was developed by students at the Naval Postgraduate School (NPS).

Net Income: Revenues less expenses.

Net Profit: Revenues minus taxes, interest, depreciation, and other expenses.

Net Revenue: Gross revenue adjusted for deductions and expenses.

Net Worth: Total assets minus total liabilities.

Newsgame: A game that highlights some aspect of news or current events.

Nondisclosure Agreement (NDA):   A contract that must be signed prior to the discussion of sensitive information, such as a forthcoming game project.

Nonplayer Character (NPC):   A game character not under the direct control of the player.

Object Management Group (OMG):   An open membership, not-for-profit consortium that produces and maintains computer industry specifications for interoperable enterprise applications.

Object Model Development Tool (OMDT):   A tool for developing HLA models for simulators.

Online Game: A game that can be played against other human players, using the Internet. Most online games are run in a PC-based browser environment.

Open Platform for ELearning (OPEL):   The Advanced Development Laboratory's evolving standard that defines SCORM compliance of games.

Open Source: Software code that can be read and modified by users.

Open System: A system capable of integrating hardware and peripherals of multiple vendors. Such systems usually are able to interact with other open systems based on standard protocols.

OpenAL: A cross-platform audio API that contains functions for playing back sounds and music in a game environment.

OpenGL: An cross-platform API specification for writing applications that produce 2D and 3D computer graphics. Comparable to Microsoft's proprietary Direct3D.

Operational Requirements Document (ORD):   A document that specifies a particular need of a military organization.

Operations: The analysis of problems associated with operating a business, designed to provide a scientific basis for decision making.

Outsourcing: Entrusting a business process to an external services provider.

Out-Tasking: A limited form of outsourcing in which a task is contracted out to a consultant or other service provider.

Overhead: The expense of running the business as opposed to the direct costs of personnel and materials used to produce the end result.

Patent: A grant made by a government that confers upon the creator of an invention the sole right to make, use, and sell that invention for a set period of time.

Patent Family: All of the patent documents associated with a single invention that are published within one country.

Patent License Agreement (PLA):   A commercial use license for patented and patent-pending technologies. PLAs are negotiated on either a nonexclusive or exclusive basis and define the royalties to be paid by the licensee during the term of the agreement.

PC Game: A game designed to run locally on a personal computer—typically a Windows- or Mac OS–compatible PC.

Performance Measure: A quantitative tool that provides an indication of an organization's performance in relation to a specified process or outcome.

Personal Digital Assistant (PDA):   A handheld electronic organizer that might have Internet access and email functions.

PERT Chart: A method for project planning by analyzing the time required for each step.

Pervasive Computing: The anytime, anyplace access of computational power and data, in an unobtrusive form.

Pipeline: A set of data processing elements connected in series, so that the output of one element is the input of the next one.

Portal: A Web site that offers a broad array of resources and services.

Postmortem: A detailed analysis written after the completion of a game project.

Preliminary Design Review (PDR):   The phase at which a design is first presented for government comment.

Prime Contract: A contract awarded directly by the federal government.

Primitives: Geometric shapes used to represent objects in a game.

Process Management: An evaluation and restructuring of system functions to make sure that certain processes are carried out in the most efficient and economical way.

Process Map: A graphic description of a process, showing the sequence of process tasks, which is developed for a specific purpose and from a selected viewpoint.

Process Optimization: The removal or reengineering of processes that don't add significant value to a product or service, impede time to market, or result in suboptimal quality.

Profiling: The process of taking a few key customer data points, such as name, occupation, age, and address, and generating best guesses about other characteristics.

Profit Margin: Net profit after taxes divided by sales for a given 12-month period, expressed as a percentage.

Profit: The positive gain from business operations after subtracting all expenses.

Program Executive Office of the Strategic Instrumentation Command (PEO STRI):   The center for training and simulation for the U.S. Army. Formerly STRICOM.

Proof of Concept (POC):   An early iteration of a game, created with the intention of determining the feasibility of a gameplay concept.

Proprietary: Owned, copyrighted, or for which exclusive legal rights are held.

Protocol: A way of doing things that has become an agreed-upon convention. Alternatively, a set of standards that defines communications between computers.

Public Domain: Belonging to the community at large, unprotected by copyright, and subject to appropriation by anyone.

Regression: A mathematical method of forecasting using line equations to explain the relationship between multiple causes and effects.

Renderware: A 3D graphics rendering engine owned by Electronic Arts.

Request For Proposal (RFP): A document that requests prospective service providers to propose the terms, conditions, and other elements of an agreement to deliver specified services.

Requirements Specifications: The document that specifies the needs that must be addressed by a particular technology.

Retained Earnings: The portion of an organization's net earnings not paid to shareholders in the form of dividends.

Return on Assets (ROA): The ratio of operating earnings to net operating assets. The ROA is a test of whether a business is earning enough to cover its cost of capital.

Return on Equity (ROE): The ratio of net income to the owner's equity. The ROE is a measure of the return on investment for an owner's equity capital invested in the shared services unit.

Return on Investment (ROI): Profit resulting from investing in a process or piece of equipment. The profit could be money, time savings, or other positive result.

Revenue: The inflow of assets from providing services to customers.

Rights: Legal permission to use an IP, either under a license, or by dint of ownership of the IP.

Royalty: Money paid to a developer or IP owner based on profits made from a game, according to the terms of a contract.

Run-Time Environment: Within the SCORM standard, a means for interoperability between Sharable Content Object-based learning content and Learning Management Systems.

S1000D: An international specification for the procurement and production of technical publications. The specification has been applied in areas other than technical publications.

Self-Paced ELearning (SPEL): When a learner uses the Internet to search for static documents that provide information and content.

Semi-Automated Forces (SAF): The forces controlled by a computer simulation that is under human direction.

Serious Game: An interactive computer application, with or without a significant hardware component, that has a challenging goal, is fun to play, incorporates some concept of scoring, and imparts to the user a skill, knowledge, or attitude that can be applied in the real world.

Sharable Content Object (SCO):   In the SCORM standard, the lowest level of granularity of learning resources that can be tracked by an LMS.

Shareable Content Object Reference Model (SCORM):   A software model that defines the interrelationship of course components, data models, and protocols so that courseware objects are shareable across systems.

Simulation: An imitation of some real device or state of affairs.

Simulation Network (SIMNET):   The military system of simulated networked tank, armored vehicle, aircraft, and other weapons systems.

Simulation Object Model (SOM):   The High Level Architecture specification for interoperability.

Simulation Training and Instrumentation Command (STRICOM): The U.S. Army command for simulation training, now referred to as PEO STRI.

Situation Training Exercise (STX):   A simulation designed to train one skill or a related set of skills.

Six Sigma: A statistically driven quality management methodology designed to reduce defects and variation in a business process, thereby increasing customer satisfaction and business profits. The stated goal is to reduce defects to a level equal to six standard deviations (sigma) from the mean.

Slack: In the context of project management, the time in which a minor process or activity can be completed in advance of the next major operation or activity that depends on it.

Small Business: For the purpose of competing for SBIR/STTR monies, a U.S. owned and independently operated for-profit company with no more then 500 employees. The principal investigator must be employed by the business.

Small Business Innovation Research (SBIR):   A program administered in part by the Small Business Administration that encourages small businesses to explore their technological potential and provides the incentive to create commercial products.

Small Business Technology Transfer Resource (STTR):   A competitive program that reserves a specific percentage of federal R&D funding for award to small business and nonprofit research institution partners.

Sneaker: A shooter that emphasizes subterfuge and precision strikes over nonstop action.

Software Developers Kit (SDK):   A collection of software utilities, documentation, and sometimes hardware that enables a programmer to build software for a particular platform.

Sprite: A two-dimensional, prerendered figure.

Standard: A process, format, or transmission protocol that has become convention by agreement of a group of users.

Statement of Work (SOW):   The part of a contract that specifies activities to be performed.

Statistical Process Control A benchmarking method based on statistical quality control.

Strategic Services: Processes that directly affect an organization's ability to compete.

Strategy: The differentiating activities an organization pursues to gain competitive advantage.

Structured Query Language (SQL): A standard command language used to interact with databases.

Subject Matter Expert (SME): The domain expert who can ensure a training system is working properly.

Sympathetic Haptics: The use of a computer model to allow people to feel the same sensation that they would experience if they actually touched another person.

Synchronous Collaborative ELearning (SCEL): A real-time, collaborative eLearning experience.

Synchronous Learning: Real-time learning at a scheduled time with learners and teachers present, much like a real classroom, but using technology for remote access.

Syntax: The ordering of and relationship between the words and other structural elements in phrases and sentences.

Tacit Knowledge: Unspoken or implied knowledge.

Taxonomy: The classification of concepts and objects into a hierarchically ordered system that indicates relationships.

Technical Design Document (TDD): A document created by the technical staff after analyzing a game development document.

Telemedicine: Practicing medicine at a distance.

Texture: An image pattern applied to graphical objects in a game.

Trademark (TM): A name, symbol, or other device identifying a product, officially registered and legally restricted to the use of the owner or manufacturer.

Training Aids, Devices, Simulators, and Simulations (TADSS) Any training device used by the military.

Transformation Technology Directorate: The part of the U.S. Army Operation Test Command responsible for transforming the U.S. Army into a smaller, more technologically advanced force.

TV Game: A self-contained, portable game system integrated with a game controller that operates on batteries and plugs directly into a TV.

Universal Description, Discovery, and Integration (UDDI): A protocol for an interoperable platform that enables applications to dynamically identify and use Web services over the Internet.

Unstructured Learning: Unexpected learning that occurs while the learner is engaged in a nonstructured learning activity.

Useful Life: The time, usually expressed in years, that a game or game device can perform a useful function.

User Interface: The junction between the user and the computer.

Utility Patent: A patent that covers inventions that function in a unique manner and produce a utilitarian result.

UV Mapping: A method of applying complex textures to 3D models.

Value Chain: The sequence of events in a process that adds value to a game.

Value Proposition: A statement summarizing the customer targets, competitor targets, and the core strategy for how a development shop differentiates its products from those of the competition.

Video Game: An interactive, graphical game that executes on a desktop or handheld computer, game console, or cellphone.

Virtual Training: The use of simulators to train military personnel.

Wallpaper: Textures applied to screen as a persistent background pattern, often themed to a game.

Warez: Pirated software.

Wargame: A game in which players put military units in direct conflict with each other.

Web-Based Training (WBT):   Training that occurs over the Internet or intranet.

Work For Hire: Creative output that is wholly owned by the party who paid the creator for it, without having to pay royalties or residuals after the work is released.

Workflow: A process description of how tasks are done, by whom, in what order, and how quickly.

Working Capital: The funds available for current operating needs. Current assets less current liabilities.

World Wide Web Consortium (W3C):   The working group responsible for developing specifications, guidelines, software, and tools for the Web.

XNA Studio: An integrated, team-based development environment from Microsoft that is tailored specifically for game development.

APPENDIX B

ACRONYMS

The serious gaming industry, like every area of specialization, has its own vernacular and acronyms. The military—a potentially significant source of serious game funding through Small Business Innovation Research (SBIR), Small Technology Transfer Resource, and other avenues—is particularly difficult to navigate without knowledge of several dozen acronyms. Following is a collection of acronyms used in the military, intellectual property discussions, business, and other areas serious game developers are likely to encounter. Some of the terms are not mentioned in the text but are included here for readers who attempt to interpret the military/government-speak associated with SBIR grants, Broad Area Announcements (BAAs), and the like.

AA Anti-Aliasing
AAA Top selling entertainment game title
AAMA American Amusement Machine Association
AAR Action After Review
ACA Associate Contractor Agreements
ACEL Asynchronous Collaborative ELearning
ACO Administrative Contracting Officer
ACR American College of Radiology
ADL Advanced Distributed Learning
AFRL Air Force Research Lab
AGDC Australian Games Development Conference
AGR AICC Guidelines and Recommendations

AI Artificial Intelligence
AIAS Academy of Interactive Arts and Sciences
AICC Aviation Industry CBT Committee
AMOA Amusement and Music Operators Association
ANSI American National Standards Institute
API Application Programming Interface
ARIADNE Alliance of Remote Instructional Authoring and Distribution Networks for Europe
ARPANET Advanced Research Projects Agency Network
ASAM&RA Assistant Secretary of the Army—Manpower and Reserve Affairs

ASW   Anti-Submarine Warfare
AVCATT-A   Aviation Combined Arms Tactical Trainer-Aviation (also ACATT-A)
BAA   Broad Area Announcement
BPM   Business Process Management
BI   Business Intelligence
C2   Command and Control
C4   Command, Control, Communications, and Computers
C4ISR   Command, Control, Communications, Computers, Intelligence, Surveillance, and Reconnaissance
CBD   Chemical and Biological Defense
CBI   Computer-Based Instruction
CBT   Computer-Based Training
CCR   Central Contractor Registration
CCTT   Close Combat Tactical Trainer
CDA   Confidential Disclosure Agreement
CDR   Critical Design Review
CEL   Commercial Evaluation License (Agreement)
CEMA   Consumer Electronics Manufacturers Association
CES   International Consumer Electronics Show
CLUT   Color Look-Up Table
CMI   Computer-Managed Instruction
COG   Cost of Goods
COGS   Cost of Goods Sold
CORDRA   Content Object Repository Discovery and Registration/Resolution Architecture
COTS   Commercial Off-the-Shelf (game software)
CPU   Central Processing Unit
CPX   Command Post Exercise
CRADA   Cooperative Research and Development Agreement
CSA   Canadian Standards Association
CSBA   Center for Strategic Budgetary Assessment
CSF   Content Structure Format
CT   Computed Tomography
CTX   Combined Training Exercise
DAB   Defense Acquisition Board
DARPA   Defense Advanced Research Project Agency
DARWARS   DARPA's War Simulator
DAU   Defense Acquisition University
DICOM   Digital Imaging and Communications in Medicine
DIGRA   Digital Games Research Association
DIS   Distributed Interactive Simulation
DKE   Digital Knowledge Environment
DL   Distance Learning
DLIELC   Defense Language Institute English Language Center
DLL   Dynamic Link Library

DMSO   Defense Modeling and Simulation Office
DOD   Department of Defense
DSB   Defense Science Board
DSS   Decision Support System
DTC   Direct to Consumer
DTRA   Defense Threat Reduction Agency
DVTE   Distributed Virtual Training Environment
E3   Electronic Entertainment Expo
ESA   Entertainment Software Association
ESRB   Entertainment Software Ratings Board
ET   Embedded Training
EXCEL   Excellence through Commitment to Education and Learning (Naval task force)
FAR   Federal Acquisition Regulation
FCS   Future Combat System
FOM   Federation Object Model
FPDS-NG   Federal Procurement Data System—Next Generation
FTE   Full Time Equivalent
GAO   General Accounting Office
GDC   Game Developers Conference
GOTS   Government Off-The-Shelf (game software)
GPR   Government Purpose Rights
HLA   High Level Architecture
HLSL   High Level Scripting Language
HSARPA   Homeland Security Advanced Research Project Agency
ICC   International Color Consortium
ICRA   International Content Rating Association
ICS   International Classification for Standards
ICT   Institute for Creative Technology
IDA   Institute for Defense Analysis
IEC   International Electrotechnical Commission
IEEE   Institute of Electrical and Electronics Engineers
IGDA   International Game Developers Association
IGF   Independent Games Festival
IMAT   Interactive Multi-Analysis Trainer
IMI   Interactive Multimedia Instruction
IMS   Instructional Management System
IP   Intellectual Property
IRB   Institution Review Board
ISO   International Organization for Standardization
IT   Information Technology
ITS   Intelligent Tutoring System
ITLET   Information Technology for Learning, Education, and Training
J2ME   Java 2 Micro Edition
JANUS   Joint Army-Navy Uniform Simulation
JFCOM   Joint Forces Command
JNTC   Joint National Training Capability
JRO   Joint Requirements Office
JRTC   Joint Readiness Training Center

JSTO   Joint Science and Technology Office
JTASC   Joint Training Analysis and Simulation Center
JTC   Joint Technical Committee
KPI   Key Performance Indicator
KPP   Key Performance Parameter
KSA   Knowledge, Skills, and Attitudes
LMS   Learning Management System
LOM   Learning Object Metadata
LTSC   Learning Technology Standards Committee
LTSO   Learning Technology Standards Observatory
MDA   Missile Defense Agency
MMOG   Massively Multiplayer Online Game
MMORPG   Massively Multiplayer Online Role-Playing Game
MOA   Memorandum of Agreement
MOE   Measures of Effectiveness
MOP   Measures of Performance
MOTS   Modified Off-The-Shelf
MOU   Memorandum of Understanding
MRI   Magnetic Resonance Imaging
MTA   Material Transfer Agreement
NAICS   North American Industry Classification System
NASGA   North American Simulation and Gaming Association
NAVAIR   Naval Air Warfare Center
NEMA   National Electrical Manufacturers Association
NES   Nintendo Entertainment System
NIST   National Institute of Standards and Technology
NPC   Nonplayer Character
NPS   Naval Postgraduate School
NPSNET   Naval Postgraduate School Network
NSF   National Science Foundation
NUWC   Naval Undersea Warfare Center
NVC   National Voluntary Contribution
OEM   Original Equipment Manufacturer
OEMA   Office of Economic & Manpower Analysis
OJT   On the Job Training
OMDT   Object Model Development Tool
OMG   Object Management Group
OPEL   Open Platform for eLearning
OpenAL   Open Audio Library
OpenGL   Open Graphics Library
ORCA   Online Representations and Certification Application
ORD   Operational Requirements Document
OSD   Office of the Secretary of Defense
OSTP   White House Office of Science and Technology Policy
OUSD P&R   Office of the Under Secretary of Defense for Personnel and Readiness

PAO   Principle Action Office
PDA   Personal Digital Assistant
PDR   Preliminary Design Review
PEO STRI   U.S. Army Program Executive Office of the Strategic Instrumentation Command
PFP   Partnership For Peace
PKC   Public Key Cryptography
PLA   Patent License Agreement
PMA205   Naval Aviation's simulation directorate
PMTRASYS   Marine Corps. Systems Command Program Manager for Training Systems
POC   Proof of Concept
POP   Point of Purchase
POV   Point of View
PS2   PlayStation 2
PSP   PlayStation Portable (Sony)
PTO   Patent and Trademark Office
QA   Quality Assurance
QC   Quality Control
QWL   Quality of Work Life
RCM   Revenue Cycle Management
ROA   Return On Assets
ROE   Return On Equity
ROI   Return On Investment
RPQ   Request for Price Quotation
RTE   Run-Time Environment
RVU   Relative Value Unit
SAF   Semi-Automated Forces
SBIR   Small Business Innovation Research
SC   Subcommittee
SCC   Standards Council of Canada
SCEA   Sony Computer Entertainment America
SCEL   Synchronous Collaborative ELearning
SCM   Software Configuration Management
SCO   Sharable Content Object
SCORM   Sharable Content Object Reference Model
SDB   Small Disadvantaged Business
SGDD   Serious Games Design Document
SGI   Silicon Graphics, Inc.
SIG   Special Interest Group
SimNet   Simulation Network (U.S. Army)
SME   Subject Matter Expert
SOBT   Submarine On-Board Training
SOM   Simulation Object Model
SOW   Statement of Work
SPC   Statistical Process Control
SPEL   Self-Paced ELearning
SQL   Structured Query Language
STRICOM   Simulation Training and Instrumentation Command (U.S. Army)
STTR   Small Technology Transfer Resource
STX   Situation Training Exercise

SubSkillsNet   Submarine Skills-Training Network
T2   Training Transformation
TADSS   Training Aids, Devices, Simulators, and Simulators
TATRC   Telemedicine & Advanced Technology Research Center
TDD   Technical Design Document
TFADLAT   Total Force Advanced Distributed Learning Action Team
TGE   Torque Game Engine
TOR   Terms of Reference
TPP   Trading Partner Profile

UDDI   Universal Description, Discovery, and Integration
UMD   Universal Media Disc
UML   Unified Modeling Language
USAMRMC   United States Army Research and Materiel Command
VAST   Virtual At-Sea Training
VR   Virtual Reality
WBT   Web-Based Training
W3C   World Wide Web Consortium
XML   Extensible Markup Language
XNA   Microsoft's game development platform

C

FILE FORMATS

As the game development industry matures, the number of unique application file formats will diminish. For now, serious games developers have to contend with multiple format standards for graphics, fonts, animation and video, audio, databases, and game engines. The following list of standard formats is included for readers new to game development who might encounter Web sites offering content suitable for a particular project, but who have no idea of the applications that can be used to open or import the content.

Advanced readers who need detailed information, such as format file structures, how to convert from one format to another, and data compression methods, should consider investing in the massive *Encyclopedia of Graphics File Formats* [MurrayvanRyper96]. Although not as detailed, Wotsit's Format (*www.wotsit.org*), which is hosted by GameDev.Net, offers free information on hundreds of different file types, as well as algorithms, source code, and hardware specifications.

The medical formats listed at the end of this appendix are offered as an illustration of domain-specific formats that game developers might encounter. The list provided here is a sample of the hundreds of unique file formats used by the medical and biomedical communities. Because many of the medical formats are differentiated by header and body information as well as extension, they are listed by name with summary information.

TABLE C.1   Animation and Video

EXTENSION	APPLICATION
AVI	Microsoft Video for Windows
BVH	Biovision Motion Capture
FLC	Animator Pro
GIF	Animated GIFs
MPEG	Motion Picture Expert Group
PCS	PICS Animation

TABLE C.2   Audio

EXTENSION	APPLICATION/DESCRIPTION
AIF/SND	Apple Macintosh AIFF
AIFF	Audio Interchange File Format
ASF	Active Streaming Format
AU	Sun and NEXT machine format
AVI	AVI Video
CDA	CD Audio
CEL	Audition Loop
DBL	Raw sound format
DWD	DiamondWare Digitized
IFF/SVX	Amiga
MID	MIDI
MP3	MPEG Audio Layer—III
MPG/MP2/MPEG	MPEG Video
OGG	Ogg Vorbis Open Format
RA/RAM	Real Audio
SAM	8-Bit Singed
VOC	Creative Labs Sound Blaster
VOX	Dialogic ADPCM
WAV	Windows Waveform
WMA	Windows Media Audio

TABLE C.3   Databases

EXTENSION	APPLICATION
CSV	Comma Separated Value File
DBF	DBase file documentation
DDF	BTRIEVE database
DIF	Data Interchange Format
FP3	File Maker Pro
MDB	Microsoft Access
PDB	Palm Pilot
TXT	Text Database

TABLE C.4   Fonts

EXTENSION	APPLICATION
TTF	Truetype Font
PFA	Type 1 Font ASCII
PFB	Type 1 Font Binary

TABLE C.5   Game Engines

EXTENSION	APPLICATION
3D	Unreal/UT
AA	Serious Sam SKA
B3D	Blitz Basic
BDY/MOT	Genesis 3D
BSP	Quake Map
BW	Black and White
DCR	Macromedia Shockwave
DTS	Torque GE
MD2	Quake2
MD3	Quake3
PSA	UT2003
PSK	Unreal Engine Skeletal Mesh
SKN	The Sims
SMD	HalfLife

TABLE C.6 Graphics Formats

EXTENSION	APPLICATION
3DMF	3D Metafile Format
3DS/AM/AS	3D Studio
AI	Adobe Illustrator
ASC	ASCII
BDF	3ds max
BMP	Windows Bitmap File
BR5	Bryce 5
BVH	BioVision Motion Capture
CAN	Object Animation
CGM	Computer Graphics Metafile
COB	Caligari Truespace
DXF	AutoCAD
EPS	Encapsulated PostScript
GIF	Graphics Interchange Format
ICB	Targa Bitmap
ICO	Windows Icon
IDD	MIDI Instrument
INFINI-D	Infini-D
ISS	iSpace Scenes
JIF/JFF	JPEG Bitmap
JPEG	Joint Photographic Experts Group
LUV	Lithium UnWrapper
LWO	LightWave
MAX	3ds Max
MDL	GameStudio
MS3D	MilkShape
MSP	Microsoft Paint bitmap
MTX	Viewpoint
OBJ	Wavefront
OOGL	Object Oriented Graphics Library
OPENGL	OpenGL
PCX	PC Paintbrush

PNG	Portable Network Graphics
PSD	Photoshop
PSP	Paint Shop Pro
PZ3	Poser
QT	Quicktime
RAW	Raw
RGB	Red Green Blue Color Space
RIB	RenderMan
SCN	TrueSpace/Calgari Scenes
SGI	Silicon Graphics Image
SWF	Macromedia Flash
TEX	Texture
TGA	Targa image file format
TIFF	Tagged Image File Format (bitmap)
VDA	Targa Bitmap
VRML	Virtual Reality Modeling Language
W3D	Macromedia 3D
WMF	Windows Metafile Format
WRL	VRML Scenes
X	DirectX
XSI	SoftImage

TABLE C.7   Medical Formats

NAME	SUMMARY
Analyze	Mayo Clinic Analyze application format: *www.mayo.edu/bir/software/analyze*.
DICOM3	Digital Imaging and Communications in Medicine 3.0 Image format: *www.nema.org*.
GE Advance	General Electric Positron Emission Tomography format: *www.gehealthcare.com*.
GE MRI Genesis 5	One of several proprietary General Electric Magnetic Resonance Imaging formats: *www.gehealthcare.com*.
PhysioBank	Archive of biomedical signal data: *www.physionet.org/physiobank*.

Protein Data Bank	RCSB Protein Data Bank repository of 3-D biological macromolecular structure data: *www.rcsb.org/pdb*.
Siemens CT	Siemens computed tomography format: *www.siemens.com*
Siemens PET	Siemens Positron Emission Tomography format: *www.siemens.com*.
SMIS	Surrey Medical Imaging Systems (SMIS) Magnetic Resonance Imaging format: *www.medical.philips.com*.

REFERENCES

[MurrayvanRyper96] Murray, James and William van Ryper, *Encyclopedia of Graphics File Formats*. O'Reilly & Associates, 1996.

SERIOUS GAMES DESIGN DOCUMENT OUTLINE

Following is an outline for a serious game design document, based on several of the serious medical games described in the text. In re-purposing this outline for other projects, the relative emphasis of the subcomponents of each section, which are keyed to the development pipeline in Figure D.1, should reflect the development environment, the complexity of the game, the serious content, and whether custom hardware is required.

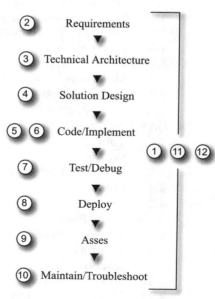

FIGURE D.1 Serious games design document outline indexed to the development pipeline.

A BRIEF BUSINESS PLAN PRIMER

A sound business plan, like a talented game development team, is critical for success in the serious games development business. The following primer is based on the authors' work developing serious games for pharmaceutical, medical education, and consumer industries, his work at Harvard/MIT, as well as his work evaluating business plans for a major venture capital firm.

Readers who intend to invest the month or more required to develop a viable business plan should consider partnering with someone skilled in the art and read through as many *funded* plans as possible. Readers should also work through the online tutorials and business plan templates freely available through the Small Business Association (SBA) at *www.sba.gov/starting_business/planning/basic.html*. An invaluable game-specific resource is Laramee's *Secrets of the Game Business* [Laramee03].

Although there is no single correct format for a serious games business plan, every successful business plan addresses six core issues:

- Vision and Mission
- Business Structure
- Product Strategy
- Market Analysis
- Marketing Plan
- Financial Plan

Often, a business plan is folded in to the serious game design document to establish the business credibility of the developer. A good business plan doesn't guarantee that the developer will manage the proposed game development in a way that turns a profit. However, a deficient business plan will prompt prospective investors to avoid the development shop, even if it has an amazing talent pool. Following is an abbreviated business plan outline that highlights the six core elements.

EXECUTIVE SUMMARY

Following is a one-page summary of the business plan, highlighting the core issues listed previously.

Vision and Mission

Present Situation: The present financial, product, and human resources status of the business. It might be a startup with no assets other than a design document or an established shop with positive cash flow and new titles ready for release.

Vision and Mission: The vision and mission of the development shop, including short- and long-term goals and objectives. The reader of the business plan should come away with a clear understanding of where the development shop is heading.

Business Structure

Legal Business Description: The legal structure of the business, as recognized by the federal and state governments. Common structures range from C- and S-corporations to limited liability corporations to partnerships and sole proprietorships.

Functional Business Description Potential: Investors want to know whether the business will be operated as a centralized operation, where all intellectual property contributors are in-house, or as a decentralized operation in which much of the intellectual property contribution is from outside sources. The business plan should make this explicit, on a function-by-function basis, as per Figure E.1.

Management Team: The management team, including the Board of Directors and Board of Advisors. Biographies relating the relevant business experience of the team, as well as an organizational chart, should be included.

Strategic Alliances: Formal and informal strategic alliances with other business and content entities. For example, the developer of a serious medical game might have ties to a hospital or academic medical center to insure quality medical content. Complex alliances should be depicted graphically.

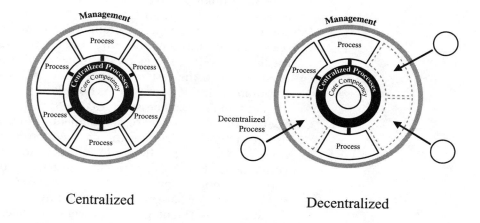

Centralized   Decentralized

FIGURE E.1   Centralized versus decentralized functional business description.

Product Strategy

Current Product: Define the product strategy that applies to the proposed serious game. An example of a product strategy in the serious medical game space is to enter one specialty, say emergency medicine, and then after the game is established, move the same or modified game to another specialty area.

Research and Development: Define the research and development strategy, including the proportion of income reinvested in research and development. Successful businesses gain traction and visibility with their initial game offerings and reinvest earning into developing the next titles.

Production and Delivery: A detailed description of production and delivery, including exactly how the development pipeline will be implemented, including software tools and how the finished game will be delivered to customers.

Market Analysis

Market Definition: Provide a definition of the market that can be used to estimate the demand of the game after it is released. This definition typically references the entire possible market and then assumes some rate of penetration, for example, 1.5 percent of a $200 million market for emergency response training for emergency medical technicians.

Customer Profile: Typical customer demographics, such as age, sex, vocation, income, and other indices that can help identify the best marketing strategies. Customer profiles might be known precisely, as in the case of serious games developed for internal corporate training. More often, however, profiles are based on market samples and guesstimates.

Competition: A definition of the competitors in the marketplace. A useful method of defining the competition is through a Porter Analysis, developed by Harvard Business School Professor Michael Porter [Porter85]. This approach analyzes the competitive forces within the serious games industry in five areas:

- Buyers—The bargaining power of buyers
- Suppliers—The bargaining power of suppliers
- Substitutes—The threat of substitutes
- Potential Entrants—The threat of new entrants
- Industry—The level of competition within the established industry

A Porter Analysis is typically depicted graphically as in Figure E.2. The entries within each of the five categories offered here reflect the industry as a whole and do not reflect a specific market niche within the serious games space. For example, the industry as a whole can be categorized as highly competitive, with confusion in the marketplace as to what the apparent oxymoron *serious games* means. The industry is also in the midst of a shakeout, with significant and frequent mergers and acquisitions.

From the perspective of substitutes, there are threats from traditional teaching, traditional computer aided instruction, training videos, and books. The industry is also at the mercy of tool makers and publishers. There are many potential buyers, but uncertain demand. The industry is fragmented, in part because of the diverse needs of potential buyers. For example, the training needs of the healthcare industry are often different from those of the military.

Finally, from the perspective of potential entrants to the industry, there are low barriers to entry, thanks to new tools that can be used by anyone in the large pool of post-dot-com Web developers. Switching costs are low for Web developers because many of the development tools are common to the Web and game development industries.

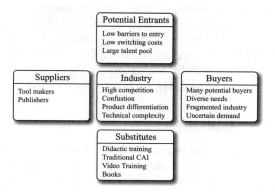

FIGURE E.2   A generic Porter Analysis of competitors in the serious games industry. An analysis for a business plan should be more focused on a particular niche in the industry.

Risk: A detailed analysis of the financial risks of the proposed game development, from technological, human resource, and financial perspectives. For example, returning to the Functional Business Description given previously, the risks inherent in a centralized model include the inability to reduce HR expenditures during downturns without firing employees. Conversely, a risk associated with the decentralized model is that the core competencies necessary for completion of the game—especially domain-specific knowledge in the military, medicine, or other serious games subject area—might reside in consultants. Faced with other demands on their time, consultants may be unavailable to contribute to the project.

Marketing Plan

Sales Strategy: Define the sales strategy, in terms of product, price, and promotion. Even if a serious game is developed for internal use within a corporation, military, or other closed environment, the intended users often have to be sold on the importance of investing their time and energy in playing the game.

Distribution Channels: Define the distribution channels, such as packaged CD-ROM ,Web download, or local area network.

Advertising and Promotion: Describe the advertising and promotion plan. As noted earlier, even if a serious game is designed for a captive audience, they usually have to be sold on not simply going through the motions of using the game.

Public Relations: Detail how the business will handle public relations, including publications in print and on the Web.

Financial Plan

Assumptions: Define the basic assumptions behind the business, including the expected rate and amount of return or, for a non-profit, the whether the operation will be self-sustaining or require a constant infusion of funds.

Financial Statements: If the business is operating, provide the financial statements showing monthly cash flow, loans, and liabilities.

Capital Requirements: Define the projected short- and long-term capital requirements for the life of the development project and provide the data behind the projections.

Exit/Payback Strategy: Define how investors will exit from the business and what guarantees, if any, the business can extend to investors.

Supporting Documents

Back-up statistics and assertions, especially those relating to market potential and risk, with references from reputable sources.

REFERENCE

[Porter85] Porter, Michael, *Competitive Advantage: Creating and Sustaining Superior Performance.* Free Press, 1985.
[Laramee03] Laramee, François, *Secrets of the Game Business.* Charles River Media, 2003.

APPENDIX

F

RESOURCES

The following collection of online and print resources includes funding sources; academic, corporate, and military resources; and developer organizations.

ACADEMIA

Academic organizations and publishers involved in serious games initiatives.

Campus Technology: A monthly publication focusing exclusively on the use of technology across all areas of higher education. *www.campus-technology.com.*

Digital Games Research Association (DIGRA): A nonprofit, international association of academics and practitioners whose work focuses on digital games and associated activities. *www. digra.org.*

Experimental Game Lab: A laboratory within UCSD's Center for Research in Computing and the Arts that is concerned with next-generation gaming. *www.experimentalgamelab.net.*

MIT Comparative Media Studies: A program at MIT that explores media technologies and their cultural, social, aesthetic, political, ethical, legal, and economic implications. *ocw.mit.edu.*

SimWorkshops: A TATRC-sponsored series of workshops designed to develop a community of researchers and educators, explore fundamental issues and barriers to simulation-based learning, and promote evaluation of simulation-based learning in clinically-related learning environments. The Readings section of the Web site provides a wealth of information on the academic evaluation of games. *simworkshops.stanford.edu.*

The Education Arcade: A consortium of international game designers, publishers, scholars, educators, and policy makers who are exploring the new frontiers of educational media that have been opened by computer and video games. *www.educationarcade.org.*

BUSINESS DEVELOPMENT

Business development resources for the serious game development community.

Small Business Innovation Research Program (SBIR):   A competitive program that encourages small business to explore their technological potential and provides the incentive to create commercial products. The SBA (Small Business Association) is the coordinating group for all ten federal departments and agencies that participate in the program. *www.sba.gov/sbir/indexsbir-sttr.html.*

Small Business Technology Transfer Program (STTR):   A highly competitive program that reserves a specific percentage of federal R&D funding for award to small business and nonprofit research institution partners. Unlike the SBIR program, an academic partner is required to receive funding from the government. *www.sba.gov/sbir/indexsbir-sttr.html.*

United States Small Business Administration (SBA):   The organization tasked with maintaining and strengthening the nation's economy by aiding, counseling, assisting and protecting the interests of small businesses. *www.sba.gov.*

Sloperama: A personal Web site with numerous links and short articles on the gaming business that pertains directly to serious game developers and development. *www.sloperama.com.*

CONFERENCES

The most important general conferences for serious games developers include the Game Developer Conference (GDC) and the Serious Games Summits. Developers should also consider attending domain-specific conferences related to the serious subject matter of their games.

Austin Game Conference (AGC):   A two-day annual conference designed to educate and inform game industry professionals on online games for PCs, mobile devices and console systems. First held in 2004. *www.gameconference.com.*

International Consumer Electronics Show (CES):   An annual event sponsored, produced, and managed by the Consumer Electronics Manufacturers Association (CEMA). Covers all areas of consumer electronics. *www.cesweb.org.*

Electronic Entertainment Expo (E3):   The annual electronic blitz in Los Angeles that includes games in the wider context of entertainment. *www.e3expo.com.*

Game Developer Conference Europe (GDC Euro):   The must-attend conference for serious games developers in Europe. *www.gdceurope.com.*

Game Developers Conference (GDC):   The annual trade conference by game developers and for developers of computer, console, hand-held, arcade, location-based, and online games. The first annual Serious Games Summit was held at the 2004 GDC. *www.gdconf.com.*

Games+Learning+Society (GLS):   An academic meeting sponsored by the Madison School of Education and Academic ADL Co-Lab. *www.glsconference.org.*

Independent Game Festival (IGF):   Established in 1988, the festival encourages innovation in game development through annual events where independent game developers compete for cash prizes and media coverage. *www.igf.com.*

Interservice/Industry Training, Simulation, and Education Conference (I/ITSEC):   Promotes cooperation among the Armed Services, Industry, Academia and various Government agencies in pursuit of improved training and education programs, identification of common training issues and development of multiservice programs. *www.iitsec.org.*

Medicine Meets Virtual Reality (MMVR):   This annual conference is the leading forum for researchers and developers of information-based tools for clinical care and medical education. The conference is normally held in collaboration with the Telemedicine and Advanced Technology Research Center of the U.S. Army. *www.nextmed.com/mmvr_virtual_reality.html.*

Milia: This annual conference, held in Cannes, France, bills itself as the leading global forum for owners, buyers and distributors of digital content and new interactive technologies. *www.milia.com.*

Association of Broadcasters (NAB):   The world's leading conference and exhibition for the converging electronic media communications industries. *www.nab.org/conventions.*

Serious Games Summit: Held annually on the east and west coasts, this is the conference for current and future serious games developers. *www.seriousgamessummit.com.*

Siggraph: Conference for researchers, artists, developers, filmmakers, scientists, and other professionals who share an interest in computer graphics and interactive techniques. *www.siggraph.org.*

Tokyo Game Show: The premiere computer entertainment show, first held in 1996. *tgs.cesa.or.jp/english.*

Video Game/Entertainment Industry, Technology and Medicine Conference (VEITMC):   A forum for serious games in medicine.

Women's Game Conference (WGC):   Focuses on women in the computer and video game industry. Held in conjunction with the Austin Game Conference. First held in 2004. *www.womensgame-conference.com.*

GAME DESIGN

Complete examples of serious game design documents are relatively scarce, in part because they often contain proprietary or sensitive information. The resources listed here, while general in nature, should be reviewed by readers new to game design.

***Game Design: The Art and Business of Creating Games, Second edition*:**   By Bob Bates, Premier Press/Course PTR, 2004. This book—one of several by a noted game industry expert—provides an excellent overview of what's involved in crafting a game design document.

Gamasutra: This online resource for game developers of all genres offers several tutorials on game design and game design documents. Notable are Tim Ryan's *The Anatomy of a Design Document, Part 1: Documentation Guidelines for the Game Concept and Proposal,* and Tzvi Freeman's *Creating a Great Design Document. www.gamasutra.com.*

GAME ENGINES

Listed here is a sample of the game engines—sometimes more appropriately called game development environments—for developing serious games and/or game prototypes for concept demonstrations. Engines such as Gamebryo, Torque, Delta3D, and Unreal are more capable and market, proven than some of the alternatives. However, these engines may be overwhelming to developers in a traditional simulation or online courseware shop who are attempting to migrate their work to a game environment.

3D GameStudio: One of the more powerful of the entry-level game engines for developers willing to climb a modest learning curve. A minor inconvenience is that some of the demos and tutorials are available only in German. The one-time license fee for the professional version is about $800. *www.conitec.net*.

Cipher Game Engine: Affordable ($100), powerful engine for royalty-free game development. Not as feature-packed as engines such as Gamebryo or Unreal 3, but it can be extended by developers fluent in C++. Source code is provided with the license. *www.cipherengine.com*.

DarkBasic Pro: Thanks to a BASIC language wrapper and a large online community, the learning curve of this development environment is extremely short, allowing developers and students to focus on overall game design. It makes a good prototyping environment on the PC, regardless of how the final game is coded. Games developed in the $130 environment are royalty free. *www.theGameCreators.com*.

Delta3D: Free, open source software from the Moves Institute. Several components are under development, but the available tools are impressive. Installation requires Microsoft's .NET environment. *www.delta3d.org*.

Gamebryo: A powerful, proven cross-platform engine and component-based toolset. See the Web site for screen shots of serious military games developed with Gamebryo. From Numerical Design Limited (NDL). *www.ndl.com*.

Game Gardens: A free, open source development toolkit for simple multiplayer games. *Gamegardens.com*.

Macromedia Shockwave Player: Developers familiar with Macromedia Director (about $1,200) can produce Internet-based 3D games that execute on the free Shockwave player. *www.Macromedia.com*.

PopCap Framework: An open source toolkit designed to create games for the casual gamer. PopCap encourages publishing any game developed with their framework on their Web site. *Developer.popcap.com*.

Second Life: Best described as a MMOG designed for modification, this subscription-based 3D online environment supports game development. An array of graphical authoring tools, a built-in physics engine, and a scripting language enable serious games developers to create interactive, multiplayer games. It's worth visiting the Web site, if only to read the full description of the 3D online world. *Secondlife.com.*

Torque: Affordable ($100), feature-packed, multi-platform engine with a track record of several commercial titles. Source code is available with the license. *www.garagegames.com.*

Unreal Engine 3:   This top-tier game engine and associated toolset features a visual scripting system, impressive physics, and advanced graphics capabilities. *www.unrealtechnology.com.*

Because game engine versions and capabilities change frequently, the best source for game engine information is online. A good source for the latest information on commercial and open-source game engines is Dev-Master.net. The site provides details of vendor-submitted product information in its 3D Engines Database, as well as a forum for independent game developers. *www.DevMaster.net.*

ONLINE INFORMATION SOURCES

The following online information sources provide an up-to-the-minute view of the gaming industry and the latest research relevant to serious games development. Many also provide information on career opportunities in the game development industry.

1Up.Com: An often-quoted Web site with news of the game industry. *www.1up.com.*

Adrenaline Vault: News, reviews, and downloads of recently released game files. *www.avault.com.*

American Association of Artificial Intelligence: This nonprofit scientific society maintains a compendium of information about artificial intelligence and computer games under the topic Video Games, Toys, Robotic Pets & Entertainment. *www.aaai.org/AITopics/html/video.html#good.*

Bluesnews: General game news. *www.bluesnews.com.*

CMP Game Group: A group within international CMP Media LLC that covers and supports the Game Developers Conference, *Game Developer* magazine, Gamasutra.com, the Independent Games Festival, and the Game Developers Choice Awards. *www.cmpgame.com.*

Digitalmill: Co-founded by Ben Sawyer, who has been instrumental in elevating public and developer awareness of and interest in serious games. Together with the Woodrow Wilson International Center for Scholars, founded the Serious Games Initiative. *www.Dmill.com.*

Flipcode: Daily game development news and resources. *www.flip-code.com.*

Gamasutra: Online game development magazine and community with weekly articles and news. *www.gamasutra.com.*

GameDailyBiz: Game industry newsletter. *www.gamedaily.com.*

Gamedev.net: General resources with an emphasis on tools and techniques. *www.gamedev.net.*

GameJobs: Provides listings of jobs in the game industry. *www.gamejobs.com.*

Game Research and Technology: An extensive Web site with links to research on the technology of games. *www.red3d.com/cwr/games.*

Gamesindustry.biz: Game development, publishing, retail, and distribution in the U.K.. *www.Gamesindustry.biz.*

Games-Match: Listings of jobs in the game industry. *www.games-match.com.* For jobs in the United Kingdom, check the sister site, *www.games-match.co.uk.*

GameSpot: Extensive library of game information for players, with useful game walkthroughs. *www.gamespot.com.*

GameSpy: Industry news and game information from the player's perspective. *www.gamespy.com.*

Gametab: A collected game news digest of many other news sites. *www.gametab.com.*

International Game Developers Association (IGDA):   A non-profit professional membership organization that advocates globally on issues related to digital game creation. The IGDA also presents the Game Developers Choice Award at the annual Game Developers Conference. *www.igda.org*

Ludology.org: An online resource for video game researchers. *www.ludology.org.*

Mary-Margaret: Jobs for game professionals. *www.mary-margaret.com.*

North American Simulation and Gaming Association (NASGA):   A network of professionals working on the design, implementation, and evaluation of games and simulations to improve learning results in all types of organizations. *www.nasaga.org.*

NPD Funworld: Sales and marketing information for manufacturers and retailers in the toy and video game industries. *www.npdfunworld.com.*

NPD Group: Sales and marketing information for consumer electronics and video games. *www.npd.com.*

Persuasive Games: Designers and builders of political/persuasive games (*www.persuasivegames.com*).

Public Interest Entertainment Corporation (PIECORP): A nonprofit organization dedicated to using the technology of games to make a difference in society, and to develop open source, open development, open publishing, and open distribution tools. *www.piecorp.org.*

Serious Games Newsletter: An online newsletter as a service of the Serious Games Initiative at the Woodrow Wilson International Center for Scholars, Breakaway Games, Ltd., and Digitalmill, Inc. *www.seriousgames.org.*

Social Impact Games: An excellent source for examples of serious games in various categories. *www.socialimpactgames.com.*

Society for Modeling and Simulation International (SCS): The principal technical society devoted to the advancement of simulation and allied computer arts in all fields. Although not a gaming organization per se, the resources available through the organization and its Web site should be of value to serious game developers. *www.scs.org.*

Water Cooler Games: This Web site is an excellent forum for the uses of video games in advertising, politics, advocacy, and other non-entertainment purposes. *www.watercoolergames.org.*

INTELLECTUAL PROPERTY

Astute developers take steps to protect their intellectual property before development even begins.

Nolo Press: Offers do-it-yourself legal solutions for copyright, trademark, and patent applications, as well as non-disclosure agreements. A good place to start, even if you eventually hire an attorney. *www.nolo.com.*

United States Patent and Trademark Office: Online tutorials, forms, and search engines for trademarks, servicemarks, and copyrights. *www.uspto.gov.*

MEDICAL ORGANIZATIONS

Medical organizations are second only to the military in funding serious games development. Organizations involved in using serious games to educate the public and healthcare providers are listed here.

American Medical Association: The largest physician's group in the U.S. is involved with a variety of distance learning activities. *www.ama-assn.org.*

American Medical Informatics Association: A nonprofit membership organization of individuals, institutions, and corporations dedicated to developing and using information technologies to improve health care. *www.amia.org.*

Center for Medical Simulation (CMS):   An educational organization dedicated to improving the quality of health care through teaching teamwork and clinical decision making using simulation. CMS offers programs for physicians, nurses, technicians, and industry personnel using its simulated clinical environment. *www.harvardmedsim.org.*

Games For Health: Promotes best practices, community building, and research into how game technologies can be used in direct patient applications, personal health education, and workforce initiatives. The organization supports an annual meeting of the same name. www.gamesforhealth.org.

MedBiquitous: An international group of professional medical and healthcare associations, universities, commercial, and governmental organizations dedicated to advancing healthcare education through technology standards that promote professional competence, collaboration, and better patient care. *www. MedBiq.org.*

Robert Wood Johnson Foundation: The nation's largest philanthropy organization devoted exclusively to health and health care. Supports the Games For Health initiative, among others. Accepts independent, unsolicited proposals. Preference is given to applicants that are public agencies or are tax-exempt. *www.rwjf.org.*

Simulation Development and Cognitive Science Lab: A multidepartmental collaboration between the Anesthesia, Surgery, and Nursing Departments at the Pennsylvania State University College of Medicine. The lab's Web site provides an extensive list of commercial and academic medical simulations that may be of interest to serious game developers in the medical space. *www.hmc.psu.edu/simulation.*

MILITARY ORGANIZATIONS

The following military organizations are using gaming technology for training and simulation, and represent opportunities for serious games developers.

> **Advanced Distributed Learning:**   An initiative sponsored by the Office of the Secretary of Defense (OSD) that is a collaborative effort between government, industry, and academia to establish a new distributed learning environment that permits the interoperability of learning tools and course content on a global scale. *www.adlnet.org.*
>
> **Telemedicine and Advanced Technology Research Center (TATRC):**   This subordinate element of the United States Army Research and Materiel Command (USAMRMC) is charged with managing core Research Development Test and Evaluation (RDT&E) and congressionally mandated projects in telemedicine and advanced medical technologies. TATRC maintains a productive mix of partnerships with federal, academic, and commercial organizations in developing, evaluating, and demonstrating new technologies, including gaming, in healthcare and healthcare support. See their Web site for regular broad area announcements. *www.tatrc.org.*

MULTIMEDIA SOURCES

Containing development costs of serious games means using prefabricated models, textures, and stock music whenever possible. The following include major sources of multimedia.

> **3-D-Models.com:**   Hard-to-find anatomical models as well as military props in all major formats. *www.3-d-models.com.*
>
> **3DRT.com:**   3D models of cars, space vehicles, and characters. *www.3drt.com.*
>
> **DAZ Productions:**   A must-visit site for Poser, Mimic, Bryce, and Mimic models and textures. *www.3dlinks.com.*
>
> **Leonardo Software:**   Royalty-free sound effects. *www.leonardosoft.com.*
>
> **Neo Sounds:**   Royalty-free music and sound effects. *www.neosounds.com.*
>
> **Opuzz:**   Royalty-free music. *www.opuzz.com.*
>
> **PhysioBank:**   An archive of more than 1000 freely available recordings of annotated, digitized physiologic signals, such as EKGs. An excellent resource for developers of medical games. *www.physionet.org/physiobank.*
>
> **Renderosity:**   Offers thousands of 2D and 3D models in every major format. Most items are of good to excellent quality and in the $10–$20 range. *www.renderosity.com.*

Sounddogs.com: Royalty-free sound effects. *www.sounddogs.com*.

SoundRangers: Royalty-free   music   and   sound   effects. *www.soundrangers.com*.

Texture Library: A private collection of freely available textures. *astronomy.swin.edu.au/~pbourke/texture/*

The 3D Studio: A good source for 3D models from independent developers. *www.the3dstudio.com*.

TheGameCreators: Offers *DarkMatter*, a collection of 3D models and textures ($40). *www.thegamecreators.com*.

TurboSquid: 3D models and textures. Some of the best (and more expensive) medical anatomy models available. *turbosquid.com*.

Ultimate 3D Links: Textures, 3D models, animations, plug-ins, and software. *www.3dlinks.com*.

MUST PLAY

Serious game designers don't just make games—they also play them. A short-list of games worth playing—and studying—includes:

Age of Empires: The epic real-time strategy game.

America's Army: Probably the most successful marketing game in history.

Animal Crossing: Think of *The Sims* for kids. In the course of game-play, kids learn about investing, bartering, dozens of insect and fish names, and the importance of establishing a social network. For the Nintendo Game Cube.

Atari Plug & Play: There's a lot to learn from the 10 retro titles on the inexpensive TV Games unit.

Civilization III: Sets the standard for computer strategy games.

Dance Dance Revolution: Experience a new type of hardware interface.

Ghost Recon 3:   One of the fist titles out that shows the potential of the Xbox 360.

Gran Turismo: The equivalent of Microsoft Flight Simulator on wheels, complete with accurate scenery.

Grand Theft Auto: See why the thought police are up in arms over entertainment video games—if you can manage to find a copy of the original version.

Half Life 2:   Amazing graphics are responsible for sales of high-end video cards.

Halo/Halo 2: The quintessential military first-person shooters.

Katmari Damacy: A pleasant break from traditional game formats.

Knights of the Old Republic: The Star Wars game that won the 2003 game of the year award.

Munch's Oddysee: Explore the power of NPC AI.

MyPyramid: Kids explore the USDA food pyramid and the importance of physical activity. *teamnutrition.usda.gov.*

Pikmin I and II: Top seller on the Nintendo Game Cube.

The Sims: A nonviolent game with amazing user control and wide appeal.

Xbox Live: Experience the emotionally intelligent side of gameplay.

Must Reads

Every serious games developer should have a working familiarity with the following titles.

Books

21st-Century Game Design by Chris Bateman and Richard Boon. Charles River Media, 2006. An excellent review of the theoretical underpinnings of practical game design. Unlike many books that stress theory, this book provides theory that can be readily put to practice.

Digital Game-Based Learning by Marc Prensky. McGraw-Hill, 2000. One of the first books to tackle the subject of game-based learning for adults. Marc is also an experienced game developer.

Game Development Business and Legal Guide by Ashley Salisbury. Premier Press, 2003. For the management set.

Game Level Design by Ed Byrne. Charles River Media, 2005. Provides a good overview of the practical development process.

Game Programming Tricks of the Trade by Lorenzo Phillips. Premier Press, 2002. Weighted to entertainment games and engines, but contains several useful pearls.

On-Demand Learning: Training in the New Millennium by Darin Hartley. HRD Press, 2000. Provides a good perspective of where games and other educational technologies have a place in education.

Postmortems from Game Developer: Insights from the Developers of Unreal Tournament, Black and White, Age of Empires, and Other Top-Selling Games by Austin Grossman. CMP Books, 2003. An excellent collection from *Game Developer* magazine.

Programming Believable Characters for Computer Games by Penny Baillie-de Byl. Charles River Media, 2004. A good mix of AI, physics, and interface design essentials.

Rules of Play: Game Design Fundamentals by Katie Salen and Eric Zimmerman. MIT Press, 2004. A bit on the theoretical side, this book provides an excellent grounding for students of game design. Eric runs a successful game development shop in New York.

Secrets of the Game Business by François Laramee. Charles River Media, 2003. A good business primer for game developers.

Simulations and the Future of Learning: An Innovative (and Perhaps Revolutionary) Approach to e-Learning by Clark Aldrich. Pfeiffer, 2003. A provocative look at developing business leadership skills with games and simulations.

The Game Asset Pipeline by Ben Carter. The title says it all. Charles River Media, Inc., 2004.

Theory of Fun for Game Design by Ralph Koster. Paraglyph, 2004. This book is as fun to read as the topic suggests. Ralph is also a regular at the Serious Games Summits.

What Video Games Have to Teach Us about Learning and Literacy by James Gee. Palgrave Macmillan, 2004. For the academics out there, James Gee lends credibility to the field of serious games.

Magazines

Game Developer: The must-read monthly on the game development industry. The annual *Game Career Guide* provides the often cited salary survey as well as a school directory.

NICHE READS

These books and magazines won't appeal to every serious games developer, but for niche areas, like embedded hardware-based game development, they're invaluable.

Books and Monographs

AI Game Development: Synthetic Creatures with Learning and Reactive Behaviors by A. J. Champandard. New Riders Publishing, 2004. A good overview of AI middleware and engines.

Beginning Game Audio Programming by Mason McCuskey. Premier Press a division of Course Technology, 2003. A necessary reference for audio-challenged developers.

Break Into The Game Industry: How to Get A Job Making Video Games, by Ernest Adams. McGraw-Hill Osborne Media, 2003. An excellent introduction to the overall game development industry.

The book features a listing of schools by state and insightful "day in the life" scenarios.

Enhancing Simulations, Models and Their Impact Using Interactive Game Design and Development Practices and Technology by Ben Sawyer. The white paper on serious games is available as a PDF. *wwics.si.edu/subsites/game/Serious2.pdf.*

Game Programming with Python, Lua, and Ruby by Thomas Gutschmidt. Premier Press, a Division of Course Technology, 2004. For readers who want to roll their own with a high-level scripting language.

Game Developer's Market Guide, by Bob Bates, Premier Press/Course PTR, 2003. An excellent overview of the game development industry, especially for readers new to the field.

Get in the Game: Careers in the Game Industry, by Marc Mencher, New Riders Games, 2002. A good resource for readers trying to break into the field. In addition to an extensive list of resources, a sister Web site, *www.gamerecruiter.com/gamebook*, provides job listings and career tips.

Mathematics for 3D Game Programming and Computer Graphics by Eric Lengyel. Charles River Media, 2002. For readers who need to brush up on vector algebra and other essentials.

Mathematics for Game Developers by Christopher Tremblay. Premier Press; Thomson Course Technology PTR, 2004. A good reference book with game-relevant examples.

Microcontroller Projects Using the Basic Stamp by Al Williams. 2nd edition. CMP Books, 2002. A great place to start learning about microcontrollers. Includes a microcontroller simulator on CD-ROM.

Physics for Game Developers by David Bourg. O'Reilly & Associates, 2002. An excellent reference. Equivalent to Conger's book.

Physics Modeling For Game Programmers by David Conger. Thomson Course Technology, 2004. It's a tossup between this and Bourg's book. Either one makes a great reference.

The Art of Electronics by Paul Horowitz and Winfield Hill. Second Edition. Cambridge University Press, 1989. This is *the* reference book for every serious games developer working on games that use embedded hardware.

The Use of Computer and Video Games for Learning: A review of the literature by Alice Mitchell and Carol Savil-Smith. A comprehensive review of the literature and recommendations. From the Learning and Skill Development Agency, UK. A PDF of the monograph is available online. *www.lsda.org.uk/files/PDF/1529.pdf.*

What's a Microcontroller? by Parallax. One of several free downloads from Parallax. *www.parallax.com.*

Young Children and Technology by Susan Haugland and June Right. Alyn & Bacon, 1997. An excellent reference for developers working in the K–12 market who don't want to repeat the mistakes of the edutainment developers of the 1980s.

Magazines

There are dozens of magazines that can help serious games developers enhance their craft and understand the constantly changing landscape of game development. Interestingly, the best magazines tend to come from the U.K. There is a premium for the imports, but they're worth it.

Animation Magazine: For the professional animator.

C++ Users Journal: A serious journal for game programmers who code in C++.

Circuit Cellar: Aimed at the serious hardware enthusiast, it's a good source for information on embedded systems.

Computer Gaming World: A monthly update on what's hot in gaming.

Computer Graphics World: For the graphic artists in the development shop.

CPU: Computer Power User: For power PC users.

Develop: The European trade monthly for game developers.

Dr. Dobb's Journal: Pearls for hard-core programmers.

Edge: A U.K. journal with great glossy photos of what's new in the gaming world.

Electronic Gaming Monthly: Gaming news and reviews. Available as an electronic subscription.

Game Informer: Another general gaming news source.

Game Pro: A multiplatform gaming magazine targeting the teen reader.

Nuts & Volts: Microcontrollers, robotics, and other electronics. Not limited to computer electronics, like most other hardware magazines.

Official Playstation Magazine: The official word from Sony.

PC Gamer: A gamer's perspective on the game world.

PC Modder: Information on the bleeding edge of computing, including how to modify PCs for maximum performance.

PCExtreme: Excellent hardware tutorials. From the U.K.

PC Pilot: The best serious flight simulation magazine on the market. Another U.K. magazine.

The Hollywood Reporter: As the distinction between movies and games diminishes, events in Hollywood are more relevant to the game developer community.

Wired: For keeping up with general technology trends.

World: A magazine from the U.K. for serious 3D art developers. The accompanying CD-ROM with demos and samples is worth the subscription.

Xbox Magazine: The official Xbox magazine. Buy it for the demo disc and play the half-dozen demos each month, just to stay on top of what's available in the entertainment market.

STANDARDS ORGANIZATIONS

Advances in serious gaming depend on establishing and following industry standards. The following organizations are resources for standards associated with serious gaming.

Advanced Distance Learning (ADL):   A DOD and White House Office of Science and Technology Policy (OSTP) initiative designed to ensure ubiquitous access to education materials tailored to individual learner needs. Responsible for the SCORM standard. *www.adl.org*.

Aviation Industry Computer-Based Training Committee (AICC):   An international association of technology-based training professionals that develops guidelines for the development, delivery, and evaluation of CBT and related training technologies in the aviation industry. The AICC actively coordinates its efforts with broader learning technology standards organizations like IMS, ADL, and IEEE/LTSC. *www.aicc.org*.

IMS Global Learning Consortium: A nonprofit consortium of hardware and software vendors, educational institutions, publishers, government agencies, systems integrators, multimedia content providers, and other consortia that develops and promotes the adoption of open technical specifications for interoperable learning technology. IMS specifications and related publications are made available to the public at no charge. *www.imsproject.org*.

National Institute of Standards and Technology (NIST):   This government agency provides a variety of resources for game developers, including the Dictionary of Algorithms and Data Structures for Programmers. *www.nist.gov*.

World Wide Web Consortium (W3C):   The XML Working Group within the W3C was responsible for developing XML in 1996, and the W3C remains active in recommending improvements to the standard. *www.w3.org*.

TRAINING AND DEVELOPMENT ORGANIZATIONS

The training and development community represents a major market for serious games. The following organizations can provide information on the industry.

American Management Association: A management education organization recognized as an educational institution by the Regents of the University of the State of New York. *www.amanet.org*.

American Society for Training and Development: Covers all areas of corporate training, with a recent emphasis on online training options. *www.astd.org*.

VENDORS

Sources for hardware and software tools for serious games developers.

Academic Superstore: Price breaks for developers in the academic community. *www.academicsuperstore.com*.

All Electronics Corporation: Surplus electronics parts for microcontroller projects. *www.allelectronics.com*.

Cyberguys: Eclectic collection of hard-to-find hardware, media, and computer supplies. *www.cyberguys.com*.

Digi-Key: Great source for electronic components. *www.digikey.com/digihome.html*.

Disc Makers: CD-ROM and DVD duplication with cover art. *www.discmakers.com*.

Dynon Instruments: Virtual instruments for microcontroller work. *www.dynoninstruments.com*.

Immersion: Force-feedback hardware for medical, aviation, and automotive simulations and games. *www.immersion.com*.

IOtech: Sells a variety of PC-based data acquisition hardware for embedded gaming systems. *www.iotech.com*.

Link Instruments: Virtual instruments, including logic analyzers and digital oscilloscopes. *www.linkins2.com*.

Micromint: Production quantity embedded microcontrollers. *www.micromint.com*.

Microsoft: The software giant has developed XNA, a game development platform targeted at containing development costs. XNA covers three areas: Content Creation, Production Processes, and Game Technologies. *www.Microsoft.com/xna*.

National Instruments: Sets the standard for virtual instruments with its LabView series. *digital.ni.com*.

Parallax: Source of the popular BASIC stamp microcontroller, prototyping kits, *free* books in PDF format, and accessories. *www.parallax.com.*

PC/Mac Connection: Offers academic discounts and a good selection. *www.pcconnection.com.*

Programmer's Paradise: Software, hardware, and books for programmers. *www.programmersparadise.com.*

Publishing Perfection: Offers a wide assortment of graphic design hardware and software that can be used for game development. *www.pubperfect.com.*

Rabbit Semiconductor: Microcontrollers for evaluation and production, with an emphasis on embedded networking. *www.rabbitsemi4wireless.com.*

SimMarket: Aircraft simulation hardware, including realistic instruments. *www.simmarket.com.*

SimWare: Aircraft simulation software and hardware, including full-motion platforms. *www.simw.com.*

The Writer's Store: Offers software solutions to help game script writers with dialogue and creating story lines with impact. *www.WritersStore.com.*

TigerDirect.com: Discounted, varied selection of hardware for networking, storage, and computer upgrades. *www.tigerdirect.com.*

Writer Online Workshops: Internet-based workshops on writing, presented by Writer's Digest. The workshops, which range in topic from script writing to basic grammar, are run by live instructors. *www.WritersOnlineWorkshops.com.*

INDEX